Performing Democracy

THEATER: Theory/Text/Performance

Enoch Brater, Series Editor

Performing Democracy

International Perspectives on
Urban Community-Based Performance

Susan C. Haedicke and Tobin Nellhaus, Editors

Ann Arbor

THE UNIVERSITY OF MICHIGAN PRESS

Copyright © by the University of Michigan 2001
All rights reserved
Published in the United States of America by
The University of Michigan Press
Manufactured in the United States of America
⊚ Printed on acid-free paper

2004   2003   2002   2001.   4   3   2   1

A CIP catalog record for this book is available from the British Library.

Library of Congress Cataloging-in-Publication Data

Performing democracy : international perspectives on urban
   community-based performance / edited by Susan C. Haedicke and
   Tobin Nellhaus.
      p.   cm.
   Includes index.
   ISBN 0-472-09760-1 — ISBN 0-472-06760-5 (pbk.)
      1. Community theater. 2. Workers' theater. 3. Theater and
society. 4. Theater—Political aspects. I. Haedicke, Susan C. II.
Nellhaus, Tobin. III. Title.
   PN3305 .P47   2000
   792'.022—dc21   00-12180

Acknowledgments

We would like to thank LeAnn Fields at the University of Michigan Press for encouraging, supporting, and guiding this project from the beginning, and Marcia LaBrenz for her expert editorial assistance at the end. We also want to acknowledge our appreciation to the Theatre and Social Change Focus Group in the Association for Theatre in Higher Education, which provided many panel slots at conferences where we could test ideas and gauge interest in the issues. This book would not have been possible without our contributors' deep commitment and unending patience. Johns Hopkins University Press kindly granted permission to include a revised and expanded version of Bruce McConachie's essay, "Approaching the 'Structure of Feeling' in Grassroots Theatre," which first appeared in *Theatre Topics* 8:1, 33–53. © The Johns Hopkins University Press. Susan would like to thank Robert A. Alexander, founder of Living Stage, for his extraordinary pioneering work in community-based theater which changed her view of what theater meant and what it could do and for his friendship and willingness to share his vision with her. She would also like to thank her family for their faith that the book would be finished and their constant encouragement. Tobin would like to thank Outi Lahtinen for her editorial assistance.

Contents

Tobin Nellhaus and Susan C. Haedicke

Introduction

What does not change / is the will to change.
—Charles Olson, "The Kingfishers"

Community-based theater is now a noticeable undercurrent within performance and activist circles. From a smattering of isolated activities just
twenty years ago, it is now reaching ever-growing numbers of audience
members—or, rather, participants—with its efforts to involve, mobilize,
and politicize, and in the process it is expanding the boundaries of what we
call "art." Community-based performance work is relying on an increasingly wide range of approaches and is occurring in an extensive variety of
communities and contexts. This vitality and growth have not come without
difficulties, conflicts, dangers, and mistakes. *Performing Democracy: International Perspectives on Urban Community-Based Performance* aims to survey some
of the recent activity around the world and to consider some of the controversies that confront it.

The growth of community-based performance is a major reason for
creating this collection. Because it traverses customary institutional lines,
community-based performance has attracted interest from an unusual range
of people: practitioners and scholars of theater, community and political
activists, social service and community development professionals, social

Susan C. Haedicke teaches drama in the English Department at The George Washington University. She has presented numerous papers and published several articles on
community-based theater and dramaturgy, inspired by her association since the early
1990s with the Living Stage Theatre Company, on which she is completing a book. In
addition, she is dramaturg for LE NEON Theatre, a French-American theater in the
Washington, D.C. area.

Tobin Nellhaus writes on theater history, performance theory, and social theory. From
1993 to 1996 he headed the Theater and Social Change focus group within the Association for Theater in Higher Education. He received an American Council of Learned
Societies fellowship in 1996–97, was a Fulbright Scholar in 1997–98, and is now the
Librarian for Drama, Film and Theater Studies at Yale University.

scientists and even psychotherapists. Their needs and concerns necessarily vary. There is much in this book for all of these groups, but theater practitioners and educators are the primary audience for *Performing Democracy*. One reason for this focus is that, despite being the ones who produce most of this activity, the practitioners of community-based theater remain relatively isolated in their practical work. But they are aware that activity is everywhere and frequently express an eagerness to hear about others' work. What innovations are being explored? Which methods should we abandon? How have problems been resolved, or at least managed? What success stories can we hear to encourage us? While the practitioners are asking these and other questions, educators (who are often also practitioners) are searching for ways to understand community-based performance work, explain its effectiveness (and its failures), devise improvements—and teach students about the work, either to expand their knowledge of theatrical activity generally, or to train a new generation of practitioners.

A complex set of needs thus faced us as editors of this anthology. Practitioners, teachers, and students of community-based theater are interrelated, and some individuals count as all three, but the positions have differences as well as regions of overlap. Our goals are to broaden knowledge about the community-based performance work that is being undertaken, to build a critical understanding of that work, and to foster its continuation. Fundamentally, we aim to represent the field to itself. That includes displaying its difficulties and weaknesses in an attempt to overcome them. Our hope is that, as the first major collection on community-based performance, *Performing Democracy* will encourage practical developments and critical reassessments by the people most directly involved with it. In this introduction we aim to clarify how we have gone about representing community-based performance within this collection.

Representing Community-Based Performance: Basic Decisions

How should one represent community-based performance? How does one determine its scope and value? The questions prove surprisingly complex, and answering them involves not an idealized definition of a fixed genre but, rather, the entire political history of community-based performance. The complexities arise partly because of community-based performance's range and variety and also because of the misunderstandings and sometimes willful misrepresentations already in circulation. British playwright and activist Steve Gooch recalls a member of London's theater board pronouncing the syllables of community theater "individually and aloud . . . to infer [sic] their similarity with 'com-mun-ism.'"[1] In the United States the phrase *community theater* often conjures up a patronizing image of untrained amateurs getting together haphazardly to put on a play with forgotten lines, ill-fitting costumes, or wobbly sets. Although revolutionary politics and lack of professionalism do both occur (sometimes together), the purely formalistic categories that look at community-based theater either as political propaganda or as third-rate entertainment do not allow for an understanding of what this kind of artistic practice involves.

Controversies over the scope and value of this work do not arise solely between the practitioners of community-based performance and their mainstream critics: some of the most important debates are among the practitioners themselves. A central issue that constantly confronted us was, what counts? What is better regarded as something else? Those doing the work don't all agree. Community-based performance is relatively new; it has emerged in all sorts of places to address a broad range of situations, and even its best-known advocates are constantly seeking new approaches. We feel it is premature—and, in any case, inappropriate—to propose some sort of definitive model. Community-based performance seems to us best understood as a range of activities bearing certain family resemblances. Among the most common traits, community-based performance often redefines *text,* initiates unique script development strategies that challenge time-tested techniques for playwriting, and introduces participatory performance techniques that blur the boundaries between actor and spectator in order to maximize the participants' agency. The last is probably the most striking strategy of community-based performance—perhaps even the feature distinguishing it most frequently. Because of it, this work regularly depends upon a dialogue between the audience and the theater company (sometimes dissolving that division altogether), producing a two-way learning process not circumscribed by actual performance event or space, and disrupting the traditional actor/audience relationship.

Within these broad outlines numerous approaches have developed. Some forms have become established as central or most characteristic, while others seem "borderline." The former are well represented in this collection, but restrictive definitions are plainly untenable. Some important activity is in genres other than theater in the narrow sense. Thus, the reader will find articles on work involving Boal's forum theater, documentary drama, agitprop, cabaret, puppets, skateboarding, presentational dance performance, and everything in between. Throughout this introduction we will simply use *theater* and *performance* as synonyms. But, if anything unites community-based performance practitioners, it is their political commitment and artistic engagement. Under often trying and sometime horrific circumstances, they muster astonishing dedication, creativity, compassion, courage, and sheer dogged persistence to illuminate, alleviate, and if possible overcome those circumstances.

Another aspect we have strived to represent is the international scope of community-based theater activities. This type of performance work is occurring all over the world. Still more important, the transmission of ideas and methods internationally has been crucial to community-based performance's development almost from its beginning. Many of the strategies and principles used in contemporary community-based performance have their foundations in the (widely varied) work of individuals and companies such as Augusto Boal in Brazil; Peter Cheeseman, Arnold Wesker's Centre 42, John Arden and Margaretta D'Arcy, John McGrath's 7:84 Scotland Theatre Company, and Ann Jellicoe's Colway Theatre Trust in Great Britain; Living Stage Theatre Company and Cornerstone in the United States; Nigerian Popular Theatre Alliance in Nigeria; PETA in the Philippines; and ToBakYi in South Korea. Most of these were active mainly during the 1960s, 1970s, and into the 1980s, yet much of the work in Asia, Africa, and South America during the 1990s is little known to English-speaking audiences, even though the exchange of ideas, approaches, and techniques remains invaluable to community-based theater's development. To this end we sought essays on projects around the world, and, in fact, performances from North America, South America, Asia, Africa, Europe, and Australia are represented.

The internationalism of community-based performance work is in a way all the more remarkable because, at the same time, the activities tend to have a decided commitment to localism. The projects almost invariably seek to explore issues of immediate concern to the residents of a specific locale (as does, for example, the East Palo Alto Project discussed in the contribution by Harry Elam and Kim Fowler) or, at the very least, adapt preexisting materials to the particular community (such as, say, Cornerstone Theater's version of *Peer Gynt,* which became *Pier Gynt* when produced in Eastport, Maine, where resetting the play to use local language and places helped to connect the production to town life).

Partly to convey this conjunction of localism with internationalism and partly to present a common set of issues and problems, we decided that the essays in this collection should explore urban projects. The most compelling reason for this focus, however, is that current concerns about community often revolve around the dynamics of city life: the city offers both anonymity and alienation, freedom and confinement. Despite the intensification of isolation, bureaucratization, and commodification that urban residents feel, city life continues to have a strong appeal. City life represents "the 'being-together' of strangers," and the city offers public spaces where "strangers encounter one another . . . often remaining strangers and yet acknowledging their contiguity in living and the contributions each makes to the others."[2] Thus, issues of community—its formation, maintenance, and disintegration—are intensified when the community-based performance occurs in city space. By the same token ambivalence toward urban life is an acute (if seldom mentioned) issue for advocates of community-based performance. At what point does the goal of reaching and empowering "the common people" slide into a longing for a simpler age free from the "shock of the new"? Can the dry-eyed effort to grab hold of the city's creativity and turn it toward our own democratic purposes wind up simply valorizing the trendy? As we begin the twenty-first century, community-based performance must face the forces of modernity—which are inextricably linked to urbanization—and one way or another respond to it, contribute to it, or both.[3]

The range of activities within the community-based theater movement and its international character emphasize one of its other aspects: the diversity of people involved. There are important differences among the people connected to the movement. Community-based performance is an important mode of work for people who are committed to activist theater and who are not specifically trained as scholars. Most of our contributors do in fact teach, although not all would consider themselves primarily academic, and, by the same token, most of the scholarly essays derive their key insights from the authors' own practical activities. Consequently, the majority of the essays in this book discuss a project in which the author was directly involved. That, of course, raises the possibility of mere boosterism, but we found much less self-aggrandizement than we might have feared, and actually the authors tended to strive for objectivity or used the opportunity for constructive self-criticism, even soul-searching. Such self-reflexivity is essential for the development of community-based performance. (In very different ways the essays by Bruce McConachie, Susan Mason, and Mary Ann Hunter are exemplary in this regard.) Other contributors discuss projects in which they did not participate or had only a minor capacity. Interestingly, the contributions from such authors tended less toward analytical scrutiny and instead usually aimed to develop the historical record of community-based performance work (an important undertaking itself).

Yet, in spite of great strides forward, especially in the past few years, critical analysis within the community-based performance movement remains relatively underdeveloped. Conference presentations have usually emphasized practical activities: some have probed deeply, and a few essays have focused on critical analysis and theorization, but those offerings have been more the exception than the rule. This tendency is not all bad: such sessions are frequently well attended, and audience members often remark on how refreshingly different they are from the ordinary fare. The "groundedness" of community-based work is one of its strongest and most invigorating features. It is difficult to say what exactly led to this "pragmatic" character, though clearly it is related to members' activist orientation. But, whatever the explanation, criticism and theory of community-based performance have developed fitfully and unevenly.

The fortes and failings within the community-based theater culture naturally appeared in the submissions we received, presenting us with a complex decision. We feel that it is imperative to bring a critical perspective to this work: without it the practitioners of community-based performance cannot surmount the difficulties that face them or determine whether it actually achieves what it claims. Yet we know that many people interested in community-based performance have an urgent need just to learn about the kinds of activities being developed. Moreover, it seemed to us that both scholars and activists would find "reports from the trenches" invaluable while, at the same time, they would benefit from essays that plumb some of the issues involved in the work. With these thoughts in mind we arrived at a difficult and in some ways controversial choice to develop two sorts of essays and, thus, to alternate interpretive or "analytical explorations" with shorter "production documentations." The analytical explorations focus on issues such as community identity, authority, or process, unpacking these issues from a theoretical perspective. The production documentations raise similar matters, but, rather than analyze them, they emphasize how those issues play out in practice. The distinction is scarcely watertight: all documentation involves interpretations of work that is itself theory based, just as analysis requires a foundation in documentary or other concrete evidence. Making the distinction thus risks suggesting (in positivist fashion) that there is a clear division between theory and practice, when nothing could be farther from the truth. Nevertheless, while theory and practice cannot be sundered on principle, the balance between them certainly varies. Some of our authors explore assumptions or implications extensively; others leave more space for readers to draw their own conclusions—and this situation, we feel, is as it should be, pre-

cisely because of the mix of people involved in community-based performance and the range of potential readers of this collection.

Finally, the process of selecting essays was shaped by the question of
how to organize them. We placed the essays into three parts, each one gathering both analytical explorations and production documentations under a
thematic rubric. This structure resulted from several considerations. Without question, constructing the collection around "issues" (race, gender,
class, age, and so forth) had its attractions—familiarity high among them.
But, on the one hand, the essays themselves, or rather the performance
work that they discuss, would not allow it: the majority concerned multiple
issues in some way, and in some cases the performance project was explicitly aimed toward uniting narrowly conceived groups and bridging categories. And, on the other hand, there seems to be mounting evidence that
"identity politics" has produced a skewed concept of personal identity
within theory and a problematic politics of competitive group identities in
practice.

This is not to suggest that recent theoretical explorations of the social
constitution of "subjects" have been simplistic, still less that collective action
by and loyalty to specific social groups are unnecessary—quite the contrary.
Yet there are reasons to believe that, for many people, agency often involves
notions of identity that reach more broadly and weigh less heavily than current theory implies. Some of this evidence comes from community-based
performance itself: the first essay in this collection, in fact, offers a striking
case in which issues that these theories posited as central to an audience's
identity formation proved almost beside the point in practice. It might even
be argued that community-based theater, even as it employs notions of
community (involving identities and exclusions) in its effort to give marginalized peoples a voice, also tends to subvert the very idea of community
boundaries through its dialogic process—and that our representation of that
work should bear this dialogism in mind. Thus, we found ourselves looking
not just at who and what the essays talk about but also how they talk to one
another. Thematic rubrics seemed to illuminate the *process* of community-
based theater in a way that issues and identities never could.

Before closing this initial overview, one additional question needs to
be considered. It did not need to play a special role in our decision making
because it confronts everyone involved in community-based performance,
but, since the question arises so often, it has to be answered directly. The
question is this: Community-based performance sounds like a great form of
community development or social work—but is it art? Given the centrality

of the work's social functions, one can hardly fault those who raise this question. Community-based performance stretches and challenges the customary boundaries and definitions of art. In it aesthetic considerations must go hand in hand with those of social activism: as many of the essays here demonstrate, rather than an aesthetics of sublimity, community-based theater pursues a *grounded* aesthetics.

Murray Edelman offers one analysis of this connection between art and activism, arguing that the twentieth century has abandoned the view that beauty is a necessary or defining attribute of art. Art, he suggests, cannot be separated from social and political ideas and activism: "Art and ideology ensure that there is no immaculate perception. By the same token, there can be no politics without art and ideology. . . . Together, art, the mind, and the situations in which they are applied construct and transform beliefs about the social world, defining problems and solutions, hopes and fears, the past, the present, and the future."[4] Edelman provides a definition of art that does not eliminate concern for aesthetic formalities but subordinates them to the art's work toward social change; to the relationships between the performers and the community and the greater society in which they both live, work, and play; and to dialogue as a form of action that constructs meaning. Thus, whether a work is "art" is determined by its involvement in and impact upon the community's cultural production.

Augusto Boal, instead of validating the sociopolitical import of art, justifies the artistic merit of performances that stretch the boundaries of art. The essence of theater, he asserts, is "in the human being observing itself. The human being not only 'makes' theatre: it 'is' theatre." Any space conjoining a stage space and an auditorium space becomes an *aesthetic space* because the attention of the whole audience converges upon it. Yet, while the actor and spectator can be different people, they can also coincide in the same person. Thus, theater, as art, does not come from the text, the performance, the sets, the costumes, or other traditional theatrical conventions, but from "the subjectivity of those who practice it, at the moment when they practice it."[5] Art is now defined not solely as a set of formal features: it also involves a set of social relationships. Insofar as community-based performance shapes a group's social relations through activities that involve images or the imagination, it is an artistic practice, even if mainstream aesthetics fails to recognize it as such.

The title of this collection, *Performing Democracy,* brings these aspects of community-based theater together. On the one hand, it is an artistic practice of performance. On the other hand, it has the sociopolitical goal of democratization and strives to use democratic means and processes of operation, that is, to act democratically. And by enacting democratically constructed theatrical fictions, sometimes in places where democracy or even safety scarcely exists, community-based performance aims to make democracy a reality.

The remainder of the introduction will consider the collection's three parts and their themes in more detail. Briefly, the first part, "Defining Communities," focuses on how performances contribute to the definition, creation, and preservation of a community, at times under extreme duress. The second part, "Authority in the Community-Based Performance Process," concerns the issues of authority arising within either the process of producing community-based performance or its relationship to the community. The final part, "Empowering the Audience," considers community-based theater's efforts at strengthening a community—the performances' interventions in social and cultural life, in local and national politics, and in individual development. The titles of the three parts do not offer any sort of taxonomy or anatomy: they simply strive to pick out certain thematic threads that tie together a set of essays and are woven into the activity itself. Community-based performance necessarily involves all three aspects (and more). Consequently, many essays, perhaps most, could fit into sections other than the ones we chose; often it was the relationship between essays in a group that we felt brought the themes forward best. Nevertheless, these themes help foreground the ways in which community-based performance strives to build democracy by building community.

Defining Communities

The essays in the first part of the book wrestle with definitions of *community* and how they are deployed or even created by community-based performance. The problems are manifold. As one writer has put it, "Community as a concept has a definite center without a well-defined periphery. The core of the concept of community is around people interacting in specific space and time; but these dimensions vary."[6] And the variations arise not only among lay definitions but also among those proposed by social scientists.

Sociologists have argued about the concept of "community" for well over a century, and definitions abound. For some scholars geographic proximity (such as a neighborhood or district) is sufficient to establish a community. Others consider any group sharing a common social position (like the homeless) as forming a community, whether or not there is significant organization, common symbolism, personal bonding, or even acquaintance among members. From another perspective a shared set of symbols provides the centerpoint of community formation; in a related analysis a community is any group of people who are in direct communication with one another (a view that encompasses on-line communities). Benedict Anderson takes this concept one step further with his analysis of the "imagined community," in which even indirect or one-way means of communication, most notably the newspaper and the novel, allow individuals unknown to one another to become bound together, so that "in the minds of each lives the image of their communion."[7] A further definition places common needs, interests, activities, or desires at the center of community (e.g., the theater community). But, as Alan Filewod points out in his contribution to this book, the term *community* in the sense of commonality is often a political and ideological instrument deployed in order to benefit a much narrower social group. According to some interpretations, a community must be long-lived, but others allow for the possibility of temporary, ad hoc community formation. By 1955 George Hillery had discovered ninety-four possible definitions of community; but in 1976 Willis Sutton and T. Munson asserted that over 70 percent of the definitions relied on "community as a structural entity—a specific population, place, or location," and less than 12 percent used social interaction as a determining characteristic.[8]

Ann Jellicoe's productions of community-based plays throughout England during the late 1960s exemplify theater that creates the "undeniable warm and friendly feel" of commonality, of shared experiences and meanings, that serve as the "common core" of most definitions, as Richard Barr observes.[9] But for Iris Marion Young this

> ideal of community . . . privileges unity over difference, immediacy over mediation, sympathy over recognition of one's understanding of others from their point of view. Community is an understandable dream, expressing a desire for selves that are transparent to one another, relationships of mutual identification, social closeness and comfort. The dream is understandable, but politically problematic . . . because those motivated by it will tend to suppress differences among themselves or implicitly exclude from their political groups persons with whom they do not identify."[10]

This view of community depends on clear demarcations between who belongs and who does not and so tends toward an exclusionary "us" versus "them." Likewise, Barr asserts that there is a movement in modern social theory and modern drama "from concepts of community conceived in terms of homogeneity to concepts deriving from heterogeneity, from community based on commonality to community dependent on difference."[11] Communities in this sense rely on Freirean-type dialogue, what Anna Yeatman calls "perspectival dialogism [that] works with and invites conflict and confrontation . . . [through] the ongoing negotiation of . . . different perspectives and the provisional settlements they achieve."[12] Many of the contributors to this volume explore these problematics both within the community-based theater process and between the community and the theater practitioners and point toward the same movement from commonality to heterogeneity in community-based performance.

In considerations of community definition, the nature and role of urban life loom large. Here again, in a collection treating communities— which in most understandings involve establishing certain kinds of social boundaries—we have been less concerned with sharply bounded definitions of "cities" than with activities, relationships, and issues that have become associated with city life, even if the municipality is relatively small. Population density, waves of immigration and/or flight, and intricate economies and social conditions all foster more numerous and more complex communities within cities and offer opportunities to form types of communities that are more difficult to achieve in rural areas, such as ad hoc or temporary communities.

Not surprisingly, then, there are variations or even conflicts over the definition of community within the community-based performance movement and so among our contributors (although they are mainly concerned with concrete communities of people who live and interact within relatively specific locales, rather than with communities in a more abstract sense). There has even been debate over the term *community-based theater*. As Bruce McConachie mentions in his essay, many of those engaged in this performance activity prefer the term *grassroots theater* as less problematic historically and politically. In England and Australia the usual phrase is *community theater,* but in the United States that expression refers to amateur play productions. From our perspective *grassroots* is at least as ambiguous as *community*. (Just who is and who isn't part of the "grassroots"? Are students? Are well-educated theater professionals? Are gay/lesbian teenagers and unionized workers all part of a unified grassroots? Does the term adequately include urban life, or does it hint at nostalgia for an agrarian past? And so forth.) We have adopted the term *community-based* as being least confusing, and it has the advantage of being increasingly current, at least in the United States.

Whichever term is used, questions abound about the nature and role of the community in community-based performance. As suggested earlier, an important issue for us in selecting essays was whether the community directly participated in the performance's production, but even this could only be a rough gauge rather than a litmus test, and in a few cases other criteria assumed greater importance. There are also questions about how community-based theater defines and establishes the communities with which it works and about its influence and appeal. In what manner and to what degree can it work within a community's own definition of its boundaries (boundaries that may appear sharp to community members but often turn out to be flexible and fuzzy)? What resources can it employ to focus—or refocus—a community's self-definition? To what extent can community-based theater actually create a community from otherwise unconnected individuals?

The point to all these questions is not that community-based performance is endangered by its lack of consensus on the most basic concepts. It is, instead, that, as a field, community-based performance has in fact grasped the most fundamental point of all: *community* is a polymorphic concept precisely because it is the product of ever-changing social alliances, and community-based theater is itself an agent of social change capable of strengthening alliances and forging new ones, along with the skills and symbols to sustain them. Consequently, it must constantly consider all types of alliance—and so should not hold out false hopes for a singular, fixed concept of community. For better or worse its history and goals enforce its multiplicity.

Authority in the Community-Based Performance Process

Performing Democracy's second part focuses on issues of authority as they arise within the process of conducting workshops or creating performances, on the one hand, and within the work's relationship to the community, on the other. The reasons for this focus again lie in community-based performance's political history. The current era of community-based performance grew out of multiple and diverse activities, but all of them had a political edge. One starting point was the revival of ideas and strategies from the 1930s, such as Bertolt Brecht's concept of a politically committed theater practice, the Federal Theatre Project's Living Newspapers, agitprop, locally focused theaters, and related performance activities in Europe and the United States. Another was the literacy campaigns of Paulo Freire, which united the inculcation of reading skills with the development of critical faculties. Other beginnings lie in activism against social and economic injustice, especially the many movements of the 1960s for racial equality, unionization, community empowerment, and national sovereignty, which for many activists made radical democracy the political bottom line. As a result, community-based theater today is not so much a coherent dovetailing of varied political programs as a protean creature whose forms bear family resemblances, and sometimes family rivalries, as its advocates question ever further levels of authority, including its own.

Indeed, the historical development from political drama to community-based performance can be understood in large part through the changes in the sorts of questions that practitioners and scholars asked. If the political views of dramatists like Shaw and Gorki were manifested in representations and/or discursive argument, Brecht and Piscator insisted that the representational process also bore political weight. Thus, questions of political content—"What is performed?"—were supplemented or even replaced by questions about the politics of style: "How is it performed?" With the upheavals of the 1960s and 1970s theater was brought to the streets, to parks, to factories, as new questions arose concerning the constitution of the audience and, closely related to this, the problem of where performances took place and the sense of who "owns" a space: "Who is it performed for, and where?" At the same time, theater companies began to explore investing political content into popular artistic forms (defined in the usual disparate ways but usually meaning senescent genres such as the minstrel show and the Scottish *ceilidh*): a first stab at the question of "Whose material?" that would bear more current fruit in subsequent years.

The reasons are not entirely clear—perhaps it was that radical social change proved extremely hard to achieve and that some forms of oppression appeared to have a deep psychological hold, and so activists found they needed to work at a fundamental level for gradual transformations—but in the 1980s and 1990s another set of issues slowly came to the surface, questions focusing on the process of producing theater, especially issues of social location, control, authority, and authenticity: "Who performs, whose material is performed, and who decides?" Those are the core questions of community-based theater now. The significance of community-based performance today is frequently in the process, not in the product, and the theater work grows out of and strives to address the present-day needs, hopes, and culture of a particular, usually underserved, community. As the center of balance shifted from product to process, in some community-based work (like that of Boal and Living Stage) the "product" in the sense of a public performance disappeared altogether.

One way these new issues became evident, marking a fundamental change from mainstream theater and high art, was in the role of the audiences at community-based performances. Rather than sitting passively in the dark watching a fully prepared play, the audiences participated at some point in the production's creation, sometimes by offering the stories woven into the text, sometimes by writing the text, and sometimes by performing as well. Thus, the dramatic text and often the performance developed collaboratively out of the community, as individual authorship by a playwright unaware of the particular community waned. Baz Kershaw defines this change as a move from *democratization of culture,* in which high art is brought to the masses—"a hegemonic procedure that aims to cheat the mass of people of their right to create their own culture, and that conspires to hold them in thrall to their own uncreative subjugation"[13]—to *cultural democracy,* in which the people participate in and even control cultural production and distribution. Through this process of empowerment through theater, communities learn about their roots, their rights, and their cultural contributions to society at large. Directly or indirectly, they develop greater agency, and so it is not surprising that community-based performance is gaining popularity.

Perhaps unintentionally, a similar practice of cultural democracy seems to have developed *within* the community of community-based performance. It has remarkably few "big names," dominating personalities, or famous theater companies. Without a doubt, one reason for this internal democracy is that most of the practitioners work with particular communities on very local matters and so tend to become isolated. But the matter goes much farther than that. When practitioners of community-based performance meet, they are eager to share their knowledge and experiences. Often two or three work together on projects. And so it is no surprise that when they write essays, they may write them collaboratively. Hence, this collection has an unusual number of essays with joint authorship and was itself the product of joint editorship.

As community-based theater strives to engage the hearts and minds of the audience participants and to improve their lives through art, questions about its value and potential dangers to the community must be asked. Art is never politically neutral, and altruistic or socially committed intentions do not shield the work from moral ambiguities. Its very immersion within community relations enmeshes community-based performance in local political complexities that may concern its own activities. Consequently, community-based theaters often struggle with ethical considerations and political conundrums. What begins as a benefit to the community can transform in an instant into a liability, and sometimes a project can teeter between the ethical and the unethical. Intervention, location, and agency, all revolving around asymmetrical relations of power, authority, and involvement, circumscribe the politics that determine the nature of the work. In community-based theater at least two groups, regardless of their form—actors and spectators, facilitators and participants—are involved in shifting social relations, defining and categorizing, understanding or misunderstanding, empathizing with or rejecting each other. Sometimes organizations such as social service agencies or university groups participate in the process as well. Inherent in the interaction between these groups is a dynamic of authority based on knowledge and/or expertise. That does not mean that such sites of exchange are doomed to failure or even that they must retain a hierarchical structure, but it does mean that the stance, assumptions, and motivations of those involved, the discourse surrounding the event, and the relationships between the groups and between language and issues of knowledge and power must constantly be interrogated.

Many of the ethical ambiguities revolve around the role of the facilitator. The model to avoid, but the one so easy to slip into, is that of colonialism, in which the invader consciously or unconsciously appropriates the resources of the vanquished for personal gain. The important questions to ask are: Does the product/process reflect the community or the facilitator? And are people's stories and lives being mined for the benefit of the facilitator? Just recovering repressed stories, which certainly may feel good to those finally given the opportunity to speak, does little to change the established power dynamic, especially if the theater/cultural worker is there to plunder, no matter how subtly. The question, of course, arises about whether this alliance can ever rid itself of colonialist qualities—a question that has to be answered in at least two ways: by examining the processes and methods employed within each project, which is the focus of the essays in part 2; and by considering the community-based theater's work toward community and individual empowerment, which is the theme of part 3.

The possibilities of colonialism reveal how the politics of intervention involve the politics of location. The latter "recognizes and interrogates the strengths and limitations of those places one inherits, engages, and occupies and which frame the discourses through which we speak and act." The ethical considerations focus primarily on the issue of representation, or the "way in which meaning is constructed through placement, positioning, and situatedness of discourse."[14] For the internal dynamics of community-based theater the looming questions ask who has the authority to speak, under what conditions, for whom, and who decides. But simply holding these questions in mind cannot safeguard a community-based performance project from exploiting a community, still less from committing political blunders out of ignorance, lack of time, or insufficient skill. The fact is, much as it may be wished for, nothing can guarantee that a project will avoid the ethically dubious. Even so, a well-designed process can help prevent, defuse, or at least minimize cultural exploitation and political endangerment.

The approach adopted by many community-based performance projects is to break down the traditional functional divisions and, in particular, to foster dialogic interactions. Major roots for this strategy lie in radical pedagogy. The performance event in which spectator becomes artist, passive subject becomes active agent, parallels an educative process that Freire calls "problem-posing education." This process emphasizes communication in which all involved are "jointly responsible for a process in which all grow" and in which the goal is to demythologize traditional "commonsense" reality. Traditional education, explains Freire, resembles banking in that the teacher deposits information into the mind of the student that discourages both original thinking and challenges to the status quo at the same time as it passes on traditions and prejudices. In contrast, problem-posing education uses dialogue as the tool that enables the speakers to learn about themselves and the world around them and see that relationship not as a static reality but as one in process.[15] Through dialogue the participants investigate other people's thinking so that they can achieve a critical perception of the world rather than accept an imposition of the values and beliefs of the more powerful or numerous on the weaker or the minority. One voice does not perpetually hold the privileged position, but, instead, multiple voices share the authority and enrich the worldview. Freire writes, "Whereas banking education anesthetizes and inhibits creative power, problem-posing education involves a constant unveiling of reality"[16] and of culture. Thus, culture becomes "a shifting sphere of multiple and heterogeneous borders where different histories, languages, experiences, and voices intermingle amid diverse relations of power and privilege."[17]

When this pedagogical model informs the performance process, when the audience shifts its role from passive observer to active artist, this "fictional" action does change lives as participants learn how to give meaning "to the dreams, desires, and subject positions that they inhabit."[18] Boal, who is internationally recognized for his work in community-based theater, calls these techniques "poetics of the oppressed," in which "the main objective [is] to change people—'spectators,' . . . into actors, transformers of the dramatic action," which in turn trains them for real action.[19] Robert Alexander, founder of Living Stage Theatre Company, explains that "audience members become creators when they talk about the experiences of the characters. If you can make choices in the imagination, you can make choices in life."[20]

Yet the obvious question is, "Can you?" Making choices in a fictional situation has very little cost, whereas in actual life the cost can be great. So, even if community-based performance displaces spectators and actors with (in Boal's phrase) "spect-actors" and fosters a dialogue within the community, ethical and political concerns remain. If the participants are falsely taught that they can change circumstances that in fact are beyond their reach, then the work not only is dishonest and cruel but also powerfully preserves the status quo by defusing the participants' anger and frustration. It offers them a temporary "feel-good" solution while robbing them of the impetus toward real action.

Hence, the dialogues that community-based performances seek to generate must occur not only within the community but also across the community/facilitator divide. Indeed, the facilitator's expertise must translate into active listening more than informing or instructing. When beginning any grassroots project, Steve Gooch insists that the practitioners must ask, "How do we 'get into' the lives of the people in our area?" He admits that the question is dangerous but considers it essential for establishing a "dynamic understanding of the relationship between producers and audience in the longterm."[21] Without an intimate understanding of the needs, desires, and beliefs of the group involved, the theater practitioners not only work at a disadvantage but can actually do harm. During a talk at Mount Holyoke College in 1996, Nobel Prize–winning Nigerian playwright Wole Soyinka observed: "When you go into any culture, I don't care what the culture is, you have to go with some humility. You have to understand the language, and by that I do not mean what we speak, you've got to understand the language, the interior language of the people. You've got to be able to enter their philosophy, their world view. You've got to speak both the spoken language and the metalanguage of the people."[22] Speaking the "language" and listening are as crucial for those originally from the particular community as it is for those from outside the community. Understanding how and why a community's history has been devalued and acknowledging how the histories of the community and the facilitator interpenetrate are essential. Ethnographer Dwight Conquergood explains that individuals who do community-based theater work "must work with real people, humankind alive, instead of printed texts," and hints at areas of tension when he admits, "Opening and interpreting lives is very different from opening and closing books."[23]

Although moral ambiguities haunt the process of community-based performance work and can go well beyond the relatively narrow sphere of the performance to spill into other areas of cultural action and community organizing, at its best this work exemplifies the praxis of liberation pedagogy. The performative techniques of recovering one's history, discovering and "trying on" several potential solutions to a particular problem, experiencing others' reactions to one's own actions, and reshaping power relations not only offer participants "skills that would enable them to understand and intervene in their own history" but also to utilize a "pedagogy of articulation and risk," a practice of "experimentation and collage" that encourages making connections and "remapping borders." Here the participants begin "to reconstruct their world in new ways, and to rearticulate their future in unimagined and even unimaginable ways."[24] For these reasons understanding and interrogating the processes used by community-based performance have far-reaching implications.

Empowering the Audience

The concerns over community-based theater's process and internal authority relations arise because of the work's fundamental aim of "empowering the people." Community-based performance seeks social and cultural change. Kershaw insists that this type of theater, which he calls "theatre of social engagement," must be "considered as a form of *cultural intervention*": these performances are "committed to bringing about actual change in specific communities."[25] A 1992 conference on grassroots theatrical activity declared that "grassroots theater is linked to the struggles for cultural, social, economic, and political equity for all people. It is fundamentally a theater of hope and often of joy. It recognizes that to advocate for equity is to meet resistance and to meet with no resistance indicates a failure to enter the fight."[26] In Paulo Freire's words: "As a form of deliberate and systematic action, all cultural action has its theory which determines its ends and thereby defines its methods. Cultural action either serves domination (consciously or unconsciously) or it serves liberation."[27]

Community-based theater intervenes toward liberation through three important functions that recur in all of its myriad forms. One is to report and articulate the struggles, goals, values, and dreams of a particular community, usually one that has been marginalized, ignored, or silenced. By telling the community's stories, the performance announces its existence—not least to itself. As another principle from the 1992 conference states: "Grassroots theater is given its voice by the community from which it arises. . . . The people who are the subjects of the work are part of its development from inception through presentation. Their stories and histories inform the work, their feedback during the creation process shapes it. The audience is not consumer of, but participant in the performance."[28]

The simple act of staging community narratives can have a profound effect. Audiences who usually avoid mainstream theater because of cost and irrelevance to their lives often express surprise and pleasure when they attend community-based performances. Writing from the vantage point of years of work in British community-based theater, Steve Gooch claims that: "Comments like 'I didn't think theatre was like this, there's so much in it, I want to see it again' . . . or 'I never thought I'd see my own life, the things I care and worry about every day, up on the stage, acted out' are typical within my own experience and that of colleagues in the same field." Gooch continues, "The degree of confirmation, of 'lift' and sheer self-respect that audiences can gain from a theatre which concerns itself with the stuff of their own lives cannot be achieved through other media, or through a theatre viewed as distant and separate."[29] So, this theatrical activity provides a space for neglected voices to speak and to be heard.

Of course, there is no guarantee that the community's "voice" will be at all univocal; more likely, in fact, it will be decisively plural, conflicted, even contradictory. That reality brings us to the second major function of community-based theater: to experiment with strategies for solving problems affecting a particular community. Diversity and differences of opinion can weaken a community, but they can also provide it with great strength—if a way can be found for its members to "put their heads together." Performance offers a way for individuals to work collectively in order to articulate positions on issues and explore solutions to problems—at its best, precisely by honoring the variety of viewpoints within the group and the fragmentary character of any particular representation. The dissolution of the distinction between actors and spectators is just one way (albeit a quite radical one) those goals are sought. Through such means the performance helps establish the personal and social bonds that create community.

Finally, community-based performance functions as a challenge to the dominant culture. Its aesthetics and social consciousness call into question not only the principles of both the commercial and the avant-garde art worlds but also the hierarchical organization of society and culture. As a result, community-based theater frequently tackles controversy; as Gooch writes, it can "lift the lid off a number of volatile issues which the established theatre, locked into its box-office system, its hierarchical management and its 'realism,' cannot hope to deal with."[30] Thus, the work of community-based theaters parallels and reinforces liberation movements. The result, as with any struggle for democratic change, is often messy. Yet community-based theater work can also create within a particular community, a model society like that envisioned by Paulo Freire: a "cultural synthesis" in which

> there are no invaders; hence, there are no imposed models. In their stead, there are actors who critically analyze reality (never separating analysis from action) and intervene as Subjects in the historical process. Instead of following predetermined plans, leaders and people, mutually identified, together create the guidelines of their action. In this synthesis, leaders and people are somehow reborn in new knowledge and new action.[31]

These three general functions leave plenty of room for heterogeneous concepts and methods. In particular, the concept of empowerment varies considerably. When community-based performance activists address these functions and work to bring power to the people, they may understand "the people" as a general audience, as a specific (even invited) audience, or as the participants (spect-actors) themselves. Within these approaches "the people" may be seen collectively as a community or on an individual basis. And work originally designed for one sort of participant or recipient may be adapted or directly offered for another, such as when the Seattle Public Theater presents forum theater to a general audience (see Westlake's essay), or a play written largely with steelworkers in mind later stands simply as a play for anyone (see Favorini's). Another issue pertains to whether the participants and/or spectators are encouraged to utilize institutions and resources offered by the dominant social order—working "within the system"—or instead to invent alternative means of political development.

Thus, among those viewing "the people" collectively, some community-based theater practitioners feel that the central issue is to help a marginalized community bring its perspective, history, and/or culture to the general public's attention—a filtering up of popular culture. One version of this approach has actors perform a play about some community; another has community members themselves perform it. In either case, however, the practice can be compatible with popular culture's commercialization. For other practitioners the goal is to encourage a community to exercise the powers to which it already has access within the existing political system but which it is not effectively wielding. That approach does not alter existing social relations, but, arguably, it strengthens the community's ability to change those relations. Another tack is to develop political expression and organize political forces outside the given system, often by using protest theater or agitprop to motivate public action. The questions haunting this kind of work are always whether it can achieve sufficient impact and even whether being outside "the system" will deny it any real impact at all—questions that are intimately tied to the performance's connection to a larger social movement, if one even exists. For yet other community-based theater practitioners the focus is to give people new skills, with the understanding that, by transforming the people as individuals, one necessarily transforms their social condition or at least the position from which they face the problems that confront them. Such is the strategy behind Boal's various techniques, from the socially oriented "forum theater" to the more psychotherapeutic "rainbow of desire." But whether increasing people's skills can truly go beyond ameliorating individual lives remains a conundrum. There are still further approaches to empowerment, and sometimes approaches can be combined in a single project.

Our point in presenting this spectrum of goals and their respective strengths and weaknesses is certainly not to suggest that one method is best. Still less do we want to intimate that, since no approach is perfect or possesses guarantees, community-based theater is ultimately doomed to failure or (less melodramatically) mere piecemeal improvements. On the contrary, strategies are always tuned to particular fields and aims, so they cannot help but be good for some things, not so good for others. For that reason each approach to empowerment has its range of appropriateness and validity: the complexity of the world means that fundamental social change probably requires using every approach available, and, even if the results are limited, they still are capable of larger cumulative effects. It appears that the community-based theater community understands that necessity, which explains the practitioners' diversity and evident tolerance for—indeed, interest in and encouragement of—alternatives to their own methods. The breadth and even disputes within community-based performance are a crucial part of its character and vitality; it was incumbent upon us, as editors, to represent these aspects too.

Community-based performance is a tremendously diverse mode of artistic practice and political activism. While driven toward common goals, its practitioners use many different approaches and sometimes disagree strongly about the appropriateness, priorities, and viability of the divergent strategies. Ultimately, this is as it should be. As the character, conditions, and needs of urban communities vary, so must the tactics that community-based performance adopts. As it questions itself, it has found ever-deeper ways to integrate a democratic agenda into its processes and products and so to promote social change at more and more levels. That desire for social transformation is what keeps community-based performance alive and keeps it searching for new ways to stay alive. As Charles Olson wrote, "What does not change / is the will to change." Community-based performance will change itself as it seeks to change the world, because it needs it.

NOTES

1. Steve Gooch, *All Together Now: An Alternative View of Theatre and the Community* (London: Methuen, 1984), 8.

2. Iris Marion Young, "The Ideal of Community and the Politics of Difference," in *Feminism/Postmodernism,* ed. Linda J. Nicholson (New York: Routledge, 1990), 318.

3. Perhaps we should note that we hope to succeed this collection with a volume focusing on rural projects, in which context the city/country contrast may be taken up more readily.

4. Murray Edelman, *From Art to Politics: How Artistic Creations Shape Political Conceptions* (Chicago: University of Chicago Press, 1995), 4–5, 22–23.

5. Augusto Boal, *The Rainbow of Desire: The Boal Method of Theatre and Therapy* (London: Routledge, 1995), 13, 18–19.

6. Linda Stoneall, *Country Life, City Life: Five Theories of Community* (New York: Praeger, 1983), 5.

7. Benedict Anderson, *Imagined Communities: Reflections on the Origin and Spread of Nationalism,* rev. ed. (London and New York: Verso, 1991), 6.

8. George Hillery, "Definitions of Community: Areas of Agreement," *Rural Sociology* 20 (1955): 111–23; Willis Sutton and T. Munson, "Definitions of Community, 1954–1973" (paper presented at the Annual Meeting of the American Sociological Association, New York, August 1976), qtd. in Stoneall, *Country Life, City Life,* 4.

9. Richard Barr, *Rooms with a View: The Stages of Community in the Modern Theater* (Ann Arbor: University of Michigan Press, 1998), 181–82.

10. Young, "Ideal of Community," 300.

11. Barr, *Rooms with a View,* 2.

12. Anna Yeatman, "Minorities and the Politics of Difference," in *Postmodern Revisionings of the Political,* ed. Anna Yeatman (London: Routledge, 1994), 87–88.

13. Baz Kershaw, *The Politics of Performance: Radical Theatre as Cultural Intervention* (London: Routledge, 1992), 184.

14. Henry A. Giroux, *Border Crossings: Cultural Workers and the Politics of Education* (London: Routledge, 1994), 221, 222.

15. Paulo Freire, *Pedagogy of the Oppressed,* trans. Myra Bergman Ramos (New York: Continuum, 1989), 67, 70, 71.

16. Ibid., 68.

17. Giroux, *Border Crossings,* 32.

18. Ibid., 32.

19. Augusto Boal, *Theatre of the Oppressed,* trans. Charles A. and Maria-Odilia Leal McBride (New York: Theatre Communications Group, 1985), 122.

20. Robert A. Alexander, interview by Susan Chandler Haedicke, 5 October 1995.

21. Gooch, *All Together Now,* 74.

22. Wole Soyinka, discussion with faculty and students at Mount Holyoke College, March 1996.

23. Dwight Conquergood, "Performing as a Moral Act: Ethical Dimensions of Ethnography of Performance," *Literature in Performance* 5, no. 2 (1985): 2.

24. Henry A. Giroux and Peter McLaren, eds., *Between Borders: Pedagogy and the Politics of Cultural Studies* (London: Routledge, 1994), 16–18, 31.

25. Kershaw, *Politics of Performance,* 5–6.

26. Dudley Cocke, Harry Newman, and Janet Salmons-Rue, eds., *From the Ground Up: Grassroots Theater in Historical and Contemporary Perspective* (Ithaca, N.Y.: Cornell University, Community Based Arts Project, 1993), 81.

27. Freire, *Pedagogy of the Oppressed,* 180.

28. Cocke, Newman, and Salmons-Rue, *From the Ground Up,* 81.

29. Gooch, *All Together Now,* 74.

30. Ibid., 74.

31. Freire, *Pedagogy of the Oppressed,* 183.

PART I

Defining Communities

Questions about the definition of community and the role that community-based theater can play in shaping communities are the focus of the book's first part. The contributors look at how communities are formed or strengthened through performance, in part by the way they define themselves. But what constitutes "community" is a contested issue. Some of the authors work with conceptions of community that center around unifying social locations or cultural roots; other definitions hinge more on shared interests or common points of resistance. Some of the communities they describe are decades or centuries old; some are temporary, disbanding after a single event. Establishing an ethical link (whether based on shared identity or on differences) seems to be a common thread connecting these various efforts. Through this link, as community-based theater explores strategies for solving problems confronting a community—however defined—the community itself begins to assume authority over its own formation.

The first two essays consider projects that are responding to sharp ethnic divisions. In Bruce McConachie's essay the project's central theme concerns historical events that nonetheless carry much living relevance: race relations in Williamsburg, Virginia, during the 1950s and 1960s. The project's two leaders agreed to use interracial casting but disagreed over the political implications of casting a white actor as an important black character. Surprisingly, for the African Americans in the audience it seemed not to be an issue at all. McConachie argues that images of a community's ethical relationships—its division of an ethical "us" from an immoral "them"—are far more important than ideological transactions, overriding even identity politics.

Sonja Kuftinec looks at an even more polarized situation, the civil war in Bosnia, which had divided a major city into ethnic enclaves and literally destroyed the bridge between them. Working in an emotionally and politically explosive context, the performance projects helped youths in Mostar overcome divisions both among themselves and between them and the international volunteers involved in the projects, to find voices that could begin speaking of reconciliation. Despite precautions, the process ran into its own ethical turning points, in which the facilitators had to learn from and be empowered by the participants.

Temporary communities are the topic of the next two essays. E. J. Westlake examines a project involving homeless teens in Seattle. She argues that the facilitators overcame their "outsider" status to create temporary communities, a mode of collectivity hovering between community in the ordinary sense (which generally assumes commonality) and coalition (which usually assumes differences). Temporary communities arose in three ways: within the workshop, during the public performance, and through subsequent spin-off communities.

Westlake discusses a performance project in which the temporary communities focused on a social condition; in Carl Thelin's essay a temporary community forms through a voluntary and even arbitrary association of individuals. People's Public Space, an art cooperative in Taiwan, seeks to foster a community to support individual spiritual quests and expression. It builds this communal creative spirit through "art parties," in which everyone is encouraged to express themselves. Thelin maintains that, despite this seemingly tenuous basis for collective identity, PPS's inclusiveness implicitly overturns social hierarchy.

Voluntary communities are considered further in part 1's last two essays. Political and social activism provides the main connection uniting the community served by a Canadian theater company that Alan Filewod investigates. The theater "company" he discusses is less an institutionalized organization than (in his phrase) a "strategic venture" allowing the ad hoc formation and dissolution of loose, temporary, contingent alliances of arts workers and activists who negotiate the production of performances to suit specific needs and circumstances. In such a framework the theatrical strategic venture almost disappears behind the group and project with which it works.

According to Donna Nudd, Kristina Schriver, and Terry Galloway, a cabaret club in Florida has constructed a voluntary community through several different avenues: the club is lesbian led and identified yet involves and performs for a much more diverse community that participates on an essentially voluntary basis. In its use of satire and parody the club resumes the issues that McConachie raised about identifying an ethical "us" distinct from—but here perhaps also overlapping—an immoral "them," for in this case an often vilified community turns the tables on dominant notions of morality and identity both: the outcasts become the standardbearers of an oppositional ethics. Thus, the question of a community's ethical identity now comes full circle, only now (one might say) standing on its feet. Whether in the midst of violence and chaos or in more "peacelike" settings of alienation, ignorance, political dissent, or submerged hostility, community-based performance strives to pave avenues of tolerance and acceptance within diversity—civic lessons through practical and participatory forms.

Bruce McConachie

Approaching the "Structure of Feeling" in Grassroots Theater

Racial Representation and the Problem of Ideology

The problem came to a head in the first week of rehearsal. I, a "white" male academic, had cast *Walk Together Children* cross-racially to challenge the Williamsburg community's racial categories and help its members to rethink their racial past. Of the fifteen cast members eight were conventionally "white," six were "black" or "African-American," and one was "Asian-American." In the show, centered on race relations in Williamsburg during the 1950s and 1960s, each actor played from three to eight characters, with "characterization" ranging from storyteller to dancing figure to fully dramatic persona. When race was a significant marker in a scene, the audience could see that about half the time the conventional "race" of the actor did not fit the designated "race" of the character portrayed. (For the "Asian-American" actor her race never matched that of the character she was playing.) Because our grassroots play was based on the oral history of the community during the gradual shift from legal segregation to desegregation in a small southern town, most of the characters in the show were black. Yet, because I had to cast the production with students from a predominately white college, the cross-racial casting mostly matched up white actors with black characters rather than the other way around.

The initial problem arose over my casting a white male actor to play a specific black person, one of the three through-line characters who recur as storytellers and dramatic figures throughout the show. I had not crossed conventional racial categories in the casting of the other two through-line characters, white and black females. It was a part of our arrangement with the Roadside Theatre Company, hired for the academic year of 1995–96 to

Bruce McConachie is the Director of Graduate Studies of Theatre Arts at the University of Pittsburgh, where he continues to practice and teach community-based theater. He has also written extensively on theater historiography and American theater history.

help facilitate our grassroots theater project, that Robbie McCauley, an African-American performer, would work with me and the cast for the first week of rehearsals. Robbie had been a part of the grassroots course during the first semester when she and I, along with Dudley Cocke and Theresa Holden from Roadside, had trained our students in the techniques of story gathering and presentation and educated them about the dynamics of local history and racism. The students had enormous respect for Robbie, both as a patient and insightful teacher and as a professional performer. By late February, when the problem emerged, they had already seen her one-woman show, *My Father and the Wars,* which explores her changing relationship to her own father as he fought abroad for the U.S. Army and against racism at home after 1945. By this time, too, Robbie and I had developed a good working relationship as theater educators and artists. She had helped to shape the work of the citizen Steering Committee and knew some of the locals. I had discussed my concept of the show with her, and we had talked about the ideas of the faculty designers working on *Walk Together.* Robbie had been particularly helpful in mediating a conflict between me and the African-American English professor who was helping us to craft a script from local history and the stories we had collected from the community.

So, when Robbie told me in late February she thought I should cast a black male instead of a white one in the role of this black through-line character, we had a lengthy discussion on the implications of this possible change. Both of us were keenly aware of the context of our discussion—the social and political realities facing young black males in the United States, which had been highlighted recently by the Million Man March. Both of us also knew that some cast members, white and black, were worried about the cross-racial roles they were playing. Robbie had floated her idea to some cast members about changing some of the allocation of roles, and a few had responded warmly. Since we were striving to operate as democratically as possible, including cast members in such general policy decisions was not an abrogation of directorial privilege.

Both of us wanted to talk this through together, however, before engaging the cast in discussions that could have such substantial repercussions for them. Robbie pointed out that casting a black student in the role of a prominent, progressive, humorous, and forceful African-American citizen would send an important message to the local black males at the college and in town. She suggested I consider recasting some other significant black characters along conventional racial lines as well. To my concern that changing the allocation of characters among the cast in that way would radically unbalance the general equity regarding size of roles that I had worked out—that, because there were so many more black roles than white ones, this recasting would invariably marginalize the white actors—Robbie responded that such a balancing act was less important than the racial marking of the black voice. From her point of view cross-racial casting must always allow for specific choices regarding the best way to designate empowered black characters. I did not disagree but pointed out that we were not starting from scratch: rightly or wrongly, I had cast all the black males who auditioned, the major roles were already allocated, and changing things at this point could exacerbate racial tensions among the cast. Robbie said that racial tensions were already higher than I probably realized and that some black males in the cast might take it as a defeat if certain roles were not recast.

Practical and personnel considerations aside, we ended up disagreeing about basic principles and potential audience response. This is not to say that our discussion mirrored the debate then emerging between August Wilson and Robert Brustein. Neither of us endorsed the racialism of the one or the universalism of the other; we both realized that the Wilson–Brustein debate, stuck in the politics of the late 1960s, spoke directly to neither of our concerns. From Robbie's point of view white appropriation and racial pride were at stake. She did not want local African Americans, many of whom had lived through the stories we would be portraying on stage, to "watch white actors represent their significant experiences, especially where that experience was positive and potentially empowering." I, on the other hand, wanted to complicate the local (and national) understanding of race, to recognize it as lived experience but also as social construction. It would be more challenging, though potentially destabilizing, for the local multicultural progressive alliance of both races (of which I was a part), I believed, to avoid identity politics along conventional racial lines by recognizing that such social designations were fluid. For me the issue was the politics of representation, not appropriation. I talked to a couple of African Americans on the citizen Steering Committee to get their input into our disagreement, but they were reluctant to get involved in what both took to be primarily an artistic matter. One told me that who played the roles was much less important to him than just telling the stories of the black community. Given the situation and our conflicting ideological positions, no compromise was feasible. Robbie and I had reached an impasse.[1]

In the end I decided to stand by my point of view and keep the initial casting. Implicitly asserting my authority as the director of the Williamsburg Grassroots Theatre Project, I announced my decision to the cast and my reasons for making it, noting that Robbie and I continued to disagree on the matter. Robbie's graciousness and professionalism kept the conflict from becoming a white-male-director versus black-woman-advisor problem and the cast was generally pleased that we had gotten through the controversy without a lot of nastiness, although some continued to be concerned, and one black cast member resented the outcome. Tensions eased, but many of the questions arising from the principles about which Robbie and I had disagreed continued to trouble several cast members. We all agreed, however, that the fundamental issue had to do with the Williamsburg community. The bottom line for cross-racial casting was audience response, not the feelings of individual cast members. Would the spectators be confused by our deliberate racial mixing of actor and character? If not, would they feel dismayed or empowered by this complication?

As it turned out, the cast and I were caught up in an ideological controversy that seems to have been beside the point for most of the community audience, black as well as white spectators. The William and Mary Theatre production of *Walk Together Children* opened on campus on 11 April 1996 and ran for four performances. Despite the past tensions and the many problems we had encountered coordinating the work of Roadside advisors, faculty playwrights, student cast, and community participants— chief among them the constant press of too little time and the consequent squeeze on democratic decision making for all concerned—the production was a success for all the major groups involved. We played to over a thousand spectators, including a significant number of African-American citizens who do not usually attend college productions. Because we had drawn so heavily on local history and set the stage with local landmarks, much spectator attention was focused simply on who and what was presented. One white townswoman who found it a "spellbinding" show reported: "I sat next to a group of local African Americans who spent intermission discussing who they recognized. I followed out other 'faculty/town' types wondering about the depiction of the college and its president [whom we had criticized for delaying desegregation in the 1960s]."[2]

Gauging general community response to our depiction of race and the history of race relations in Williamsburg is more difficult. Not surprisingly, the local newspaper reviewer barely recognized the racial content of the show, stating only that the script effectively recreated "pain and injustice without resorting to rhetoric." In notes to me after we closed, friends and acquaintances were more forthright but not any more enlightening about the ideological controversy that had racked our rehearsals. One longtime resident who had helped the community to desegregate, an Asian-American sociologist at the college, wrote that it was "poignant to be reminded of just how tentative and fragile black/white relations were—even among those who were well meaning."[3] A student in the cast who had been concerned about the identity politics of the production for blacks admitted that, for the most part, her parents and friends did not share her views after seeing the show. My friends on the Steering Committee and other local African Americans told me they had no problem with white actors standing in as and relating stories about their younger selves and others they knew; but neither did this practice get them thinking about how Americans define race. While I believe these respondents were telling the truth, I have no way of knowing what other truths might have emerged if we had decided to cast the show differently.

Instead of focusing on the meanings and ideological implications of our show, most of the community spectators we talked to in story circles following performances spoke of the visual and aural images that had given them pleasure. These comments often took the form of: "I liked the bit where . . ." or "I enjoyed the musical number when . . . ." The talk was of images, formed through judgment and feeling, and only secondarily of meanings. In these story circles and elsewhere, many black residents thanked me and others for presenting the show and expressed their interest in participating in future productions of the Williamsburg Grassroots Theatre Project. It was clear that our production had empowered them, although this was not a word anyone used. Some of the most significant images for the spectators had to do with the aura of an inclusive community that the show had generated. One post-show letter to me by an African-American community leader, a woman of great hope and fervent faith, summed up the feelings of many local spectators:

> We really have missed out on what we could have shared together to make this a peacefully [sic], happy, safe, productive and progressive community. . . . Blacks are a part of our community (an important part). Whites and other nationalities are a part of our community (an important part). Yes there are social and economic diversity [sic], but each can learn from the other. We *need* one another. REAL love for your fellowman does not have color nor social and/or economic boundaries. There is only one GOD, who created us (all) in HIS image (HE *can not / will not* be divided).[4]

A long-time white resident, a local architect and political moderate, expressed similar sentiments to me about community inclusiveness (minus the Christian gloss) in private conversation. For many citizens utopian hopes for a single community were what *Walk Together Children* was all about.

Most current discussions of "grassroots" or "community-based" the-ater, however, slight this general emotional response to these kinds of per-formances to concentrate on the purported ideological meanings read by the audience. The "central assumption" of Baz Kershaw's *Politics of Perfor-mance* is that "performance can be most usefully described as an *ideological transaction* between a company of performers and the community of their audience." Richard Owen Geer follows Kershaw's lead in his essay about his work with a small town in southern Georgia. So too does Sonja Kuftinec's insightful analysis of Cornerstone Theatre productions in several locales since 1986.[5]

Certainly, "ideological transaction" is a part of every performance, but the mutual making of meaning is not all that occurs in theater, and, arguably, it is not the part that matters most to its primary participants in community-based shows, local performers and spectators. I am aware, of course, that audience interest in theatrical images has been no deterrent to theater scholars (myself included) interested in understanding the ideologi-cal implications of audience response. But for community-based theater especially, when close attention to spectator desires and anxieties is a neces-sary part of the ongoing process, the emphasis on meaning apart from judg-ment and pleasure can lead astray those of us particularly concerned with furthering the goals and practice of grassroots theater. To be sure, all images have political implications, but they are often much more ambivalent and even ambiguous for audiences (and performers) than most analyses focused solely on ideology tend to comprehend. And, when the stakes center on racial representation and/or appropriation, ideological meanings can be slip-pery indeed.

It was evident to me and others that several white actors in the William and Mary cast gave black audience members "a good night out" by relating stories from their local history.[6] I believe this is because the community-centered images of the show, based mostly on the aural stories and truths shared by the African-American community and then told back to them by the cast of *Walk Together,* became more important to the spectators than the visual images tied to racial characterization. The production's emphasis on an orally defined community allowed audiences to relax temporarily their usual anxieties focused on visual racial markings and to judge and enjoy the show's images as potential citizens of an ideal locale.

Following a summary of my general point of view concerning the response of community audiences to grassroots theater, I will analyze selected images from *Walk Together Children* through this lens. In some ways I am not the right person to be writing this essay. Certainly, given my intense involvement as director of the Williamsburg Grassroots Theatre Project over the course of a year, I am in no position to comment dispassionately and at length on the structure of our work, the process we used (and that used us), and the artistic success we may have achieved. Probably my continuing hopes and anxieties about *Walk Together Children* will also undercut my attempt to move beyond ideological intentions and effects in analyzing some of the visual and aural images of the show in the context of our grassroots theatrical conversation. Nonetheless, in addition to some theoretical distance I can claim the local knowledge of an insider achingly familiar with the production. I also have the excuse that, if I didn't write about the images of this show, no one else would.

A Grassroots "Structure of Feeling" and Community Dynamics

Raymond Williams used the term *structure of feeling* to designate the emotional bonding generated by values and practices shared by a specific group, class, or culture. The concept includes ideology, in the sense of an articulated structure of beliefs, but also ranges beyond it to encompass collective desires and concerns below the conscious level. Williams, for much of his academic life a professor of drama at Cambridge University, applied *structure of feeling* both to the general dynamics of culture and to the specific interaction that occurs in theatrical communication. The term suggests both the rich images that spark immediate "feelings" from audience members and the underlying "structures" that generate these images.[7] Is there, then, a general *structure of feeling* in successful community-based theater, and, if so, how might one describe and analyze it?

Clearly, any such emotional structure pertaining to a wide variety of theatrical experiences—Kershaw documents fifty troupes doing "community" theater in Britain in 1984–85, and the actual number may have been higher[8]—must result from the general aims and orientation of this kind of theater. They are effectively summarized in the "Matrix Articulating the Principles of Grassroots Theater" written by participants at a symposium of practitioners, critics, funders, and others at Cornell University in 1992. Instead of arriving at a single definition, these advocates constituted community-based theater as a patchwork quilt of related sources, goals, and structures:

> Grassroots theater grows out of a commitment to place. It is grounded
> in the local and specific. . . . The traditional and indigenous are integral
> to grassroots theater and valued for their ability to help us maintain
> continuity with the past, respond to the present, and prepare for the
> future. . . . Grassroots theater strives to be inclusive in its producing
> practices. Presentation of the work is made in partnership with com-
> munity organizations. . . . Grassroots theater is linked to the struggles
> for cultural, social, economic, and political equity for all people. It is
> fundamentally a theater of hope and often joy. . . . Grassroots theater is
> given its voice by the community from which it arises. The makers of
> grassroots theater are part of the culture from which the work is drawn.
> The people who are the subjects of the work are part of its develop-
> ment from inception through presentation.[9]

Stitching together the separate components of this matrix is one embedded
thread: the processes and products of grassroots theater are built on a strong
alliance (and, at times, a complete merging) of theater workers with a local
community.

Many advocates of grassroots theater would keep *community* in quotes
or avoid using it at all because the word carries too much historical baggage
and evokes so many contradictory meanings and emotions. The participants
at the Cornell symposium, for instance, preferred *grassroots* over *community-
based* to designate their kind of theater. For some, *community-based* suggested
an endorsement of a conservative, tradition-bound politics. Several believed
that "the idea of community itself is in transformation" and concluded that
it was pointless to build their theater on shifting definitional sands. Others
felt that social forces beyond the community—racism, capitalism, imperialism—had so reduced the influence of face-to-face interaction that it was
foolish to try to work at that level.

In her analysis of Cornerstone Theatre's productions Kuftinec notes
the group's frequent evocation of communal commonality but sharply
questions the representational truth and long-term effectiveness of this
"mythology." From her point of view, using terms like Victor Turner's
communitas, the temporary bonding that occurs among participants in a ritual, to describe the effect of a grassroots show conceals very real differences
of race, background, gender, and belief. Cornerstone's adaptation along
racial lines of *Romeo and Juliet* for a small town in Mississippi, for instance,
apparently did little to alter the racial divisions in the town. "When Cornerstone and residents of an area participating in a production speak of the
work as celebrating community or unifying community, it is essential to

bear in mind the unstable and temporary nature of this community," Kuftinec concludes.[10] (The same might be said of *Walk Together Children* in Williamsburg; when local residents spoke of "community," most knew they were blurring social reality with their hopes and ideals.)

Nonetheless, Kuftinec notes that many of the people in the small towns that hire Cornerstone plus the troupe itself continue to use the language of community to describe their interventions. Kershaw reports that some of the most successful grassroots theater in Great Britain in the 1980s came out of Ann Jellicoe's work, self-described in the title of her popular book, *Community Plays: How to Put Them On.*[11] Despite its problems for critics and practitioners, the discourse of "community" seems wedded to descriptions and analysis of this kind of theater. I believe this is because the dynamics of community building in the late twentieth century provide the significant *structure of feeling* for grassroots theater.

As real communities—cohesive social groups engaged in sustaining their members' identities through face-to-face interactions—dwindle in significance in people's everyday lives, the imaginative construction of community assumes a greater importance. Actually, as Anthony Cohen points out in *The Symbolic Construction of Community,* people have always created images of community in order to shape and maintain their sense of belongingness and self-worth. Raymond Williams notes, too, that communities provide "the necessary mediating element between individuals and large society." For these reasons the term *community* operates as a "God word," according to Cohen, a power invoked to provide symbolic unity in the face of real differences within the group.[12] To assert membership in a community, individuals must disregard these differences and assert commonalities that separate them from other groups. Together and over time, people in communities create boundaries between what is to be included in and what must be excluded from their social group.

They do this, asserts Cohen, by agreeing on emotion-laden symbols that carry major significance for their lives. Religious insignias, for example, serve to define and differentiate many "communities of interest," Cohen's term for groups united by a common ideology, such as a church congregation. In "communities of location," however, where ideological commonality is typically weak, the symbols of community unity often cluster around geographical or historical images. In neither type of community is it usually important for community members to agree on the meanings of their symbols. Rather, says Cohen, members need only use the same symbols to proclaim their uniqueness and sharpen their differences. The image of a local school mascot, for instance, often evokes strong emotions but carries a vari-

ety of meanings for community members. In the context of a school basketball game, however, it clearly separates "us" from "them."

The symbolic work of community building is never done; including
some symbols and excluding others is a lifelong task. In the recent past,
when most people living in the industrial world were reminded of their
local ties through dozens of symbols in their everyday lives as well as
through commonplace interactions, they had less need than now for the
kind of imaginative community building that might occur through performance. Even so, parades, high school graduations, sports events, and school
plays provided potent performative symbols of "communities of location."
Today in the postindustrial world the psychosocial desire for the sustaining
power of community remains, but the practices and symbols of everyday
reality provide fewer assurances of its reality and support. The structures of
international capitalism and modern communications move people around
more frequently, isolate them from their neighbors, and fill their heads with
multinational corporate images, not local symbols. Surely, part of the reason
for the recent successes of grassroots theaters is that they provide images for
their audiences that help them to do the symbolic work of including and
excluding that constitutes a community. No performance by itself can alter
the routines of everyday life, but community-based theater can provide
"what if" images of potential community, sparking the kind of imaginative
work that must precede substantial changes in customary habits.

How, specifically, might this occur in the performance of a grassroots
play? Part of the answer lies in what Kershaw, following Elizabeth Burns,
calls appropriate rhetorical and authenticating conventions for the performance. These conventions, "the means by which the audience is persuaded
to accept characters and situations whose validity is ephemeral and bound to
the theatre" (rhetorical) and the semiosis of the play, the signs that "'model'
social conventions in use at a specific time and in a specific place and
milieu" (authenticating), must connect the audience to the possibilities of
community experience in their own lives.[13] Simply put, *how* the show is
communicated and *what* is communicated must draw on conventions that
are locally familiar. In this way residents can be induced to put their imaginations to work in the symbolic building of community during the show.
(Within the definitions proposed by Kershaw-Burns, Robbie McCauley
and I disagreed about whether cross-racial casting would provide an appropriate "rhetorical" convention for *Walk Together*. Specifically, would
African-American spectators accept white actors as valid representatives of
black life in Williamsburg?) Rhetorical and authenticating conventions

include modes of singing accessible to the community, specific stories rooted to the locale, visual symbols drawn from familiar scenes, speech and diction patterns that call forth time and place, ways of walking and gesturing specific to a group. Practitioners of grassroots theater could supply hundreds of similar examples of rhetorical and authenticating conventions that have proven successful in their work.

Kershaw knows that many of these conventions are based in the oral traditions and practices of the community, but he does not emphasize this point. In terms of what Viv Edwards and Thomas J. Sienkewicz call the oral-literate continuum, grassroots theater draws heavily—both in its creative processes and final performances—from the oral end of the spectrum. The well-told tale is at the center of most community-based theater. Because the dynamics of storytelling are so deeply embedded in this form of performance, the human voice (often regardless of the visual image of the speaking actor) has great power to evoke a web of sympathetic connections. And, if the audience experiencing these narratives is attuned to orality, it may be able to accept several different kinds of performers as voices of their community.[14]

While this orientation toward orality and the general conventions of community-based performance are clear enough in many descriptions of the form, the ways in which these factors are usually brought into play by the performers and "regarded" by their audience to create a *structure of feeling* typical of grassroots theater are not. *Regarding theatre* is the term used by Alan Read in his *Theatre and Everyday Life* to designate the primary activity of an engaged audience. From his point of view spectators at a live performance do much more than look and passively consume when theater is working as it should. Rather, audiences rely mostly on their immediate feelings to make ethical judgments continually about the "images" in play. These images, though initiated onstage, are part of an ongoing transaction, "an economy of symbolic exchange," between audience members and performers. The images that interest Read combine the nexus of bodies, props, and light that form material images onstage and the mental pictures and sounds in the heads of spectators regarding them. Located in an idealized space between spectator and performer, the images oscillate, says Read, "between the material and metaphysical."[15]

Read's insights, based primarily on Michel de Certeau's mix of phenomenology and materialism, are particularly helpful in understanding the dynamics of grassroots theater. In part this is because Read uses his own experience of nine years as the director of an East End London community-based theater to generalize about the communal basis of all theatrical exchange. All theater is local for Read, bound up with the ethics of every-day life. Ethics, believes Read, quoting de Certeau, "defines a distance between what is and what ought to be. This distance designates a space where we have something to do." Adds Read, "This is the place where the-atre occurs. Both ethics and theatre are concerned with possibility." Bor-rowing from Richard Kearney's *The Wake of the Imagination: Ideas of Cre-ativity in Western Culture,* Read sees theater as the best medium to alter the face-to-face ethical relationships of community because theater puts live people in a room together and asks them to imagine themselves living in one another's shoes. Thus, he states, there is a "structural acquaintance" between the theatrical process of image creation and "the dynamic of com-munities to imagine themselves." Read concludes that "images and the imagination are . . . the means through which the material needs of com-munities form and disperse. . . . It is precisely through images that the first tentative transformation of everyday existing realities is first conducted."[16]

The cognitive psychology of George Lakoff and Mark Johnson extends Read's insights into these communal images and provides persuasive evi-dence of their importance. Building on the empirical evidence of cognitive science, Lakoff has been examining how human beings categorize their experiences to create meaning, while Johnson has investigated the philo-sophical ramifications of their work. Both, like Read and de Certeau, are phenomenological realists. Lakoff and Johnson hold that certain presemiotic patterns in our minds come between perception and conception to structure human understanding. These patterns are distinctive "image schemata," singly defined by Johnson as a "recurring, dynamic pattern of our perceptual interactions and motor programs that gives coherence and structure to our experience." The path schema, for example, which humans learn kinesthet-ically at a young age by crawling from one location to an end point, struc-tures certain events in our experience as a narrative with a beginning, mid-dle, and end. As this example suggests, image schemata are linked to primal human interactions with the world—an infant's experiences with contain-ment, gravity, and mobility shape the images and basic-level categories in its mind. All humans share the capability for developing the same range of image schemata, but different cultures, societies, and historical eras empha-size different patterns. Together with basic-level categories, image schemata structure all perceptions, including those constructed in performance.[17]

Lakoff and Johnson's tentative list of image schemata provides a sug-gestive chart of distinctive performance images that can aid analysis. "Balance," for instance, occurs when spectators experience performers attempting to maintain some kind of equilibrium, be it physical, vocal, psychological, or some combination of these and other types. Audience perception of a tightrope walker or of a singing quartet working for harmonious balance are examples. With "surface," audiences are led to focus on similarities and differences in two dimensions, rather than three, as in the experience of much modern art and television viewing. Regarding "scale," spectators are induced to rank performed actions on a vertical hierarchy of importance. Any sports activity that measures winning on the basis of points scored involves "scale," as does much dramatic theater that ordinates differences by gender, race, and class. The experience of "counterforce" invites audiences to identify with performers exerting their will against an aggressive power. Lakoff and Johnson understand these image schemata as patterns of perception, but for my purposes they can provide a rough grammar of primal images that link audience experience directly with performance activity and provide the structure of feeling for a performance.

Of central importance in the generation of these shared images is the live presence of actors. Like Read, Jon Erickson conceives of embodied stage images as the mutual creation of spectators and performers. In *The Fate of the Object* Erickson states, "The tension between the *body as object* and the *body as sign* gives birth to an awareness of *presence* as the tension between basic corporal being and the becoming of signification."[18] This tension between corporeal materiality and semiotic possibility is inevitable, believes Erickson, because it is impossible for spectators and performers to perceive performed images as either pure bodies or pure signs; they are always both. Thus, actors live at the dynamic center of image schemata experienced in the theater. Reading Erickson in conjunction with Read, we can conclude that performers and audience members enjoy the dynamic oscillation between corporeality and signification in the embodied images they have constructed together in the theater. This experience occurs in all theatrical events that "work," grassroots theater included.

What seems to be somewhat unique about the experience of community-based theater are the kinds of images generated and what the audience does with them. Prompted by the rhetorical and authenticating conventions that are a part of grassroots theater, spectators are induced to turn their imaginations to the ethical relations that might constitute their local, face-to-face lives. Specifically, following Anthony Cohen, it is possible to hypothesize that audiences use the symbolic exchange of the theatrical experience to make judgments about the kinds of images to include or exclude from their ideal community. Community-based theater, then, is less about representing the realities of actual or historic communities—although markers of these realities need to be present to "authenticate" the experience—and more about imagining and constructing the relationships of an ethical community for the future. The images generated in a grassroots show provide a structure of feeling that induces the audience to divide an ethical "us" from an immoral "them" and then to examine who "we" are.

The image schemata of Lakoff and Johnson help to clarify how this works. Understood within their grammar of images, community-based theater relies primarily on the image schemata of "containment." As Johnson discusses it, "containment involves necessary relations among an 'inside,' an 'outside,' and a boundary dividing them." He summarizes five entailments that derive from this schema:

> (i) The experience of containment typically involves protection from, or resistance to, external forces. When eyeglasses are *in* a case, they are protected against forceful impacts. (ii) Containment also limits and restricts forces within the container. When I am *in* a room, or *in* a jacket, I am restrained in my forceful movements. (iii) Because of this restraint of forces, the contained object gets a relative fixity of location. For example, the fish gets located *in* the fishbowl. The cup is held *in* the hand. (iv) This relative fixing of location within the container means that the contained object becomes either accessible or inaccessible to the observer. It is either held so that it can be observed or else the container itself blocks or hides the object from view. (v) Finally, we experience transitivity of containment. If B is *in* A, then whatever is *in* B is also *in* A. If I am *in* my bed and my bed is *in* my room, then I am also *in* my room.[19]

Shifting these entailments into the arena of grassroots theater provides general insight into the kinds of images and experiences typical of this kind of theater: (1) Community-based theater can evoke images of protection from forces outside of the community. (2) It can sharpen perceptions of conflict within the community. (3) Grassroots theater can celebrate or problematize location. (4) It can provide images that reveal or block realities below the surface of community life. (5) It can move spectators and actors to experience smaller and larger images of contained communities, from neighborhood to nation to (perhaps) world. None of these "entailments" relating to community-based theater is particularly surprising. They simply systematize what cultural workers in grassroots theater have known for decades. But they do provide a firm basis for distinguishing this kind of theater from other types and for leading performance analysis toward a better understanding of its aesthetics and politics.

As Read knows, when spectators imagine the possibility of an ethical community, politics cannot be far behind. Citizens who construct ideal futures for their community during theatrical interaction will likely be more interested in local politics. And the kinds of imaginative choices about inclusion and exclusion they have made while enjoying the show, plus the many images of containment they have regarded, may influence their political choices. Hence, community-based theater has the potential for helping to shape a more inclusive democratic process with more equitable results at the local level. Many grassroots advocates and practitioners—including Kershaw, Geer, Cocke, and McCauley—understand this possibility and work toward it in their productions.

Given the structure of feeling in these plays—their images of containment and their inducements to include and exclude—however, a progressive result is not inevitable. Conservatives and reactionaries have ethical principles that could also form the basis for an imagined community in the future. The communitarianism of Amitai Etzioni emphasizes the common good over personal freedom, group responsibilities over individual rights, and civic virtues over capitalist incentives—all values that foreground images of containment and hence could emerge from participating in a grassroots project. Yet there is much in communitarianism that would trouble many advocates of grassroots theater. In short, there is no guarantee that community-based theater will produce progressive community politics.

All that can be affirmed is that grassroots performances will probably help to turn local residents into better citizens, in the sense of Michael Oakeshott's understanding of citizenship as a kind of consensual identification. Oakeshott defines *politics* as "the activity of attending to the general arrangements of a collection of people who, in respect of their common recognition of their manner of attending to its arrangements, compose a single community."[20] In a liberal democracy a political community only exists, in other words, among citizens who recognize its procedures and attend to its business. All adult residents may have a vote in local elections, but not all voters become true citizens, in Oakeshott's sense. Certainly, the dynamics of grassroots theater can turn more voters into citizens, but community-based performance in general does not mandate a specific direction for the "attending" that citizens practice.

Walk Together Children in the Context of Williamsburg

While community-based theater in general has no specific political orientation, each grassroots performance of modest coherence and success within a
local community invariably animates ethical images that move its audiences
in certain political directions. For "communities of location" these directions are unlikely to be ideologically specific, as noted earlier. Moreover,
because audiences have as much control as theater workers over the mutual
images constructed and experienced, the local context always inflects the
specific structure of feeling that emerges in performance. Like any group of
spectators, local folks bring a wide variety of desires, anxieties, and agendas
with them to the theater; there is never a single context shaping the
response of local citizens to a community-based production. Nonetheless,
in the contained space where notions of citizenship and community ethics
intersect—the space of grassroots theater—there is often a rough consensus
about an acceptable range of general ethics and future goals. And among the
majority of residents who are likely to spend their time at a theatrical performance, this taken-for-granted spectrum of values may not range very
widely. This spectrum necessarily shapes local perceptions about the ethics
of images understood to be inside or outside of the community as they are
ostended during the production.

Williamsburg, Virginia, is typical in this regard. Where community
ethics are concerned, locals tend to hold views shaped by individualistic
capitalism and Christian belief. On a Left-Right political continuum most
observers would probably identify Williamsburgers as moderate to conservative. This general picture holds across racial lines, although local blacks,
who constitute about a quarter of the area population, have somewhat different beliefs when it comes to the importance of religion and racial solidarity. With regard to the local citizens attending *Walk Together Children,*
they were generally older than average, better educated, wealthier, and
more liberal in their social and political views than the rest of the region.
Despite our best efforts to draw more local working-class families into the
theater, the audiences for our four performances, though more racially integrated than usual, remained predominately "middle-class." Given the general demographics of theater audiences in America, none of this is surprising, even for grassroots theater.[21]

While we were developing *Walk Together,* a local group of concerned
citizens calling themselves "All Together" gathered to advocate changes in
the racial status quo in Williamsburg. Formed in response to local racial

divisions evident after the Simpson verdict and the Million Man March, "All Together" began as a small interracial group of community leaders in October 1995 and by June 1996 had a mailing list of over two hundred Williamsburg-area residents. Many of the citizens who shared their stories from the 1950s and 1960s with students in the Grassroots Theatre Project also participated in the three general meetings called by the leaders of "All Together." I attended all of their meetings and was invited to speak about the techniques and goals of our Grassroots Theatre Project at one of them. We included their mailing list when we sent out flyers inviting the community to attend our production. Articles about "All Together" appeared near articles for *Walk Together* in the local newspaper before the show. In short the discourse of "All Together" provided a major context within which many Williamsburg citizens (in Oakeshott's sense) might regard (in Read's sense) the images of our grassroots show. Significantly, this discourse also marked out specific limits within which acceptable dialogue about race might occur in Williamsburg. These limits, then, impinged upon the images of local community that most citizens helped to construct when they enjoyed our production.

The discourse of "All Together" spoke primarily to local concerns about attitudinal divisions between black and white residents. Its "Statement of Mission and Goals" announced this focus near the beginning of the document: "The crisis our generation faces encompasses *a sense of* division, separation, fear and distrust. These unhealthy frustrations, which endanger our common future, must be challenged so that *attitudes* are positively altered."[22] Out of this concern emerged what the statement termed "our mission": "To bring people together to share openly our similarities, differences, strengths and weaknesses, leading to positive changes in attitudes enabling us to solve community problems." More specific goals followed, which included: "Foster improved human relationships," "Bridge religious, racial [and other] differences," "Work cooperatively to identify and attack the root causes of the problems confronting us," "Improve all forms of communication." In sum, the document assumes that racial divisions in Williamsburg are mostly a product of uncivil and unhealthy attitudes, that more human interaction across racial lines could change these attitudes, and that more "positive" attitudes will enable the community to "solve" many of its problems. In some tension with these assumptions is the statement's assertion that there are some community problems with "root causes" that apparently lie beyond racial bad attitudes. But what these might be and how one might uproot them remain unspoken.

Entirely missing from this "statement" is any acknowledgment that structural relations of power embedded in circum-Atlantic, national, and regional history have shaped and continue to dominate the discourse and practice of race relations in Williamsburg. The document turns its back on this massive reality; the real problem, according to the statement, is the "sense of division, separation, fear and mistrust." Real division and separation along racial lines is a mirage, a false reality, that merely requires the new eyeglasses of a positive attitude to see through. A genuine community of racial togetherness beyond the unfortunate but unimportant circumstances of history and power waits only for the right vision to recognize its validity.

This naive hope, clearly derived from Christian faith but with little input from democratic experience, is reflected in other documents from "All Together." One later statement, a listing of "Problems" and "Solutions," clearly recognized some of the major sources of discord in Williamsburg: "racism," "economic disparity," "too few blacks and women [in powerful positions]," "access to hospital care," and "housing," among them. But the solutions to these social and political problems never got past: "treat each other with dignity," "assemble data," "encourage blacks and women to become more active," "increase mentorship activity," "more positive coverage in the newspapers," and "[create occasions] to celebrate our diversity."[23] Another document urged action "to bring about fairness and equity" but at the same time asserted the essential fairness and equity of existing community institutions: "We have systems in place for a civilized society—justice, education, political, welfare, banking, and health. All who are affected need to be involved in making it work."[24] As might be expected, some of this discourse reflects the mindless boosterism of any small town concerned about its self-image. Also at play, however, are the numbing denial and hypocrisy that infect American talk about race.

Nonetheless, this myth of an ideal community, troubled but fundamentally unstained by racism, capitalism, and other long-term inequalities, continued to sustain the energy and commitment of the citizens participating in "All Together." The leaders of the community group, some of whom did not completely agree with the sunny certainties of its discourse, apparently understood that this kind of talk was necessary to build a following in Williamsburg. Despite (and partly because of) its shallow and dishonest social analysis, this discourse did give its believers a sense of empowerment and entitlement in attending to matters of race in local affairs. "All Together" began, and for others continued, a process of turning voters into citizens that *Walk Together Children* would also facilitate. Its limitations—the limitations of many groups of concerned citizens in the United States—also contained the kinds of images that local citizens would coconstruct while participating in our production.

I will focus on significant moments within three major scenes from the production to examine the mutual making of images during the show and their implications for the ethical construction of community. One significant symbol ostended by the performers in *Walk Together* was an interracial circle of citizens sharing their personal stories with one another. Each of the two acts of the show began with this "story circle," a suggestive symbol of containment that was actually a half-oval of actors sitting on a rounded apron stage and open to the audience. In these scenes, set in the present, each student performer, many cross-racially cast, played a single man or woman who remembered images from the 1950s and 1960s. The actors, dressed in partial costumes to indicate their older characters, sat on black and white folding chairs and related their stories. Gradually, the circle broke up (although many of the chairs remained in place) as the performers moved offstage or to other stage areas to perform roles in scenes set in the past and requiring more physical action.

In our conception of the show we had decided to anchor each act of *Walk Together* in the process the students had actually used to gather the stories. We expected that audience members who had been community participants in the project would recall the story circle they had been a part of. Other spectators, we hoped, would get a sense of the authenticity of the stories told and perhaps be moved to participate in a story circle in the community at a later date. By emphasizing the oral tradition that grounded the production, we (unintentionally) decentered the visual cues marking racial characterization to suggest the potential commonality of citizenship. Of course, our onstage symbol of a story circle did not match the actuality of any community meeting that had occurred the previous fall. Through dialogue, clothing, and gestures the performers signaled a group that was much more diverse—in class, education, and background, in addition to race—than any that had met. For dramatic purposes their stories were less rambling and more interesting than any actually told.

In act 1, following self-introductions around the circle, the conversation shifted to race relations under segregation, with brief personal stories about cross-racial friendships, racial antagonisms, and white guilt. Probably the story that set the tone for the scene was the first long narrative, remembered by a black woman, now in her fifties, who spoke about a time when the "whole community," primarily white neighbors, pitched in to help her mother when her ten children, the narrator among them, had accidentally contracted ptomaine poisoning. "We all came together in a tragedy" was the theme of her story.[25]

What image might Williamsburg citizens, responding from within the general orientation of the "All Together" discourse, have constructed from this scene? Probably an image of racial inclusiveness, only slightly modified, if at all, by social and historical understanding. The mental picture painted by the black woman telling the story mostly matched the stage picture while the actor was speaking. That is, the audience saw an actor whom some may have identified as Asian-American but most probably took to be a light-skinned African American talking to other student actors, both white and black, playing other characters sitting in a half-circle who, through their eager faces, friendly gestures, and patient listening, were helping the "black" woman to tell her story. The story itself, while it probably happened to the local resident who told it, may have been embellished by her desire to link her own memory with the myth of the security and cohesiveness of the archetypal American small town of the past. This myth has particular local salience because "Colonial Williamsburg," the restored eighteenth-century village at the center of modern Williamsburg, is still portrayed and per-ceived locally as an idealized community, despite the recent incursions of unpleasant social realities into the historical interpretation told to visitors. It is unlikely, however, that many Williamsburg citizens complicated their image of a racially inclusive community in this way.

Nor, probably, did their image include thoughts about the economic and sexual realities that led the narrator's mother to have such a large fam-ily in the first place, without the prospect of medical insurance or an ade-quate income to take care of them. From the narrator's point of view the episode of ptomaine poisoning was a "tragedy," not an avoidable event, and the audience saw little onstage to question this image of a black woman under segregation grateful for neighborly Christian charity. In retrospect we might have done more at the top of the show to help the audience toward a complicated image of the segregation past, but our primary goal in this first scene was to ease them into the recognition that blacks and whites had helped one another in the past and might again in the future. Besides, there were several strong scenes of racial injustice still to come. The dialogue and staging probably helped the audience toward the ethical judgment that Williamsburg is a racially diverse community and citizens must help one another through the difficult parts of their lives.

On the other hand, the cross-racial casting of many of the characters in the story circle may have prompted some in the audience to wonder about the nature of this past and future "help" across racial lines. We had deliberately jumbled the race of many actors and characters in this first scene, in part to alert the audience that this rhetorical convention would recur throughout the show. Spectators told us later that this apparent "mismatch" between several actors and characters—taken to an extreme when one white character played by a black actor recalled how his daddy had employed many "colored folks" to work in his fields—led them to pay very close attention. In Erickson's sense of "presence" we had increased the tension between the body as object and the body as sign. Suddenly, for the audience, a black body might signify a white character. Or a body that seemed ambiguously racially marked, such as the Asian American in the cast, could somehow become an African-American character. Ironically, the heightened presence of these racially "confused" bodies drew audience attention to their speech; oral narrative, not visual cues, became the primary mode of understanding.

As I mentioned earlier, it is not clear to me how the cross-racial casting finally played out in the experience of the audience. But in the instance of the initial story circle and the ptomaine poisoning narrative, when the audience was still adjusting to this rhetorical convention, it may have destabilized racial categories sufficiently to allow some spectators to probe the historical situation and question the seemingly Christian and liberal act of community whites helping a black family through a tragedy. Even if this were so, however, the first scene of *Walk Together Children* did little to challenge or extend the limited imagination evident in the discourse of "All Together." Although the scene was ideologically undemanding, the audience had to listen closely as well as see to judge and enjoy the images.

Several spectators told me that one of the most moving incidents of the first act was what we in the production had come to call "the crow scene." It began with a black female teacher, played by a white actor, narrating the story of a student's summer job on a construction team as told to her and his classmates by the student on his first day back from summer vacation. A black actor playing Calvin, the student, picked up the narrative thread:

> They had a white boy, same age as me. And you know, it looked like every time there was a hole to go in, I would be the one to get in that hole. And it seemed to me like some of those holes were gettin' deeper and deeper. Sometimes you could be over a sewer line or something that you didn't know was there and we'd have to dig all around it. One day I was so far down in the hole I couldn't see anything but blue sky. I was workin', workin', and then I heard this strange noise. Then I looked up, I craned my neck all the way up to the sky and saw that

there were crows flying overhead. One of the larger ones—seemed like
one of the larger ones—perched just on the edge of that hole and he
went "Squawk! Squawk!"[26]

While Calvin was speaking, four other actors, initially Calvin's high school
classmates, transformed into an image of the hole by joining hands around
Calvin, crouching on their chairs, and then slowly rising to create an
impression of Calvin's descent (see fig. 1). Their arms continued to rise after
they stood, and then their hands parted and opened on "blue sky." Next,
their eight arms and hands became crows' wings and their voices picked up
Calvin's "squawks," turning them into menacing screams as they "flew"
around him. Finally, the group squawks transformed into words, indistinguishable at first but building in intensity and finally heard, in a mocking
chorus, by the audience as "Look at the nigger in the hole!"[27]

When the class first heard the crow story in the fall, told during a story
circle by a Williamsburg teacher, we knew we had a powerful scene. Several students had already worked up the piece for quick production at a pot-
luck dinner in November to show the community participants what we
were working on. Even without music, lights, and further shaping in
rehearsal, the scene evoked gasps for its nightmarish evocation of the experience of racism. The sharp verticality of the image, oppressive figures on
top and a sympathetic victim in the "hole," coupled with animalistic noises
becoming a vicious human attack, would have rattled almost any audience.

Yet to what effect? Certainly, most spectators felt the helpless terror
that occasionally accompanied black life under segregation. For some local
citizens the crow scene was probably a bit like watching film clips of liberated concentration camps after the Holocaust or hanging bodies lynched by
the Klan; a shocking image of degraded humanity dominated the picture. In
terms of the inclusion/exclusion dynamic keying spectators' response, the
crow scene gave them a type of villainy to exclude from their ideal community of the future: No one who makes black youth feel that way should
be allowed in an ethical Williamsburg! I suspect that our use of a circle of
containment—the arms around Calvin keeping him inside the hole—
heightened the impact of the scene. Human circles that had been friendly
and supportive for most of the show suddenly turned malign.

On the face of it there's nothing wrong with the simple human
response of "Never again!" to the experience of oppressive inhumanity. Yet
a certain smugness can accompany this response and the image inducing it
if the spectator believes that such incidents are safely in the past, that there
is little she or he must do to ensure that such incidents do not recur in the

Crow Scene in *Walk Together Children,* Phi Beta Kappa Auditorium,
College of William and Mary, April 1996. Photograph courtesy of
Department of Theatre and Speech at the College of William and
Mary.

future. In this regard the response of black citizens in Williamsburg to these
scenes may have varied significantly from that of many white audience
members. Although set in the past, *Walk Together Children* encouraged audiences to find some similarities between past and present situations. I know
from my conversations after the production that many African Americans
drew on their experience to make these connections during and after the
performance. In the crow scene, however, there was little shown clearly by
the performers in the primary image itself that might have jarred white spectators into the recognition that blacks continue to experience racism in this
way in Williamsburg. While the discourse of "All Together" recognized the
continuing degradations of racism, its focus on "attitude" denied the legitimacy, on one level, of black fear and rage in the face of racist oppression; in
effect, the discourse partly blamed the victims of racism for their bad attitudes toward the rest of the community. The image in the crow scene

allowed white citizens to experience that fear, but the discourse of "All Together" undercut the legitimacy of black rage.

There were, however, several other scenes in the production that showed a white power structure from the past directly oppressing local blacks. Plus, some scenes recognized that black citizens in Williamsburg continue to hold most of the low-paying and menial jobs in town. Sensitive white spectators might have understood the crow scene in this wider context and recognized their responsibility for ensuring that "never again" in the ethical city of the future would young blacks experience racism so overtly. Yet general concern about the future can occur with very little real knowledge of the present. The structural realities of Williamsburg's tourist traffic allows racism to work hand in glove with economics to keep most local blacks "in their [historical] place." Our production did little to address these present structures. Most whites remain insulated from the recognition that current realities in Williamsburg continue to churn up the emotions of being "the nigger in a hole" for a quarter of its citizens.

Our general intention in structuring *Walk Together Children* was to combine mostly sympathetic and upbeat stories to pull in the audience during act 1 and then hit them with harder, more intractable situations in act 2. White spectators may have been able to dismiss some of the images of the first act as belonging to the bad old racist past, but we made this increasingly difficult for them by our focus on race relations in education in the second act. As in many American small towns (and many larger cities), the schools continue to be flash points in many conflicts inflected by race; Williamsburg is no exception. By national standards and according to local conventional wisdom, Williamsburg had handled school desegregation fairly well. After a slow start the local school board had fully desegregated the schools by 1968–69 with no headline-grabbing incidents, maintained a generally high quality (by regional standards) of instruction, and minimized white flight to private schools. Yet it was also evident from the local history we read and the stories we heard that genuine integration had not occurred. African-American teachers had been forced to adopt the "superior" instructional techniques of their white colleagues, and black students, outnumbered three to one in most schools after desegregation, lost positions of school leadership. These historic injustices continued to rankle black groups in town. With desegregation complete, busing to ensure racial balance across the school system, and the homogeneous grouping of students regardless of race and ability in the early grades, many whites worried about what they perceived as the decreased "quality" of education for their youngsters.

In the months leading up to our production both races found much that touched their group identities in local controversies about schooling. The town and regional newspapers featured stories about fights at the high school, the possibility of a revised disciplinary code for students, and new plans for school redistricting. Little concerning race was ever reported in these stories, but all parents of school-age children and most other residents knew that race was never far from the center of these issues, at least in the minds and emotions of Williamsburg citizens.

Act 2 of *Walk Together* included scenes about the trashing of student trophies from the formerly black high school when "integration" occurred, the distrust and outright disdain shown by white teachers and administrators toward new black colleagues, the hurt caused by racist slurs among grade-school children, and parental action to maintain school safety after a racially motivated fight in the high school. We structured the act to build toward our version of a raucous community meeting centered on a racial incident that had occurred in the fall of 1969. Following a football game, the white athletic director of the high school was in his office counting gate receipts when an interracial fight broke out nearby that injured a white teacher. A group of students, most of them black, entered the director's office to which the teacher had fled. Apparently, the athletic director panicked and drew a pistol on the students, later claiming he did so to protect the teacher and the gate receipts. With the support of the school board, the superintendent demoted the athletic director for carrying a weapon in school. Many whites in Williamsburg, however, forced a community meeting to demand his reinstatement. Although led by the superintendent and involving many liberal-minded reformers, the meeting was dominated by "upper-county rednecks" (the superintendent's term), who turned it into an attack on school desegregation.

We based our dramatization of the event on newspaper reports and an interview with the former superintendent, who was still living in Williamsburg. In our version the meeting began with careful statements from both sides of the controversy but soon dissolved into rumor mongering, name calling, and finally minor scuffles. The cast and I built this scene out of improvisations and decided to keep it mostly improvised in performance to preserve its rough edges. Another reason for keeping it unscripted (though structured) had to do with the antagonisms of the scene and our cross-racial casting. Visually, we divided in two the chairs for the meeting space, and the cast members seated in them (minus the actor portraying the superintendent). Those whom the cast called the "good citizens" sat (and later stood) on one side of a center aisle, while the "rednecks" (a term we excised from actual performances) gathered on the other. Not surprisingly, most of the black actors and several of the whites in the cast found it very difficult to take white racist roles and hurl the accusations and epithets that we all knew should be a part of this scene. So, near the end of the rehearsal process we arrived at a compromise: the actors would alternate roles and locations onstage at every performance, switching between good citizen and racist. This alleviated the psychological burden and had the added benefit of keeping the improvised action more spontaneous. With improvisation also came more attention to dialogue, for the audience as well as the performers. (More attention, however, did not always bring more success. At one performance a cast member playing a racist unthinkingly introduced himself as "Jack Daniels." It brought down the house.)

For the spectators this scene probably stretched their ethical imaginations for a future community, less because of its content than because of our chosen rhetorical convention. Like the response to many plays that end in a courtroom battle, the audience had little doubt about the right and wrong of the situation; most were on the side of the good citizens and against the racists. Of course, we tried not to stereotype the working-class whites, nor did all of them who spoke to defend the athletic director end up as unthinking racists. We also gave them the best reasons we could for opposing desegregation, reasons still heard today: fear for the safety of their children, concern about increased taxes, an interest in upholding educational standards, and desire to protect a friend (the athletic director). Nonetheless, those defending the decision of the superintendent held the moral high ground: a teacher had brandished a weapon against a group of students, a clearly indefensible act regardless of the circumstances. The audience may have appreciated the complexities, but few of them could side with the upper-county whites.

On the other hand, the scene presented several working-class whites as reasonable and cautious, people who could not be realistically excluded from a future ethical community. Further, our cross-racial casting scrambled the spectators' ability to link morality to race. As occurred in several other scenes, this strategy enhanced the "presence" of the performers, in Erickson's sense of the term. One black actor who played a white racist for two of the four performances got quite violent and had to be restrained by others on his side of the aisle. African-American citizens and middle-class, liberal whites who might have excluded poor whites from their ethical community could not so easily do so after experiencing this tension between materiality and signification. Again, physical presence led to heightened listening. Clearly, our show stood against racism, but some good characters opposed desegregation and a few of the racists even had black bodies. The discourse of "All Together" cannot accommodate these complexities. In particular, it has little understanding of blacks who move from victimhood to racism and no room to accommodate the anxieties of working-class whites caught up in the historical undertow of classism and racism. Perhaps *Walk Together* stretched the moral imaginations of Williamsburg citizens in this scene. But I have no way of knowing.

After the shouting and noisy exiting in this scene, the superintendent narrated a brief ending. He noted that the athletic director was not reinstated and that the school board passed a rule forbidding guns in school. Then he added: "These measures settled the controversy at the time, but the larger problem remains. Racial tensions continue to pervade our schools and our community."[28] With his exit the stage remained nearly empty for a while, except for five musicians far upstage, one playing a blues harmonica, and folding chairs painted black and white in disarray. During the course of the performance, the chairs—with or without people sitting in them—had come to represent the citizens of Williamsburg, their arrangement suggesting several variations on the image of a contained community. I expect that the Williamsburg audience understood this stage picture and its musical analogue as a symbol for a broken community, its inner tensions having shattered its sheltering container. The implicit challenge of this scene was how to put the pieces back together again—especially the large piece symbolizing "alienated poor whites."

We provided some closure for this community problem at our curtain call, which featured cast members holding hands and singing a reprise of the title song. Local citizens probably felt better about themselves and their community when they joined in on the final chorus. I would like to be able to say that several spectators came to me afterward and admitted that Christian faith, individualistic capitalism, and better racial attitudes could not create our ideal community of the future, but of course that did not happen.[29]

NOTES

1. Robbie McCauley and I have conferred about my recollection of these events and my representation of her point of view on them. In a telephone call on 8 November 1996 Robbie suggested that I elaborate her beliefs about cross-racial casting. These changes, indicated in quotations, are now part of this essay.

2. E-mail communication from Ann Smart Martin to Robin Veder (16 April 1996), forwarded to me (17 April 1996), included in the "Walk Together" Children Papers (WTCP), Swem Library, College of William and Mary, Williamsburg, Va.

3. Ann Efimetz, "Cast Walks Together to a Success," *Virginia Gazette,* 20 April 1996; and private letter to Bruce McConachie from Satoshi Ito, 24 April 1996, WTCP.

4. Private correspondence from Deborah T. Jackson to Bruce McConachie, 18 April 1996, WTCP.

5. Baz Kershaw, *The Politics of Performance: Radical Theatre as Cultural Intervention* (London and New York: Routledge, 1992), 16; Richard Owen Geer, "Out of Control in Colquitt: Swamp Gravy Makes Stone Soup," *TDR* 40, no. 2 (Summer 1996): 103–30; and Sonja Kuftinec, "A Cornerstone for Rethinking Community Theatre," *Theatre Topics* 6, no. 1 (March 1996): 91–104.

6. See John McGrath, *A Good Night Out—Popular Theatre: Audience, Class, and Form* (London: Methuen, 1981).

7. See Raymond Williams, *The Long Revolution* (1961; rpt., Harmondsworth: Pelican, 1984), 64, for Williams's initial use of the term *structure of feeling.* In *Drama from Ibsen to Brecht* (1968; rpt., London: Hogarth Press, 1987) Williams reads two "structures of feeling" within the tradition of modern drama.

8. Kershaw, *Politics of Performance,* 49.

9. Dudley Cocke, Harry Newman, and Janet Salmons-Rue, eds., *From the Ground Up: Grassroots Theater in Historical and Contemporary Perspective* (Ithaca, N.Y.: Community Based Arts Project of Cornell University, 1993), 81. I have slightly rearranged the order of these statements in the matrix for emphasis.

10. Kuftinec, "Cornerstone," 95.

11. Ann Jellicoe, *Community Plays: How to Put Them On* (London: Methuen, 1987), 185–88.

12. Anthony Cohen, *The Symbolic Construction of Community* (New York: Youngstock, 1985), intro.; and Williams, *Long Revolution,* 65.

13. Kershaw, *Politics of Performance,* 25–26.

14. See Viv Edwards and Thomas J. Seinkewicz, *Oral Cultures Past and Present: Rappin' and Homer* (Oxford and Cambridge, Mass.: Basil Blackwell, 1990).

15. Alan Read, *Theatre and Everyday Life: An Ethics of Performance* (London and New York: Routledge, 1993), 63, 62.

16. Ibid., 90, 96, 101.

17. Mark Johnson, *The Body in the Mind: The Bodily Basis of Meaning, Imagination, and Reason* (Chicago: University of Chicago Press, 1987), xiv. See also George Lakoff, *Women, Fire, and Dangerous Things: What Categories Reveal about the Mind* (Chicago: University of Chicago Press, 1987); and George Lakoff and Mark Johnson, *Metaphors We Live By* (Chicago: University of Chicago Press, 1980).

18. Jon Erickson, *The Fate of the Object: From Modern Object to Postmodern Sign in Performance, Art, and Poetry* (Ann Arbor: University of Michigan Press, 1995), 62.

19. Johnson, *Body in the Mind,* 22.

20. Michael Oakeshott, *Rationalism in Politics and Other Essays* (New York: Basic Books, 1962), 123.

21. See Susan Bennett, *Theatre Audiences: A Theory of Production and Reception* (London and New York: Routledge, 1990).

22. Statement distributed at a public meeting of All Together, 15 December 1995, WTCP; my emphasis.

23. "*ALL TOGETHER:* OUR CONCERNS," mailed to addresses on mailing list, dated 17 March 1996, WTCP.

24. "*ALL TOGETHER*—OBSERVATIONS SO FAR," mailed to addresses on mailing list, 22 February 1996, WTCP.

25. All quotations from the production are in the prompt book. See Hermine Pinson and Bruce McConachie, *Walk Together Children,* WTCP, 5.

26. Ibid., 24–25.

27. Ibid., 25.

28. Ibid., 61.

29. A shorter version of this article appeared in *Theatre Topics* 8, no. 1 (March 1998): 33–54.

Sonja Kuftinec

The Art of Bridge Building
in Mostar

Since 1996 Scot McElvany has worked with Bosnian youth to bridge a divided city through theater. Projects developed within, outside, and across the physical boundaries of Mostar give form to a chaotic postwar situation, providing sites to rethink cultural borders and to reanimate the urban community. Performances in a summer camp, an abandoned hotel, a youth center, and on a bridge give voice to youth in a way that subverts political divisiveness. The theater projects challenge efforts to enforce religious affiliation as the predominant aspect of identity in Bosnia, literally and figuratively reforming the community of Mostar.

Before war broke out in 1991, Bosnian youth rarely recognized ethnoreligious labelings of difference. Beer drinking "Muslims" and secular "Catholics" shared friendships and intermarried.[1] The 1991–95 war in former Yugoslavia permanently altered these relationships. Although initiated by individual drives for power, the war nominally focused on, and in many ways created, differences among Bosniak "Muslims," "Catholic" Croats, and "Orthodox" Serbs.[2] The war also physically devastated the entire region of Bosnia-Herzegovina, cities and villages alike. Nowhere is the material evidence of division and destruction more visible than in the urban center of Mostar.

Located in Herzegovina, the southeast territory of Bosnia-Herzegovina, historic Mostar once featured the prized architectural structure of a centuries-old bridge. The Stari Most (old bridge) united the older east side and newer western areas of the city, and the people who inhabited both. This union ended in 1993. After fighting together against the Bosnian Serb army in 1992, the "Croatian Defense Council" turned against Bosnian Mus-

Sonja Kuftinec, an Assistant Professor of Theatre at the University of Minnesota, has been creating theater with youth in the former Yugoslavia since 1995. She has written extensively on these projects, the ethical dilemmas of creating community-based theater, and the (re)formation of identity through performance.

lims in Mostar. A general in the council destroyed the Stari Most in late 1993, effectively completing tactics of eviction, deportation, and murder that divided the city.

As the bridge collapsed, so too did marriages, friendships, and families. Teenagers in particular suffered difficult choices, sometimes having to move in with one parent or another, fight on the front line against former friends, or witness the deaths of others. The Stari Most had once reminded Mostarians that differences in the city could be traversed; its destruction symbolized the collapse of that possibility. In 2000 the city remains divided. Bosnian "Croats" now live mainly on the west side of the city, while Bosniaks (Muslims) live mainly on the East.[3] The theater projects engaged by McElvany and youth within the city give voice to this context of divisiveness while redefining and bridging community divisions, aided in large part by an integrated youth center, Mladi Most.

In its name alone Mladi Most defies Mostar's divisions. The center, literally "youth bridge," stands in contrast to the destroyed old bridge, Stari Most, encouraging young people from both sides of the city to commingle. Mladi Most is structurally integrated as well, run by a coalition of international volunteers and local workers from both sides of Mostar. In 1996 Mladi Most worked with a German youth organization to coordinate a summer theater camp outside of the city, in order to provide further opportunities for Mostarians to intermingle. The camp also included German teenagers, as Mostarian and international organizers felt that this cultural interaction would enlarge the experience of all participants. Three theater projects conceived at the camp proved memorable for international and local youth alike, animating community through process and presentation.

I worked on the first of three performances developed from daily workshops. This piece explored social identity, family, home, and material culture with a mixed group of Germans, Mostarians, and international volunteers. A second piece evolved from McElvany's work with British NATO soldiers helping in the camps. The third grew from the Mostarian youths' desire to create a performance reflecting their war experience. In each case the workshop, rehearsal process, and final performances reflected the divisions and fluidity of community boundaries among the youth from within and outside of Mostar.

Outside of the divided space of Mostar, and outside of the rehearsal process, many of the teenagers asserted divisions of national rather than local culture, illustrating the complexity of negotiating identity politics in former Yugoslavia. When faced with a group more "other" than themselves, most Mostarians asserted their cultural commonality rather than internal differences. Mostar's youth disdained food cooked by the Germans or neglected to share their Bosnian coffee. Language differences and interests contributed to separations between the two groups at mealtimes and leisure hours. Freed from their desert city, the Mostarians skipped the first morning workshop to swim at the beach. In the afternoon the Germans swam while the Mostarians worked. An evening workshop brought the two groups together, but by this time some individuals had decided not to participate. Among those who did, individuals asserted similarities as well as differences, as the workshop process revealed a context for the social disruption through which the Bosnians had lived.

We began the workshops with partners interviewing each other about ways they identified themselves. Many of the comments illustrated commonalities among the youth, whose interests focused on leisure activities. Megi from Mostar studied medicine and hoped to coach basketball; Kenet spoke of his love of violin, biology, and drawing; Ariana was enthused about 1980s music; Mikhael announced his interest in pottery; Florian attested to his devotion to sports and ancient Greek. The introduction of my partner, Aki, from Mostar, stood in contrast to these responses. "This is Aki," I explained, "he works for Mladi Most in Mostar and wants to study architecture. And he spent six months in a Croatian concentration camp building bunkers on the front line." Aki's remark delineated a difference between the teenagers, drawing attention to the specific context and difficulties faced by Mostarian youth in the war.

A section on "home" once again illuminated similarities and differences among participants. Kenet created a visual sculpture illustrating Mostar's chaos and ugliness as well as his own love for the city. Kathy Tasker, a volunteer from London, presented a place of crowded noisiness, and Mladi Most volunteer Shin Yasui sculpted his Japanese hometown as a place of difficult conformity. After seeing these other visions of home, Megi acknowledged that "it's good to know everyone has problems." Ariana offered that sharing the work "builds a sense of community."

The performance of the piece for the camp audience also contributed to this building and separation of community. Some Mostarians who had not participated in the show's development jeered, while others expressed delight at the emotional impact of the piece. Regardless, many Mostarians chose not to work with McElvany and Tasker on the next piece, developed and performed mainly by German teenagers and British NATO soldiers. Following the performance of this piece, however, a number of the more skeptical Mostarians approached McElvany about developing a project of their own. In a report following the second performance McElvany quotes some Mostarians: "We like what you're doing. We want to show we're involved too, and we want you to help us make a performance about our experiences in the war."

McElvany underlines the significance of the Mostarians' approach to him. One of the many ethical issues confronting community-based theater workers is that of agency and the potential abuse of emotional narratives for dramatic purposes.[4] In this case the Mostarians sought the theater artist's help in lending dramatic shape to their experience rather than the director digging for dramatic material to shape. From his knowledge of the group McElvany suspected that the Mostarians wanted to illustrate their lives as action movies. He thus agreed to work with them on condition that the piece not focus entirely on violence, that participants agree to engage in all the warm-ups and seemingly obscure abstractions of the theater-making process, and that the German youth be allowed to participate if they chose. (The Mostarians agreed to work with the Germans, and many Germans and international volunteers began contributing to the development of the show. After the first day, however, these participants expressed their desire to become audience members, or witnesses, to the Mostarians' work rather than directly contributing to the development of the piece.)

Despite his precautions, McElvany confronted an ethical dilemma with the group almost immediately, underlining the importance of process in community-based theater making. McElvany had asked participants to think of the most common questions they asked themselves during the war. Developing a technique we had earlier established together of juxtaposing everyday rituals and text, participants combined this exercise with one in which they used water to mime simple daily activities. McElvany describes the result: "Supa, crouched down over the water bowl, slapped water to his face in the gesture of smoking, looked up, paused and asked, 'Why did I lose my brother . . . do you know why?' Ersan then rose, threw water in the air as a soccer ball, kicked it angrily and asked, 'Why do I live here?'" Ersan then paused, sat down, and said he couldn't continue. McElvany stopped the workshop to reflect on the process with participants. He asked whether they wished to proceed and, if so, requested their permission to continue asking questions. In a reversal of the common terminology of community-based theater work, the participants had to "empower" the facilitator. Ersan looked to Supa, the acknowledged local leader of the Mostarian group. With a nod from Supa and some reflection among themselves, all the youth asserted their desire to continue developing the performance. "This is the only way we're going to do this together," insisted Supa, initially one of the Mostarians most skeptical of the theater work.

Taking care not to overemphasize the emotionally devastating aspects of the war, McElvany encouraged the group to develop moments focusing on safety as well as fear. The title of the piece, *Podrum* (Basement), reflected a duality of confinement and refuge; during bombing of the city its residents had to retreat to this windowless haven. In the final scene of *Podrum* Hajdi told of singing so loudly in the basement that the grenades outside could not be heard. She turned to the rest of the group, huddled together in a circle, and they sang "Volim Te" (I Love You).

The performance in the camp held as great an impact on observers as the process had on the participants. The Mostarians performed *Podrum* in both English and Bosnian, yet the effect on the German audience members seemed to overcome barriers of language. They watched in stunned silence, many later relating how they had felt, for the first time, something of the Mostarians' experience beyond mediated accounts of the war. Following the silence Supa gathered the spectators and participants together for a group "howl in peace," and the evening continued, breaking down barriers of difference set up during the week, as Germans and Mostarians shared songs and talk far into the evening.[5]

Podrum's success within the camp soon provoked a difficult decision for the Mostarians, reinforcing the limitations of theater's ability to unite the Mostarian youth. An international youth festival invited the group to perform *Podrum* in Mostar. Within the camp, outside of the contested site of the city, Bosniak, Serb, and Croatian youth could work together as "Mostarians." A return from the relatively safe confines of the camp to the site of urban conflict once again conjured boundaries and breaches.

The divided city of Mostar maintains no neutral space, and the festival took place on Mostar's Muslim east side. Thus, some non-Muslims, who rarely crossed the city's dividing line, felt frightened and dropped out of the performance. Participants also had to confront the more chaotic atmosphere of the urban environment, physically destroyed by the war. The group performed *Podrum* in the broken remains of the Hotel Ruza. Once an opulent architectural structure, the shell of the building stood as a symbolic reminder of the recent conflict in the city. The site had also become a playground for the children of east Mostar, who continued their recreation during the performance. While the urban performance did not, therefore, have the same impact as the camp presentation—uniting participants and observers as one momentary community—it represented the first time in four years that a group composed of youth from both east and west Mostar had publicly performed together. Thus, the performance enacted at least a temporary reformation of community.

Nino Dvizac, just before the bombs fell in the final scene: "My mother said I would go to Hvar. I asked if she would come, she said she would try. I knew she was lying." *Podrum,* developed by Scot McElvaney and ensemble. Performance in Hotel Ruña, Mostar, 1996. Photograph courtesy of Uli Loskot.

This enactment of community expanded as the mixed youth group continued working together throughout the remainder of 1996. Two very different performances evidenced the extent and limitations of such collaboration. *A New Vision of Cranes* in November illustrated intercultural cooperation, while the December production of *Mladi Most Carol* revealed the intracommunity borders remaining in Mostar.

Arising from Mladi Most volunteer Shin Yasui's desire to introduce Mostarian youth to a global intercultural awareness, *Cranes* developed into a transhistorical commentary on issues of violence, war, and peace. Yasui related the story of Sadako, a Japanese girl suffering from leukemia caused by the atom bomb's fall on Hiroshima. In the hospital Sadako recalled a Japanese legend that the folding of a thousand paper cranes would result in the granting of a wish. Sadako folded her cranes in a wish for peace. McElvany and Yasui recounted this story to youth center visitors, volunteers, and students throughout the city, who all helped to fold the thousand cranes. They then attached poems to 350 cranes and distributed them in cafes, on cars, in the European Headquarters, to police officers, and to various volunteer organizations in the city. The group also worked on the performance of a Japanese Noh play relating the story of the feuding Minomoto brothers. "Japanese Cultural Day" included this performance as well as a processional to the Carinski bridge, recently rebuilt to connect the east side with the west. The performers drew intercultural parallels between the divisions in Mostar and the Minomoto clan, followed by releasing the cranes, with their messages of peace, on the border between the two sides of the city. This performative gesture enacted community on a border of difference.

The group of young participants concluded their year of performances in 1996 with an interactive, processional, bilingual adaptation of Charles Dickens's *Christmas Carol,* performed in the Mladi Most youth center for a small group of visitors, friends, and volunteers. *Mladi Most Carol* related Dickens's nineteenth-century tale to the contemporary context of Mostar and the youth center. Marley acknowledged his guilt at not having followed through on the agreements of the U.S.-sponsored Dayton Peace Accords. "Business? Peace and justice and advocating for the capture of war criminals was my business!" Twins Nino and Dino played Ignorance and Want as a teenage soldier and a beggar, both commonly seen on the streets of Mostar. A young Scrooge spoke of the "freedom of a child," as actor Shin Yasui traced his finger along photographs of the city's decay, taken by youth in the center. Yet efforts to create a religiously "inclusive" adaptation showed codirectors McElvany and me the real dangers remaining in the performance of togetherness in Mostar.

One of the obvious difficulties faced by adapting Dickens for a multireligious group is the text's focus on Christmas. While most youth in Mostar grew up celebrating Christmas, regardless of their religious heritage, an international volunteer suggested that we include Islamic references in our adaptation. Thus, McElvany and I blithely drew the Islam moon and star beside a cross on Scrooge's gravestone. Frantically working within a three-day rehearsal schedule, we completed the design on the day of the performance. At the dress rehearsal we led the participants outside the house for the final scene. As McElvany, playing Scrooge, turned the gravestone to face the audience, we heard a collective gasp. "Do you want us to be shot?" asked several shocked participants. The cries arose from Muslims and Christians alike, each aware that to present Islamic symbols in public on the west side of Mostar presented a threat to all members of the house. Grenades and stones had already been thrown at the house by individuals antagonistic to the youth center's mission of remaining a neutral space. We removed the Islamic symbols from the gravestone.

Mostar remains a city divided. In February 1997 a peaceful memorial processional to a mixed graveyard on the west side was interrupted by shooting from Bosnian Croat police. International officials forbade travel across the city's bridges for several days, and west Mostarians evicted several Muslims living on the "wrong" side of the city. Yet the Mladi Most youth continue to build and cross ever more difficult bridges. In March 1997 they traveled to Budapest to meet with teenagers from Banja Luka, a Bosnian Serb enclave. In the summer of 1997 a mixed group of Mostarians developed a show about the ongoing reconstructing of history in Mostar, *Re-Membering Mostar*. In 1998 and 1999 Mostarian youth continue to engage in theater workshops with participants from Banja Luka and cities around the country. Community-based theater will not resolve the political divisiveness in the city or in the state. Yet collaborative performances remain a symbol of the possibility and struggle to cross and reevaluate these borders of difference. In a city where difference can mean life or death, this gesture seems a beginning toward reconciliation and reanimation of community.[6]

NOTES

1. Political analyst Tin Gazivoda states that 20 to 25 percent of marriages in Bosnia-Herzegovina crossed religious boundaries. Personal interview, 11 June 1996.

2. *Yugoslavia*, literally "Land of South Slavs," referred to a region encompassing several territories and intermixed groups. Within Yugoslavia, Croatia, Serbia, and Bosnia-Herzegovina harbored residents of similar ethnic origin who spoke, for the most part, the same language but who varied in religious affiliation and practice. While mainly Eastern Orthodox Christian Serbians live in Serbia, and mostly Roman Catholic Croatians inhabit Croatia (with significant exceptions), Bosnia was home to Roman Catholic (Bosnian Croat), Eastern Orthodox (Bosnian Serbs), and Muslim (Bosniaks) as well as Jewish and Gypsy inhabitants. This delineation is complicated by the fact that many citizens of former Yugoslavia did not actively practice their religions. The term *Bosniak* allows secular "Muslims" a group identity that does not depend on religious affiliation.

3. While few Croats live on the eastern side of Mostar, a large number of Bosniaks (Muslims) live on the west side of the city. These families suffer constant danger of eviction as evidenced by numerous objective reports, including Human Rights Watch and the Organization for Security and Cooperation in Europe (OSCE), a Vienna-based intergovernmental organization.

4. Ted Conover reports on the documentary filmmaking of *Faces*, a drama group in New York grappling with issues of violence and abuse among its teenage participants. Responses to the 30 March 1997 article include letters chastising the potentially abusive use of "psychodrama" to create emotionally compelling theater and film. See Ted Conover, "The Film Makers and the Abuser," *New York Times Magazine*, 30 March 1997, 30–35; and "Letters to the Editor," *New York Times Magazine*, 20 April 1997, 2.

5. Anthropologist Victor Turner explains this reaction in part through the notion of *communitas,* in which a ritual or performance event allows for the temporary breakdown of boundaries of difference. Turner emphasizes both the importance and temporariness of this condition. See Victor Turner, "Liminality and Communitas," *The Ritual Process: Structure and Anti-Structure* (Chicago: Aldine, 1969), 94–130.

6. This essay is dedicated to Shin (1972–98), who always "embraced the contradictions."

E. J. Westlake

The Children of Tomorrow: Seattle Public Theater's Work with Homeless Youth

The codirectors of Seattle Public Theater (SPT) began the company in the mid-1980s performing scripted work. Influenced by the work of Augusto Boal and forum theater, the group later put more emphasis on creating forum theater events around a variety of current, local issues; homelessness emerged as a central concern.

The annual workshops with homeless youth began in 1992 and culminated in a performance called *Children of Tomorrow*. In January 1997 SPT put together a forum theater workshop with fifteen homeless youth and five staff members from the five different youth centers. Marc Weinblatt and Cheryl Harrison from SPT facilitated. I observed the workshop and the performance at the end of the workshop, which was open to the general public.

Initially, I wanted to examine how the facilitators' status as "outsiders" in the community of homeless youth would affect the workshop and performance. In my own view I saw community-based theater projects led largely by straight, white men, whereas the communities themselves, especially the homeless youth, were anything but. Weinblatt also saw this trend, and, because he acknowledged this, he could approach his work with some self-consciousness. For this reason SPT offers courses for community leaders to learn to do forum theater in their own communities. Weinblatt noted with a laugh that he was training himself out of a job.

Nevertheless, I expected the workshop and performance with home-

E. J. Westlake is on the faculty at Bowling Green State University. Her recent work focuses on the formation of community identity. Currently, she is studying the process of memorialization by the riders and organizers of the Twin Cities–Wisconsin–Chicago AIDS Ride. Recently she participated in a seminar at the American Society for Theatre Research, where she talked about her work on the arrest of Seattle artist Jason Sprinkle for terrorism and the law as performance of municipal identity.

less youth to reveal some of the problems of outsiders leading members of marginalized groups. The processes of forum theater, however, enabled the group to overcome the outsider/insider division. Rather than aspiring to form a permanent homogeneous community, in which staff would profess to understand what it was like to be a young, homeless person, the facilitators succeeded in creating a temporary community of diverse elements joined together for the purposes of the project through the use of Boal's forum theater.

The facilitators formed a temporary community through this process on three levels: (1) they formed a community within the group participating in the workshop; (2) they formed a community within the performance for the general public, although there were serious difficulties with this part of the process, in part because of the physical space of the performance; and (3) they formed several spin-off communities that would either continue a connection or continue the work itself in some fashion.

It is important to note the temporary nature of the community formed by this community-based theater. *Community,* as Sonja Kuftinec points out, implies both a commonality among its constituents and a difference between the constituents and the outsiders.[1] For each of the levels of community formed during this project, no commonalities could be assumed. Therefore, the facilitators from SPT did not set out to create a community in this sense so much as they attempted to bridge differences for a limited period of time in order to establish a dialogue. The facilitators succeeded in building a temporary community by building alliances across perceived community boundaries. Weinblatt wanted to build connections between youth and staff as much as he wanted to acknowledge the diversity of the youth. The temporary community lies between community building and coalition formation.

Whereas community building assumes commonalities, coalition formation assumes difference. Catherine Gallagher describes the coalition formation as a process to reach political objectives that evolved out of the New Left movements of the 1960s and 1970s.[2] While the New Left continued to view solidarity as necessary to achieving its political goals, solidarity ceased to mean identification with the oppressed and instead came to mean a "recognition of shared oppressions."[3]

SPT facilitators could not purport to understand the oppression experienced by the homeless youth, and they did not attempt to identify with them. Nor did they present a totalizing metanarrative about homeless youth to the general audience. Rather, by recognizing oppression as universal, as something that touches the lives of all the participants, the facilitators focused on oppression shared by members of the group.

Yet this was more than a temporary alliance to achieve a goal. SPT used Boal to highlight differences but also to find common ground. Individual stories were enacted and reenacted by each of the members of the group. The participants, through forum theater, agreed to search for commonalities, to be a community for the time being.

Augusto Boal's forum theater serves as an ideal vehicle to build such a temporary community. Although originally used for somewhat homogeneous populations,[4] forum theater enables participants and audience members to bring their diverse experiences to bear, closing the gap between actor and audience. In the words of Boal it enables people to "reassume their protagonistic function in the theater and in society."[5] The facilitators from SPT use this form to build a temporary community by empowering the participants to take responsibility for the workshop, providing an environment within which the participants feel safe to share their stories, helping the participants see commonalities in their stories as well as helping them acknowledge and value individual differences.

SPT held the weeklong workshop in the basement of Pilgrim Congregational Church during weekday afternoons. During the hard rains and heavy snowfall of the week before, the basement had flooded. The floor was still dirty, and the damp air was chilly. The church used the basement for a variety of functions that served the homeless, from serving meals to holding meetings.

We began each day at noon. I arrived early to help the SPT intern from Evergreen College unload the donated food that we served for lunch. Everyday it was different: pizza, submarine sandwiches, pasta. Lunch was served for the first half-hour. The participants could come and eat first if they wanted to, but everyone was expected to be ready to work at 12:30. Weinblatt went over the policies about lunch, arriving late, the closed nature of the workshop, and pay. All actors who completed the workshop and performance would be paid fifty dollars. Weinblatt lamented that this wasn't much, but he wanted to be able to pay the participants for their work. The participants were not volunteers.

The first day appeared chaotic. About thirty homeless youth and several center staff members arrived. The day was devoted to establishing ground rules, allowing the participants to get to know one another, and helping the participants become comfortable with being physically expressive. Indeed, several of the youth seemed rather uncomfortable with some of the exercises. I thought I could pick out which ones would drop out. I also thought I could see the divisions between facilitators, staff, the youth, and me, the silent, observing ethnographer.

To establish a safe environment the facilitators closed the workshop to everyone but the participants, SPT staff, me, and an occasional journalist. Also, anyone who was late or who missed a day was not allowed to come back. This reduced the group to a few committed youth. Weinblatt stressed that no one would have to do anything they physically or emotionally did not feel comfortable doing so long as they remained engaged. To introduce the participants to SPT and to Boal, Weinblatt and Harrison used a variety of Boal's techniques. They began with rudimentary body work, what Boal has termed "knowing the body" and "making the body expressive," and moved gradually into image theater and forum theater processes.

The facilitators led a series of ice-breaking exercises geared toward knowing the body. The work helped the participants get used to moving around. It also helped them to develop trust and become comfortable with one another. I watched and took notes most of the time and participated only occasionally. The physical activity went quickly from mere movement into making the body expressive. A simple game of tag became an expressive exercise when Weinblatt insisted that the two involved in the chase act as predator-prey. Each time the new It had to come up with a bigger and more ferocious predator. The tag began with a cat and mouse and evolved into a dog and cat and then a dog being chased by a bigger dog. Participants were not allowed to just play tag. They were coached to follow the predator-prey. These exercises also enabled participants to find expressive ways to convey their feelings. Every day at the beginning of the workshop participants would give a sound and a motion that expressed how they were feeling that day. The others in the group would reflect that sound and motion back. The participants could then see their feelings interpreted and validated by the others.

I noticed the first day participants continued to pair up with people they knew from their home youth center, rarely getting into groups with youth from other centers. This was especially true of the youth from Lambert House, a center for gay, lesbian, bisexual, transgendered, and questioning youth.

After the first series of exercises the facilitators did a brief introduction to the forum theater format. The intern and Harrison did a scene from the checkout line at a grocery store. One person waits in line, while the other person cuts in front of her to be with the next person. Weinblatt invites the participants to intervene. Joey got up and told Harrison that she had dropped some money. When Harrison looked down, Joey got in front of her. Other interventions ranged from pretending not to speak English and not letting Harrison pass to confronting Harrison. Paul, a Lambert House staff member, pretended to have a heart attack. When Harrison bent down to see if he was okay, he got up in front of her. This scene drew laughs from the Lambert House youth.

After a break Cheryl Harrison delegated the responsibility of establishing and observing the ground rules (e.g., confidentiality, not putting down others, no cliques, respect for one another's personal items) to the participants, and any later enforcement of the rules was also delegated to the participants. During this meeting I got more of a feeling for the individuals participating in the workshop. A participant from Lambert House suggested a rule against cliques. Morgan, a transgendered youth, feared that youth from other centers would exclude people from Lambert House out of homophobia. She was able to voice that concern and make other participants aware of any tendency to exclude others they perceived as different. Later, when the Lambert House participants immediately grouped together for one of the exercises, others were able to point to the rule to make the Lambert House youth aware of their own internalized homophobia.

In addition to suggesting rules, several of the youth asked questions about who funds the project, how big the audience will be, why people come. To the last query Weinblatt suggests: "Some people don't know what it's like to live on the streets and they're fascinated." This draws a surprised reaction from the youth. "Seriously," he continues, "And this is your chance to educate them." The facilitators passed around the flyers announcing the performance. They read: "*Children of Tomorrow:* A Theater of Liberation (An interactive performance created by and featuring homeless youth)." Dawn reads the flier and mutters: "Oh, fuck. Now everyone in Seattle can know that we're homeless."

Keeping the group closed and giving responsibility for the workshop to the participants enabled the group to develop the cohesion necessary to make the workshop successful. Participants knew that they would not be put on the spot and that they had a voice in the way the workshop was run. The nature of the exercises also helped to develop the cohesion necessary for building the temporary community. But, as the flyer circulated, the name of the project, *Children of Tomorrow,* created some dissension among the youth. "Children!" Matt later confided to me, "We're not children! And we won't be children tomorrow." Weinblatt acknowledged that some didn't particularly like the title, but the company had to publicize the event weeks in advance. There wasn't time to agree on a name. The tension over the name raises the possibility that the SPT project in some way fetishizes the homeless youth: the teens and young adults being labeled children and the romantic notions of a word like tomorrow placing the youth elsewhere, a place other than the real space of here and now. Although I don't fully know the history of the name, a name given to the project by someone affiliated with SPT, I believe that such an impulse was not at work here. The possibility does exist, however, that this may feed into the media's objectification of the youth. Misha Berson, in her feature in the *Seattle Times,* referred to the youths' "adventures on the street," "several promi-nent facial rings," and one youth's "hand-to-mouth, footloose existence."[6]

Image Theater

Boal divides the third stage of theater of the oppressed, "theater as language," into three degrees. The facilitators employed the second and third degrees, "image theater" and "forum theater," the most often in the course of the workshop. Image theater provides a transition into the actual problem-solving work of forum theater. In image theater the participants express their thoughts by using objects or bodies to "sculpt" an idea or an image.

On the second day of the workshop the facilitators began to focus more on image theater exercises. One of the first exercises involved six chairs, a table, and a water bottle. Participants could sculpt an image of "power" with the objects. Morgan placed the chairs in a pyramid shape on top of the table with the water bottle on the seat of the top chair. Dawn placed five of the chairs so that they were bowed down to one on the table and the water bottle on top of the chair on the table. Several of the sculp-tures involved height as a means to show power. Harrison placed one chair on the floor to the side of the table, and at the other end the chairs were placed in a jumble. The water bottle was the only object on the table.

The participants began to debate where the power lay in the sculpture. Dawn, who had been very quiet and had not felt comfortable participating, made the suggestion that the power lay in the chair by itself: "The reason something has power is because they are unique. The rich are few and have money, and the poor are many and have nothing." Weinblatt reminded the group that someone had said earlier that there was power in numbers. Dawn countered: "But if you have numbers, that's nothing if you're poor." In this way the facilitators followed each exercise with some reflection that showed the multiplicity of readings of any image or scene. The group felt comfortable debating the various readings, which highlighted both the trust and cohesion of the group as well as the variety of viewpoints.

After sculpting inanimate objects, the group began to build a sculpture of power using themselves. Each person would enter the sculpture by striking a pose that would make them the most powerful person in the sculpture. The group would vote about whether the new person had taken the most powerful position and could stay. For example, the second person to become part of the sculpture stood pointing a gun at the first. Everyone agreed that the second person took the power and could stay.

The first few participants tried to take power by using guns or threatening poses or by being the tallest. Eventually, this approach broke down, and participants changed tactics. One participant struck a pose of seduction. Another kneeled in the middle of the more violent images and struck a pose of prayer. Some of the participants noted that power is "a continuous chain, there is always one better," and that "sometimes submissive is powerful."

Joey, one of the youngest participants, could not find a more powerful pose in the sculpture. He had been trying to strike poses of intimidation. He gave up and went to sit down again. "Try again!" one of the participants shouted. The others encouraged him to keep trying, and he finally took power by standing in front of the praying person and striking a pose of giving a benediction. The others agreed unanimously that this was the most powerful position in the image. Through the encouragement of the others Joey learned how to change his perception of power.

Some of the more reticent members began to be more vocal. Sam and Dawn, friends who squatted together, often sat out of some of the exercises. By now they would involve themselves in some small ways. In one instance the participants got into small groups to make fast statues. Harrison began to shout out a number of a group and a word. That group would have to then create a statue that would convey that word. Initially, the words were general like *parents* and *family.* Then she began to take words from a list of issues the youth had identified as being important to them, words like *homelessness, self-respect,* and *power.* Sam remained in his group, but he did not move to help create the sculpture. The group began to work around him, creating the statue by using him without his direct participation. Sam didn't seem to mind being included and participated in an indirect way. In this sense the group honored differences in the method and level of participation.

Image theater exercises dealing with power help the participants to recognize and express power and powerlessness in images dealing with their own lives. They can then apply this to forum theater work and begin to find solutions to their own problems. The facilitators also used image theater to help the participants understand how to interpret the stories of others and how to visualize solutions. Rather than presenting a metanarrative, which ultimately everyone would have to reject as not being relevant to their lives, Boal's theater created an opportunity for dialogue. Within the search for commonalities, the bonds that form the temporary community, there was room for difference. Within the communal story was a dialogue about social change.

The facilitators employed Boal's concept of making sculptures of an "actual image," a "transitional image," and an "ideal image."[7] In an exercise called "pilot/copilot" a "teller" and "listener" use the other participants to sculpt a story from the teller's own life. After the initial sculpting they have a short amount of time to change the image to fit three wishes they may have for the outcome of the story.

Rashleigh and Jewel volunteered for this process. By the images the two women created it was evident that the story was about being an outsider. In the first sculpture Rashleigh, who was the teller, put one person standing apart from a larger group. In the first two changes she put the outsider into the group and put onlookers in poses that showed that they were shocked. In the third change the group was empowered by their unity and confronted the onlookers who had to yield.

Jewel also showed an outsider apart from a group, but in the images that followed she showed the outsider being accepted. Rashleigh said of Jewel's images that she thought that Jewel had misinterpreted what she had said. Weinblatt explained that in this process others bring in their own story to add to the one you may have started with.

In this sense the exercise was part of the preparation for forum theater in which the "spectators" bring in their experiences to try to solve the problems posed by the scene. Regarding the performance at the end of the workshop, Weinblatt stressed that the audience members who intervene in the scenes might not know anything about what it is like to be homeless or even understand the issues being raised but that they have their own stories, and the stories of forum theater become the stories of the entire group.

By the third day the group was remarkably transformed. Several of the youths had not returned after the first day, and by now the group was starting to enjoy working together. Seven of the fifteen participants were now from Lambert House. I noticed staff members and youths from different centers mixing in group work. The group also began to take ownership of the ground rules. On this day Joey showed up about an hour late. The group discussed whether he should be allowed to stay and voted to stick to the rules. A staff member from Orion Center came with Joey on the fourth day to plead his case. Evidently, she felt it was her fault that Joey had missed his ride. She had given him a bus ticket the day before and told him that the group wouldn't mind that he was late. The group debated for over an hour about the consequences of allowing him back in. Morgan said that she thought Joey was disruptive and that she would be distracted if he were allowed back in. Rashleigh defended him and said he was really trying. A staff member from University District Youth Center said that his behavior shouldn't be the criterion. Angie thought he should be allowed back in if he really wanted it that badly. After a vote he was allowed in.

When Weinblatt and the staff member went to talk to Joey, he had changed his mind. It seemed like the staff member had been more invested in Joey's acceptance back into the group than Joey had been. Being hyperconscious of manipulation by outsiders, I wondered if Joey would have come at all if the staff member hadn't convinced him twice to return.

Forum Theater

For the purposes of the performance the group had to narrow down the list to three central issues. The group selected the issues of getting a job and police harassment but could not agree on the third issue. They had discussed love, power, soul-searching, and getting kicked out of the house.

The group had spent a lot of time on the fourth day working on a story about how Brandon was kicked out of his house by his abusive stepfather. While everyone agreed that this was important, roughly half of the street youth were from Lambert House and felt that coming out was a priority. Morgan pointed out: "This is a very diverse group of people and whatever we come up with everyone will support, we will all be looking out for each other."[8] The group decided that it would focus on finding a story that rang true for most of the members. A consensus was reached that the story of being kicked out of the house had many of the same elements as a story about coming out, since many of the queer youth were also forced to leave their homes because they had revealed their sexuality to their parents. The group used a personal story to reach a solution that acknowledged the diverse backgrounds of the youth while recognizing a shared oppression.

The Performance

On the fifth day of the workshop the participants met at the Oddfellows Hall on Capitol Hill. A variety of arts groups including SPT share the building. The acoustics in the particular room of the rehearsal and performance were particularly bad. It was hard to keep rehearsal under control. The participants were nervous and energetic, and Weinblatt was exhausted. Finally, Weinblatt fell silent for a moment, losing his patience. As he looked down, Matt made a jerking-off motion. I thought the cohesion of the group was threatening to come apart.

Later, Matt and I were outside smoking. He was complaining about Weinblatt's authority and once again about the title of the project. "It should be called something cool," he said, "something that has something to do with street life. It should be called something like *Sketch What*." I asked him what this meant. He explained: "It's a street term for like 'How's it going?' or 'What's Up?' But it can also mean 'Look out' or 'Heads up, there's a cop coming.'"

The group presented the three forum scenes on the last night of the workshop to a general audience.[9] The audience was a mix of homeless people and those affiliated in some way with the homeless issues, supporters of Seattle Public Theater, and several people who had read about the event in the *Seattle Times* but had no previous experience with SPT or with the homeless.

In addition to the coalition of participants formed within the workshop, SPT facilitators hoped to forge a broader coalition between the workshop participants and the diverse elements within the audience—the second level of coalition building. In SPT's application of forum theater, members of the workshop perform a scene, and the audience members list the problems they see in the situation. The scene is performed again so that the audience can intervene when they feel someone lacks power. They can attempt to change the scene through the character's actions. After they have tried an intervention, the audience may debate its effectiveness. Where the workshop participants felt empowered with some ownership of the process, they understood that true empowerment would come from their ability to generate a dialogue with the audience.

There were some difficulties with the performance. Aside from the problem with the acoustics, a much larger audience turned out than the facilitators had anticipated. A feature by the *Seattle Times* drew an unexpectedly large turnout of over three hundred people, making a close, intimate dialogue very difficult. Weinblatt maintained control over the flow of the evening and made certain that as many people as possible were engaged. Also, the youth and the audience seemed focused on connecting and reaching an understanding about the issues being raised.

Although people often identified with and took the roles of the homeless youth, audience members brought their own stories to the scenes and, in doing so, often took on roles that were surprising to the workshop participants. For instance, in the first scene, in which a sexist boss refuses to hire a young, homeless man, two people took the role of the boss, feeling that he was the person lacking power. In the scene about police harassment one woman even took the role of the police officer, feeling that the young, homeless woman did not show the officer enough respect.

In the story in which the young man, Matt, is kicked out of his home by his abusive father for being gay, most of the interventions focused on the character of the mother, who often deferred to the father. One woman stood up to the father, stating, "It's my house, too, and he's our son, and he has a right to be here." When the father kicked Matt out anyway, the mother left with Matt. Someone pointed out that now she was homeless, and someone else observed that the mother had just abandoned her daughter. Another woman took the mother's place and turned the young men away at the door. She gave them some money and told Matt to come home later. While one person felt that she was still giving her power to the father, others felt that she was choosing her battles and protecting her son.

A man who took the mother's role told Matt that things could be unpleasant if he brought his friend in, and he warned the father that if he became abusive he would call the police. When the father threw the men out, the mother told them to wait outside while he called the police. One person in the audience noted that the mother gave everyone options. Another person expressed that he hoped people were now more aware of the issues facing gay kids.

I was really surprised that some of the members of the general audience took roles other than those of the homeless youth. I hadn't thought the other people were oppressed, and I thought maybe the audience was confused. I thought maybe the youth would think so as well and view the audience as ignorant outsiders.

Several of the youth I spoke with said that they felt that the audience clearly understood what they were trying to convey. One young man told me that he felt the audience was really engaged and that it was interesting to see the interventions they tried. I realized much later that I was the only one who saw a division. I was trying to make the audience and the youth fit into a paradigm that they did not see. It was surprising to watch which characters audience members identified as powerless, identifications that did not always coincide with those of the homeless youth. Homeless and non-homeless audience members took a variety of roles, which goes against the possible assumption that the non-homeless were simply shy about taking roles of homeless youth while "real" homeless youth were present. The audience brought stories with them that allowed them to identify oppression across the board. By committing themselves to an active dialogue, the audience and the youth worked together to find solutions to the scenarios. Forum theater resists the universalizing impulse of formal theater by doing away with ownership of a specific plot or character. It deprivileges representation and allows room for direct intervention and political action. As the audience member stands up to intervene in a forum theater scene, a connection can be formed by the sharing of stories and ideas across formal community boundaries.

Beyond the Performance

The third level of the process of building temporary communities involves a transformation in the community outside of the theater, where the work resonates beyond the performance event. While one can theorize that the group of the "general audience" of the event may feel less removed from the group of "homeless youth," there are other more tangible effects of the workshop and performance.

Some friendships were formed between youth from different centers. Paul, the staff member at Lambert House, said that he thought the workshop helped to smooth over some previous animosity between staff and youth there, that his own participation had helped him connect with the Lambert House participants. Also, some of the group members were able to continue their work due to a grant secured by the staff at Capitol Hill Youth Center. One audience member I spoke with works with young women at risk and thought she might try some forum theater techniques with them.

The forum theater work performed by Seattle Public Theater forges connections between people who might not have seen themselves as allies. It defies the homogenizing effects of formal theater by refusing to subscribe to representation coming from the mind of a single author. On both micro and macro levels it builds coalitions for political action through the use of stories that are simultaneously individual and collective.

NOTES

1. Sonja Kuftinec, "A Cornerstone for Rethinking Community Theater," *Theater Topics* 6, no. 1 (1996): 92.

2. Catherine Gallagher, "Marxism and the New Historicism," in *The New Historicism,* ed. H. Aram Veeser (New York: Routledge, 1989), 40.

3. Ibid.

4. Marc Weinblatt, personal interview, 4 November 1996.

5. Augusto Boal, *Theater of the Oppressed,* trans. Charles A. and Maria-Odilia Leal McBride (New York: Theater Communications Group, 1985), 119.

6. Misha Berson, "Theater Becomes a Tool for Awareness," *Seattle Times,* 24 January 1997, D3.

7. Boal, *Theater of the Oppressed,* 135.

8. One participant said in an interview: "I think it's intensely uplifting to realize from the first day that the gay and straight kids are working together and don't give a shit about their sexuality or each others'. They're here to work" (qtd. in Ruth Fox, "All the World's a Stage: Street Youths Perform in Theater of Liberation," *Real Change,* 15–28 February 1997, 13). Morgan stated in a *Seattle Times* interview, "It's great to know people for who they are, not who they appear to be" (qtd. in Berson, "Theater Becomes a Tool," D3).

9. Generally, it is uncommon for a forum theater workshop to develop forum scenes for a performance open to the general public. SPT ends the workshop with a performance, however, for several reasons. The performance offers a goal for the workshop participants to work toward. It allows SPT to publicize and raise public awareness about the work it does. And it offers an opportunity for the homeless community to open a dialogue with the "general public."

Weinblatt also believes that this dialogue is an important and exciting part of SPT's work. Marc Weinblatt wrote in an e-mail to me (17 October 1997) that our culture is so diverse that

> it is so hard to get a homogenous audience which is what "pure" Forum calls for. We do it sometimes and we do it with (the more common) heterogenous audiences as well. Yes, there are dangers in this. Like doing a scene on Racism for a mostly white audience. Has the ability to re-wound. But what a shame to rule out the possibilities that come from that kind of cross fertilization of ideas. We teach and learn from each other. The important thing in performing for heterogenous audiences is (and this is an adjustment I have recently started making) that an awareness of this fact is brought to light. I now ask spect-actors to simply be aware that if it is not their story up there (if they have never been homeless, for instance), that they aren't coming from a place of experience. They are stepping into someone else's world. We did one of our Friday night performances a few weeks ago and the scene we Forumed had a blind character. Some people wanted to play that role and I simply pointed out that if they have never been blind, their advice has a different weight. An outsider's point of view. Come up and try your ideas but just remember, you aren't blind (you aren't homeless, you aren't black, etc.)

Carl Thelin

Art Party Vision:
The People's Public Space
as Social Acupuncture

Taichung is a city of 850,000 located in central Taiwan. In tourist pamphlets it is called Taiwan's "City of Culture," ostensibly because it is home to numerous universities and colleges. In fact, many Taichung residents joke that the only culture in their city is "barbershop culture." In Taiwan most barbershops are fronts for brothels, and *barbershop culture* refers to whoring and drunkenness. The fact that many Taichung residents feel that their city lacks culture is perhaps symptomatic of the radical changes that have completely reshaped Taiwan's urban landscape over the last thirty years.

In the city center sparkling steel and glass buildings sprout beside two-story shop fronts left over from the Japanese colonial occupation. Outside the center the transformation has been even more radical. Huge residential developments and whole new commercial districts, built with little or no sign of planning, have displaced rice and sugarcane fields, all in the space of a single decade, from the mid-1980s to the mid-1990s. In the mid-1980s Taichung's streets flowed with motorcycles and small locally produced cars. Today those vehicles remain but are becoming lost in an ever-expanding tide of BMWs and Saabs. McDonald's opened Taichung's first foreign fast-food restaurant in 1985. By 1995 the more than thirty McDonald's locations were competing with everything from Pizza Hut to Ponderosa. This very rapid twinned urbanization and Westernization has had a major impact on Taichung's cultural mind-set.

Carl Thelin was born and raised in Taichung and returned there to teach English and Theater at Tunghai University from 1991 to 1995. He attended his first People's Public Space art party in 1993 and was peripherally involved in several more art parties before being asked to direct *Death of a Seed*. He has also worked with several PPS friends on unrelated performance projects. In 1995 he left Taiwan to pursue graduate studies at the University of Hawaii and now lives in San Francisco.

Taichung has the same social problems as any urban center, but they have been exacerbated by rapid economic development and the sudden flush of new wealth. Residents frequently complain about traffic congestion; safety, air, and water pollution; and crass materialism, as people pour themselves into ever greater "get rich quick" schemes. They are also concerned about rampant political corruption, the power of the local mafia, and vast generation gaps between themselves and the generation before or after them.

Small wonder that in the face of such rapid change and social turmoil, some people would begin to feel a lack of culture. Many younger people have abandoned traditional religious practices, as well as traditional performance and art forms, without really embracing anything else. A number of new theater and art groups have begun to try to fill this void. One such group is the Renmin Gongshe (People's Public Space, or PPS).

The PPS is an art cooperative. Founded in 1990, its membership is a loose and constantly changing group of people coagulating around founder Ah-huan and his closest friend, Xiao-lien. Ah-huan does not use the word *member* at all, preferring *friend*. Friends have included teachers and students from local high schools and universities, nightclub musicians, Daoist priests, Buddhist monks, carpenters, insurance salespeople, advertising industry professionals, and many others. Their "art space" was until recently made up of two old-style Taiwanese shop fronts, one of which is a living and eating space, while the other is the performance/gallery space. (For the last few months, as of this writing, the PPS has been in financial difficulty and has been forced to sublet the art space shop front.) Anyone who wishes is welcome to stay and eat in the living quarters side, so Ah-huan and Xiao-lien often have homeless or socially marginalized people staying with them.

The PPS (the English name is Ah-huan's translation) takes its name from a pun on the Chinese term for "workers' commune" (*renmin gongshe*) and the old word for "inn" or "tavern" (*gongshe*). Although the pronunciation (and English romanization) of the words for commune and inn are the same (*gongshe*), the characters used to write them are completely different. In its name the PPS uses the first three characters from workers' commune (*renming gong*) and the last character (*she*) from the word for inn. Although this name means something like "people's public inn," the name's obvious reference to Chinese communism makes it politically charged. Taiwan is governed by the Chinese Nationalist government, which governed all of China from 1911 until it lost a civil war to the current Communist Chinese government in 1949. After retreating to Taiwan, the Nationalists vowed to retake China, and officially the two governments are still at war, although no real military actions have been taken by either side for many years. This history gives Taiwan a sensitive political climate in which a seemingly Maoist name such as Workers' Commune is calculated to be provocative.

The PPS was founded at the end of a period of social unrest in the wake of the "Houseless People" protests of the late 1980s. These protests happened when the government launched a massive urban renewal drive, buying up land in order to widen roads and build new city parks and other municipal facilities. People were compensated at the "public use price" for their homes and property. The public use price was often as low as one-tenth of the market value of the property, meaning that the people displaced by the new construction not only lost their nest egg but usually were unable to buy a new home to live in. Ah-huan, the thirty-year-old founder and self-proclaimed "comrade-in-chief" of the PPS, was at that time living with his parents, and they were among the people who lost their houses. This occurrence and the subsequent mass protests sensitized Ah-huan to the importance of having a space of one's own. "Younger people in Taiwan today seldom have their own space," he claimed in a recent interview.[1] Since most single young adults still live with their parents and work for someone else and neither Taiwanese parents nor employers are generally great respecters of privacy, there is truth to this claim. "My generation is radically different from our parents'. Taiwan has changed so much in the last twenty years," he said. "We needed our own space, where we could just screw around." (It should be noted that early "screwing around" at the space took the form of some very groundbreaking artwork.) It wasn't until after the founding of the space that he began to articulate a wider agenda.

Despite its inflammatory name, the PPS eschews formal politics, and *friends* run the entire political gamut from outspoken advocates of Taiwan independence to scholars of the Chinese classics who speak glowingly of Han Chinese unity. In fact, Ah-huan eschews any kind of political or social agenda. "There are no social problems," he says, "No good or bad, no right or wrong, everything simply is." This rather Zen-like statement does not give us the whole picture, however. In the midst of Taiwan's intensely competitive and materialistic environment the PPS seeks to foster a special kind of local community consciousness, to initiate an attitude of tolerance and support for individual spiritual quests and individual expression. Ah-huan says: "People need to create and we need others to support our creative spirit. This is the only way to reach spiritual harmony." The group builds this communal creative spirit by engaging in "art parties," in which everyone is encouraged to express themselves as an individual in a shared space. These art parties are frequently sparked by some incident in the life of the PPS community, so they are celebrations of its shared history as well as exercises in communal creativity. "We want to be sharp like an acupuncture needle," Ah-huan claims, "We puncture one small point, and irritate it for the benefit of the whole body." An examination of one series of events involving two art parties allows us to see how their social acupuncture works.

In May 1993 a man named Mr. Lin came to live at the People's Public Space. He claimed to be a cultural representative of President Lee Teng-Hui and said that he could lead the PPS into a "new age in art." Mr. Lin divided his time between writing about religion and collecting things that other people had abandoned by the roadside, ranging from bars of used soap to old shoes to coffee table art books. He lovingly packed all of these objects, along with his own writing and charcoal drawings, in cardboard boxes.

In July 1993 a tattoo-covered man arrived to stay at the PPS. According to Xiao-lien, he had an "aggressive, playful disposition." He was a recently released convict who had spent twenty years in prison. Mr. Lin was afraid of him and abruptly disappeared, leaving all of his possessions at the PPS. Ah-huan kept these things in storage in case Mr. Lin came back, but they were in the way, and a new place had to be found for them each time a new art event was staged. As time went by, some of the boxes began to smell. Finally, when he needed the storage space for an upcoming project, Ah-huan organized an art party to "celebrate Mr. Lin's existence and contribution to our lives."[2] The celebration took place just over a year after Mr. Lin had departed and was celebrated as the first anniversary of his disappearance.

This art party, called *Mr. Lin's Secret Treasure,* was held on 9 July 1994. All of Mr. Lin's boxes were placed in the center of the art space. The party began with people gathering to hear Xiao-lien tell the story of Mr. Lin's stay there. Other friends who had known Mr. Lin then shared their memories with the group. Not all of this sharing was verbal. One PPS friend arrived with a plastic bag full of small scraps of paper, which he distributed to everyone. He later said that this act was his protest against the art party, which he felt was a defamation of Mr. Lin's memory. He chose to pass out his scraps of paper, while Mr. Lin did not choose to subject his possessions to public scrutiny.

After memories were shared, participants began opening the boxes and passing their contents around. Participants were encouraged to play with the objects and to let them inspire the creation of new art. Out of Mr. Lin's cast-off life, many new works of art began to take shape. Some people began to sculpt the objects into new shapes, while others juxtaposed unlikely pairs of objects or nailed them to the wall in an interesting pattern. One person created a mobile out of several pairs of scissors, hangers, and a mutilated calendar. Other people simply drew pictures inspired by Mr. Lin's "treasure." Some of the art was performed; for example, several people read simultaneously in English and Mandarin from a bilingual Bible found among Mr. Lin's possessions. Even when the works of art were not performed, this event as a whole was intensely performative. According to Ah-huan, participants derived as much from the atmosphere of creativity and from watching others at work and helping them as they did from their own projects. One participant described the art party this way: "Just sheer creativity for the fun of it. And fun there was! Laughing children, dancing through the room, their joy shared by surrounding eyes; hands working . . . seemed to be acting on sudden impulse rather than according to any conscious decision. . . . There was no gap between art and life. Art was 'lived' and everyday life became art."[3]

In November of the same year a second art party, *Death of a Seed,* was staged to celebrate the publication of a book about the first party. This performance grew out of Ah-huan's reading of Mr. Lin's writings about religion. This event was to be a bit more formal and more structured than others. Various friends were asked to be responsible for different aspects of the performance. I was asked to direct it, although the term *director* must be interpreted very loosely at any PPS event, since, as always, friends were encouraged to find their own voice in the performance. The performance eventually involved four separate independent but related elements. The main performance was accompanied simultaneously by an ensemble of classical Chinese instruments and a Western-style rock band, both of which improvised off of the events taking place in the main performance. The fourth element was supplied by a performance artist who took photographs of a group of people planning to come to the show and made masks out of the photos, so that some members of the crowd were wearing masks of their own faces, which they removed at the end of the performance. These four elements came out of four individual visions of what should happen at the performance that emerged at a planning meeting. Ah-huan told all four people to run with their ideas, and there was no real effort to coordinate them. Each one added a dimension to the performance.

As participants (hereafter I use *participants* to mean the unrehearsed spectators) entered the space, they were greeted by women dressed in the uniforms of department store salesclerks. These women, who we called angels, led the arriving participants toward actors representing various religious figures. Each religious figure moved aimlessly through the space, chanting slogans associated with their religion. The figures represented Buddhism, Daoism, Islam, Christianity, and Confucianism. We had

attempted to cast actual believers as their respective faiths. Our notable successes here were that we had a Daoist spirit medium playing Daoism and a
devotee of the Chinese classics playing Confucianism. All of the religious
figures had ropes dangling from their waists. The angels asked participants if
they would convert to each of the various religions. Each time they said yes,
they would be tied by the wrist onto one of them. Many people were tied
onto two or three different religions at once. Since the religious figures
were constantly moving, this resulted in a giant human knot. Finally, Ah-
huan, who tied himself to all five religions, shouted: "Free yourselves! We
are stupid not to untie ourselves!" Everyone tore off their ropes and began
to dance. Several other scenes followed, including the distribution of the
books and Ah-huan's speech of celebration, but the human knot was
definitely the centerpiece of the event. Eventually, the whole thing turned
into an informal dance party, completely obliterating any remaining distinction between performer and participant.

We can see traits in both of the art parties that typify much of the work
the PPS does. An event shared only by their community, the junk collecting and subsequent disappearance of Mr. Lin, served as the inspiration and
impetus for both parties. No high artistic ideals or risky statements about
political issues were proclaimed here. There was simply an assertion of Mr.
Lin's importance to the community. Holidays are an important part of how
any community defines itself, and in celebrating the anniversary of Mr. Lin's
disappearance the PPS was proclaiming a kind of local community holiday.
Within the context of each event an ad hoc community is built through
participation in the event. Advance publicity always emphasizes the participatory nature of PPS events. Each event is structured so that participants are
naturally involved and so that the success of the event depends on them. In
Death of a Seed, for example, the moment participants entered they were
greeted by the angels and invited to join a religion. In *Mr. Lin's Secret Treasure* participation was encouraged through speeches by Ah-huan and others.
The bonds of this temporary community are strengthened as the various
participants open up and express themselves through their creative work.
They see others expressing themselves, and sometimes an atmosphere of
shared confidences is created. One participant commented, "We're in here
just about going crazy while just outside in the street people are driving by
or selling things, having a humdrum day."[4] The atmosphere at the end of an
art party is typically euphoric. People are often reluctant to leave, and, when
they do leave, they often go to a pub or teahouse with a group of people
they may have just met at the event. After *Death of a Seed* most participants
stayed for two or three hours of dancing, and, when the dance party finally

dissipated, I went out to a pub with a group of people and ended up talking for another four hours with two people I did not know before the event. Our conversation was wide ranging, covering everything from politics to Daoist thought to bizarre childhood experiences, and we spoke with a frankness unusual in contemporary Taiwan. PPS art parties consistently seem to generate this kind of connection between participants.

Ah-huan believes that the key to generating this feeling of community is fostering individual creative expression in a supportive communal context. We have seen how the PPS does this in several ways. The person protesting the violation of Mr. Lin's private belongings was given space to do so as part of the celebratory event. Both art parties relied for their character and success on the active participation of everyone present. They were thus communal and involved the observation of others realizing their visions while realizing one's own. Even in a more structured event like *Death of a Seed,* radically different ideas were given a place in the structure of the party, and audience participation was still integral.

Most important, Mr. Lin is never dismissed as a homeless crank. In fact, the only time there is any disagreement about him among the PPS friends, the dispute is over whether he is being accorded enough respect. Despite the fact that he is a vagrant rather than an artist in the eyes of almost everyone outside the PPS community, they extend to him the same support and legitimacy that they do to any friend. This fact makes the PPS a genuinely revolutionary entity, rather than just a bunch of artists performing and applauding for one another. Everyone is genuinely welcomed in, and they seem genuinely interested in each person's vision. There is an implicit overturning of social hierarchy in this inclusiveness. Their policy of letting anyone stay at the space ensures that a steady stream of marginalized people become involved in the PPS, and these people are given a voice many of them could find nowhere else. The diverse range of backgrounds represented among PPS friends attests to the appeal of the cooperative's vision of community among more than just the socially marginalized.

Socially, then, the PPS is a distinct community within Taichung's urban landscape. The community has its own sense of history and holidays. For at least the duration of each event the participants see themselves as distinct and apart from the city around them. They have a value system different from, and perhaps antithetical to, that of the city. Where the city prioritizes the pursuit of wealth and marginalizes the homeless, the PPS prioritizes individual expression and respects and upholds the marginalized.

The one governing aesthetic principle at the PPS is that personal expression and the support of the personal expression of others are good.

The PPS is an aesthetic community in that its members share their personal expression with one another and applaud one another's work. PPS friends are usually not established artists but, rather, ordinary people who need a creative outlet.

The city, the force that spawned the PPS, is usually not explicitly addressed in the group's work but is addressed indirectly in a variety of ways. Homelessness is a relatively new phenomenon that has arisen as people have moved from large family homes that could accommodate several generations and their in-laws to small urban efficiency apartments. In the past if you had a family, even in the form of distant cousins, you had a place to stay. This is no longer true. The PPS's "everyone can stay here" policy is a response to this new urban phenomenon as well as to the Houseless People protests. Many of the raw materials used in art parties are salvaged from dumps and trash piles. The treasure in *Mr. Lin's Secret Treasure* is a case in point, but many of the props, costumes, lights, and musical instruments used in *Death of a Seed* were also salvaged. The PPS friends do not salvage waste specifically because of its urban nature, but the fact that they create their work using the city's waste is an implicit reassertion of their own special marginal status within the city. In a sense this salvaging is also a return to an older, pre-urban lifestyle. Thirty years ago trash was not simply dumped but carefully sorted and recycled. Raw materials were scarcer then, and junk could be a very valuable commodity. Certainly, the most significant way in which the PPS sees itself as a response to its urban environment, however, is as a provider of open space. The group seeks to provide physical and emotional space to anyone denied it by the city. People create and go to art parties to express themselves in ways that they cannot in the course of their normal urban lives.

The PPS effectively provides this space to those who need it. They are providing social acupuncture at one small point in the heart of Taichung. And perhaps they are having an effect on the larger body of society as well.

Mr. Lin, by the way, has been sighted at art openings elsewhere in Taichung. He still claims to be the president's cultural envoy.[5]

Epilogue

In August 1997 the People's Public Space closed for good. There were several reasons behind the closure, but mainly it was due to continuing financial hardship and the landlord wanting to develop the site that the group's building was on. In true PPS form Ah-huan and Xiao-lien threw a final art party to commemorate the closing of the space. This final party included a performance involving the cleaning of the space, and other performance events lit by a bonfire built out of everything they were throwing away. Ah-huan is philosophical about the closure: "The Space was an important part of my life and the lives of its friends. We developed it and it developed us for a while, but now we must find new paths to fulfillment."[6]

A variety of other artists and groups have been influenced by the work of the PPS. Perhaps the most notable example of this influence was an event held during the month of May 1995 by one-time PPS friend Wu Chong Wei entitled *Taipei Mid-Air Fractured Festival*. This was a month-long gathering of artists from all over Taiwan held on the banks of the Danshui River in Taipei County. The artists gathered there built a shantytown and welcomed anyone who wished to stay with them to do so as they created and performed their art. Wu's own artistic contribution, from which the event took its name, involved lifting large pieces of junk such as discarded washing machines into the air with a helium balloon. When the balloon reached a certain height, the piece of junk would be released to come crashing down to earth.[7] The open invitation to live on premises and participate in the creation of art is characteristic of the PPS, as is the central emphasis of the main event, the creation of art out of urban detritus. This event was important in that artists from all over Taiwan participated and also because it marked the first time that an event of this type received government sponsorship. Ultimately, however, the best indication of the success of the PPS probably lies in its impact not on other artists but on the lives of its friends, especially those who are not artists outside of the context of PPS art parties. This impact will never be tangibly measurable, but it is surely significant.

NOTES

1. Ah-huan, telephone interview with Manfred Sablotny, 27 March 1997. All further quotations from Ah-huan are taken from this interview unless otherwise noted.

2. Spoken at the performance of *Mr. Lin's Secret Treasure*. PPS, 9 July 1994.

3. Anonymous participant, quoted in Lin Jinhuan (Ah-huan), ed., *Lin Xiansheng de Mimi Baobei* (Taichung: Renmin Gongshe, 1994).

4. Casual conversation with a PPS friend in November 1994.

5. The writing of this essay would not have been possible without the invaluable assistance of Manfred Sablotny and Adam Benatovich.

6. Telephone interview, 2 August 1998.

7. Victor Wong, "Taipei Bohemians," *China News*, 28 April 1995.

Alan Filewod

Coalitions of Resistance: Ground Zero's Community Mobilization

This account of Ground Zero begins with the caution that *community* is arguably the most misused word in contemporary political discourse. As a rhetorical instrument, it is an empty signifier that demands allegiance and marks value without specificity. *Community* implies a system of shared interest, but the word is often deployed as a strategy of ideological mapping that centers the subject in a field that masks individual interest. Communities in these terms exist as subjunctives, objects of invocation, and sites of recourse. They are invariably "imagined," as Benedict Anderson has said famously in reference to nations.[1] At the same time, community is the locus of political action and both site and object of political intervention theater. By its very constructedness theater work enacts and exposes the social formations that create communities, but it can—more often does—replay essentializing and totalizing fictions of sentimentalized communities, of geography, ethnicity, class, and gender, that dehistoricize the work of political resistance.

The sentimental quest to rediscover a sense of community, allegedly lost in the alienated world of postindustrial transnational capital, has framed much of the political theater work of the past two decades, particularly in North America, where *community* frequently erases *class* in popular discourse. This has produced the familiar condition by which theater artists form companies that model idealized community structures. Throughout the industrialized world politically engaged theaters have shown a tendency to see themselves as the vanguard of political change and have as a result

Alan Filewod teaches Canadian drama and political theater at the University of Guelph, Ontario. He is the author of *Collective Encounters: Documentary Theatre in English Canada* (1987); and coauthor (with David Watt) of *Workers' Playtime: Studies in Theatre and the Labour Movement in Australia, Canada and the United Kingdom, 1970–1997* (2001). His introduction to community activist theater began as a member of the Mummers Troupe in Newfoundland in the early 1970s; subsequently, he was one of the founders of the Canadian Popular Theatre Alliance.

expended a great deal of energy on the complexities of their own organizational politics, negotiating class and gender politics, issues of collective structures and artistic processes, and the recurrent contradictions of sustaining oppositional work in semisubsidized arts industries that contain activist cultural work in perpetual states of economic crisis.

In this model the political theater mirrors the complex of the mainstream arts organizations, which, as Loren Kruger has noted in her study of national theaters, summon representative audiences to enact metonymic communities.[2] Just as national theaters enact ideology through simulation, political theaters work to embody oppositionality. The crises that result from this metonymic strategy are painfully familiar. The history of twentieth-century political theater in the world of capital is one of lost causes (think of Piscator's disappointment that the working class would not support its own theater) and romantic naïveté. Consider Clive Barker's caustic description of the British political theater of the 1970s, characterized by "groups of students explaining to carworkers how the carworkers were exploited, a subject on which the carworkers were experts and the students were not."[3]

If *community* has in this historical model proved to be a discursive trap—an always deferred reference to something that the theaters must "reach" to justify their radicalism—it has also been the method by which a less established but ultimately more effective model of theater activism has produced concrete results. In Canada this method has been known as the "popular theater" process; it is historically related to the notion of theater for development in the underdeveloped world and has begun to enter the mainstream of institutionalized theater practice though the work of Augusto Boal. As the term has been understood in Canada, popular theater work engages with local communities defined not by essentializing characteristics but by political struggle. The recurring operative principle has been the partnership of theater workers with activists in which the theater does not attempt to model the social conditions of struggle but, instead, works to achieve specific tactical ends.

That process has exposed the ideological fiction materialized in the very notion of the theater company. In our study of theaters working with organized labor groups, from which this account of Ground Zero Productions is largely extracted, David Watt and I argue that contemporary interventionist theaters tend to be loose, temporary, and contingent alliances of like-minded arts workers and political activists engaged in a constant process of negotiation and adaptation to changing contexts.[4] Because they constantly rework the components of theatrical production (including performance space, the theatrical tools of style and technique, and the administrative tools of company structure and management) we propose the notion of *strategic ventures* as a more useful term than *company*. The notion of the theater company—of a structure that collapses administrative and financial management onto the continuity of an artistic ensemble—has always been a tool primarily of cultural managers and theater historians, because it provides a way to narrate, fund, and contain theatrical practice; it allows for the individual artistic temperaments that create theater work but depersonalizes their contexts. Arts councils (at least in Canada) repeatedly make the point that they fund companies, not individuals; theater historians narrate structures in which biographies play out their meanings.

If we mediate the notion of community as an ideological weapon that points in all directions at once and repudiate the material fact of the theater company, a strategic venture like Ground Zero becomes virtually invisible. It is in fact the case of Ground Zero that leads to these qualifications, because Ground Zero is a theater that is not a theater, a company that is not a company, working with communities that are not communities, often employing actors who are not actors, producing plays that are not plays. In each of these contradictions Ground Zero exposes problems of ideology routed through language; in each case it exposes a crisis in the way culture is institutionalized in capital society. In the interstices of these crises Ground Zero has developed an interventionist theater practice that has for almost two decades built effective coalitions of resistance and action.

A Theater That Is Not a Theater . . .

By identifying Ground Zero as a theater that is not a theater, I am circumventing a deeper problem of narrative, because Ground Zero is largely the work of one man, its founder and director, Don Bouzek. At the same time it is not reducible to that one man because his work has been produced with the collaboration of many gifted actors, administrators, puppet makers, painters, writers, and activists. Ground Zero is neither a theater nor an individual: it is an ongoing business structure that enables an artist to make a living and help others make theirs in the arena of political change. For most of its history Ground Zero has existed as a small office/studio crammed with old computers, video editing machines, and boxes of the detritus of theatrical work. It has also been, on occasion, Bouzek's living space. The important point here is that, while Ground Zero is in a sense the external identity of Bouzek's theatrical practice, it is at the same time an ongoing structure that cannot be personalized. And yet the two identities, of artist and company, are deeply intertwined. It is because of this complex that Bouzek has been able to succeed where many other have failed, in establishing an ongoing role for theater work in the social justice and labor movements in Canada. Bouzek the artist deploys Ground Zero the company to create work, often with arts council grants, with other artists, building a repertoire of traditional plays, *ceilidhs,* parades, and processional performances; Ground Zero the company pays Bouzek the artist to undertake video and performance commissions from labor organizations; together both claim a space in the theatrical community, offering opportunities, solidarity, and moral support for artists from marginalized communities.

A Company That Is Not a Company . . .

In order to establish a company that could exist as a series of mobile projects in a cultural system that forces arts groups to "sink roots" and institutionalize, Bouzek had to invent an administrative structure that would enable an artist-controlled theater to operate on an ongoing professional basis within a partially subsidized theater system that has historically marginalized political theaters. Ground Zero's fundamental administrative principle, reiterated annually in grant applications, is that the company does not undertake work on a given project until all financing for it is secured. To do this Bouzek has broken the cycle of dependency on public funding. While Ground Zero continues to apply for and receive grants, they are earmarked for specific, non-revenue-generating projects or for infrastructure support, while the bulk of the work is undertaken as commissions from sponsoring organizations in the labor and social justice movements.

Because it locates its place within a community of activism around the issues in which it intervenes, Ground Zero reaches out to allied organizations: educational offices of trade unions, community development groups, local action programs, and minority cultures (notably Filipino, Latin American, and First Nations groups). In effect, Ground Zero has repudiated the essentialist notions of community that have informed Canadian popular theaters in favor of a tactical populism that recognizes the need and possibilities of marketing its services.

Operating until the move to Edmonton out of a single office/studio in downtown Toronto and Bouzek's home in Peterborough, Ground Zero has avoided the major trap of most theaters, which struggle to fill a house and employ a company of artists and technicians. Ground Zero has maintained its financial stability through three primary means: by operating on a project-to-project basis, by subsidizing theater work with commissions for educational videos for labor groups, and by selling its shows to host organizations in lieu of selling tickets, which in practice means that the company's books have never had to forecast box office revenues. For most of its history Ground Zero has had only two full-time employees: Bouzek and an administrator. Much of their work has drawn on the active collaboration of a wide group of actors, puppeteers, designers, musicians, and visual artists who work on a project basis. The flexibility of hiring on a project basis has meant that Bouzek could gather together the artists most appropriate (in terms of cultural background, gender, or work experience) for a given project.

Plays That Are Not Plays . . .

Bouzek began his approach to political intervention theater while working as a media producer for the Development Education Centre in Toronto. He had already had ten years of theater work (with an emphasis on postmodern performance) behind him, but his foundational piece, which provided the outline of a theatrical vocabulary for Ground Zero, was a presentational, multimedia exploration of a Canadian radio pioneer called *The Fessenden Animation*. Bouzek cites Robert Wilson, Laurie Anderson, Pina Bausch, and Mabou Mines as artistic influences but found "their lack of content . . . depressing."[5] Wanting to find "a way of having content exist in imagistic work," he began working with puppetry, music, video, and photography.

Ground Zero (at this point still unincorporated and occasional) moved into the sphere of political action in the early 1980s, when Bouzek joined other volunteers to help Theatre Ontario, a nonprofit support agency for community-based theater, lobby against cutbacks to the Ontario Arts Council. That campaign brought home to him "the importance of the political process in our work"[6] and introduced him to Catherine Macleod, then executive director of Playwrights Union of Canada, who had a background in the labor movement. Through her he began to meet labor activists and produced a documentary performance on nuclear power entitled *St George / The Dragon*. Produced as a support piece for Performing Artists for Nuclear Disarmament, Bouzek took it to the Canadian Labour Congress's summer training institute at Port Elgin, Ontario. As he later recalled, that was the turning point that showed him a conjunction of constituency and mission:

There were three important things I learned in Port Elgin. The first is what it is like to play for an audience that is concerned with content first. People afterwards talked about "when this character said that, I disagreed." A long way from the discussions about the costume concept I was used to. Second, connected to the above the Labour Movement is an oral culture—people hear and remember things. It places more emphasis on the spoken word, and less on writing. Third, it was critical to set the work in a performance venue where the audience felt comfortable. Having big guys in tank tops come into a union hall and get a beer before they sat down scared hell out of us as theater people. But that meant they took the play on their terms, and made it work all the stronger.[7]

After five years of building networks with activist groups and artists, Bouzek had built the artistic track record required to make a bid for funding status as a company. He had also consolidated his artistic methods, so that in his application for charitable tax status, he could write that "we meld live performers, multi-layered soundtracks, projections, video and other elements into shows designed to play spaces like convention centers or community centers at reasonable cost."[8]

He had also by that point consolidated his principles of politically interventionist artwork. In 1989 Ground Zero held an invitational retreat in Peterborough, where two dozen popular theater workers and activists examined ways to clarify principles and establish working and workable linkages across cultural differences. The retreat produced a statement of principles that defines the relation of performance work to community struggle:

1. We do theatre for, with and by specific communities who have not been given access to resources in our society.
2. We act in partnership with organizations committed to social change (and sometimes other organizations when they are undertaking projects which may assist social change).
3. The cultural and aesthetic standards manifest in our work are shaped by those of the intended audience(s). *Note:* When we evaluate our work, the power and effectiveness of the presentation's engagement with the audience is considered in equal measure with the execution of traditional theatrical "production values."
4. Our work is engaged in a process of Popular Education which has its own traditions and methods of work.[9]

These principles radicalize the relationship of artist and community by re-siting fundamental terms of cultural authority. The popular theater process acknowledges the leadership expertise of activists within communities of struggle, but this can lead to complex negotiations in which artists and activist partners must find ways to educate one another. Activists must trust that artists know their tools (a particularly complex issue when artists like Bouzek breach the comfortable walls of narrative realism); artists must trust that activists know the issues and their constituencies. Activists fear losing their membership support if the cultural work is too "out there"; artists fear the loss of artistic autonomy. As Bouzek found, the foundation of solidarity that enables such partnership usually overcomes these difficulties.

By the end of the 1980s Bouzek had established a system of development that allowed for quick reaction to emerging issues while maintaining focus on long-term projects. In his applications for arts funding he included a succinct definition of this process:

> We begin work on an issue by selecting a creative team which will typically involve writers, performers and musicians with a director. . . . [This] begins a research process which will draw on written material, interviews and workshops with people directly effected [*sic*] by an issue. This source material will be brought together at rehearsals as scripted scenes and scenarios for improvisations. From this a first draft will be set for presentation at a reading at an appropriate community event. . . . Based on feedback . . . revisions will be made and some staging added prior to another event. Usually after about half a dozen such sessions the script has been solidified.
>
> The script is then mounted. We rehearse for about two weeks and add the production elements [which] typically involves the collaboration of visual artists. The show is then performed a number of times at community venues in Metro and vicinity. This allows for final feedback and any necessary revisions. . . . Finally, the show is made available for touring as widely as possible.[10]

Ground Zero's theatrical vocabulary is eclectic but invariably reflects Bouzek's early interest in postmodern performance. The techniques of postmodernism—including genre play, decentered character, split focus, and the disruption of image/text—proved to be highly effective and portable. They also provided a working method of play development in rehearsal that could draw on the tradition of collective creation that had been so important in the development of postcolonial Canadian theater. And they offered a dramaturgical process that escaped the trap of overly familiar social realism that has become conventionalized in "art and working life" political theater through-out the English-speaking world. A typical Ground Zero performance might include quoted documentary text, hand-held puppets, actor-manipulated signs, satiric songs, short dialogue bits, and voice-overs. Usually, they would be done in a show context that sets up and strikes quickly in found space—a union hall, a hospital cafeteria, a parking lot.

A useful example of how Bouzek employed these techniques in a process of political intervention can be seen in Ground Zero's collaboration with organized labor in 1990, when it embarked on a union funded project to raise public awareness of health care underfunding. *Where's the Care?*—later described by Bouzek as "one of the most successful agit-prop things we've ever done"[11]—began with a chance meeting and materialized because of an unexpected election call by the Liberal government of Ontario in 1990. Late in its term in office the center-right Liberals decided to call a snap election, which they unexpectedly lost to the social democratic New Democratic Party (NDP). *Where's the Care?* was Ground Zero's contribution to the substantial social justice activity that surfaced in that campaign. It is a paradigmatic example of the effective use of agitprop in alliance with labor, and it is a rare example of a production funded entirely by a union.

The subject of *Where's the Care?* was the Liberal government's down-sizing of Ontario's comprehensive public health care system. In Ontario, as in the rest of Canada, health care is a provincial responsibility. All citizens are provided with free health care paid for by a massive public payroll insurance plan, and there is no private "second-tier" health care system. By the late 1980s Ontario's health system was in financial trouble: in 1990 the Ontario Hospital Association (OHA) reported that over eight hundred beds had been closed in that year, with another thirty-three hundred shorter-term closures. The OHA forecast a fifty-two million (Canadian) dollar deficit for Ontario's hospitals. The overall health care system in 1990 consumed a third of the entire provincial budget, and the government responded by freezing operation increases at the rate of inflation. Consequently, public apprehension about the future of health care became a major issue in the election.

Ground Zero's intervention began when Don Bouzek met Steve Eadie, a maintenance worker and organizer involved in the Canadian Union of Public Employees (CUPE) local at Toronto's Hospital for Sick Children. Eadie, along with other delegates at a CUPE convention, had seen Ground Zero perform at an anti–free trade rally at Toronto City Hall.

Clips from that performance had made the national network news, demonstrating the tactical effectiveness of media-oriented political theater. Bouzek and Eadie then came up with the idea of a one-off show for his local. As Bouzek recalls: "The show went really well. It was in a hotel meeting room, and there must have been a hundred people or so. We thought it was pretty good, but I think Steve was dreaming of 400 or something. I always thought the purpose of this stuff was the media attention, and was less sure of the slant, to put it crassly, of getting bums in seats at members' meetings."[12]

That performance (which presented a series of puppet and agitprop scenes about the effects on underfunding in one hospital) established the basis of a more planned project. When the government called its election later that summer, Eadie proposed a plan to CUPE for a traveling show that could be used to attract local media attention to the health care issue during the campaign. As Eadie remarks, the idea of a theatrical performance was not easy to sell: "The first reaction was out and out fear and hatred and loathing of anybody who would bring this idea forward. . . . The hatred and loathing passed in two minutes. The fear remained. What we were trying to do was set up something that people were not familiar with and had never done before."[13]

In a rare move CUPE accepted the plan and contributed most of the fifteen thousand (Canadian) dollar budget needed for a two-week process of research, script development, and rehearsal and a two-week tour of major regional centers. To put that figure into context, Ground Zero's budget for a union video normally falls between twenty and forty thousand (Canadian) dollars. For CUPE the theater event was a bargain. The plan that Bouzek and CUPE devised was to use a fifteen-minute performance as a media hook for press and television coverage of CUPE's demands that the government reopen two hundred beds slated to be closed, open four thousand new beds across the province, and change the restraint policy. As Eadie remarks in the video Ground Zero made of the project, "One of the initiatives was to use media and theater events as the method with which we would attract public attention."[14] CUPE had entered into a coalition with other health care interest groups, including the Ontario Public Service Employees' Union, the Service Employees International Union, the Association of Allied Health Professionals of Ontario, the Office and Professional Employees International Union, and, in an uncommon alliance, the Ontario Medical Association. For the most part, however, the project developed through CUPE networks.

The union early on identified the goals of the project. The plan was based around two complementary objectives: to encourage activism by coalitions expressing local responses to the cuts and to integrate local action with centrally distributed media releases. Eadie suggested that Ground Zero begin by talking to Charlene Avon, president of the CUPE local at St. Joseph's Hospital in Peterborough. In the video Avon explains the process from her end:

> The fact that we would have some input into it, and then we actively go out and recruit our members and the public to take part in this was the big thing that sold us on this. I think it's fantastic, and it makes the issue really alive then.
>
> I got busy on the phone and phoned various presidents of hospitals and homes in the area, and also other labor people in the area, made them aware of the issue and what was going to happen, seeking their support. We then went to the memberships of both hospitals in the area, as well as getting information from some of the satellite hospitals and met with Ground Zero in the cafeteria of the hospital.[15]

For her the value of the project was not just in its media impact but in the effect the process had on the participants:

> It was really encouraging because it made you realize that you could do this, that you could stand there, you could talk to the media, that you could say what you felt, that you knew the issue. You just needed that confidence, and I think that's where the confidence came from, somebody saying, "hey, you can do it, and this is what it's all about, and we're here to help you. But go for it."

While researching the show through such networks Bouzek assembled a team of artists to bring it together quickly. The show was devised by him, two actors (Rhonda Payne and Gwen Baillie), designers Diana and Jerrard Smith, and country musician Washboard Hank. According to Bouzek:

> Essentially the piece was constructed as a storyboard of photo ops. We worked the interview material into the images and added the song to get 15 minutes. . . . Steve wrote a generic speech with space for local examples to be delivered by community spokespeople in each city.[16]

Performances took place between 21 August and 4 September, the day of the election, in nine cities. Performance venues varied: a shopping center in Hamilton, a public library in Windsor, outside a hospital in London, labor halls in Thunder Bay and Toronto, a hospital in Peterborough, and parks in Kingston and Sudbury. This staging called for a show that could be quickly erected and performed in adverse conditions and which could pick up and move in the event of inclement weather. This, of course, is a useful reminder that agitprop techniques are produced by necessity.

The text of *Where's the Care?* is a compact and highly effective tactical agitprop that builds on familiar conventions of popular theater practice in Canada. These conventions derive from the movement of community documentaries in the 1970s, which spawned a gestic dramaturgy based on the montage of songs, emblematic theatrical routines, and, most important in the Canadian tradition, authentifying presentational monologues. Bouzek's characteristic stylist touch results from the use of puppets (including hand-held masks and larger, bunraku style figures) and multimedia.

The performance typically began with an introduction by the president of the local hosting the show. In one taped performance, at the Peterborough Labour Day picnic, the local host invites the audience to "enjoy the skits." This is an entirely appropriate naming because in small-town Ontario the skits at church parties and school concerts are the most familiar form of theater. A skit is in effect a performance made by real people inside a community with no attempt at marking culture as something outside the community experience.

The frame of the show is a montage of songs, photo-op agitprop moments, and presentational monologues. The song is simple and catchy, so that audience members can pick it up quickly:

Where's the care?
Has it vanished into thin air?
Where's the care
All we want is our fair share.
Where's the care?[17]

The "Spirit of Care" is represented by an actor in a wheelchair, who identifies herself by protesting weakly (in one of the Monty Python quotations that often creep into Bouzek's work), "I'm not dead yet!!"

Along with puppets, songs, and iconic business (the international language of agitprop), the show includes audiotaped sound effects not as a stylistic nicety (although it does give the performance a technically sophisticated soundscape) but, rather, as a useful technique that enables under-rehearsed and nervous local members to participate in the performance. For example, two ambulance attendants (an actor and a local member) carry in a puppet on a stretcher, traveling around the audience under taped dialogue:

> (*Sirens*)
> AMB. ATT.: We've got a cardiac case coming in.
> HOSPITAL: Our cardiac unit's been closed, you'll have to go to Civic.
> AMB. ATT.: Roger. Civic do you read?
> HOSPITAL 2: Loud and clear.
> AMB. ATT.: We have a cardiac case now.
> HOSPITAL 2: Sorry. We have no beds at present.

Eventually, they reach a hospital and put the puppet to "bed" vertically against a backdrop beside a sign that says (with each word on a separate card): HEALTH CARE SYSTEM. One of the attendants remains onstage and addresses the audience in a low-key, natural delivery that suggests a desire to erase the performative distinctions between professional actors and local participants:

> I'm an ambulance attendant in a small town. We're on a central dispatch system. So last week we get this call to pick up a guy who lived on Maple Street—one block away from our station. We get there in two minutes only to find his wife frantic—she had called over an hour ago. How it took one hour for the call to get from dispatch to our station I'll never know.

He finishes his story in stages, interrupted by iconic agitprop bits. (The Ogre, a two-faced hand-held puppet mask, reaches up and removes the CARE card, leaving the legend HEALTH SYSTEM on the backdrop; the Ogre reappears as a lying politician, promising more beds and announcing closings.) The show ends with a refrain of the song, performed by actors and local members and broken by statements of solidarity and militancy:

> We're tired of listening to broken promises. But we're not giving up. I'm wearing my button on September 4th [election day]. And I want to see everybody in this province wearing the button, everyone who works in our health care system and everybody who uses our health care system.

The audiences for the shows were not large; a room with twenty or thirty people was common. But, as Bouzek insisted, the real target audience was not the local union membership but the media. The performance transformed a routine meeting into a news conference and a media event. Consequently, the performance was received by the media not as an entertainment but as an expression of popular militancy. Typically, *Northern Life* reported the show under the headline, "Ontario's health care system in danger of 'Americanization,' say union members."[18] The article never mentions Ground Zero; instead, it states that "the play was put on by a coalition of front-line health care providers, including nurses, doctors, ambulance attendants, technologists and hospital clerical staff." The disappearance of the theater company is one of the most striking indicators of the success of the project.

Such media pick-up provides a quantitative measure of the propagandist value of agitprop when it personalizes large political issues. In Ground Zero's agitprop work, the media response is part of the aesthetic totality of the process. Explicitly in *Where's the Care?*—but no less so in a rally—the audience is literally part of the performance: as onstage performers, as demonstrators, and as a meta-performance staged for media use.

The strategy of localizing and personalizing a major political issue may have contributed to the significant role the health care issue played in the defeat of the Liberal government. But, as later events showed, the NDP was no more adept at managing the health care crisis in its term in office. Its awkward attempts to grapple with the deficit alienated the labor movement, which paid the price of its defection five years later, when the NDP was replaced by a hard-right conservative government that pushed the health care crisis to a new phase. In the late 1990s, when the Tories began shutting down hospitals across the province and sought to remove the right to strike in the public sector, the closing of a few thousand beds seemed like a minor problem. Ground Zero's intervention may have helped win a battle, but in the long run it was a small skirmish in a struggle that would become much larger and complex. Bouzek himself had no romantic illusions:

> We were only part of a real campaign to get social issues—like health care—front and center. Obviously, we didn't win the election for the NDP by doing a play. But we were a piece of that. . . . What we did do was show that you could use theater to get a provincial message out by focusing campaigns at the local level.[19]

Communities That Are Not Communities . . .

As the experience of *Where's the Care?* indicates, Ground Zero identifies not with particularized communities but, rather, with emergent coalitions of resistance, communities activated by the political moment. Bouzek has worked closely with particular partners—health care unions; the giant Communications, Energy and Paperworkers Union; the Carlos Bulason Cultural Workshop (a Filipino expatriate theater in Toronto); the Ontario Federation of Labour; and the Toronto Labour Council, to name some of his closest partners. But even these groups cannot be reduced to totalizing concepts of community. The labor movement in particular needs to be addressed not as a political bloc (the "labor community") but as an extremely diverse and culturally plural alliance of local organizations crossing through and reconstituting existing communities. On the level of cultural action, groups like Ground Zero reclaim the concept of "community" as a strategy of mapping sites of political change. The more successfully they do so, the more they are disallowed and penalized by the agencies and structures that constitute the cultural sphere.

In 1998, after relocating to Edmonton, Alberta, several thousand kilometers west of its original home in Toronto, Ground Zero was informed by the Canada Council that its annual funding request had been denied because the company's niche in the local "cultural ecology" was unclear. In fact, Ground Zero by its very history challenges the fundamental precepts encoded in the concept of "cultural ecology." That is a concept that neatly frames bureaucratic policies in an undifferentiated community "served" by the arts and which the arts in turn reflect. The rhetoric of community in cultural policy is closely related to the familiar rhetoric of the cultural "garden," in which the arts sink "roots" in the community, which they nourish and which in turn supports them. This is a rhetoric that disallows politicized art because the liberal humanist ideology that it articulates perceives engaged art as disruptive of the unifying value of community unless it addresses issues that bring communities "together." Hence, the expression of resistance is encouraged in those domains that do not challenge the material structures of policy. For arts council bureaucrats political art is "viable" if it has a community to support it. This is obviously and easily true of the numerous issues of identity politics; it is less obviously the case when speaking of class, which disrupts the fiction of the subsuming national community and which locates identity in economic determinants that are not only changing and changeable but which cannot be reduced to narratives of essential identity.

When Ground Zero moved to Alberta, it destabilized the fundamental relation of art and community that governed Canadian arts policies for decades, by showing that the theater is more than a narrative space that anchors a community by transforming ideology into cultural geography.

Instead, Ground Zero's move highlighted the idea of the strategic venture that adapts to the contingencies of the political moment and which helps connect/reconnect communities as they appear, reform, and mobilize in struggle. Or, as one writer/performer at Ground Zero's popular theater retreat said of this relationship of cultural work and political action, "If you resist, you are my community."[20]

NOTES

1. Benedict Anderson, *Imagined Communities: Reflections on the Origin and Spread of Nationalism* (London and New York: Verso, 1991).

2. Loren Kruger, *The National Stage: Theatre and Cultural Legitimation in England, France and America* (Chicago: University of Chicago Press, 1992).

3. Clive Barker, "Alternative Theatre / Political Theatre," in *The Politics of Theatre and Drama,* ed. G. Holderness (London: Macmillan, 1992), 32.

4. Alan Filewod and David Watt, *Workers' Playtime: Studies in Theatre and the Labour Movement in Australia, Canada and the United Kingdom, 1970–1997* (Sydney: Currency Press, 2001).

5. Bouzek to Caroline Lulham, correspondence, 17 November 1986. This six-page letter outlining his personal history and principles was written as a response to a questionnaire sent to popular theater workers by a student at Mount Allison University.

6. Ibid.

7. Bouzek to Filewod, correspondence, 10 October 1997.

8. Ground Zero to Department of National Revenue, 7 May 1986. Ground Zero Archive, McLaughlin Library, University of Guelph.

9. Popular Theatre Workers Retreat, "Statement of Principles," MS, n.d., Ground Zero Archive.

10. Ground Zero Productions, "Artistic Director's Letter," Canada Council Application, August 1992, 4.

11. Bouzek to Filewod, correspondence 26 October 1997.

12. Ibid.

13. Steve Eadie, in Ground Zero Productions, *Where's the Care?* videotape, 1990.

14. Ibid.

15. Charlene Avon, in Ground Zero Productions, *Where's the Care?*

16. Don Bouzek, interview with Scott Duchesne, Toronto, June 1996.

17. Ground Zero Productions, *Where's the Care?* production typescript, 1990. All subsequent quotations from the text are from this typescript.

18. *Northern Life,* 2 September 1990.

19. Bouzek to Filewod, 26 October 1997.

20. Hector Bunyan, in "Cultural Workers Community Forum, Draft #1," MS, n.d., Ground Zero Archive.

Donna M. Nudd, Kristina Schriver, and Terry Galloway

Is This Theater Queer?
The Mickee Faust Club and the
Performance of Community

There is plenty of evidence to claim that the Mickee Faust Club in Talla-hassee, Florida, is a lesbian performance company: the club was founded by a lesbian couple; six of the present-day eight members of the board are les-bians; currently half of the forty-odd members of the club describe them-selves as lesbian or bisexual; for the last decade the company's local biannual cabaret shows have been filled with gender-bending performances with gender being bent for the most part by women; and its national perfor-mances in Washington, D.C., and Miami have featured material with pre-

Donna Marie Nudd is an Associate Professor and Chair of the Department of Commu-nication at Florida State University. She teaches and writes in the areas of performance, women's studies, and pedagogy. She has served as Director and Dramaturg for both of Terry Galloway's shows that have toured throughout the United States and abroad. For Mickee Faust she performs, directs, designs posters, and makes many trips to the Magic and Fun Shop.

Kristina Schriver is the Director of Forensics and faculty member at California State Uni-versity—Chico, where she teaches classes in argumentation, communication criticism, and feminist rhetorical theories. Kristina joined the Mickee Faust cabaret in 1991 while attending graduate school at Florida State University. At first a performer, Kristina later began to write song parodies and skits for the troupe. Schriver has written several essays about community performance and collaboration.

Terry Galloway is a writer, performer, director, and teacher. She helped found two comedy cabarets; has published plays, books, articles, and monologues; and has per-formed throughout North America and England. She has received grants from the National Endowment for the Arts, Pew Charitable Trusts, Florida Commission of the Arts, Texas Institute of Letters, Ralph A. Johnson Foundation, Dobie Pasiano Award, and Able Trust. She has been a Visiting Artist at several universities, most recently the University of Texas at Austin.

dominantly lesbian and gay themes. Lots of evidence, yes, but without denying the many lesbians and gays, real and honorary, who have been and still are a creative, energizing force in the company, this essay will argue that Mickee Faust is something more inclusive—a queer performance company.

> Queer is not a conspiracy to discredit lesbian and gay; it does not seek to devalue the indisputable gains made in their name. Its principal achievement is to draw attention to the assumptions that intentionally or otherwise inhere in the mobilization of any identity category, including itself.[1]

To be queer, then, is to be unable or unwilling to regard "any identity category" as single, fixed, or unyielding. When even such a seemingly fixed, "real" category like gender, for instance, is regarded as dynamic, pluralized, multiple, and shifting, then automatically all the other less seemingly fixed, real identifiers are assumed to be just as dynamic. To the queer mind there is no natural or unnatural identity, no real or unreal one. Rather, identity is seen as an act of engagement, a conscious performance.

We are a queer theater, then, and not just because many of our non-lesbian company and audience members could describe themselves thus: "To the best of my knowledge and understanding my mind frame is best labeled as queer, though sexually I am not."[2] We are a queer theater because we use theater in a particularly queer-conscious way that questions individual and cultural notions about "who we are." And we are a queer theater because we believe it is by engaging ourselves and our community in those performative acts of questioning that who we actually are as individuals and members of the larger communities to which we belong can be discovered, articulated, and celebrated or changed.

In this essay we argue that Mickee Faust is queer not just from our personal experience (which is intimate and extensive) or our conversations with other members of the company and its audience (just as intimate and extensive) but also from a seemingly more "objective" knowledge base, the sixty surveys we collected from company and audience members. We've divided this essay into five sections. The first is a brief overview of the company and its playground—who Faust is, what kind of theater we do, where we are doing it, and for whom. The second section describes our queer beginnings, our theatrical intentions as expressed by an early gender-bending performative model. The third section examines how by questioning sexual/gender identity we have been led to question other indices of identity like class, race, and disability as well as our professional and political identities. The fourth section looks at our audience and the community sensibility we share with them. Lastly, of course, we explain how we are made queer, drawing our own conclusions about what all these performances, queer or otherwise, might mean.

The Company and Its Playground

The name Mickee Faust derives from two sources: a certain unctuous rodent living in his own little magic kingdom in Orlando and Goethe's good German doctor whose struggles with the devil were said to mirror the group's own. The leader of the club is Mickee Faust itself, a foul-mouthed, cigar-puffing rat who is in real life Terry Galloway, a pipe-smoking, deaf, woman performance artist. In 1987, Galloway and her partner, Donna Nudd, a professor at Florida State University, produced *Skitz from Hell,* the first of the now biannual two-hour cabarets to feature the writing and performing talents of twenty-seven residents of Tallahassee, Florida, who elected to call themselves the Mickee Fauskateers. The debut performance featured a raucous and wily kind of theater, which has since become Faust's hallmark: a mix of political and sociosexual satire, literary and cinematic parodies, old vaudeville, new vaudeville, original and adapted songs with some fully-staged bad jokes thrown in for good measure. One hundred and seventy-five to two hundred people a night (a number that has remained constant throughout the decade) attended those first six nights of performance, which were presented at The Warehouse, a poolhouse bar located on the fringe of this small town's industrial district.

    The site that hosts this "thinking person's answer to corporate mickeyism" is located in the Florida Panhandle, or what is commonly referred to as "the redneck Riviera."[3] The Tallahassee terrain is different from what many would consider an urban playground. Lodged firmly between the Georgia state line and Florida's Alligator Point, the city's towering trees canopy many of the major avenues. In fact, the Chamber of Commerce touts these "canopy roads" as one of the city's most distinguished features. Springtime Tallahassee is the largest government-sanctioned "community" event, bringing hundreds of thousands together at downtown parks, in carnivalesque fashion to celebrate spring with art, crafts, music, fair food, and a parade valorizing slaveholder and Native American oppressor Andrew Jackson. In all, the noise and feel of Tallahassee are befitting its slogan: Florida with a Southern accent.

    But, despite its traditional, Southern accouterments, Tallahassee is an urban center. The town houses two major universities: Florida State University (FSU), with its student population of nearly thirty thousand, and Florida A&M, a prestigious historically African-American University. Tallahassee is also the state capital. The phallic tower housing state activities is one of the few buildings forming an anemic skyline. The three major institutions, FSU, Florida A&M and the Capitol represent the locus of state and local activity, but this triad is not without tension. The edge of the Florida State University campus is less than a mile from the gate of Florida A&M, but the two schools (ironically separated by train tracks) form few alliances. It is Tallahassee's urban quality and its highly institutionalized framework that contribute to both the town's activism and the town's conservatism. The narrower, more provincial forms of the Old South—the organizers of Springtime Tallahassee, for instance—often collide with its progressive undercurrent, a subterranean community once so politically motivated that Tallahassee in the 1960s was called "the Berkeley of the South."

It could be argued that Faust in its first five years of existence could have had no clear or fixed theatrical identity—weird, queer, or otherwise—in part because the group itself kept changing and in part because, while it did have a place to present its finished productions, it did not always have a permanent "home," a space that existed exclusively as a playground for the members to meet, brainstorm, create, rehearse, and play. But, while the identity of Faust may have shifted and changed as individual members left or joined and while the creation of a permanent space has given the group a structural locus, nonetheless, Faust has always had a recognizable "self," a core of intention that was engendered by the founding group but which took on new shape and resonance as the group and its audience began to cohere. That intention was simply to give voice theatrically to an alternative community identity that might otherwise go unheard. The institutional setting of Tallahassee has, in many ways, mystified theater, theatricality, and performance in general. Florida State, a top-ten theater program, stages large technical productions and a few offbeat productions every now and then at an "annex," but for the most part the theater it stages is professional and somewhat moribund in its polish. The Tallahassee Little Theater (the local community, i.e., amateur, theater) attracts "stage-ready" talent from Tallahassee's working population and imports theater for that community via Samuel French.

Looking for a format that could incorporate a more original, local, and contextualized voice, Faust embraced the cabaret format as one broadly accessible but also politically and sexually risky. To seem distinct from a kind of theater that is exclusive, imported, and intimidating, the company, without any official deliberation, took to calling itself "indigenous theater" rather than "community theater." This identification meant that whoever finds him- or herself drawn to the alternative sensibility should be free to participate in it. The collective expectation was that those who joined would work, embrace the cooperative structure, encourage the structure to take risks, explore themselves, push boundaries. In return the fledgling Faustkateer could expect the opportunity to perform and have his or her performative talent nurtured, no matter how uncertain or raw.

Queer Beginnings: The Implications

The nexus of the complicated identity exploration that Faust did and continues to do could be found in its earliest productions. Among the early shows of the Mickee Faust Club was a parody of the tough-talking detective genre that featured a lesbian as Jake Ratchett, Short Detective—a brash operative who talks like Bogart and looks like Chaplin. Jake's love interest, Rose Simper, Spoiled Debutante, was played by Toni D., a cross-dressing emcee at a local gay bar who was then in the early stages of the transsexual male-to-female process. The local paper carried a picture of the two in full drag and mad embrace with a caption that simply advertised the dates and times.

To much of that early audience Jake was obviously a parodic role, but Toni was closer to the real thing—a tall, beautiful, buxom brunette with a sweet Southern lilt to her husky voice. Toni had always been out about her transsexualism, had always been herself on her job as a local librarian, wearing her long hair down, using makeup, wearing skirts and blouses and a bra. She was one of the first heroines of the transgendered community here. But few people outside of the lesbigay community knew her, and most of that audience had no reason to think, no basis for knowing, that Toni was in fact a man playing a woman, even as he was in fact becoming a woman.

The audience simply accepted Toni as a woman playing what had always been traditionally a woman's role even in parody—the femme fatale in a tough guy's fiction. In that role of Rose Simper, Toni had an exchange with Jake Ratchett about identity, an exchange central to the mystery. It went like this.

(*Jake and Rose are about to embrace again when Rose pushes him away. He goes flying.*)
ROSE: Stop it, Jake. I can't let you do it.
JAKE: Do what?

A Man and a Woman. Mickee Faust Club, Tallahassee, Florida.
Photograph courtesy of Beatrice Queral.

ROSE: It. I lied Jake. I am what I am but I'm not what you think I
am.
JAKE: So what do you think I think you are?
ROSE: Does it matter what I think you think?
JAKE: I should think so. So?
ROSE: Whatever I think you think I think you think, I know what
you think ain't even close to what I really am.
JAKE: Sweetheart, it don't matter what you think I think you are,
'cause no matter what the hell you seem to think I do think, I
think you're pretty much what you seem to be.

ROSE (*and on this line Toni lowered her voice about ten octaves and the
sound that came out was unmistakably He-male*): Well, I'm not.[4]

And at that point the audience roared, a collective "hah" of the kind that is
said to enlighten. They were surprised. The audience had been taken in by
the performance onstage, but what had really taken them in was the more
complicated fiction, Toni's true life's performance of gender. It was that
complicated fictive/real layering of performance that allowed the audience
to be surprised into recognizing their own habitual assumption that "gender" is a stable, fixed state of being, easily recognizable and therefore easily
categorized.

Yet it wasn't just the straight audience who had been surprised into
questioning their own assumptions. The gay males in the audience con-
fessed to a kind of shock themselves. Toni was renowned for keeping a tight
grip on her female persona: she never dropped character, she never dropped
her voice, not at the library where she worked by day nor at the gay bar
where she worked by night. Her performance as Rose Simper marked one
of the rare times that Toni let go of her private act, lowered her voice, and
let some hint of her own personal complications be heard.

And it wasn't just the audience that had been nudged into such questioning. The group itself was brought face to face with its own ignorance,
its own habits of thought. When Toni arrived for the dress rehearsal she
found that she had been allotted a space in the men's dressing room. It was
an entirely uncomfortable space for her to be in, but it was somewhat
beyond the group's experience to realize what they should be sensitive to.
But her distress was noticed, the oversight was corrected, apologies offered,
and a space was cleared for Toni in the women's dressing room, where she
proceeded to give a few of the lesbians and one of the young preteen performers hair styling tips and some lessons in flare.

Yet our embarrassment at having unintentionally hurt Toni led to
some deeper questioning. Why, we asked, had we even bothered to have
separate dressing rooms in the first place? What was the intention behind
this conventional segregation? To protect the women from the men? To
separate groups who have an assumed attraction for each other? We were so
dismayed by the implications of our unthinking behavior that we literally
broke down the walls: the different but equal rooms were made into a single unsegregated space.

This multilayered exploration of gender identity in Faust was led by a
lesbian and a transsexual. But it didn't end there. It simply expanded to
include all kinds of gender role playing, gender configurations. So now, as

one member notes, Faust has "women playing men, men playing women, straight men playing gay men, straight women playing lesbians, gay women playing gay men, lesbians playing straight women and scripts such as the one that has a straight man 'coming out' to his lesbian moms."[5]

This kind of performative questioning didn't stop at *gender* and *sexuality*. Once those two terms were exposed as being neither fixed nor stable, neither easily recognized or categorized, every other fixed, stable identifier was up for grabs. It was as if starting at a radical extreme opened the door for us to question all those other assumptions about race, disability, and occupational and regional self.

Further In-Queeries

One of the most powerful ways in which Faust posits those questions is also its simplest: noncomment casting. Just as women have been nonconventionally cast as men and men as women, so too are people of color cast as the Nordic leads in a parody of an Ingmar Bergman film, for example—roles that are not culturally identifiable as "theirs" but which they come to possess through the power of their performances. The same kind of repossession occurs when the disabled member who uses a chair is cast in roles that are not culturally identifiable as "hers." Often the chair itself becomes part of her performance, adding new, unexpected theatricality to the roles: the mystery of a moving throne makes the Pharaoh all the more miraculously divine, just as having his very own, bite-sized tank makes the stereotypical, mad military general all the more ridiculous and threatening.

Yet these kind of questions about the nature of assumed realities—the theatrical as well as the cultural ones—are also asked through the casting of real people in fictional skits, skits that often mirror their exterior lives as well as their interior fantasies. "Women of the Year of the Women," for instance, was a satirical competitive pageant touting the accomplishments of powerful contemporary women like Janet Reno, Mrs. Doubtfire, and a talk show guru and pitting them against one another. It was a conventionally funny piece with some obvious gender bending (a guy in drag as Reno, a woman in double drag as Robin Williams as Mrs. Doubtfire). But its impact came with the introduction of the final contestant. She was nobody famous; her story had in actuality been culled from a newspaper account of the life of a young black woman who had been physically assaulted in her home. But the contrast of her "true" story enacted realistically threw the accomplishments of her parodic counterparts into a different, more critical light, and the piece itself took on added power from that juxtaposition—the accomplishments of powerful white women, one of whom was actually a man, all of whom were being amply rewarded for their "struggles," were contrasted to the never-ending struggle of a young black woman for whom the only reward in life was being allowed to continue to live. The audience who had been laughing at the easier humor was brought up short by the realism, the sincerity, with which this last young contestant was being acted. But the group, too, was being brought up short by the piece, in part because the originator was a young straight African-American woman who felt somewhat conflicted about her role in the prevailing white/lesbian power structure of Faust and in part because that role itself was being enacted by an African-American single mother of four who in fact worked long, hard hours at a difficult, physically demanding job that left her right on the financial brink—a woman who knew the life she was performing.

This blurring of the boundaries that would separate our "real" lives from our theatrical selves is most evident in our performances onstage. But it is actually integral to our whole creative dynamic. The members of our club are often outsiders in an insider's world, but, as one commented, "I am the one who gets to intrude on that world and expose it, warts and all." The woman thus quoted is a journalist whose ethic of "objectivity" prevents her from publicly offering her own personal and political opinions on the legislative sessions, criminal hearings, and press conferences that she covers. But in the skits she writes for the company, she destabilizes the "public" perceptions of the governor, state officials, senators, representatives, university presidents, and state and local activists by caricaturing them. Her parodic skits about the state legislative committees who rule on everything from school prayer to homosexual rights become a form of eavesdropping as she feeds her broad, comic creations snatches of overheard, off-the-record dialogue. And when these caricatures utter their lines on the Mickee Faust stage, it is not surprising that lines that were never officially "reported" (i.e., the ones that were actually uttered by the public officials but never made it into journalistic accounts), those pilfered lines, always seem the most absurd and always get the biggest laughs.

Yet this reporter is more the rule than the exception. Many of the members of Faust, even those who could be regarded as "upstanding citizens"—the professors, the lawyers, the accountants, the small business owners, the health professionals—also view themselves as marginalized: they may work within institutions, but they are not "of" them. A parody of the Promise Keepers written by a straight, white, male sports announcer was at once an acknowledgment of his own obsession with sports and a critique of the ways its cult status can become overgrandized and perverted. "The Hookers' National Anthem," adapted from "The Battle Hymn of the Republic," was, to the former hooker who wrote it, a way of defying and complicating the imposed definition of what was once her "identity." The female professor at Florida State University who was highly critical of the zealous position taken by her university president on long-distance learning played a female professor at Florida State University confronting that president in a piece that ridiculed his obsession with distance learning as well as his eagerness to "corporatize" the classroom. She did this in front of an audience, many of whom had ties to that particular university, one of whom was her dean, whose area of expertise is distance learning. When the events that shape our lives become part of the theater we create, when they are given dramatic shape and shared with others who are sitting in a room with us, talking back to us, telling us what they think of how we enact ourselves onstage by their applause, their silence, their boos or their cheers, then our lives are no longer just our own; for better or worse they have become part of a community experience.

Queering the Community

As mentioned earlier, the identity of Faust was complicated by the lack of a home, a space in which the company could play. As Faust established a routine (fall and spring shows), acquired a stable locale for its productions (a pool hall with a stage), and rehearsed in a space the members were transforming into their own theater (a double garage in a railroad art district), they then had a position from which they could predictably interact with the community. But this predictability revealed identities nested by virtue of their place, or notions of what it means to live in a particular playground. As a regular audience grew and recognition swelled, the theater faced, faced off, and ruptured a set of community identities both troublesome and tightly bound—those notions of what it means to live in a Southern town and "go to the theater." Although our audience survey responses suggest it is Mickee Faust, the cabaret, that is responsible for the rupture, we wish to acknowledge that our audience, both loyal and growing, makes the theater possible. The practice of "this different kind of theater" would still be situationally interesting if it played to small crowds or supportive relatives. The size of the audience, however, makes the mobilization of community identity quite relevant.

Faust is recognized as community theater not simply because its performers are pulled from the alternative community at large but, rather, because Faust provides a location where a disordered, questioning group of sullied spectators meet several times a year to smoke cigarettes, drink beer, laugh, boo, and give life to a cabaret and fictionalize the notion that a particular spirit will always be overwhelmed by the most powerful identity working at its location. Put differently, our audience author their own performance of community. Many sit quietly, some jeer quite loudly, still others find Faust an occasion to see old friends. For these people the reprieve of intermission is a time to move through the aisles hugging, talking, and kissing little-seen acquaintances. The audience moves around the theater space with the same freedom with which the performers intermingle with the audience. The incestuous interplay between audience and cast is partly motivated through the performative venue. The most loyal fans not only attend the cabarets but also all the Faust hosted events. They compete against one another in the annual "From Bad to Verse" poetry competition; they dress up for the "Feast of the Customs Collector"; they bring their rotting Halloween leftovers to "The Pumpkin Chuckin' Contest." And many, like this year's pumpkin chuckin' "honorable mention" recipient, find their way onstage.

Yet even the most passive spectator is unavoidably moved by the experience of Faust. Because even having an audience for this kind of theater articulates a community identity, or, as one audience member remarked, "hope for the future, in that there are others younger than I who look at life like I do."[6] Others have suggested that the entire performance of a Faust show—the skits, the audience—both in number and action, the subterranean locale, textures community life. Although Faust is undeniably altered by its Southern situation, the urban landscape, too, is altered by the presence of Mickee Faust. When asked if Faust changed the way one imagined Tallahassee, only two spectators benignly answered. Most offered these altered descriptions of place: "more hip, more sophisticated, more artistic,"[7] "more metropolitan,"[8] and "eccentric."[9]

There is at these shows a sense of complicity between audience and performers that is palpable, a determination, perhaps, to subvert the idea that to be in the South is to be a part of a certain Southern culture that is white, conservative, and oblivious. The audience members and company, sitting together, laughing together, open themselves to one another. As one survey respondent wrote, "Thank god not everyone in this town is a rabid, southern conservative sports fan."[10] In other words, it says something about you if you attend a Faust show. Time and again we have witnessed a peculiar ritual that would seem to support this claim: as the ticket line queues up and begins to snake out past the front room bar, a barfly will eye it and ask the server, "What's going on back there?" Almost always, the bartender says, "it's a cabaret," and then leans over to whisper a more thorough explanation into the ear of the inquirer. They might have read about Faust in the newspaper, as the company has thrice been the cover story in the entertainment pullout of the local paper; the whispers suggest, however, that something more seedy, edgy, and questionable is afoot. Do they whisper "they're lesbians" or "they're liberals" or "she's deaf, you know"? It hardly matters. For to place yourself inside the whispered and questionable means you can never passively spectate. Or, more pointedly, you can never keep that kind of theater contained, separate from yourself. To be there is to engage in the work of the theater. To be there is to be implicated.

How We Are Made Queer

When a group of people who call themselves "queer" create and perform that notion of themselves on a stage within a geographic space that is identified as Southern, backwater, and culturally deprived, the questions they are posing are about their identity within that space—but they are also questioning the identity of theater in that space. What do we mean by theater? Are we talking about an artifact of history? An entertainment? A money-generating tool? A profession exclusively for the beautiful or the brilliant? The unapproachable domain of the people who make it their life's work? We are a queer theater because our answer is not only that theater is simply what we will make of it but also that we are made by that making. Perhaps, then, we are made queer because we are recalling the deeper assumptions of theater itself that it is performance that exists in those junctures between the self and the other; that it is through performance that we can acknowledge the multiplicity, the otherness, of ourselves; that it is through performance that we carry on the never-ending internal dialogue with those selves through which we question and articulate our individual and cultural notions of identity; that it is indeed through performance that we can enjoin those notions into being.

NOTES

1. Annamarie Jagose, *Queer Theory: An Introduction* (New York: New York University Press, 1996), 126.

2. This quotation comes from a response to one of the survey questionnaires that the authors wrote and distributed to company members through e-mail and personal contact. Completed surveys by company members will be referenced as "Survey, Faustkateer." This quotation comes from Survey, Faustkateer, no. 15. Surveys were also placed on the Mickee Faust listserv and Web page as well as being randomly distributed at a cabaret performance in Tallahassee, Florida, at the Warehouse, 12–13 September 1997. Completed surveys by audience members will be referenced as "Survey, Audience."

3. Survey, Audience, no. 24.

4. Terry Galloway, *While the Cat's Away . . . ,* performance, Warehouse, Tallahassee, Fla., 22–23 April 1988.

5. Survey, Faustkateer, no. 23.

6. Survey, Audience, no. 1.

7. Survey, Audience, no. 12.

8. Survey, Audience, no. 11.

9. Survey, Audience, no. 16.

10. Survey, Audience, no. 14.

Authority in the Community-Based Theater Process

Community-based performance has strong ties to struggles for democratization. But it is reasonable to ask: How democratic is its own process? Who has authority, who has power? Why, how, and toward what end do they use it? The issues of representational authority arise implicitly within many of the essays in this collection and occasionally form an explicit subtheme (such as in the disagreement that opens McConachie's essay). In part 2 we give these issues special focus. There are two main aspects: the process of producing community-based theater—a process that involves relations of authority within the performance production or workshop itself; and the interactions between the performance work and the community it seeks to benefit through that work. This focus is part of a general shift toward giving "process" primacy over "product." In some instances there is no final product at all. But even within this larger trend there are significant differences in approach, some of them ultimately pointing to different concepts of democratization.

In the first two essays representational authority is the crux of the discussion. For Laura Wiley and David Feiner community-based theater should not seek "authenticity" (often an abstracted or selective notion of what "truly" belongs to a culture) in the final performance product but, instead, locate it as an aspect of the process through which performances are developed. Ultimately, they argue, community-based theaters using this model do *not* earn and maintain the authority to represent a community: on the contrary, such performance work seeks to decentralize this authority throughout the community. Their argument suggests that, through radical, dialogic cultural democratization, community-based theater can usefully *undermine* the identity politics that its commitment to a community would seem to foster. It becomes increasingly vital to frame a theatrical representation as just one among many from a heterogeneous population—one based on a specific history and social position that exists within a dynamic framework of relationships to others.

Against this backdrop Susan Mason's essay offers a cautionary but invaluable tale of how disastrously things can go wrong, despite the best of intentions, when the process of creating a performance does not sufficiently interrogate the lines of authority and community position. The effort to develop a play based on interviews with immigrant families in Holland became overladen by groups and individuals with cross-purposes, inadequately articulated and incompletely fulfilled needs and agendas, and the pressures of a deadline. Here, too, identity politics played a damaging role, as a film crew documenting the project sought to focus on race relations to the vocal opposition of the students who were interviewing the immigrant community. The essay underscores the importance but also the difficulty of building a sense of inclusion within and ownership of a community-based performance project, especially when it requires a complexly interlocking set of communities.

Although Wiley and Feiner rightly caution against seeking authenticity even in performances that have been produced with the participation of the community, some sense of authenticity remains necessary for many community-based theater projects, particularly if it culminates in a performance depicting the community to others or to itself. Such theater work is a widespread form of community-based performance. It is usually what mainstream subsidized theaters mean when they speak of doing community-based theater, but (as several essays show) it continues to have a valid raison d'être among activists. Even in these cases, however, the location of authority varies in distinctive ways. Often the central source of a performance's authority resides in the sources used in its production, but the identity of the performers and the performance's endorsement by respected institutions can also play a role.

The Micronesian youth theater that Daniel Kelin presents gains an important part of its authority from its revival of indigenous cultural traditions, which serve performances concerned with recent social ills. But the youth's participation in the production of the shows is also vital. As Kelin observes, the youth think through the entire issue (causes, effects, potential solutions) in order to create scenes that would speak to the youth in their audience. Thus, the performance has the authority of having been produced and performed by the audience's peers. In the process the youth themselves are trained to be educators, so that the performance work becomes at least as important for the performers as the audience.

Like the Micronesian youth theater, Jane Heather's project utilized oral sources of authority buttressed not by documents but by institutional and personal authority. The project consisted of a play commissioned by a

Canadian labor union. Since it was not possible to have union members perform, other sources of representational authority were needed. Heather's own history of activism provided part of that: she was known within the labor community and accepted as part of it. The union's backing also afforded her the authority to obtain interviews with workers and arrange performances of the play.

In John Somers's project, because the events depicted are long past, documents alone provide material for a play on the history and culture of an English town during the Victorian era. Nevertheless, historical recovery created a sense of heritage for the schoolchildren and adults involved and so served celebratory as well as educational aims. According to Somers, the school's functions gave it a special role in the community, allowing it to become a fulcrum for reinstating a sense of community identity. In this instance the institution supplied an important function in establishing community identity.

A performance representing the more recent past has additional options. Employing a process of combining documents and oral history into "community plays" that was established in the 1960s, in the mid-1970s Attilio Favorini and Gillette Elvgren devised a play on the steel industry and the steelworkers of Pittsburgh, performed by university students, who were often steelworkers' children. In the early 1990s, however, the play was revived with a professional cast in a city where steel had ceased to be a major industry, and so the performance became disconnected from its community. Even though the dramatic product embodied the same authority of documents and recorded memories, its relationship to the community it represented shifted "under its feet." What had been a community-based performance became a history play. Thus, authenticity must be paired with a living connection to the community for the performance project to remain community based.

The point is underscored by Harry Elam and Kim Fowler's analysis of a project they conducted in East Palo Alto, California. There again, documentary research and oral histories together formed the basis for two one-act plays; in this project, however, the plays were written by professional playwrights. The plays' ties to the community endured nevertheless: the key element, Elam and Fowler maintain, was that the project and its dramatic products respected the voice of the community and addressed its real needs—these qualities are essential if community-based theater is to promote social change.

In part 2's concluding essay the role of the professional artist is at its height. According to Jan Cohen-Cruz, the Liz Lerman Dance Exchange exemplifies "community-centered professional performance," which aims to produce "community-informed" dance works. Lerman and her company, drawn from a cross-section of ages and ethnicities, work on materials gathered from or about different sorts of communities and craft them into a form that strives to balance artistic imperatives with community sensibility. Here we return to issues of authority within the community-based performance's production process but now with attention drawn to the professional artist as having certain needs that should not be ignored. Cohen-Cruz defends this approach, emphasizing that community-based performance must itself be diverse.

Laura Wiley and David Feiner

Making a Scene:
Representational Authority
and a Community-Centered
Process of Script Development

Representational authority has been a buzzword in several academic disciplines of late, but the ideas behind this jargon term have concerned community-based theater practitioners in the United States since the current U.S. incarnation of the movement began in the 1960s and 1970s. Indeed, in some ways the whole movement centers on representational authority. Theater companies that formed in allegiance with liberation struggles such as the Freedom Movement in the southern states and the Chicano Movement in the western states and groups that developed in working-class communities (many initiated through employment and opportunity programs) shared a recognition of the relationship between representation and power. Their theatermaking proceeded from an understanding of artistic expression as one means for people traditionally removed from power in U.S. society to define themselves and the world in their own terms rather than accept an oppressive status quo. A good example is Roadside Theater. As a leader in community-based theater for over twenty-five years, Roadside is the theatrical arm of Appalshop, a multimedia arts and educational organization that has been serving the mountain communities of Appalachia since 1969.[1] Roadside's director, Dudley Cocke, states the importance of representation

David Feiner and Laura Wiley are the founders and codirectors of the Albany Park Theater Project, a teen-centered community-based theater in Chicago's multiethnic Albany Park neighborhood. Prior to his involvement in community-based theater, David worked at the Yale Repertory Theatre as a dramaturg and at Arena Stage, where he coordinated the humanities programs and served as the theater's first archivist. Laura previously worked at the Chicago Dance Coalition, Yale Repertory Theatre, Cornerstone Theater Company, and the Goodman Theatre. She has also worked with a variety of youth-focused social change organizations.

in life-or-death terms: "To deny a people their cultural expression is to deny them their existence."[2] This conviction drives Roadside's work. The company expresses not only its own vision but also one of the fundamental principles of community-based theater in general when it describes itself as making theater "on the premise that mountain communities can assume a larger measure of control over their own lives if they can gain control over the definition of their culture and the tools of cultural transmission."[3]

In this essay we will use our own community-based theater work in Chicago as a concrete context for examining "representational authority." In particular, we will discuss how this issue has informed our efforts to employ and expand methods of community-based scene development, in which community members participate fully in turning stories they tell and collect into performance.[4]

Behind the term *representational authority* there are two interconnected questions: who has the power to represent whom? and who should have the right to represent whom? These questions became vital as people recognized the role of representation in the definition of culture. As the Roadside example shows, one of the central goals of community-based theater has been to increase opportunities for marginalized and oppressed groups to represent themselves and the world around them as a means of asserting their own identity and achieving "cultural, social, economic, and political equity."[5] In our analysis we will look specifically at how theater can be used toward cultural self-definition. This will lead to an exploration of two levels of representational authority that have not received much critical attention. Turning our focus from the relationship between a community and the dominant culture, we will look at representational authority *within* community-based theater practice. First, we will address the matter within a company of community-based theater makers: how is the authority to represent apportioned, and what effects does this arrangement have? Then we will look at the negotiation of authority between a company and its community in which the question becomes: who has the right to represent *for* whom, or how does a community-based theater group earn and maintain the authority to offer representations of the world in the name of a community?

As a preface to these questions, it is useful to consider the issue of "authenticity," which is frequently treated as an objective of community-based theater and related cultural empowerment movements. Focusing on authenticity can obscure or cover up fundamental concerns such as community self-expression and self-definition. It can thereby have the effect of stripping potentially radical acts of at least some of their power, reinscribing them in dominant culture discourse as quaint displays of tradition rather than outbreaks of agency from the margins.

The term *authenticity* refers to the genuineness of a cultural product, the "truth" of its belonging to a particular culture. Ironically, the term owes much of its popularity to social science and cultural studies scholars who suggest that the world is now beyond authenticity—that, in a globalized world where every culture interacts with other cultures and all are constantly exposed to mass culture, the possibility for cultural purity no longer exists (assuming it ever did). In *The Predicament of Culture* historian James Clifford writes about this situation and its impact on how cultural difference is made, lived, and encountered:

> This century has seen a drastic expansion of mobility, including tourism, migrant labor, immigration, urban sprawl. . . . In cities on six continents foreign populations have come to stay—mixing in but often in partial, specific fashions. The "exotic" is uncannily close. Conversely, there seem no distant places left on the planet where the presence of "modern" products, media, and power cannot be felt. "Cultural" difference is no longer a stable, exotic otherness. . . . Twentieth-century identities no longer presuppose continuous cultures or traditions. Everywhere individuals and groups improvise local performances from (re)collected pasts, drawing on foreign media, symbols, and languages.[6]

Despite the doubt Clifford and others throw on authenticity, the idea survives in discussions surrounding community-based theater as one means of evaluating work. Indeed, some have used the idea of authenticity almost to grade work, with whoever elicits the purest expression of "the people" earning the highest marks. Most often this is an externally applied measure (though not always), coming from the likes of newspaper reviewers, scholars and researchers, and mainstream theaters or other arts presenters hosting and publicizing performances by community-based groups. Such an approach focuses on the performed products of community-based theater, looking at the plays presented and practically pinning a ribbon on the ones that can be confidently labeled "true." Clearly, authenticity has relevance when looking at the work of a movement that fights for the right of communities to represent themselves. But the typical use of authenticity has more to do with the outsider's appetite for "the real deal" than with the effects of the work on a community.

We propose that the search for authenticity should focus on process rather than product. Such a reorientation will reveal that the critical issue for community-based theater is community self-representation—representational authority—not the purity of the artifact produced. This is not merely a matter of aesthetic accuracy in terminology or of theoretical abstractions that have little to do with "the work" itself. It is strategic. There is a risk to community-based theater and, more important, to the communities it serves in allowing authenticity of product to continue as a perceived goal or measure. As James Clifford argues, when the emphasis is on "pure products," people's cultural difference "remains tied to traditional pasts, inherited structures that either resist or yield to the new but cannot produce it."[7] The danger then is that nonmainstream communities are dismissed as "endangered authenticities,"[8] relics of a past that, in the prevailing Western metanarrative, will soon vanish entirely in the wake of global homogenization. Through the lens of authenticity, community-based theater appears as a way of memorializing a traditional past rather than shaping an empowered, democratic future. Clifford proposes an alternative to the dominant vision of progressive and inevitable Eurocentric monoculture. He sees new orders of difference emerging, in which groups everywhere "invent local futures" from the traditions of their collective pasts and from the myriad influences of the interconnected present. In this vision, cultures and communities are not fixed entities but, rather, continuous creative processes. Such a vision encourages a new understanding of authenticity as located not in the purity of cultural products but in the ongoing process of community making. Refocusing questions of authenticity from product to process makes it clear that community-based theater is not some kind of living museum but one means by which people are inventing Clifford's local futures.

Here our case studies become useful in illustrating how community-based theater fosters the definition of culture. Our primary example is the scene development process that produced "A Cambodian Ghost Story," a piece created by an ensemble of six teenagers in Chicago's Uptown neighborhood. To explore some ways we are building on the "Ghost Story" process, we will also look at our current work with the Albany Park Theater Project, a teen company we founded in 1996. Both examples demonstrate processes whereby neighborhood teens participate fully in all aspects of collecting community stories and turning them into theater that they perform. Professional facilitators collaborate with the teens throughout but do not take any components of the theater making out of their hands.

We employ this democratized process not to guarantee an authentic product but in order to decentralize representational authority. Sharing the authority to represent among the group maximizes the opportunities theater can generate for the kind of interactions within which the definition of culture occurs. In the social sciences one tradition views cultures as semiotic systems, ever-changing networks of symbols and meaning through which groups of people make sense out of their experiences.[9] As sociologist Ruth Horowitz explains:

> The uniqueness of a subculture rests in its symbols . . . through which group members appraise and evaluate their behavior and that of others. Cultural symbols acquire meaning when people talk about something, when they agree or disagree about the definition of a situation. People not only use meanings to make sense out of situations but change or reinforce prior meanings in interaction.[10]

The dramaturgical process—conceiving, scripting, and staging a performance—is especially fertile for creating such interactions. When a group of people comes together to decide what stories to tell and how to tell them, they engage in a formal definition of *culture*. They learn one another's values, experiences, taboos, and dreams, and they form new, shared perspectives and histories as they deliberate and collaborate to arrive at agreed-upon ways of representing their lives and the world around them. As they negotiate their play making, they are also negotiating and renegotiating community identity and culture.

Such a process has a particular value in today's urban neighborhoods. Recent history has forced changes in the meaning of group identity, or "community." Patterns of migration and immigration have dispersed communities and cultures once located within more or less distinct geographic boundaries, transforming them into diasporas while at the same time creating possible new communities in small geographic areas—neighborhoods—now shared by a variety of ethnic groups. In both Albany Park and Uptown, two unusually diverse Chicago neighborhoods, we have found that many residents do indeed define one of their community "affiliations" by geography: they consider themselves members of "the Uptown community" or "the Albany Park community." Yet often they don't interact much with many of their neighbors—their fellow community members—if they do not also have a shared racial or ethnic community affiliation.

During the planning discussions that led to the Albany Park Theater Project, many residents expressed a desire for more local institutions through which people in the neighborhood interact and develop relationships across ethnic, racial, and religious lines. They wanted to build on the fact that Albany Park's inhabitants share more than geographic proximity, common services such as police and schools, and designation as part of a government statistical unit, "Community Area 14–Albany Park."[11] Many of Albany Park's residents have a shared experience as immigrants or refugees (over 50 percent of the population is foreign born)[12], as U.S.-born Americans who migrated to Chicago looking for better economic conditions, or as "native" Chicagoans forced to move from gentrifying neighborhoods in search of affordable housing. Many also have common histories of persecution, whether in former homelands or from racial, ethnic, and economic prejudice encountered in the United States or both. Despite various economic histories, many are currently working class or poor.[13] These commonalities create the potential for collective action, both internal and vis-à-vis the dominant culture and power structure. Strong community connections across racial, ethnic, and religious lines don't just result in a more neighborly neighborhood; they establish a foundation for mobilizing potential collective action into community development. By providing one forum for the negotiation of community identity and culture and for the exploration of collective concerns, community-based theaters in urban neighborhoods like Albany Park can contribute to this process. In our discussion of the Albany Park Theater Project we will look at some of the ways in which APTP has been designed to serve this purpose on an ongoing basis in one neighborhood.

"A Cambodian Ghost Story" began when an afternoon's brainstorming session with a group of participants from a community-based project in Chicago's Uptown neighborhood turned to the topic of ghouls, ghosts, wizards, and sorcerers. While the discussion was laden with references to fantastical comic book characters and warriors from the movie *Mortal Kombat,* the talking spurred a young Cambodian immigrant, Chit Chak, to share a "real" story told to him by his father.

The story takes place in the aftermath of the Khmer Rouge's oppressive regime. A ghost, disguised as a member of the tyrannical army, leads Chak's father from his modest straw-thatched home deep into the woods that form the border between Cambodia and Thailand. There, on the spot where the mysterious figure suddenly disappears, he discovers the physical remains of his best friend, from whom he was separated several years earlier in battle. Although he had held out hope that his long-lost friend was still alive and had escaped to another country, he assumed that in fact his friend was dead—murdered by the Khmer Rouge and dumped somewhere like garbage. While saddened to have his worst fears confirmed and unnerved by his enigmatic guide, Chak's father is happy for the chance to provide his friend a proper burial, at last allowing the murdered soldier's restless soul to find peace.

Chak's story, performed by an ensemble of teenagers, became a simply staged but powerful piece about a man's death in war-torn Southeast Asia. But it was also about the experience of a teenager sharing a story of his family and his native culture with peers rooted in other cultures. The peers were a group of young people united by geography (all lived in the same Chicago neighborhood) and by an interest in theater. They nonetheless were a heterogeneous group representing many different cultures—African-American, Anglo, Bulgarian, Cambodian, Colombian, Cuban, and Mexican—and many different life views stemming from class, gender, and experiential variations.

The development process of "A Cambodian Ghost Story" had at its heart the transcript of Chak's original telling of the story. After the group read through the transcript together, we as facilitators asked the cast simple questions with multifarious answers: who are the central characters? what are the key images that stick with you? what do you feel when you hear the story? what would you want an audience to feel? The transcript thereby made way for discussion, which paved the way for structured improvisation that evolved into scripted material, which was then set down on paper, rehearsed, and performed.

The entire process, of course, also entailed discussion about the context in which the story took place and in which it was to be performed. Much the way a "professional" playwright's social climate and literary style would be analyzed by a professional artistic team of director, dramaturg, and designers, here, too, the "text" and life material of the performers as well as the storyteller were examined and discussed—by the whole group—in order to arrive at the desired method of representation.

In the final performance version of the story, much of the dialogue came verbatim from the ensemble's scene development process, with the group's questions, interpretations, physical reactions, and ideas for visual images becoming integral to the script. Within a context of diversity and plurality as well as commonality, the process brought out a richness of exchange rarely afforded in conventional theater practice. The transcript of Chak's story became the launching point for honest, open-ended conversation about many topics; inspired by Chak's tale, and with guidance from the facilitators, the cast talked about war, death, mourning, afterlife, poverty, community, religion, topography, and, of course, ghosts. The intimacy of interaction allowed for authentic negotiation of community identity and representation.

When Chak spoke of his father seeing the ghostlike figure wearing a red rag around his head, it was important that his friends raised in the

United States on a steady diet of Saturday morning cartoons conjure up an image not of the cherubic, marshmallow-colored Casper but of a chameleon force, mystical and spiritual in nature. The potent image of the red rag itself was reinforced by Chak in his poetic, understated way as he tried to explain during a rehearsal why his father would be so instantly drawn to following a figure who bore the emblem: "Let's say you went to war, right, and you was doing *a lot* of fighting, and your enemy wore a red rag, right?, around their head. In the future, even though the war was over, you see a guy wearing a red rag, it remind you of something, right?" The group decided that an ordinary red bandanna would be the defining costume attribute worn by the actor playing the role. In working together to figure out how the ghostlike character would move, the ensemble relied heavily on the instincts of one cast member who felt a particular affinity with the apparition. The actor is not confident verbally but is a beautiful physical artist, and he chose stylized movements inspired by his martial arts training and the story's Asian setting. As the piece was double-cast, the part of the spirit was also played by a teenage girl who lacks confidence in her corporeal abilities as a result of her struggle with multiple sclerosis. She relished the opportunity to shed her reputation as a klutz, and the rest of the group supported her in taking on the challenge of adapting a role with few lines of dialogue but tremendous physical presence.

When Chak spoke of the forest, it was important that his collaborators conjure up not the image of a benign, suburban forest preserve where schools take field trips for picnics but, rather, a dense, dark, frightening yet magical place, a domain not within human control. Chak evoked this image in describing the way the forest engulfed his father: "Soon it was dark because the woods are really, really deep like the deepest of night. And all you could see was black, right?, blackness, and that was all. The figure led him into the woods far, farther than he knew his way back from." We experimented with methods of creating the forest, first by improvising the sounds of the animals and the movement of the trees and trying to recreate the sensation of being in almost total darkness during the day. We discussed the sense of claustrophobia Chak's father might have experienced, increasingly feeling closed in by the dense woods, unable to see but a few feet ahead at a time. We talked about times we had felt profound fear, either for ourselves or for someone else. We shared thoughts about the possibility of a purpose so compelling that it drives you on despite your fear.

Similarly, when Chak spoke of his father's army service, we heard no mantra of "Be All That You Can Be" playing in the background. There was no vision of exuberant youths in crisply ironed fatigues marching off to state-of-the-art military facilities, preparing to defend lofty principles on the shores of exotic lands. The vision Chak revealed to the group was of a war-ravaged country in which poor people signed on to loosely organized fighting units, stirred by a personal sense of political injustice and fear about their people's survival:

> In the story my father told me, he was in the army. He wasn't in the army because he was drafted or to get money for college. He was fighting for Lon Nol's regiment because he despised the Khmer Rouge. He thought they weren't doing the Republic any good, especially for the peasant farmers who he believed were the most hard working class in Cambodia.

As the cast members learned about Cambodia's history from Chak, they were motivated to relate examples from their own lives that paralleled some of the same themes. They were eager to incorporate the anxious tenor of their discussions about the killing fields of Cambodia and the gang violence on the streets of Chicago, about the poverty of the peasant farmers in Cambodia and Mexico and their recently arrived relatives working on assembly lines, about the dictatorial communist rule in Bulgaria and Cuba and the "new world order" rhetoric of U.S. leaders. In part this was achieved through lighting and sound designs that seemed to evoke at once both an eerie, untamed forest in the Far East and the percussive rhythms of Western urban architecture and gangsta rap videos.

Our experience working on a story of racism and prejudice shows in a more pronounced way how collaborating in scene development allows a group of people to share experiences and negotiate values. The story was a post–civil rights era Rosa Parks tale in which a "mean old white woman" sitting toward the front of a Chicago Transit Authority bus shoves a black girl out of the neighboring seat and declares that "niggers don't belong here." Again, the group was ethnically diverse, composed in this instance not only of teenagers but also younger children and adults, many of whom lived in a low-income supported housing complex.

The discussion and improvisation process here became an opportunity to explore not only one specific painful story but a whole painful condition within contemporary society. The group ultimately worked to create some consensus both about how the piece might be played as well as about expectations for treating one another with sensitivity and fairness.

As facilitators, part of our strategy was to avoid eliciting mere platitudes about the evils of racism and to avoid an oversimplified story about one person's injustice toward another. As a group, we read through the transcript, which was rich in emotion but contained few fleshed-out details. As facilitators, our goal was to work with the group to navigate between what was already provided in the story—the hard, cold "facts" so to speak—and what might be, either buried in between the lines or in the future. This interplay between reality and invention, flexing both memory muscles and imagination muscles, defined the course the group undertook.

As facilitators, we decided that, while the narrator's voice (the teenage cousin of the girl who was shoved) was important, we needed to hear the story from the perspective of its other characters. We asked each member of the group to assume a given character and to pretend that they had just returned home that day from this bus trip and were reporting to their family over dinner what had happened. The rest of us—the "audience"—would then assume the role of the family and ask questions to pull out more distinctive aspects of the character's experience. We all took turns, with several different people playing each character to try to draw out different possibilities.

In one portrayal "the black bus driver" expressed tremendous guilt over not speaking out in support of his fellow African American who was being unfairly treated. He explained, however, that, while some might have viewed him as being in a position of authority because he was the driver, he actually felt quite helpless, fearful that the white woman or another passenger would lodge a complaint against him. He didn't trust that his boss would be sympathetic to his position, and he feared losing his job. Deciding that keeping his steady job and providing for his family was more important than battling acts of racism outside his immediate sphere, he decided not to rock the boat.

In another portrayal "a white teacher" who knew the teenage girl and her cousin from school explained to her husband that she chose to wait until the incident was effectively over and then approach the girls. Mostly, she just felt so embarrassed, so uncomfortable, to hear one human being talk to another that way. She thought about intervening but didn't want to be "Super Whitey" stepping in to save them. After the incident the girls were obviously very upset. So she went up and put an arm around them and let them know that she thought the way they were treated was wrong and that she thought they handled themselves very well.

A white teenage boy played "the old white woman" first. Despite their preconceived notions, the group was moved by her story. She returned home from the bus stop and shared the day's news with her cat. She recounted how she had made the long trek to the cemetery on the anniversary of her husband's death to leave some flowers, even though she could not really afford them, and to fill him in on what had been happening. By the time she was returning home, she was greeted with a less than ample seat on an overpacked bus for her more than ample body that was racked with arthritic pain. And then the little colored girl—oh, she knows she's not supposed to use that word or the other word, but it's hard. It's what she knows, that's all. And anyway, the girl was so giggly and fidgety, swinging her legs back and forth. And the seats are hardly big enough to begin with. She could hardly believe she was being so mean to just a little girl. But she was so tired, and everything is so complicated now, not like when she was growing up. The old woman just wanted to get home.

Part of the benefit of this method of script development is that it allows time for people to explore motive. It allows company members to uncover and understand the way a person's life experiences and larger community circumstances influence ideas and behavior. It allows time to create new, collective experiences that shape opinion and action—that build community. Thus, one goal of community-centered script development is to create a process wherein what is usually a luxury ill afforded—getting beyond quick judgments and stereotypes—is standard practice.

Certainly, there were uncomfortable moments as company members wrestled with their own ability—and their collaborators' ability—to make a distinction between giving voice in a story to a character with unsavory beliefs and condoning those beliefs. They struggled to understand the difference between saying abhorrent words yourself and saying them as a character in the context of a play about racism. Allowing people to invent on top of the material offered in the raw transcript provided a forum for a more complex exploration of racism. What was revealed was a different face of racism—not out-and-out hatred but buried animosities that bubble up to the surface in times of stress. While some in the group were concerned that this process was excusing the old woman's behavior, others tried to drive home the point that she was a three-dimensional character, difficult to stereotype or dismiss so easily. Along with deepening the group's understanding of this particular story and its characters, perhaps more important, the conversations opened up the possibility of racism below the surface even within *our* group and encouraged us to begin a process of reconciling conflicting attitudes with one another. We went into the process assuming a certain level of trust already existed among those of us working on the story, preparing the way for the group to embrace the material creatively. Yet in some way the trust required to work collaboratively on such difficult material was earned by going through the process of working collaboratively on such difficult material.

The ongoing process of defining and refining community identity was highlighted in a different way when issues of nationality—what it means to be an American—and immigration were the focus of our work. Laura worked on a project with a group of girls aged nine to fourteen who had emigrated from either Rumania or Mexico. They all resided in a lakefront high-rise called Carmen-Marine, a building owned by the Department of Housing and Urban Development but in the process of being sold to the tenants.

We quickly found the cornerstone to our process in one evening's story-gathering session on the topic of the differences between the girls' native and U.S. cultures. As a logical extension, a discussion blossomed on the theme of their use of their native languages versus their use of English. The girls seemed surprised but fascinated to hear the similarities and differences in their perspectives:

> —I like to speak Rumanian because it makes me feel unique.
> —I like to keep up my Spanish because when I go to visit my grandmother in Mexico it's the only way I can talk with her.
> —I like to be able to talk in Rumanian because sometimes you can speak it at school or hanging out with your friends if you don't want everyone to know what you're saying.
> —I like speaking Spanish and understanding Spanish just because it's a beautiful language.
> —I have to try to remember my Rumanian because my father wants to move back there some day when it's safe again and after he's saved more money and so we have to be ready. "We're just visitors here," he always says, "and we have to remember who we really are."
> —I don't speak very good Spanish anymore. We never speak it at my house because my parents want us to be Americans now. They always say, "This is your home now, forget about the past."

The girls developed a trilingual performance piece based on their stories of what they most liked and disliked about being girls, of their experiences in coming to the United States, and of their adjustment to life in Chicago. Refining the piece in rehearsal, the girls had fun comparing how different languages express the same idea or feeling or object. They learned from one another to gently make corrections on an exact word choice or turn of phrase. They shared their joys and frustrations of existing in between various colorful worlds, of resisting at times the ambitions the adults in their lives held for them. And they delighted in being able to tell the boys clamoring at the door to "keep out!" of the girls-only class.

While "A Cambodian Ghost Story," "Marcella's Bus Story," and "A Carmen-Marine Fairy Tale" were interesting stories in and of themselves, what was most powerful in all of these examples was the way in which authority was shared in the process of bringing the stories to life on the stage. Facilitators did not exclusively own authority and bestow it upon individual group members when deemed appropriate (as if it were a static entity to begin with). Nor did final authority rest with a professional playwright thought uniquely qualified to take the interesting but raw material and make it presentable. The assumption was that everyone came to the proverbial table with inherent expertise and valuable life experience that conferred upon them the credibility to participate in decisions that affected the group—whether artistic decisions about how to stage something or more personal decisions about how to interact with their collaborators.

Chak discovered his talent to transport his diverse colleagues from inner-city Chicago to his native Batdambang Province and savored the chance to experience pride in being an immigrant rather than the discomfort in being labeled an "outsider." At every turn the artists who worked on "Marcella's Bus Story" infused the rendering of the story with their own ideas about civil rights, race relations, personal versus communal responsibility, and the power of words to both inflict and heal hurt. As the girls of Carmen-Marine were contemplating their individual futures as adolescents on the brink of womanhood, they listened intently to one another make sense of the choices they and their families had made about allegiance to their native cultures and desires to assimilate into the perceived U.S. culture. The resulting finished products in all these instances were highly idiosyncratic meldings of culture, syntheses of seemingly disparate strands woven into one (not *the*) unique cultural expression of a community. The script development and rehearsal process is not merely the means to an end—entertaining and meaningful public performance—but the lifeblood of the transformative experience and the locus of authenticity and authority in community-based theater.

These processes were not, of course, without their limitations. In "A Cambodian Ghost Story," while every member of the ensemble participated in scene development and the group as a whole determined the content, tenor, mood, and presentation of the piece, the two of us as facilitators exercised a higher level of authority over certain aspects of the process. We brought the group an approach to the story at the inception of scene development and, after six weeks of group discussion, improvisation, and rehearsal, the two of us assembled the array of material produced by the group into a script. The ensemble provided all the content and inspiration for this work and critiqued and revised what we brought them, but in these two situations they received something the two of us fashioned outside of the group as a whole.

Our concept for the scene derived from the context in which Chak originally told the story. His interaction with the group and their involvement in the story fascinated us as much as the story itself. As we've indicated, in telling his father's story Chak provided editorial comments designed to explain Cambodia to this multicultural group of Uptown Chicagoans. These kinds of interactions gave us the idea to stage not only the story Chak told but also Chak's telling of the story—to have Chak and the ensemble simultaneously in and out of the story, playing the story and also playing their experience of the storytelling. We formulated this approach between the time we heard Chak tell the story and our first day of work with the ensemble. While we talked as a group throughout the process about how we were staging the story, we only really discussed the approach to the scene overtly when people seemed to seek approval from the two of us as the "theater experts" that it was okay to perform a play in this unfamiliar manner, with Chak narrating the story and playing his father in it and other ensemble members playing roles in the story and playing themselves listening to and talking about the story.

The two of us assumed more direct control over putting a performance script together from the material that came out of these six weeks of ensemble work. We did so out of necessity rather than principal: performances were approaching, and we needed to move from making a scene to rehearsing one. So one night we sat down with transcripts of Chak telling the story and notes on the various discussions and improvs during scene development, and we pieced together a script. We followed the order of Chak's original storytelling, inserting group interactions in their appropriate places, using the language from the transcripts, and building the piece dramatically around the ways in which the group had improvised various sections.

When we brought the script to the full group, people expressed their delight at seeing their work and their words inscribed as a play. We presented the script as a draft and encouraged revisions. All told, revisions were minimal, with no structural or conceptual changes. While we hope this owed in part to the group's satisfaction with our work on the script, it also undoubtedly came out of respect for our perceived status as theater experts, not to mention the authority of just having a script—once the group's work was codified in one manner, people were likely to think along those lines and unlikely to consider substantial changes unless they were especially unhappy with the text we offered.

Our concern with the control we as facilitators exercised over these two aspects of the process centers on the way our authority inhibited the potential participation of others. By coming into scene development with a preformed approach to presenting the story and by assembling the script ourselves, we limited the degree to which these two tasks would necessitate the kind of intragroup negotiations we've portrayed as fundamental to theater's community-building potential. With the Albany Park Theater Project, we have begun trying methods for making scene development even more broadly interactive. After working on the various Uptown projects, we founded APTP in order to implement a community-centered method of script development on an ongoing basis and to work intensively day in and day out within the same community. We formed the company in the belief that community building would happen not just as a result of the heated climax of periodic production but from the kind of sustained, consistent group interaction afforded by the regular interaction sought after in the scene development process.

In our effort to make scene development even more democratic, facilitators no longer embark on a scene with an approach in mind. Group discussion of the raw material now literally begins the process, with the group together developing an approach to the story or a number of approaches with which to experiment. As members of the company, facilitators still contribute ideas but within the context of group collaboration rather than as leaders delivering preplanned strategies. We also have a number of ideas we have yet to try for expanding participation in the scripting process. As many teen participants come to APTP new to theater, we want to begin by pairing a youth ensemble member interested in a particular scene with a facilitator. Together these two would shepherd a story through scene development and assemble a script draft from the material generated by group discussions and improvs. This approach expands participation in the obvious way of creating additional roles for ensemble members. We anticipate that it will also encourage a less restrained revision process, with extensive participation from the full group, in which the script draft serves as a launching point for continued discussion and collaborative work. We hope that the involvement of a peer in scripting will render the script less authoritative—less untouchable—than when it comes to the group only as the work of facilitators. Looking even further down the road, we expect the group will develop members who can draft ensemble work into scripts on their own, without facilitators, and can partner with newer participants in this process, thereby making scripting even more of a collaborative group endeavor. The goal is not to remove the facilitator as some kind of corrupting presence but to empower the full group by demonstrating the expertise and leadership of every member and that every step need not involve a facilitator.

Our approach to the negotiation of representational authority between a company and its community is driven by the same goals as our effort to democratize authority within the company. We've already shown that the theater-making negotiations of "A Cambodian Ghost Story" and APTP are also negotiations of collective identity among the ensemble. APTP extends this definitional activity beyond the APTP company into the community at large. As a company of neighborhood teens collecting community stories and turning them into plays,[14] APTP appears on the surface to make theater—to represent—on behalf of the rest of the community. But within Albany Park, APTP aims to serve as a catalyst for widespread cultural self-expression throughout the community and for the culture-defining negotiations such formal, public, collective expression necessarily involves. Of course, as Ruth Horowitz's model suggests, culture-defining interactions happen without theater all the time as part of everyday life—when people talk on the phone or meet on the street, at schools, in stores. In making theater together, however, community members engage in a more formal, concerted, and conscious definition of themselves and their community. As we've discussed, theater can also foster interactions among community members who might not normally come together. In these ways theater can help maintain and expand the public sphere within a community at a time when the public sphere in most places has eroded. Moreover, theater brings a special quality to the public sphere, providing a safer, more comfortable place to negotiate community than many other public sphere activities—a place where the stakes don't seem as high, where people feel they're merely "playing" rather than deciding important issues they know will affect their lives.[15]

APTP has a number of ways of extending the democratization of representational authority beyond the members of the teen company into the community at large. Most visibly, APTP's public performances combine the presentation of scenes created and performed by the company with interactive components that directly involve audience members in sharing stories with one another and even improvising performances from these stories. APTP performances thereby become occasions for fresh interchange, collaboration, and collective creation rather than just presentations of the work of a relatively small group of community theater makers. The company holds these performances in a variety of community settings: parks, churches, community centers, schools, the local library, vacant lots, the neighborhood bank, and restaurants.

Outside of performances we involve community members who aren't part of the company in APTP's creative process. (Here it is important to emphasize that the APTP company is not a closed, set group of people; any teen in the neighborhood who wants to join the company can.) Story gathering is an ideal way of bringing noncompany members into the process. APTP teens often collect stories from others in the neighborhood. We also have neighborhood residents lead workshops in various performance skills, especially traditions from community members' native or ancestral cultures. These kinds of opportunities to dabble in the company's theater making serve as an impetus and a means for more widespread participation, creating an ever-growing circle of people who come together in various ways as collaborators in APTP's community theater making.

In trying to catalyze widespread community cultural expression rather than merely represent on behalf of a community, APTP joins and draws upon a long tradition in community-based theater. While Roadside is a full-time, internationally touring ensemble, the company constantly seeks to involve its Appalachian audience in its theater-making process. As Dudley Cocke describes it, "The community participates in the creation of new plays first as a resource for the script and later as respondent and critic during the various stages of play development."[16] Roadside's accounts of its own work show that the company gauges its success in part by what happens *after* the metaphorical curtain has come down. Writing about an evening of performances Roadside helped organize, company administrative director Donna Porterfield beams that "the audience's response was enthusiastic and emotional. Many people stayed afterward to swap stories and gathered in small groups singing songs."[17] According to John O'Neal, the Free Southern Theater considered it essential that its performances inspired audiences to get directly involved in the company's work. Indeed, O'Neal portrays cultivating such involvement as the company's "job":

It would not be enough simply to perform. We felt a need for a way to really get involved with, and to involve, the residents of local communities. The Community Workshop Program, an ongoing, year-round program geared specifically to the participation of local people, was developed to meet this need. . . . [T]he job of the touring company . . . is to catalyze the involvement of local people in the workshop program.[18]

Augusto Boal argues throughout his work that the barrier between active performers and passive spectators "intimidates" and "represses" the audience. According to Boal, this system can only serve to maintain a status quo, for it encourages passivity and acceptance in people.[19] Roadside, Free Southern Theatre, and APTP provide three of many possible examples of how a like-minded conviction guides much community-based theater practice. To fulfill its goal of helping mountain communities gain control over the definition of their culture, Roadside does more than create and perform for them, on their behalf, as their agents. The same is true for FST, Albany Park Theater Project, and other community-based theaters. These companies also provide an ongoing impetus and opportunity for people throughout their communities to engage in processes of defining their culture—or, to adapt James Clifford, inventing their local futures. If we accept Boal's argument, for community-based theaters only to create for audiences (rather than prompting "audiences" to create as well) would, in fact, be self-defeating.

The answer, then, to the question of how community-based theaters earn and maintain the authority to represent on behalf of their communities is that, in a sense, they don't. On the contrary, their work explicitly aims to decentralize such authority in the community. But what about when they perform for outside audiences? Then they literally represent their communities in both senses of the word, depicting them and acting as their ambassadors. Indeed, companies' missions often include such ambassadorship. By touring outside its own community, a company can offer homegrown images of the community as an alternative to the frequently demeaning mainstream images and can work at developing dialogue and relationships between communities. There are, however, pitfalls even in substituting a complex and constructive image for a simplistic and destructive one, pitfalls similar to those surrounding authenticity. One possibility is that people see the community as a fixed entity, contained entirely in the image presented, rather than as a heterogeneous and ever-changing amalgam of experiences, values, and relationships among real people. Although no longer contained in the debilitating mainstream representation, the community is nonetheless still contained in a sole representation. There's also the possibility of exoticism, that outside audiences will see performers as little more than exotic others on display to entertain and titillate them.

So what are community-based theaters to do? The thoughts we offer here are some preliminary ideas as we begin thinking about this difficult issue, to which an entire essay of much greater length could be devoted. One strategy we can imagine and that we believe community-based theaters use (though not necessarily consciously for this purpose) is to emphasize their performances as singular representations, with emphasis on the singular, as opposed to comprehensive images of their communities. For instance, many groups detail in their performances the specific origins of the stories they tell. Roadside's play *Red Fox / Second Hangin'* begins not with the Red Fox story but with stories about some of the people who told the tales from which Roadside compiled its version of Red Fox's story:

> we've come here to tell you folks a tale. It's a true story about a man who lived down home back in the 1890s . . . told from court records and 100 years worth of memory. . . . Of all the old people down around home that love telling bits and pieces of this story, I reckon I'd rather listen to an old man from up on Kingdom Come Creek over in Kentucky. Everybody up Kingdom Come Creek called him Pap, and to tell you our story, we've got to tell you a little bit about Pap and his time.

Roadside makes the origin of the story clear practically down to the address of the man who told it to the group. Similarly, "A Cambodian Ghost Story" dramatized not only Chak's father's story but also the process whereby the company created the piece. "Ghost Story" audiences experienced the story itself, the origins of the story, and the origins of the play. John O'Neal says he makes a point of providing this kind of genealogy with the stories that make up his Junebug performances: "When I get a story from someplace, and tell it again somewhere else, I try to tell who the people were I got the story from, so that one gains insight into the life of the people and the place where the story comes from."[20] Such "insight" demystifies the performance, revealing it as something constructed by the company (in a manner not unlike Brecht's *Verfremdungseffekt* [alienation effect]). We believe one possible outcome of this approach is that audiences understand the play as merely a glimpse of the community, a brief and only partial view, and recognize that "there's much more where that came from."

Another method is to underscore the heterogeneity of the community. On a very simple level, revealing a performance's origin with specific people in a specific place and time does this by implying the obvious but forgettable fact that the community is full of other people with other stories to tell. Likewise, many performances consist of numerous stories with tremendous casts of characters. Junebug and Roadside storytellers digress almost incessantly, leaving one story momentarily to tell another, often keeping several going simultaneously. APTP performances are collages of typically unrelated scenes performed back to back with no effort to weave them into a narrative whole. Thus, a single performance may contain stories that present radically different images of the community or contradictory views on a subject. This kind of multivocality practically defies an audience to reduce the community to a snapshot or soundbite. Casting choices may achieve a similar effect. For example, in "Ghost Story" a young Bulgarian woman from the ensemble alternated with Chak in the role of the Storyteller. Her appearance and Eastern European accent made it clear she was not Cambodian, not the originator of the story, thereby highlighting the diversity of Uptown and begging the question of what stories she herself might have to tell.

Breaking down the audience/performer division with opportunities for interchange between audience members and performers is another common practice that we think reveals performances as only partial and provisional views of a community. Residencies, workshops, and related activities allow people to meet company members as human beings instead of icons, reminding them that the community represented onstage is actually a network of real people. Most groups combine tour performances with interactive components whenever possible. The American Festival Project is a national coalition of companies that sets up periodic festivals throughout the United States expressly to enable more prolonged interaction and exchange (as of this writing, member companies include Pregones Theater, Robbie McCauley and Company, El Teatro de la Esperanza, Liz Lerman Dance Exchange, Urban Bush Women, A Traveling Jewish Theatre, Francisco Gonzalez y su Conjunto, Carpetbag Theater, plus founders Roadside and Junebug Productions). Festivals consist not only of performances by AFP companies but also of residencies, workshops, discussions, and collaborations with artists from the host community. Festivals may last several weeks or more often stretch over a number of months or even years. Planning, too, becomes an integral way that festivals induce exchange, bringing together AFP company members with planners from throughout the host community over an extended period of time.[21] Some theaters also put interactive elements on the same bill as performances, ensuring that audience members who don't attend separate workshops have that part of the experience. Roadside, for example, has followed performances with story swaps featuring local people the company had met during other residency activities.[22] Similarly, APTP often asks audiences outside its community to share stories with one another and improvise performances just as it does in its Albany Park appearances. In addition to introducing performers as real people, these various practices also get audience members thinking and talking about their own relationships to communities. Stimulating this kind of self-awareness may prompt audience members to bear in mind the complexity of community and to imagine other communities and people's relationships with them as intricate, just like their own.

What these various practices share is that they each limit or undermine the company's representational authority, thus avoiding narrow interpretations of its community. They demonstrate that the company and its performances are part of something larger, incomplete on their own. Indeed, our entire discussion has focused on practices that avoid the containment of representational authority in any one place or by any one group. Community-based theaters do this by decentralizing theater culturally and providing opportunities for cultural expression by people and groups typically denied equal participation in dominant culture discourse. We've explored practices aimed at democratizing authority within community-based theater making itself, both among the participants and in the relationship between a company and its community. We have focused on our own work not because we believe it is especially unique or pathbreaking but because we feel it's important that community-based theaters make their processes more accessible to others. Process over product (or, at least, process as well as product) has long been a community-based theater mantra. Yet in the United States there remains far too little public dialogue about process, too few in-depth descriptions and analyses of how and why groups do their work. Organizations, publications, and events such as Alternate ROOTS, the late *High Performance,* and the 1992 "Grassroots Theater" symposium at Cornell have played an important role, but much more is needed. We feel this is especially critical given the current prevalence of mainstream theaters and arts organizations adopting the prefix *community-based* (and its widespread usage in general). We hope this analysis of the connections between the goals of our work, the processes used, and the resulting outcomes contributes to the development of new ways of talking about and evaluating community-based theater by those who make it, those who study it, and the many people who do both.

NOTES

1. Roadside prefers the name *grassroots theater,* disavowing *community-based* as vague and apolitical. Other practitioners prefer different labels. Though *community-based* is currently in widespread use, there is no consensus on a name.

2. Dudley Cocke, "Appalachia, Democracy, and Cultural Equity," in *Voices from the Battlefront: Achieving Cultural Equity,* ed. Marta Moreno Vega and Cheryll Y. Greene (Trenton, N.J.: Africa World Press, 1993), 39.

3. Donna Porterfield, "Arts Presenting and the Celebration of a Community's Culture," *High Performance* 64 (Winter 1993): 65.

4. We use the word *scene* rather than *script* because text and staging are created together as part of the same process.

5. *From the Ground Up: Grassroots Theater in Historical and Contemporary Perspective,* ed. Dudley Cocke and Harry Newman and Janet Salmons-Rue (Ithaca, N.Y.: Community-Based Arts Project, Cornell University, 1993), 81.

6. James Clifford, *The Predicament of Culture: Twentieth-Century Ethnography, Literature, and Art* (Cambridge, Mass.: Harvard University Press, 1988), 13–14.

7. Ibid., 5.

8. Ibid., 5.

9. See, for example, Clifford Geertz, *The Interpretation of Cultures* (New York: Basic Books, 1973); Anthony Cohen, *The Symbolic Construction of Community* (New York: Youngstock, 1985).

10. Ruth Horowitz, *Honor and the American Dream: Culture and Identity in a Chicano Community* (New Brunswick, N.J.: Rutgers University Press, 1983), 20.

11. Chicago was divided into seventy-five "community areas" in 1930 by the Social Sciences Research Committee at the University of Chicago. Since 1930 the only change to the original map has been the addition of two community areas. The City of Chicago, the U.S. Bureau of the Census, and social science researchers still rely on the original community area divisions today. For more information on Chicago's community areas, including the considerations used to make designations, see *Local Community Fact Book: Chicago Metropolitan Area, 1990,* ed. Chicago Fact Book Consortium (Chicago: Chicago Fact Book Consortium, 1995).

12. *Local Community Fact Book,* 397.

13. It is not, of course, merely coincidence that, after (im)migrating to or within Chicago, they have come to find themselves living in the same neighborhood. The housing options available in certain neighborhoods and the housing options *not* available in some neighborhoods determine in large part who will live where. See Dwight Conquergood, "Life in Big Red: Struggles and Accommodations in a Chicago Polyethnic Tenement," in *Structuring Diversity: Ethnographic Perspectives on the New Immigration,* ed. Louise Lamphere (Chicago: University of Chicago Press, 1992), 99.

14. *Company* at APTP has an unfixed meaning, with the group's composition fluid and the door always open to anyone who wants to participate.

15. Anthropologist Victor Turner calls this the "ludic" quality of theater, drawing on the Greek word for "game." See Victor Turner, *From Ritual to Theater* (New York: Performing Arts Journal Publications, 1982).

16. Cocke, "Appalachia," 38.

17. Donna Porterfield, "Arts Presenting and the Celebration of a Community's Culture," *High Performance* 64 (Winter 1993): 67.

18. John O'Neal, "Motion in the Ocean: Some Political Dimensions of the Free Southern Theatre," *Drama Review* 40 (Summer 1968): 74.

19. Augusto Boal, *Theatre of the Oppressed,* trans. Charles A. and Maria-Odilia Leal McBride (New York: Theatre Communications Group, 1985), ix–xiv, 46–47.

20. Kate Hammer, "John O'Neal, Actor and Activist: The Praxis of Storytelling," *Drama Review* 136 (Winter 1992): 17.

21. Ibid., 15.

22. Janet Salmons-Rue, *Storytelling Theater: Culture, Communication and Community* (Ithaca, N.Y.: Community-Based Arts Project, Cornell University, 1993), 13.

Susan Mason

Finding the Edge:
Multiple Community Goals

During the first three months of 1993 I participated in an urban community-based theater project in Utrecht, the Netherlands. The project, *On the Edge,* was designed, facilitated, and organized by Eugene van Erven, professor of American Studies at Utrecht University, using the Philippine three-part community theater model he documented in *The Playful Revolution.*[1] Our project differed significantly from the Philippine model, especially in the number of different communities we were working with simultaneously and the resulting multiple, and often conflicting, goals of the project. Ultimately, defining the "edge" depended upon whose goals were or were not being addressed.

Our project also differed from the Philippine model because we neglected to include a crucial step wherein participants define their expectations early in the project and then periodically review the process to determine if their goals are being met. Two years later, in 1995, when van Erven and I were creating a workbook/video package documenting the project, he realized this significant omission.[2] Consequently, since the various communities involved in the project had different and often incompatible goals that were neither clearly identified at the outset nor periodically reviewed during the process, frustration, confusion, and resistance impeded the project from the beginning. At least a year after its conclusion, however, we began to review and evaluate the project and have continued to do so periodically over the next four years, and this has become a significant part of

Susan Mason, Professor of Theatre at California State University, Los Angeles (CSULA), was Performance Review editor of *Theatre Journal* from 1993 to 1995. She has published articles on Dutch theater and is editing a book on the San Francisco Mime Troupe. She recently worked with French director/playwright Pascal Rambert, who is reconceiving his community-based play *Race* in Los Angeles with students from CSULA and actors from the Los Angeles Poverty Department, a skid row theater company.

our project, giving participants an opportunity to reexamine mistakes and
suggest improvements.

Our primary community was a group of nine students in the International Theatre in Education program at the Utrecht Art Academy (HKU),
one of several postsecondary professional training programs in the arts in the
Netherlands. Training these students in the Philippine process of community-based theater as one course in their program that winter and creating a
play out of this process was our goal. Theirs was to fully participate in and
own their creative project as well as to complete an assigned course at their
school. An overlapping community was the HKU, where the students continued taking classes besides ours with teachers who are the regular faculty of
the academy. The HKU teachers wanted to ensure that our course was satisfying their students' educational and creative needs. They also wanted the
play created by the students to tour to local high schools later that spring.

A smaller and more geographically scattered community was made up
of several immigrant families the HKU students interviewed. Our goal was
to facilitate the students' contribution to creating a play based on these
interviews; the play would be performed by the students in a staged reading.
Because most of the immigrants who were interviewed came from different
countries, lived in different cities in the Netherlands, and had never met one
another before, during, or after the project, their only common goal may
have been to tell the students their stories about adapting to Holland, their
new home. Their goals may have been more complicated, however, such as
wanting to placate the student interviewers while withholding information
about their reasons for moving to Holland or about their difficulties in
adapting to Dutch culture.

Another layer of community was Utrecht University, where van Erven
teaches and where I had a Fulbright lecture assignment. The university's
Studium Generale was cosponsoring a three-month lecture project—"The
Edge of Existence" (*De Rand van het bestaan*)—with RASA, an intercultural
center in Utrecht. This series examined life in extreme conditions in four
megacities and among four groups of nomadic people. Our play reading in
April 1993 would be one event in this series about "life on the edge." This
performance aspect of the project created the need for another community:
the production team, which included me (director of the staged reading), a
stage manager, composer, and the nine student performers.

The community making most of the decisions was that of the project
leaders: van Erven, me, Ton van Vlijmen from the HKU, and Elroyce
Jones, a playwright van Erven had brought over from the United States
with support from the U.S. Embassy. Creating a play was our common

goal. We met only a few times with van Vlijmen, however, and Jones joined the project after one month, so van Erven and I were the primary project leaders, facilitators, and decision makers. I was nominally the project dramaturg and was completely ill prepared to facilitate because I had never done this kind of work before.

Van Erven got partial financial backing to have the process documented, so a final community consisted of the producers (who got more backing), director, crew filming the students' process, and van Erven. While our common goal with this community was project documentation, their goal was also, among other things, to meet the specific conditions upon which their project was funded. Although their participation caused numerous problems *during* the project, the thirty-two-minute film they created has given us the opportunity for ongoing evaluation that is rarely part of community theater work.

Consequently, our project involved seven communities, each with different goals neither clearly communicated nor periodically reviewed until much later. Furthermore, because all participants did not hold equal authority, some communities—namely, the students, their HKU teachers, and the immigrant subjects—were marginalized throughout the process.

The Philippine model begins with a get-to-know-you phase, during which the goals of the project are described and agreed upon and participants become acquainted using theater games. We rushed through this phase in one week—a mistake. Had we taken more time to get to know one another, we might have found opportunities for student input in the project goals, but, because of a tight schedule and predetermined project goals, there was no room for negotiation.

The project, we explained, was for the students to interview immigrants in the Netherlands; these stories would be crafted into a play about the difficulties of adapting to a new country and creating a new home. Some of the students were immediately troubled by the goals of the project. How could they identify immigrants? Should they question people on the streets who are not white? What about people who are not white who are citizens from former Dutch colonies? While some immigrant organizations were eager to participate and thus identify an immigrant population, some students would interview people in their neighborhoods. Holland is a commuter country, and the students lived in various cities. Their concerns were never thoroughly discussed nor satisfactorily resolved.

The underlying problem was that the students were *assigned* this project and had no voice in its design. Ideally, the group of participants will choose to participate, and the concluding event will be something they have created out of their own experiences. Because HKU students follow a designed program of study, their teachers expect resistance and spend early class meetings soliciting input from the students in a motivational phase. Had we worked with the HKU faculty, we might have been able to incorporate some of their methods, but we chose to exclude the HKU teachers from our work with the students, meeting only as a larger group for weekly plenary sessions. These sessions were facilitated by Bodine de Walle, one of the HKU faculty, who was also handling student frustrations in sessions alone with them. Later, reflecting on the limited role of the HKU, she wrote: "Although we were supposed to have been the guardians of the pedagogical aspects of the project, we actually only played a marginal role. For projects of this kind, marginal tasks do not exist."[3]

The film crew was present at the first meeting. Although they introduced themselves, they maintained an essentially objective relationship with the students until one stormy plenary session about three weeks into the project when the students insisted on voicing their concerns: they didn't feel like the project was *theirs*. They wanted to redefine the project: how anyone creates a home anywhere. Why did they have to focus on immigrants? What about their own experiences living abroad? The students had quickly noticed that the film crew began to single out the one black student in their group and two other students who were interviewing third world immigrants. The film director (who never intended to participate in discussions) explained that race relations in Holland and third world immigration were the basis on which the film was funded. But race was the issue most of the students did not want *their* project to be about.

In this and other conflicts that arose, the students' protests were never significantly addressed. Commitments had been made to the "Edge of Existence" lecture series and to the film sponsors defining the product in a way that denied the students creative latitude and ownership. Clay Toppenberg, one of the student participants who later worked on community theater projects in Trinidad and Curacao in 1994, said the project "had too many objectives. I must emphasize that I deeply believe in this way of working. It is too bad that things went sour a bit due, I think, to unperceived cultural differences and hidden agendas. And we as players were kept dangling between structures we didn't really know too much about."

The second phase is fieldwork: drawing stories out of the community that will become the material for the play created in phase 3. This phase was extremely frustrating for the students who had stories of their own to tell. All the students had lived in other countries, and each had experienced adapting to an unfamiliar culture. But, because the lecture series was about "life on the edge" and the film was about race relations in Holland, the subjects specifically sought by the film crew and project leaders were poor third world immigrants in the Netherlands. While some students conducted interviews, several became irritated and uncooperative with the project goals as defined by the project leaders. The film crew continued rewarding (with attention) those who cooperated.

The moral and ethical issues involved in interviewing the immigrants were clearly felt by the students but remained essentially unacknowledged by van Erven and me. To *take* this "raw material" collected by the students and craft it into a play and a film raises issues of exploitation and ownership. Were we sending the students out as colonial anthropologists? Some of the students thought so. Ownership and ripping off kept emerging as issues in this project.

In the third phase of the Philippine model the participants create a play out of the stories they have collected. Sometimes a playwright facilitates this process. With the support of the U.S. Embassy, van Erven brought in an African-American playwright, Elroyce Jones. For financial reasons he didn't arrive until late in phase 2, which was a mistake. He was unaware of the students' frustration about their lack of ownership in the project and therefore exacerbated an already tense situation. Although he met with the students to discuss the material they had collected, after a week he unveiled the play he was writing: *The Threaded Sand*. It was a fictional play using an Antillian family he had met as the characters. He had begun working on a play before meeting with the students and disregarded all their fieldwork. Because we overlooked the periodic goal check and because Jones arrived three weeks into the project, he didn't know what was expected of him. He had never worked collaboratively before and had recently participated in the O'Neill Playwriting Conference, which is totally focused on the playwright and development of the play. In retrospect, bringing in a playwright was one of our two biggest mistakes (the other was the external commitments). If the students had been given the opportunity to craft the play out of their interviews, they could have had some sense of ownership. Now they had none.

In an effort to include the students' fieldwork and to prevent a complete revolution, we commissioned several scenes from Jones involving people the students had interviewed and bits and pieces of their stories. We dictated characters and locations, and he wrote about five different scenes. Two of the students chosen by their peers to represent the group worked with us, commissioning, editing, and structuring a play out of this new material and some central scenes from *The Threaded Sand* during a long weekend one week before the play reading at RASA. We broke the scenes up into beats and cross-cut back and forth between them. The resulting play was called *On the Edge*.

The following week we had four days of rehearsals culminating in the staged reading and a reception sponsored by the American Embassy. Although most of the students continued working on the play in order to tour it in high schools that spring, our project ended with the reading. Even though the audience responded positively to the reading, our work with the students failed in every respect. For most of them it had been an extremely negative experience in which their needs, ideas, and experience were ignored. Nevertheless, three have continued with community work. Two years later, when van Erven and I reviewed the project while writing the workbook, I realized the students' own stories could have been integrated into the immigrant play and still fulfilled our external commitments. I also saw that the theme of being marginalized continually informed the process; we had repeatedly marginalized the students and their teachers. There was our edge.

The workbook includes commentary from student participants and others involved in *On the Edge* as well as the transcript from a 1995 Association for Theatre in Higher Education conference session in which about twenty people viewed and evaluated the film. One of the HKU students, Majella Perry, who later worked with the Irish Youth Federation training youth workers in community theater for social change, wrote: "Ownership is crucial to any collaborative creation and that ownership hinges on having the opportunity to contribute at all levels and stages of the project. . . . In *On the Edge* the process was so focused on an end result we neglected to address the real difficulties and frustrations we were having. . . . If I were to run a project such as this myself . . . I would work directly with the community who are the subjects of the project. It is possible to do a project like this without the target group actually performing, but in that case the community must be much more closely involved in the research and in the creation of the play."

Creating the workbook has proved to be the most informative part of the project, and, although the film documentation created additional problems, it has given us the opportunity to review the process with various audiences in an ongoing effort to understand what pitfalls to avoid and how to improve this kind of work. The commentary provided by those whom we silenced and their continuing participation in community theater work have been especially meaningful.

NOTES

1. Eugene van Erven, *The Playful Revolution: Theatre and Liberation in Asia* (Bloomington: Indiana University Press, 1992).

2. *Edgy Storytellers*, ed. Eugene van Erven and Susan Mason (Houten: Atalanta Publishers in collaboration with IDEA, 1997). The package includes the workbook and the film *The Storytellers: A Film about Multicultural Theatre Project, "On the Edge"* (Utrecht: Stichting Ocean Film Productions, 1993).

3. This quote and those following are in *Edgy Storytellers*, chap. 3.

Daniel A. Kelin II

Jodrikdrik Ñan Jodrikdrik Ilo Ejmour: A Performing Arts Tradition Is Born

On a tiny island in the Pacific, at the edge of a serene lagoon, bright light suddenly fills the darkness as a burst of song shatters the still air. The many children running about playing suddenly rush to the edge of the plywood stage facing the lagoon. The people milling about the graveled lot talking quickly jostle for a good seat on the wooden slats under a tented roof.

A large group of young people, brightly dressed, dance onto the stage. Singing at the top of their lungs, these young people yelp and cheer in an effort to draw the crowd's attention to the stage. A woman with a hand-held microphone encourages the audience to applaud. The musicians, now at the side of the stage, retune their instruments. Another song begins, but this time the youth dance slowly onto the stage in formation. They are now wearing more traditional Pacific garb. A young woman steps to the edge of the stage beginning a story of the "long and long time past" as the youth create a frieze of ancestral life on a remote Pacific island.

Each summer in the Marshall Islands this scenario repeats itself. It is a new "tradition" of performing arts, focused around issues of concern for the islands' youth and reviving among the younger population performance traditions of those islands. It is a tradition that has made all from dogs to the very president of the island nation sit up and take notice. It is the tradition of an organization little more than a decade old, but one that has had greater impact than any other organization (health, social, or cultural) in that tiny

Daniel A. Kelin II, author/poet, playwright, and theater educator, works for the Honolulu Theatre for Youth. His writing has appeared in numerous journals, including *Pacific Islanders, Kamehameha Journal of Education, Hawaii Review,* and *Parabola.* Under a Rockefeller Foundation grant Daniel developed a play based on Marshallese songs, dance, and folk stories. The American Alliance for Theatre and Education awarded him the 1995 Youth Theatre Director of the Year.

island nation. It is the tradition of Jodrikdrik ñan Jodrikdrik ilo Ejmour (JNJIE, Youth to Youth in Health), a nongovernmental organization (NGO) dedicated to the health and cultural well-being of young people throughout the Marshall Islands.

The Marshall Islands consists of some twelve hundred tiny islands formed into twenty-nine atolls spread over nearly eight hundred thousand square miles of the Pacific Ocean. Nearly half the total population of the republic lives on the capital island of Majuro—twenty-five thousand people in less than three square miles of land. The vast majority are employed by the overinflated, financially strapped government that once canceled school lunch programs to complete a ten million dollar, first-class hotel.

In the past Marshallese elders and parents taught their children the ways of life and dealt with problems as a family in order to keep the community running smoothly. With the beginning of urban life, family units have begun to dissolve. Young people of the outer island communities regularly move to the "easy life" of the capital island. This urban drift brings with it problems plaguing other such urban centers, including one of the world's fastest population growths, a high male suicide rate, increased teenage pregnancy, sexually transmitted diseases, large numbers of school dropouts, crime, and gangs. These realities have escalated far faster than the government is able to deal with them. Seventy percent of the population now is under twenty-five, so many young people bear the burden of serious health and social issues with no family (or parents too young) for support or information. The youth, left mostly to their own devices, choose between "accepted" activities: sexual promiscuity and/or prostitution, bar hopping, and, for younger ones (as young as six or seven years old), gangs. There is little else.

Jodrikdrik ñan Jodrikdrik ilo Ejmour, founded in 1986 by Darlene Keju-Johnson, strives to offer an alternative, providing young people the information and support they need, training them to be role models for their peers, and giving them a voice in a society that places little value on its youth. Jodrikdrik trains young people to lead outreach programs in improving deteriorating family health and tackling urgent youth social problems and cultural deterioration. They are innovative in their approach in the Pacific. Through community and school (both elementary and high) programs, the youth bring recognition to such topics as AIDS, suicide, the social effects of alcoholism, abuse, and the importance of cultural continuity. The organization has the needed support of the World Health Organization, Bread for the World, and the Australian and New Zealand governments, all of which have played an instrumental part in the phenomenal growth of Jodrikdrik. Additionally, the business community of Majuro rallies around Jodrikdrik as it does for no other organization. Every project is inundated with donated materials, food, labor, and facilities.

Jodrikdrik began under the Marshall Islands Ministry of Public Health. It is now an NGO, although still affiliated with the Ministry. Jodrikdrik's (adult) director is a government employee assigned to JNJIE. The assistant director and staff of five are all past Jodrikdrik trainees who oversee and work with the volunteers. They are all youth aged nineteen to twenty-eight. The volunteers are recent trainees who have demonstrated responsibility and leadership qualities. Assigned to a staff member, volunteers assist with organization, cleaning, scheduling, preparing food for breaks, video-taping, and picture taking. During formal training volunteers assist with small groups of new trainees to develop projects and scenes. Highly self-motivated volunteers can become paid staff members.

The staff create the outreach programs for schools, are trained media specialists who produce television and radio shows promoting their work, travel to many of the outer islands to run workshops and follow-up programs, assist various professionals who lead workshops for the organization, and train other youth in their annual summer training.

Each summer Jodrikdrik hosts two training programs for youth: the first for youth that live in the capital island, the second for a gathering of youth from the outer islands. The young trainees become the future members of Jodrikdrik, the basic tenet for broadening the impact and outreach of Jodrikdrik. In the first ten years of the organization about four hundred young people graduated from the summer training. Many of the capital island youth have become regular volunteers at the Jodrikdrik office. Others are called upon to assist in various ways in the many programs that Jodrikdrik hosts and/or participates in. The outer island youth take back to their own islands the skills necessary to run mini-programs based on the Jodrikdrik model.

The first part of the summer training features mini-workshops led by social, health, and cultural specialists on topics ranging from AIDS to teen pregnancy to cultural pride. From these workshops a foundation of information is laid down as preparation for the drama workshops, which form the second part of the summer's overall training.

Originally developed under my direction, the drama training begins with basic performance skills and technique exploration, focusing on improvisation, storytelling, physical expression, pantomime, and the metaphoric use of tableaux, music, and dance. Once a vocabulary of skills has been built, the group then imagines, devises, and develops an issue-ori-

ented drama scene with the drama specialist. This demonstrates a model for
creating scenes improvisationally focusing on how best to apply the skills
earlier explored. The trainees then separate into smaller groups and, with a
Jodrikdrik staff member as leader, create their own smaller-scale, issue-ori-
ented scenes based on topics from the first part of the training.

The first obstacle to overcome in the drama portion is the Marshallese
reluctance to "take center stage," especially in front of someone non-Mar-
shallese (i.e., the drama specialist). Two aspects in particular deal with this
problem—first, having the Jodrikdrik staff spend much of the time with the
trainees developing the pieces and, second, creating pieces improvisationally. By having the Jodrikdrik staff work directly with them, the trainees feel
a lot more comfortable. When they share their developing scenes with the
drama instructor, energies are focused on development, as the trainees look
to the drama specialist to help make their scene a more dramatically viable
piece. Confidence is gained almost as an afterthought. By the time the scene
is ready to be presented, the trainees have already spent a lot of time performing for others.

Improvisation is used as the main process for creating scenes because it
utilizes the trainees natural talent for "talking story." In a country where few
people read, information is gained and passed on through conversation.
(The Marshallese word bwebwenato means both "story" and "conversation.")
Also with improvisation, loose structures are developed that allow for freedom within. This gives the trainees a great amount of power and responsibility. They realize quickly they must contribute, or nothing happens. This
often means a lot of switching trainees within developing scenes to find out
who is more equipped to delve deeply into a particular piece. Oddly
enough, however, trainees get more involved if they jump in as a reaction
to another trainee's lack of ideas than if they start the process themselves.
Yet, when trainees take that kind of responsibility, the training becomes
easier and more self-sustaining. Improvised scenes also help if any of the
youth are unable to perform. Several times trainees have not shown up for
the performance or gotten sick backstage and had to be whisked off to the
hospital, or a case of laryngitis has laid a performer up. Other performers
step quickly and easily into the actorless role and play the scene in a similar,
but newly improvised, way.

One very popular social issue scene was "Pregnancy Man." Onstage a
man is fast asleep, while a pregnant woman cooks (pantomimed). She wakes
him, he berates her, then says he's going out. When she questions him, he
physically abuses her. The man goes off to a bar. When his wife arrives
there, his friends laugh at him. He slugs her swollen stomach as they con-

tinue laughing, then he chases her out. A freeze, and music begins as the story restarts. In pantomime the man wakes and discovers he's pregnant. He runs from his now unpregnant wife to the bar. He tries to hide his stomach, but his friends discover it. They laugh at him and hurt him. Alone and sad, his wife enters and gently cradles him. A freeze, music ends, and the story restarts (with dialogue). The woman (pregnant again) wakes her husband. He discovers he is no longer pregnant. Ecstatic, he hugs his wife. He cradles her and tells her from now on he'll take care of everything. He lovingly caresses her stomach, jumping about in joy. End.

A constant reflection of the issues by the youth is necessary to create the most effective performances. It also contributes to the young trainees' better understanding the impact the issues have on their society. The youth are put in the position of thinking through the entire issue—cause, effect, and possible solutions—in order to create scenes the audience can understand and appreciate. As the performers are being trained to be peer educators, the importance of fully understanding the issues cannot be underestimated, and theater offers participants the chance to look at the issues in a detail that classroom lectures cannot. The dramatization of the issues, then, is almost more important for the performers than for the audience. Yet the audience, too, becomes engaged by the work, both for its surface content and for the simple fact that the youth are so involved in its creation and performance.

In the final part of the training the entire group comes back together to stage a Marshallese legend. While the health, social, and political issue scenes tend to be more realistic, confined storylines with small casts, the folklore pieces are more "epic" in nature, involving more characters, song and dance, and research into the correct ways of recreating life of the distant past. For this reason we begin the summer training with the issue pieces, both as a way to satisfy the stated goals of Jodrikdrik and as models of dramatic structuring for the trainees. The acquired skills can then be applied easily to the chosen legend. The trainees do not have as much freedom improvisationally with the folk pieces, and more time has to be spent combing out the strands of the story so that each trainee understands the overall flow of the piece, so the process is slightly different.

First, the legend is presented orally. Written sources are not used as the trainees will often rely on the printed words. The legend is then deconstructed, examined, and broken down into scenes and then reconstructed improvisationally. During this process the group learns songs attached to the particular tale and/or collectively creates new songs. They teach one another dances that accompany the songs. The outer island youth become teachers for the less "cultured" capital island youth, introducing them to the songs and dances of their specific island. Older people are often consulted as resources, detailing to the young performers the ways of living from the long-ago past and demonstrating dances and songs and sharing stories. The elders hardly get a chance to sit down as the youth ask them to go over the dances again and again.

The legends are large-scale, involving up to forty trainees and staff. Combining oral tradition with music, dance, and very theatrical staging, a narrator relates the story as it is performed. One of the most satisfying of them concerned a young man named Leli, who, shunned by neighbors as a "momma's boy," wanted to be a warrior. Through a frustrating and enlightening series of adventures, he gained a magical power that transformed him into a giant who defeated the enemy. To theatricalize the story the war was danced; canoe sailing was a combination of music, original song, and rhythmic movement; and Leli's ultimate triumph (transforming into a giant and defeating the enemy) was created by elevating the actor behind palm leaf screens while having him "kill" the others in a highly stylized slow-motion sequence set to music.

A key element in the drama training is creating a sense of ownership in the participants' own cultural heritage. That heritage is a primary teaching tool and has been a way to develop a unique performance style for the islands. Storytelling, song, and dance are the most lasting traditions of the ancestors of the Marshall Islanders. A performance style combining song, pantomime, and dance is documented in the journals of European "discoverers" of those islands, but there is no record of a formal tradition of theater in the Western sense. The oral tradition, however, has not been able to keep up with the quickly developing tradition of television and videotapes. Nor does dance seem to be holding up against the infusion of Western culture. Music and songs are still very much a part of daily life but are being challenged by church music on one side and rock on the other. All are slowly slipping from the collective memory of the Marshallese. The drama training has attempted to instill a respect for a culture in the midst of this change while trying to stop the materialistic attitude of tossing out the old for the new.

The revival of these skills and cultural treasures, however, does not end there. By combining Western-style theater techniques with Marshallese dance, legends, and music, Jodrikdrik celebrates its cultural heritage by bringing the past to full life in a way that is engaging and fun but, most important, in a way that makes it theirs; their stories, their dance, their language, and, as it is improvisationally built, their own form of interaction and humor. The youth learn the skills but find ways to use those skills to touch their audience as other media cannot. It is a selective syncretism that has

Jodrikdrik Ñan Jodrikdrik Ilo Ejmour. Photograph courtesy of
Giff Johnson.

fired a need within the youth to seek out their unique traditions of storytelling, dance, and song. It has made the organization search for the oldest,
documented Marshallese performance elements to enrich this new tradition;
they are now exploring their ancestors' ways of performance by (re)intro-
ducing percussive instruments.

The culminating event of the summer training is the annual *Showtime!*
presentation, a showcase of the work developed by all trainees, both capital
and outer island. As described in the opening paragraphs, *Showtime!* is held
lagoonside under the stars. The overall performance begins with a dance.
The brief social issue scenes generally begin with a tableau of some sort and
end with a song to signify the beginnings and ends of each piece clearly.
The legends most often use dance at the start. Transitions between all scenes
are covered by music and an MC encouraging applause while mentioning
tidbits of what is yet to come. The overall evening is constructed so the legends are scattered throughout the evening with the popular one in the middle (for older people who can't stay late). Performances always end with
everyone singing.

A simple plywood stage accentuates the pounding of the step dances
generously sprinkled throughout the performances. Gaping doorways offer

wide entrances to the stage so the actors can crowd backstage to watch the other performers and to ensure that none of them misses an entrance. Speakers, microphones, and video cameras and a couple of powerful outdoor lamps litter the front of house area to record the event and to ensure the audience can hear the performers over the crunch of gravel under other audience members' feet. Two to four Jodrikdrik members are assigned as stage crew. Throughout the evening they can be seen scrambling on and off the stage in between the various scenes setting chairs, woven mats, and cleaning up spilled food or dropped props. They are the backbone of the evening, keeping it quick and engaging.

Most often the audience is filled with people who know or are related to the trainees, not so surprising in such a small community. The children in the audience are often heard screaming out the name of their relative, or certain sections of the audience laugh at seeing their child or cousin in a way they're not used to.

Showtime! is a coming together of the community, a coming together that affirms a place for the past, present, and future of the Marshallese and their culture. They take charge of the stage as they learn to take charge of their lives, learning from the old as they create the new. Many of the youngest audience members chant bits and pieces of the performances for up to a year after the show. Their enthusiasm for Jodrikdrik's presentations are replaced only by the following summer's *Showtime!*

After overcoming the nervousness of the first performance, the second night of *Showtime!* is always a wild performance for the youth. They have discovered their power. They milk everything for what it is worth, be it the comedy or the issue they wish to address. And the audience responds in kind. One year a third night of performance was added at the last minute. From word of mouth only, over twenty-five hundred people attended that Monday night performance—10 percent of the population of Majuro.

From informal performances for family and friends to the big *Showtime!* performed lagoonside at the end of summer, the youth are constantly in motion. Their low-tech, idea-oriented productions are transported all about the island and performed on basketball courts, parking lots, and the local hangout underneath the national museum. Throughout the year those youth who are not in school (nearly 50 percent of high school–aged students are not) volunteer as performers for the school outreach programs. Drawing on the short performance pieces developed in the summer, the youth perform in every school on the capital island, adding follow-up workshops for individual classes. Often the youth are requested to perform at government symposiums, anniversary celebrations of local businesses, and cultural fairs of the nation's museum. Jodrikdrik regularly greets incoming

dignitaries at the airport: when then Secretary of State George Schultz visited the islands, a picture of him dancing with one of the youth was printed
in newspapers around the world.

Jodrikdrik goes where the people are, and the people always gather for
the youthful exuberance. A presentation Jodrikdrik offered in tiny Woja
Village was held on the bare cement slab of a basketball court behind a
church. A sign on one of the basketball hoops welcomed the youth to the
village. Jodrikdrik set up its usual microphone stands and laid props here and
there about the cement. The group began with a song, dove right into a few
of the short dramas, and then performed one of its newly created legends. In
the midst of the last, it started raining. Everyone, audience and performers
alike, scattered (children first, adults after, and finally the performers, who
seemed unsure about whether to continue or not). After the rain let up, the
youth hooked up the microphones again and continued the show. All the
little kids ran back onto the cement slab and promptly sat right down in
the puddles. The performers ended up sitting in puddles as well, as parts of
the show required sitting on the ground—a typical night for Jodrikdrik.

Having toured Hawai'i, Australia, and Guam, Jodrikdrik is possibly the
most well-known nongovernmental organization in Micronesia. The group
has been courted to help create similar organizations in other Micronesian
countries. Jodrikdrik created and performed a "Marshallese musical" based
on a well-known legend of the islands for the twenty-seventh South Pacific
Economic Forum. The youth, sixty-five of them, performed right next to
the cultural treasures of the Marshall Islands, a sign that maybe the government is beginning to recognize the power of its own youth. It is an organization that has certainly changed the state of the young population in those
islands. In the more than ten years the organization has been in existence,
population growth has gone down, clinic visits by youth have gone up, discussion has opened up on such taboo subjects as sex, child and spousal
abuse, and youth issues in general. It is an organization the youth enjoy and
possibly even what they want, although there isn't a full enough understanding of choice in those islands for them to know that they can want. A
flood of emotion and personal accomplishment, however, comes out in
drama when the youth identify the issues, create the ideas, and are pushed
to explore them as far as possible. Through the dialogue, performance, and
cultural revival they discover a sense of power, of being able to do something, be heard, have others listen. It is a new tradition flavored with old
that is accessible, hip, and highly sought after by youth and celebrated by
both the capital island community and the entire nation.

Jane Heather

Dramatic Union: Workers' Theater in the 1990s

In the fall of 1994 I was approached by two locals of the Canadian Union of Public Employees (CUPE) to write and produce a play about the effect of privatization on their members and on the services in the city. The two locals were city of Edmonton outside workers (sewer workers, garbage collectors, maintenance workers, etc.) and school janitors. I researched and wrote the play *Running,* directed it with a cast of both professional and amateur actors, and it ran at the Edmonton Fringe Theatre Event, 1995.[1]

Community-based theater is a means by which groups of people who are deprived of effective voice by the social and economic relationships of power can speak and be heard. Working people are one such community. This project was initiated by a particular community (public service unions) with specific objectives (the fight against privatization of their jobs). Over time the project grew to include several other excluded communities: nonunionized workers, the working poor, seniors on fixed incomes, new immigrants and established immigrants, the young stuck in "McJobs," the unemployed, unionized workers, and left-wing political activists. The process also pulled together two groups that have historically found common cause but of late often occupy mutually exclusive spheres: theater workers and labor organizations. Community-based theater also creates community.

Two elements are central to understanding the project and its success: (1) the dominant discourse (what are we fighting against?); and (2) the development of the resistant voice (how do people become "politicized"? who are our allies? what must we do now?). This essay is divided into two

Jane Heather is a popular theater worker who has created community-based theater projects with senior citizens, prison inmates, aboriginal youth, teachers, counselors, women's groups, and a wide variety of social agencies and organizations. She is a sessional instructor in the Department of Drama at the University of Alberta, Canada. She lives in Edmonton with her husband, son, and mother.

sections, social context and representational authority, that basically follow the process of the project.

Social Context

Alberta is a deeply conservative province, a place where rugged individualism, the self-made man, cowboy pride, and rural self-sufficiency figure large in the mythology. The reality is a bit different. The population is no longer predominately rural and agricultural. The discovery of vast petroleum deposits in 1947 has been the single most important factor in the development of economic, social, and political life. Alberta has always been an antiunion province, and only about 12 percent of working people in the private sector are unionized. Every year or so, "right to work" legislation is seriously discussed by the government. Minimum wage is five dollars an hour, the lowest in the country.

A monumental lurch to the right began when the Progressive Conservatives won a very solid majority with a new leader in 1993. Since that election the neoconservative agenda has been ferociously pursued, resulting in public sector job loss and wage cuts, huge cuts to all government services, increased user fees, corporate tax cuts, and privatization of public services. Politicians try to sell privatization and contracting out as a way to increase the efficiency of service delivery by introducing competition into these areas. Underlying this argument is the stereotype of public sector workers (and unionized workers in general) as lazy inefficient drones, insulated from the economic realities other Albertans face daily. CUPE was looking for ways to get its views on privatization and the voices and stories of its members out into the public arena.

The call from the union was the first bright and hopeful thing on my horizon since the landslide election. I did, however, have some doubts and concerns. Committees are as cautious and conservative as their most cautious member, and internal politics and turf wars can kill a project. And theater and unions? Not here, brother, not in living memory.[2] Was I dealing with a lone enthusiast in a sea of reluctant skeptics? Would I be expected to try to convince a bunch of redneck sewer workers that rank and file dues should go to pay for something as flaky as theater? Also, there are misconceptions that plays appear miraculously, that since actors like their work it isn't "real" work, that productions can be written and put on very quickly, and that it's cheap if not free. The education process can be difficult and lengthy. Simultaneously a dream come true and a potential nightmare. At the first meeting representatives from both locals expressed huge enthusiasm and support for a theater project. They had done some leafleting about privatization issues at the Fringe Theatre event the preceding summer, and the response had been positive. They felt a theater presence at the event would be a direct, engaging, and unique way to get their members' point of view out to the public. Fun was also a factor.

I presented a proposal and budget with every possible job I could think of identified and assigned to me or members of the locals. I presented a quite generous budget that included not only fees for cast and crew but also the entire production expenses. We rehearsed without charge in the CUPE hall and had full access to photocopying, phone, and fax. The union agreed to take care of all the publicity, poster, program, press release, radio and television spots, interviews, and newspaper articles. The commitment of volunteer time, constant enthusiastic support, sheer positive energy, and belief in the project were overwhelming. Dismissed and vilified as "greedy," "self-serving," and "whiners of the week," the men and women in these two locals had been silenced. They chose theater as another way to resist the neoconservative agenda, to speak their resistance and their story.

Representational Authority: Who Are You to Speak for Me? Research, Writing, Casting, and Rehearsal

There are major ethical questions that arise in this work around the relationship between the community and the facilitators/interpreters. Have you come to steal my story? and who are you to speak for me? are important questions. This problem is often circumvented by having members of the community create and perform their own material. As this option was not open to me, the issue of gaining representational authority was urgent. The depth and veracity of the research and therefore the work can be impacted by how much a community accepts you as "family." I cannot outline a step-by-step "how to" for others, but factors such as class, political involvement, longevity in a community, and the parties I have attended and joined (or not joined) influenced my credibility and adoption into the family. Despite claims to the contrary, we live in a society riddled with class inequity and bias. Class is still largely determined by what your Daddy did or does, and mine was a railroad worker. I put a lot of performative energy into "passing" (particularly in some university settings), but sooner or later my roots always show. Over the last twenty-three years most of my theater work has been in the area of popular theater for public education and social change. That work, combined with my involvement with the women's movement, aboriginal issues, Marxist study groups, a small independent labor newspaper, picket lines, demonstrations, rallies, protests, and food and housing co-ops, means that it is just as likely that somebody will know me and my work in any gathering of union people as in a gathering of theater people. I had always assumed that my politics were of little interest to the theater community and my theater work mostly invisible to my political community. I was wrong. My personal history, experience in community theater, and politics made me "family" of the extended sort. Consequently, the process was comfortable, in a code I understood, and we got to the center of things fast.

To begin my writing process, I collected names of members willing to talk about their jobs and experiences around privatization. I also read all the articles the two locals had produced about the issues. The stories I collected in conjunction with the paper research from the unions formed the basis of the play.

The union committee identified several needs and objectives for the play: a representative from each local must appear as a character onstage, the effects of privatization on workers and their families need to be portrayed, the facts about the economics of privatization have to be made clear, and, finally, anti-union rhetoric needs to be challenged. When a group decides to use theater as a tool, the process of enacting events transforms an "issue" into human lives, wound up with contradictions, joy, anger, and uncertainty. A play is not a speech or a slogan or a panel or a round-table discussion. Part of my research is to hear not only what community members are saying but also what they are not saying. In addition, the theater workers' agenda and objectives always live in the play, consciously or not. As I researched, I added several things not identified by the union. One of these was the need to represent who was taking these newly privatized jobs.

Who is taking our jobs? One school custodian I met told the story of being on an information picket line some months before. The school board had decide to hire contract workers to clean her school over Easter vacation. Phyllis had been working as a school janitor for many years and had gone from being "nothing" (in her words) to someone with real pride and skill in her job. She had become very involved in the union over time, and it had "changed her life." She was more than willing to volunteer for an information picket line and try to convince the contract workers not to go into the school. It was her description of who came—"young guys, some East Indians and that, Chinese girls. . . . I was mad but I kind of felt sorry for them too, you know?"—that gave me the central character and the main action and contradiction of the play.

The unionized workers that I wrote about work in jobs particularly vulnerable to privatization because replacement contract workers are so easy to find. The reserve labor pool of desperate young immigrants can be quickly trained (management believes) to clean schools, pave roads, dig sewers, and collect garbage. The tendency to scapegoat and blame new immigrants is tempting and in part based on fact. I needed a central character with politics sophisticated enough to deal with this contradiction in a clear way. Using stories lent to me by Phyllis and by members of the expatriate Chilean community, I created Ninfa, a Chilean woman who had fled the coup in 1973 and now works as a school custodian. She meets a new immigrant, Joji (a young Filipina nanny), when Joji comes to the school to pick up the child she cares for. Ninfa befriends her and gives her advice about surviving the immigrant experience, including giving her winter clothes and English lessons. These two women with so much in common must take opposite sides when privatization forces them to fight for the same job.

Is it true that privatization is cheaper and more efficient? The character of Steve, a retired garbage man, functioned as the representative of the outside workers' union, labor historian, and researcher. There is significant research from several urban centers in North America (including Edmonton) about the effects of privatization on the collection of garbage. The two major corporate players, Browning-Ferris Industries (BFI) and Waste Management Inc. (WMI)—WMX Technologies since 1993, both have long rap sheets of price fixing, low-ball bidding, and improper handling and disposal of hazardous waste. The character of Steve spoke directly to the audience and provided statistics about privatization that are rarely published and not generally known. Steve also illustrated some of the effects of the cuts on seniors' income and health care services.

What are the effects of privatization on workers and their families? The true story "His Job Went Down a Hole" was taken from written research and transferred point by point to the play. In the story and the play Roland has been laid off from a city sewer job and hired back by a contractor. He knows the danger of this job and refuses to go down a sewer without the proper safety measures in place. He is fired. He and his wife separate over the conflict of how to survive the layoffs and firings.

What good are unions and political action? Ninfa's daughter Sarita carried the story of the young women working in retail clothing boutiques.[3] These young workers are very vulnerable to exploitation, and one of Sarita's coworkers is trying to unionize the mall boutique. Ninfa, Steve, Sarita's father, and Pablo Neruda all try to convince Sarita to support the union drive actively. Sarita is offered a management position and makes the argument to her mother that union organizing is time-consuming, that it targets you to the boss, and that having a union is no guarantee of keeping your job. It is difficult for Ninfa to refute her daughter's criticism of unions and political action because in Ninfa's life they are all true.

At the climax of the play all these characters (except Steve, who is too ill) meet, with all their contradictions and anxieties about the future and their survival, at the information picket. Ninfa is trying to prevent contract workers from going in to clean the school. Joji, the Filipina nanny, and Roland, the laid-off sewer worker, both show up to take the contract work. Ninfa tries to convince them not to go in, but their determination, driven by despair, carries them past her, over her, and through her. Sarita arrives in time to witness her mother being trampled by people she had helped. This seems to harden Sarita's resolve to take the management job she has been offered and abandon her coworkers. Sarita is left with this dilemma, and the play ends.

The play went through two drafts. Each draft was read by the CUPE committee, theater workers, and friends in other unions.[4] I rewrote the play based on comments from all. By early May I had a draft I could take to rehearsal, and I was ready to cast. Alberta conservatism certainly extends to the artistic community, and I worried—unnecessarily, as it turned out—that I might not be able to cast at all. Soon after I began to phone actors, they began to call me. I was able to cast experienced and talented actors with a desire to break the silence that implies complicity.[5]

Over the many weeks we rehearsed in the hall, executives, office staff, and members had a close look at how a play is put together. Several times we requested technical assistance and equipment to make the work scenes authentic. A tremendous ease and respect grew between actors and union people. In most cases these two worlds had had no previous contact with each other. The unreserved support and enthusiasm of the union for the play expanded and solidified during this time. My early fears had disappeared but served to remind me how deep dominant culture's stereotypes are and how difficult it is to resist and challenge them, even when you know better. As we rehearsed, the union mounted a large publicity campaign. Postering, press releases, a public preview, press coverage, front of house, set moving, T-shirt sales, and promotion of the show on site were handled by union volunteers. As a result, all eight performances sold out.

The successful reception and quite unprecedented coverage of the play can be traced to several key factors. Permission to speak on behalf of members, nonmembers, and other working-class people was granted incrementally, with many check points and opportunities to respond. The theater workers had a political and emotional commitment to the material. The rehearsal of the play was on union turf and transparent. The production company and the union had specific tasks assigned to them, and the groups worked in concert. The existence of the Fringe allowed this community-based theater to reach a wider audience. Theater hadn't been tried before, and so energy, enthusiasm, and curiosity were generated and sustained throughout the process.

What now? The issues raised in the play continue to be vital to working people in Alberta. The play continues to have value as an organizing, educational, and mobilizing tool. Theater, however, is ephemeral, and, unlike video, it can't be pulled off the shelf and plugged in anywhere, anytime. A remount of the show is always a possibility, but the time, money, energy, and focus it would require is difficult to muster in the current siege climate. A consistent and long-term alliance between unions and the arts and a constant public presence would be required to begin to achieve significant impact on social and economic issues. A long journey with many steps, *Running* is one.

NOTES

1. The Fringe Theatre Festival is the largest and oldest such event in North America. For two weeks every August there is theater in nine to twelve indoor venues continuously from noon to midnight. Streets are closed to vehicle traffic and carnival takes over. Through the Fringe an opportunity is created for community-based theater to be seen by a wider audience.

2. This is not the case in some other parts of Canada. Ontario, for example, has a provincial government fund for labor/arts projects based on the Australian model.

3. I based this character and her story on an article by Naomi Klein about the first attempt in Canada to organize retail fashion outlets in shopping malls. Naomi Klein, "Salesgirl Solidarity," *This Magazine* 28, no. 6 (1995): 12–19.

4. Union representatives: Doug Luellman and Alf Hyrciw. Consultants: Valeska Gonzales, Patricia Hughes, Lucy Salucop, Tom Fuller, and Robert Clinton.

5. The cast consisted of Edith Mitchell, John B. Low, Sandra Paddick, Jimmy Hodges, Diane Dichoso, and Trish Agrell-Smith (stage manager).

John Somers

Discovering Seminal Stories: Community Theater as Cultural Memory

The project I describe here was carried out in Exwick Middle School, Exeter, and its surrounding community in the county of Devonshire, UK, in 1989–90. At the time I was teaching in the School of Education at Exeter University, and each year teacher education students specializing in English and Drama take part in cooperative projects with schools in southwest England. I was actually working with fourteen university students who were split into two groups of seven. One group worked with two teachers and sixty students from year six (ten- to eleven-year-olds) to produce a live performance dealing with Exwick in late Victorian times. The other group helped two teachers and thirty students from year seven (eleven- to twelve-year-olds) develop a broadcast radio play based on happenings in Exwick around the time of World War II. The radio project is not dealt with here.[1]

Both projects were based on the notions that school drama productions add greatly to the learning experience of the students who take part and that, through their celebratory, ritualistic nature, they enhance generally the quality of school life. In UK schools such productions are often based on well-known, extant dramatic texts pitched at the age group concerned and containing a suitable range of parts for large numbers of performers of varying abilities. I intended to break away from this conventional approach. The project described here was intended to:

John Somers is a member of the Drama Department at Exeter University, specializing in bringing drama to community settings, including alcohol and drug education in schools; tours to France and Slovakia; and conducts cooperative work in Turkey, Brazil, and Poland. He has a special interest in research, directs the international conference "Researching Drama and Theater in Education," and edits the journal *Research in Drama Education*. He is director of an MA program in Applied Drama.

- further the research skills of the students in the discovery of interesting events to do with the history of the community in which they lived;
- involve a large number (sixty) of students in devising dramatic material based on chosen events;
- provide opportunities for the students to learn appropriate skills to allow them to perform the resultant play;
- give students, through the research and drama-shaping processes, a familiarity with Exwick as a predevelopment community;
- allow students to broadcast to the community the play that they had made;
- provide a forum for the community to consider and discuss its past; and
- empower students through an understanding of how they can be makers of significant cultural events.

These aspects of theater, history, research skills, aesthetics, social dynamics, community awareness, and active learning were to coalesce to provide a cultural experience rooted in memory but related through the students' involvement to their sense of now.

The School and Community

Exwick lies just northwest of Exeter, a city of 110,000 people, and is separated from the city by the River Exe. It was once geographically, socially, and culturally distinct, but, with the expansion of both city and village, administratively and in many other ways, it is now seen as part of Exeter. Exwick has expanded fortyfold in the last thirty years, and the hillsides that overlook the river are covered in modern housing developments. Some old buildings, remnants of the old village, are embedded in this enlarged community.

The students were able to identify a number of former farms, their landless farmhouses now mostly converted to suit late-twentieth-century urban living. They found one where the retired farmer, his holding reduced to just a garden due to housing development, talked to us as he sat with his dog in the old barn. The village also has a mill, Priory Mill, originally built by monks in the thirteenth century and working as an animal feed concern until quite recently.

The original school was built in 1890. A new school was built above the flood plain in 1971, the old school becoming a community center, a function it still performs. The village hall and church are nearby, and the old school rubs shoulders with a toll house, built to house those who collected the dues for crossing the Exe using the "new" bridge. Until that time people forded the river in summer or made long treks up- or downstream to cross by existing bridges. The river was a constant threat until the completion of a flood prevention scheme in the 1970s. Although the city is a short walk away, Exwick retains a certain separateness for, although it is poorly served for shops, its pub, community center, church, and school still allow residents—especially those with young students—to feel part of a, albeit sprawling, community.

Theater and Community

The parents of the students involved in this project were mostly newcomers to the village, and they possessed little knowledge of its history. One of our prime aims was to create opportunities for the students to discover and understand aspects of Exwick's past and to articulate their knowledge to the community. We wanted to use the performances as a focus to celebrate and broadcast a shared culture. Unlike other parts of the world (the United States, e.g., where it means amateur theater), in Britain *community theater* is a term given to theater that attempts to feed off a community's seminal stories.

Ann Jellicoe has created community plays in many West Country towns, and she recognizes the importance of this function: "Communities need community events to continually refresh them. Community drama can be a celebration of community; discovering the nature of a community; articulating it *to* that community."[2] Jellicoe's organization, the Colway Theatre Trust, goes into a community up to eighteen months before the play is performed. Professional and amateur local researchers dig out the interesting people and stories, and a professional writer is employed to focus on one or more of them to create a play for the community. Amateur directors work alongside a professional to bring the work to the stage. Her work is famed, particularly in the southwest of England, where magnificent community plays have been developed and staged. In Ottery-St-Mary in 1985, for example, a well-known happening, the burning down in 1866 of much of the village's thatched properties, was researched, and a number of stories associated with this event were woven into the exploits of a rich family, the Farleighs, and a poor family, the Hakes, to produce a play entitled *The Ballad of Tilly Hake*. One hundred and sixty adults and young people were involved in realizing this promenade play, and its effects on the community were very marked. Fourteen years later, for instance, a local amateur community theater company, set up in the wake of the Colway Theatre Trust's work, still commissions plays about local history.

Benedict Nightingale notes theater's ability to work within a community to heighten people's awareness of where they live: "Isn't it good that a community should learn more, more about the past that has shaped its present, the roots that have determined its identity? Isn't it good that it should deepen its understanding of itself; entertain itself?"[3] The model that I chose had to satisfy the needs of the seven university students with whom I was working. They took part in a process that expanded their notion of what drama was for and what it could achieve. It could also be transferred to professional contexts in which they might find themselves after graduation. The school also looked on the project as in-service training for the staff involved.

We were aware that there were several communities associated with the work of the project. Predominant was the population that had entered Exwick since the early 1970s housing expansion. They were, in the main, young marrieds who, even though they may have moved from elsewhere in Exeter, had little knowledge of the village as it existed before expansion. In their sheer numbers they overwhelmed those who had been previously resident. The latter group, by definition, were generally older and therefore tended not to have children in the school. We estimated that the ratio of "newcomers" to "previous residents" was around forty to one, which, given the lack of social activity and meeting places in Exwick, meant that the community with knowledge of old Exwick was overwhelmed by those who saw it as a dormitory settlement and, effectively, part of the city of Exeter.

The third community was the students themselves. Unlike their parents, who traveled out of Exwick to work, they spent the greater part of their waking hours in the settlement. They knew it in the way that only children can—through playing, walking, and going to school here. Given that the majority would progress to adolescence and adulthood here, they had an investment that their parents could not have. The other defined group involved was the teacher education students. They had an interest in making this ambitious project work and in exploring its professional relevance to their future careers. The teachers involved formed another subset. They were looking for a professional challenge, knowing that the work would demand of them more effort and time and that the activities associated with the project were intentionally disruptive to their normal routines. They were of that band of precious professionals who welcome this sort of stimulation.

Finally, my interest was in originating, setting up, and facilitating a sophisticated educational venture that put into practice emerging notions of how drama could form the focus for a cross-curricular study that energized and benefited all those who had dealings with it.

The Project

The two teachers covered a variety of material having to do with the period under study, relating the topic to most school curriculum subjects. The aim of the history work was to set the local study, which was to be the focus of the project and the drama, within an effective understanding of national and world events. General curriculum work on the topic was under way for some weeks before the notion of the play was introduced. The usual resources—books, videos, transparencies, maps, documents from the County Record Office, local museum collections, and field visits—were available, and teachers made good use of material that was brought in from the few families whose forebears had lived in the area since Victorian times and before. Older people who had lived all their life in Exwick were invited to talk. The students gained an understanding of the nature of Exwick life and the place of the school in the community through time.

The Roles of Those Involved

Six months before the project started, I approached several schools in Exeter with the idea for a community production that would involve teachers and school and university students under my leadership. The headteacher of Exwick Middle School, Ken Turner, telephoned me as soon as he received the letter asking me if I would carry it out in his school. When I went to discuss it with him, he intimated that he wished to counter what he saw as the mechanistic and bureaucratic requirements of the recently introduced English National Curriculum for schools with the mounting of an imaginative and challenging activity, engaging significant numbers of his students and staff, that would celebrate the creativity and cooperative energy of education in his school. I accepted.

By enthusiastically embracing the potential of the work, he gave license to the five school staff involved (four teachers and a music specialist) to give time and commitment to the project. A very important factor was that he gave the work priority and status, something he continued to do throughout the months of this cooperative effort. He dropped in on research and rehearsal sessions, openly encouraging everyone in their efforts to achieve an outcome about which they could be proud. His attitude was fundamental to the success of the work, and anyone contemplating similar projects should take this to heart.

The teachers were professionally able, outgoing, inventive, and resourceful. They ranged in experience from a young male recently graduated from my department to a senior teacher who had an important management role in the school. This blend of differing experience was fundamental to the in-service function of the project, allowing relatively junior teachers to work alongside those of considerable experience. The teachers met with me and the university students at the end of most days to review the progress of the work and to plan its development. Within the overall project structure they, as did all involved, had autonomy in deciding how to facilitate the creativity of the students. Significantly, they were able to access appropriate resources that would aid the project, ranging from hardware such as slide or overhead projectors to negotiating with colleagues for the use of rehearsal spaces.

The students understood the nature of the task from the outset. Within the given framework they were encouraged to call on their imaginative powers to create the play that was the expected outcome. They interviewed older residents, transcribed tape recordings, researched archive material, read selected logbook entries, and much more to dig out the intriguing stories that formed the basis of our play. These stories were explored through improvisations, aspects and adaptations of which found their way into the final production. Their work was the engine of the project. They understood the parameters of the exercise, and this knowledge gave their efforts structure and security.

The university students understood that their role was to facilitate the work of the younger students. They guided, advised on, and acted as sounding boards for the emerging work. They also provided leadership and structure when groups were, for example, trying out ideas through improvisation. They were the vehicles for the teaching of specific skills. Some of this teaching was planned at our after-session meetings, while other instruction was an intuitive response to the perceived needs of their group as work was in progress.

My role was to conceive the nature and organization of the project and to ensure the impetus that would establish it firmly in the life of the school.

Significantly, I also had to radiate the professional credibility that would persuade the school that this was a well-conceived, challenging, but realizable project.

Developing the Drama

After one month of curriculum work, the notion of the play was introduced. This involved inferring stories from the intriguingly sparse descriptions of events contained in the school's logbooks (head teachers in British schools are required to keep records of significant daily happenings). Previously, I read all the logbooks for the relevant period and photocopied those entries that appeared to have most dramatic potential. The selection was presented to the students in booklet form in which the entries covered the period 1892 to 1924, when all were written by the formidable headmaster, Mr. Adolphus Herbert Rousham. Groups of students, each working under the guidance of a university student, chose particular entries as starting points for exploration. Here is one from 30 August 1910: "Edith Cornall, Standard III, aged 10 yrs, was drowned in the River during the dinner hour today. She was present at school this morning." An enlarged copy of the extract was glued to the center of a large piece of card. The students then identified key questions raised by the entry. We hoped that speculation about the answers would create convincing detail to clothe the skeletal statements from the logbook. The drowning entry prompted such questions as:

> Who was Edith?
> Where did she live and in what sort of family?
> What was she doing down by the river?
> What time of day did she drown?
> Who was with her?
> How did the teachers find out about the incident?
> Who told the family?
> What was said to the other pupils following Edith's death?
> Were new rules established by the teacher?
> Who found Edith's body?

Individual questions were written around the logbook entry. Each question was explored through discussion and dramatic improvisation, and, as the work progressed, the web of detail grew, each new decision informing subsequent ones. The card served as a working document on which the students jotted salient ideas. The boxes on the card gradually filled with details about Edith and the events surrounding her death.

From the work done on the extract the group decided that Edith was the youngest of five children. Her mother was a widow who took in washing to earn just enough money to keep the family from the workhouse (an institution to which the old and destitute were sent and of which there is a particularly large example standing in Exwick to this day). On the morning of her death Edith had been reprimanded by the teacher for not paying attention to her lessons. Rebelling against this, she persuaded a group of her classmates to leave the schoolyard and, against school rules, accompany her to the nearby river. There, on the bank of the swollen river, they played a game of piggy-in-the-middle with a shoe. When the shoe accidentally ended up in the river, Edith, the strongest swimmer, was persuaded to retrieve it, and, in attempts to do so, she was swept away and drowned. At the start of the afternoon, her friends were too frightened to tell their teacher what had happened. When two of them eventually plucked up the courage to report the incident, the teachers ran to the riverbank where the headmaster, Mr. Adolphus Herbert Rousham, carried Edith's body from the swirling shallows.

These events had power even from the first exploratory improvisations, and the scene that resulted found its way into the play, the students performing it with great skill and sensitivity.

Reconstructing lives and events from the past is a matter of considered conjecture based on a careful examination of available evidence. We could only make an educated guess about the background to the drowning. Our performance triggered additional information. An elderly woman who came to the play remembered, as a young child, Edith's death. According to this woman, Edith had not waded into the river to retrieve a shoe but to recover her hat, which had been thrown into the water. She would not say who had thrown it in—the perpetrator and our informant will carry that secret to the grave. This woman's mother had used the death as a warning to her daughter not to go near the river. The students were very interested in this revelation and were intrigued that their reconstruction had come so close to the truth.

The authenticity of the material with which we were dealing was an important aspect of the work. There was a special moment when the students realized the significance of the logbook records to the environment in which we were researching them and would create our performance. The old school, now a community center, was to be our performance space, and, as we stood in the largely unchanged main schoolroom, I read selected extracts from the logbooks that described physical features that could still be identified. I read, for instance:

> A new curtain rail was fitted to divide the school-room into two.

The students were asked to look for evidence to support this entry and discovered the original brackets that held the rail. This process was repeated with entries such as:

> New cast iron grilles were fitted to the ventilators today.

These grills were still in place, and the students were able to open and close them just as the predecessors they were researching had done.

> Flood water reached to the window sills in the school-room today.

We measured the height of the window sills to understand better the extent of the flooding.

> The cloakrooms near the girls' entrance are to be out of bounds to the boys at all times in future.

We went to the cloakrooms and imagined what sort of behavior had led to this decision.

> Gas burners were removed from the walls today as our new electric lighting was switched on.

The positions of the gaslights were more difficult to find, but intrepid detective work by the students resulted in them discovering imperfections in the paintwork at eight points around the walls, and these sites were designated as the locations.

Events such as these helped the students realize that their play was about the reality of the events they were researching and representing. One girl said to me as we walked back from the old school to the new, "They are a bit like us," and an interesting discussion followed concerning similarities and differences between the lives of students in the early part of the century and their own.

Each of the other groups developed further scenes based on other logbook extracts. A brief description of a Christmas Prize Distribution of

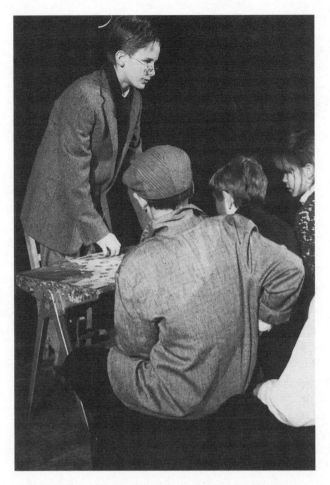

Edith's teacher discovers she has not returned to afternoon school. *When I Was a Boy,* Exwick Middle School, Exwick, 1990. Photograph courtesy of John Somers.

December 1906 gave rise to a scene in which a boy steals a beautiful potted plant from a fellow pupil and wins first prize with it; a second came from an entry concerning the overwhelming victory of a girl in the June 1911 May Queen election and explored the rivalries and jealousies involved; a third sprang from a description of how "Empire Day" was celebrated in May 1905 and depicted the nationalism and pomp involved; a fourth centered on an announcement to the assembled school of the death of Queen Victoria in January 1901; a fifth came from a logbook entry of 1910 that detailed the symptoms associated with scarlet fever, described the treatment current at the time, and mentioned the names of children who were seriously ill with it; a sixth concerned the physical abuse in May 1901 of a pupil by her parents; and the last a detailed description from September 1917 of the planting and harvesting of potatoes in the school garden as part of the national war effort. Each extract was worked on in the way described for the drowning incident, allowing the students to create further sections of the play.

The university students facilitated the exploratory work of the groups during improvisations. The emphasis was on creating an atmosphere in which all group members felt able to contribute to discussion and practical work. Students made sound recordings of their final improvisations, and, with the help of the university students, they transcribed them into a written script, which formed the basis of the performance.

The Performance Framework

The performance of *When I Was a Boy* was achieved by joining the resultant scenes together to form a continuous drama. We needed a linking narrative to give continuity and to fit the individual incidents into a coherent story line. We decided to use a device based on the students' own data collection. We supposed that a group of them who were doing research on local history was going to interview Fred Hannaford, an elderly former pupil of the school, about his memories of childhood. This idea was prompted by the children's enthusiasm for the help given in the research phase by an elderly local historian. Fred was played by Gary Read, one of the teachers involved in the project. The play opened with their arrival at Fred's house. After a brief explanation of why they have come, they are invited into Fred's home, and their questions trigger Fred's reminiscences of his childhood. As he begins to talk animatedly about particular incidents, the scene cross-fades from the living room discussion to an enactment of what he is remembering—a flashback.

This device allowed us to build the apparently disparate incidents into a coherent drama. Transparencies, some of them related to album photographs Fred was showing the students, were projected on to two screens, and live instrumental music, songs, live and taped sound effects, lighting, simple staging, costumes, and props were used to support the drama. Parents were involved in and informed of as much as possible in all phases of the production. Regular newsletters were sent home, giving progress reports and rehearsal information and asking for assistance. They were produced in the style of the play, with appropriate typography and graphics.

Tickets for the performances—all sold out—took the form of a six-teen-page program that contained additional information useful to the audience as context for the drama. Decisions about the content were made by the students. It was desktop-published with the help of the university students. As it went on sale two weeks before the performances, our audience was encouraged to read it before coming to the performance so that they could absorb some of the contextual background to the drama.

On performance nights we mounted an exhibition of artifacts, photographs, posters, and students' work in spaces surrounding the old schoolroom. Live and taped music and effects were played as people looked at this exhibition, and students in character enacted incidents around the old school and in the playground as the audience arrived—skipping games in the playground; an argument between two pupils over a game of marbles; a teacher remonstrating with a pupil, for example. The performances were magical experiences for some. The audience members, many of them coming as a result of special invitations to older residents, were enthralled, and the performance and the exhibition triggered considerable reminiscing by audience members. As much as possible, these memories were collected and added to the school's archive. In addition to the public performances, the play was presented to the rest of the school, including all the teachers, and the pride with which the young actors carried this out was palpable.

Reflections

At the end of the project everyone was left in a state of satisfied exhaustion. The performance had drawn an impressive commitment from each individual, and there was a shared sense of having created something significant both in terms of the drama and its affect on the community of Exwick. Gary Read, teacher of one of the classes involved in the project, commented after it was all over: "It was the drama element which enabled us to make the leap from acceptable class teaching to an educational, social, and cultural experience, the effects of which will remain with those who took part for a very long time." What cannot be wholly evaluated is the value the students derived from the experience, but the pride they felt after the live performance was manifest: "I felt good when we were doing it for my granddad because he went to my school a long time ago, when he was taught in the room where we did the play, and he said it was just like that. It's the best thing I've ever done."[4]

From the evaluations we carried out, it was clear that the students felt that they had taken part in an experience that had touched them and their classmates, the whole school, and the community in general.[5] An evaluation that was carried out during the whole period of the project showed that this was an event of major significance in this community. Follow-up discussions with some of the students two years later bore this out. They had vivid memories of the work and their part in it.

Since doing this project, I have been able to use the approach in other settings. My local village school, Payhembury Primary, has devised two such plays. One was based on the World War I period of the village's history. They too searched the school's logbooks and talked to local residents who remembered the period and its aftermath. The research had a particular poignancy as the war memorial bore the names of the fathers of some of the older residents. The play that resulted was one of the most powerful pieces of theater that I have ever seen.

More recently, in 1997, this school decided to take the world-famous road protest at nearby Fairmile as its topic. A group of tunneling road protesters, led by the mythical "Swampy," constructed a network of underground chambers and treehouses as a protest against a new road that was to push its way through the beautiful Devon countryside. The events were the focus of media attention for best part of two years. Once again the play, complete with original music, was a huge success educationally and theatrically. It also managed to deal sensitively with a topic that split the community down the middle, as some wanted the new road to overcome traffic queues and accident blackspots, while others saw it as an unnecessary despoliation of the environment.[6]

School plays are regular occurrences in British schools. Students are introduced to performance from as young as five, taking part in enactments of well-known stories and Christmas Nativity plays. Older students generally perform standard texts—either musicals such as *Oliver!, Grease,* or *The Boyfriend* or set texts from examination courses. There is some devising within most drama examination syllabi for sixteen- and eighteen-year-olds, but these performances are usually no longer than ten minutes. A full-length play that results from a devising process, in which the students are valued as coworkers, empowers those students. Although it has been several years since the Exwick work was completed, the participants remember it clearly and with pride. When the material that is being dealt with within the drama is drawn from events that have happened within a local community, there is a special power in the drama.

Recently, I went back to Exwick School to develop a drama from curriculum study of the Black Death, a plague that killed between one-third and one-half of Europe's citizens in the fourteenth century. Once again it was set in the Exwick locality. The archaeologist's box we used as a starting point for the drama story contained fragments of documents and other material that had been dug up on the site of the current school. The story that resulted therefore had a particular association for these students.

Schools often form an essential focus within communities. Students are deeply affected by their attendance as they grow to adulthood, and the school provides a shared focus for their parents. Through drama a school can reach out to embrace those that surround its location, and, in acting as storytellers, students reinforce their sense of the community's bonds with times and people of the past. That is a very special responsibility for the teachers but one that can bring huge satisfaction and pleasure.

There were many testimonies to the efficacy of the project. Among them were the tremendous motivation of the young people, the warmth of the response from the community to the performances and associated material, the "buzz" created in the school, and the immense satisfaction felt by the university students in learning how to set up sophisticated learning opportunities in which children are active partners. Widespread conversations with many involved and with members of the community, especially parents, convinced me that the most telling legacy was the strengthened self-image of many of the students. They appeared to have discovered how they could be an essential part of this sprawling community of Exwick. They knew it better through their encounters with the people of the past, and the adults—both in school and in the community—seemed to respect that. The project seemed almost to form some kind of community initiation.

Schools are situated in diverse communities all around the world. At a time when the globalized narratives of the big studios, TV stations, and publishing houses spread around the earth, I hope that this project description might inspire others to see how the making of theater can help define the uniqueness of each of those communities and the individuals who inhabit them.

NOTES

1. For more details of the radio project, see John Somers, *Drama in the Curriculum* (London: Cassell, 1994), 158–87.

2. Ann Jellicoe, *Community Plays and How to Make Them* (London: Methuen, 1987).

3. Benedict Nightingale, in *New Statesman,* 9 October 1985.

4. An Exwick student.

5. Students' open writing tasks and interviews with students and teachers.

6. For more details of this project, see John Somers, "Get the Show on the Road," *Times Educational Supplement,* Music and the Arts Extra, 14 November 1997, v.

Attilio Favorini and Gillette Elvgren

I Sing of Cities:
The Musical Documentary

Despite an abundance of regional drama in the United States, very few plays have addressed the urban experience site specifically and with the documentary severity and reality-driven protocols of the historian. Best known among them are the dramatization of Studs Terkel's *Working* (1978), which, though not strictly site specific, engages city life; Emily Mann's *Execution of Justice* (1984), which is as much about San Francisco as it is about the murder trial of Dan White; and Anna Deavere Smith's *Fires in the Mirror: Crown Heights, Brooklyn and Other Identities* (1992) and *Twilight L.A. 1992* (1993). In a similar vein is Thomas Gibbons's unpublished *6221* (1993), which depicts the protracted conflict between the city of Philadelphia and the radical African-American group MOVE. All of these plays are heavily reliant upon verbatim excerpts from public records and/or interviews conducted by the playwrights. Preceding them, and itself preceded and inspired by site-specific theatrical documentaries created for the Victoria Theatre in Stoke-on-Trent, is *Steel/City* (1976), a musical documentary memorializing the history of the steel industry in relation to Pittsburgh and its environs.[1]

    Steel/City (written by the authors of this essay) was initially performed for the University of Pittsburgh Theater season in March 1976 as part of the university's celebration of the American Bicentennial. That summer it was

---

Gillette Elvgren has written over 80 plays in addition to *Steel/City*. His social action dramas for children and youth deal with everything from AIDS to violence prevention and are being performed by professional companies throughout North America. He headed the MFA program in directing at the University of Pittsburgh and was Staff Director for the Three Rivers Shakespeare Festival. He is presently Professor of Theater Arts at Regent University in Virginia Beach.

Attilio "Buck" Favorini founded and chairs the Department of Theater Arts at the University of Pittsburgh. He also founded the Shakespeare Festival and served as Editor of *Theatre Survey* for 10 years. He has written and produced several Pittsburgh-based documentaries and published an anthology on documentary theater.

revived for a six-week run with most of the original student cast (now paid for their services). The "Today Show" on NBC, produced regionally around the country during that Bicentennial year, broadcast twelve minutes of *Steel/City* live, and the full production was invited to the Smithsonian Institution's Festival of American Folklife in August. The following summer it toured the steel towns of the Monongahela River Valley on a performance barge. The year after, a local professional troupe, the Pittsburgh City Players, performed the third act in senior citizen centers. In the summer of 1992 it was revived for a month's run under the auspices of the Three Rivers Shakespeare Festival, the professional adjunct of the University's Department of Theatre Arts, to coincide with the centennial of the Homestead Steel Strike, which forms the climax of the play's second act. It was also presented at the Carnegie Library in Homestead, a stone's throw from the site of the 1892 strike. The play came to the attention of Lynn Williams, then president of the United Steelworkers of America (USWA), who requested a performance of the third act for the fiftieth USWA Convention in September 1992.

To our delight the play has had broad-based support, as local workers and their families, with names like Davich and Kluz, Zahorsky and Magdic, came to the theater for the first time to see the story of their city and their clans represented through music and spectacle and especially to hear their own stories told by actors—word for word.

As a documentary, *Steel/City* partakes of a dominant modality in twentieth-century art. Reality-driven visual arts, film, television, theater, and even opera have never been more prevalent. In the theater, documentaries have ranged from the propagandistic (Erwin Piscator's *In Spite of Everything* [1925]) to the celebratory (*Quilters* [1982]) to the liturgical (Dan Berrigan's *Trial of the Catonsville Nine* [1971]), and their subject matters have been as diverse as the Italian-Ethiopian War (*Ethiopia* [1936], the first "Living Newspaper"), the Holocaust (*The Investigation* [1965]), and the Anita Hill–Clarence Thomas hearings (*Unquestioned Integrity* [1993]).[2]

Alongside the documentary tradition runs a more community-based modality that is regionally indigenous and but often less reliant on the primary source materials favored by the strictest documentarians. For example, while the Federal Theater Project spawned hundreds of plays by local playwrights of largely local interest, they were generally not reality driven, as were the Living Newspapers such as *One Third of a Nation*. At the same time, the Living Newspapers were national rather than local in character.[3] In England regional documentaries may be distinguished from the community play movement, whose chief contemporary proponent is Ann Jellicoe. The

contemporary play movement, in Jellicoe's formulation, employs a professional playwright, director, and designer to create a script of local historical
interest. Amateurs in the community are the performers and producers.[4]
Such practices recall the populist theater ideals of Romain Rolland, community pageants, and Soviet mass spectacles celebrating the Revolution.

   Steel/City derives from the British documentary tradition that under-
went a remarkable resurgence with Joan Littlewood's *Oh What a Lovely War*
in 1963. While most of the early British attempts at documentary theater
(*Busmen* [1937], *Crisis* [1938], *Uranium 235* [1946]) were directly influenced
by the American Living Newspaper, Littlewood enjambed documented statistics and photographic projections of actual battle scenes with the nostal-
gia-laden conventions of music hall to stage a confrontation of memory and
history—ultimately forcing the audience to look through all the false
romanticism and the gushing, tearful patriotism at the face of war.

   In the audience of the West End production of *Lovely War* one evening
in 1964 sat Peter Cheeseman, the energetic director of a small, professional
repertory company occupying the Victoria Theatre in Stoke-on-Trent.
Inspired by what he saw, Cheeseman immediately started work on a musical documentary of his own entitled *The Jolly Potters,* which told the history
of the potteries industry in Stoke-on-Trent and the "five towns," an area
noted for its exquisite Royal Doulton, Wedgwood, and Spode china. Its
initial success generated yearly docudramas at the Victoria dealing with such
topics as the history of the local rail line (*The Knotty*), the federation of the
six towns (*Six into One*), the life of Hugh Bourne, the founder of Primitive
Methodism (*The Burning Mountain*), the history of Staffordshire during the
Civil War (*The Staffordshire Rebels*), down to the recent *Nice Girls* (1993),
which celebrates three women who occupied a coal mine in the region to
oppose its intended shutdown.

   In 1971–72 Gillette Elvgren spent close to a year in Stoke studying
Cheeseman's approach to documentary drama, its relationship to the community, and its realization via the theater-in-the-round staging at the Victoria. Cheeseman's achievements, which have been unaccountably ignored
by theater historians, throw light upon the Elvgren/Favorini script of
Steel/City as well as on its mounting at the University of Pittsburgh in 1976.

Musical Documentaries at Stoke-on-Trent

The imperative of giving voice to the voiceless, of reclaiming for history the
forgotten past of an unheeded community, is strong in the musical docu-

mentary tradition. In this regard labor history has been a rich source of material, from the lives of Canadian farmworkers to Pittsburgh steelworkers and Staffordshire railroaders. The documentaries produced by Cheeseman at the Victoria,[5] like the documentary plays of John Arden and Margaretta D'Arcy, John McGrath and 7:84 Scotland (notably *The Cheviot, the Stag and the Black, Black Oil* [1973]), are often driven by political commitment and contemporary event. But his documentaries nevertheless retain a provincialism in the best sense, being plain spoken, workmanlike, and rich in regional history. The enactment of making or crafting that so enlivens the American musical documentary *Quilters* in performance was anticipated by twenty years in Cheeseman's work. Furthermore, among such practitioners Cheeseman stands out for his radical historiography and longevity.

The distinct character of the Stoke documentaries derives not only from their highly specific and localized subject matter but also from their creation at the hands of a group rather than a single author as well as the self-imposed rule that "the material used on stage must be primary source material. . . . If there is no primary source material available on a particular topic, no scene can be made about it."[6] Typically, the primary sources of the Stoke documentaries include both archival material and oral histories recorded from local individuals with special knowledge of dramatized events.

Like ancient rhapsodes (from *rhaptein,* "to sew together," and *oide,* "songs"), Cheeseman is concerned with creating an audience of listeners:

> One of the things wrong with our society is that too few people have a sense of history. We have lost in our society the sort of natural structure whereby old men pass down knowledge to the young in a community. . . . In this sort of atmosphere it seems to me that our obligation is to show people . . . that they [do] not stand alone in the present but are part of a historical perspective.[7]

Conceiving of his work as a channel or conduit from the past to the present, Cheeseman goes so far as to maintain: "You can't write a documentary—it's a contradiction in terms. You can only edit documentary material."[8] While refusing to accept authorial credit for the plays created under his leadership and leery of the encroachment of ideology, Cheeseman does not deny that the inevitable arrangement, editing, and abridgment involve subjectivity and personal judgment. But he does intend that the compositional pains taken by his company inoculate his productions against political narrow-mindedness and naïveté. The rule of primary source materials, he asserts, "ensures that a multiplicity of voices are heard"; the collective creation "tends to preserve the contradiction of viewpoint inherent in every historical event."[9] In historical writing, observes the French historiographer Michel de Certeau, the plurality of original sources is diminished to the singularity of the historical discourse because the citations do "not assume the form of a dialogue or a collage."[10] Cheeseman, however, does his utmost to preserve the plurality, and the Victoria documentaries show the marks of accrual and encrustation—again like the work of the rhapsode. Indeed, it is difficult to say where Cheeseman is drawing on the collective memory of the people of Staffordshire and where he is adding to it.

Music and song play a key and unique role in the Stoke documentaries. Sometimes the shape and character of the developing script are strongly influenced by the presence of musically talented cast members, as was the case with Ben Kingsley and *The Staffordshire Rebels* or Jeff Parton (a local folk singer) and two actresses, Gillian Brown and Anne Raitt, and *The Knotty*.[11] Parton lent a particularly balladic feel to *The Knotty,* which jostles along from its opening song like old rolling stock of the North Staffordshire Railway:

JEFF (*unaccompanied*): There's a story I will tell you, if you'll listen to
   my song,
I hope that it will please you, and it will not keep you long.
I'll tell you how the railway through the Potteries was planned,
How the N.S.R. built and changed the face of the land.

(1)

The Knotty encompasses more than one hundred fifty years of railroad history, reckoning the profits and losses to the Staffordshire economy and environment along the way. The songs often supply narrative links. Cheeseman's method permits a departure from primary source materials in the invention of song lyrics, on the grounds that songs stand apart from the action, though traditional melodies or new ones composed in traditional musical language are preferentially employed. The script is politically aware without ever being doctrinaire—perhaps owing to its collective creation— and keeps its own seriousness in perspective, as in an early sequence in which the conventions of nineteenth-century melodrama are used to put the "villainy" of land grabbers in quotes. Even when Cheeseman commits his theater to political issues that are still developing as he chronicles them, the Stoke documentaries are "far from pious exercise[s] in raising radical consciousnesses and reactionary hackles," as Benedict Nightingale wrote of *Nice Girls.*[12]

Cheeseman's mature documentary style can be well illustrated by the script of *Nice Girls,* which reached the stage in a matter of months after the events it documents. The four women whose heroics inspired the script attended rehearsals and are pictured in the playbill, leading the actresses who portrayed them to the site of the action or adjusting a gesture for authenticity. As with all of his documentaries relying on oral history, Cheeseman is at pains to represent the actors of his theater as workers laboring side by side with other working members of the community.

The play opens with Bren, Brid, and Gina, who occupied a shaft of the Trentham Colliery, and Rose, who remained outside and directed communications, recounting the origins of their plan: "So shall we go from there, and then work up when it actually came about."[13] Spoken by the actresses in direct address to the audience, the scene not only establishes an instant intimacy in the theater, but it gathers to itself metonymically a larger communal context: the four actual women whose words are repeated verbatim; the unseen and unheard interviewers from the New Vic; Cheeseman himself, who (though he claims no authorship) transcribed the tape recordings and compiled the script; the thirty-year tradition of documentary making at Cheeseman's theater; and the oral history telling traditions of the region. *Nice Girls* thus tells two stories: that of the occupation of the mine shaft and that of the story made about the occupation.

The former is spiced with a good-natured tension between men and women over what to do about the imminent closing of the mine. The tension is introduced in scenes of overlapping dialogue in the thick Midlands accent and in songs created for the production:

> The first time I went speakin' at a meetin'
> My husband said "I think you've done enough
> Things can go too far love, next time you'll want the car
> You're gonna end up common, loud and rough."
>
> ("Caravan," 9)

It is resolved with a hilarious episode in one of the final scenes. Rose thinks Gina's husband, Mick, is going to ask for Gina to abandon the occupation, when he takes Rose seriously aside. She prepares herself for bitter disappointment with a brusque "Right, duck, what's the problem?" to which Mick anxiously replies: "Is it all right if a put coloured in with whites in the wash? A'm really worried about it" ("Final Scenes," 1). Mick is further flummoxed when Rose wants to send him to buy Tampax for the women, who have all begun menstruating together in tense solidarity during the occupation.

GINA: Well 'e doesn't know where they go even.

ROSE: Probably stick 'em in 'is ears. . . . All right Mick, a'll come up with yer. 'E's 'ad one trauma with the washin. A conna give 'im two.

("Final Scenes," 2)

Disarming candor thus alternates with unflinching righteousness. The women can laugh over shopping for toilet paper— "BREN: What if they've only got that paper stuff, you know, that orrible . . . / ROSE: Oh no we couldn't av that on the bum" ("Wilkinsons," 1)—but their determination carries them forward. Gina suffers from claustrophobia, Bren from vertigo, and they end up by accident in Shaft 2, not knowing they are just yards away from the control room, which, had they pushed onward to it, would have allowed them to shut everything down ("Occupation," 6). Nonetheless, these and other comic mishaps in no way undermine the staunch courage of the women nor detract from their heroism, which is all the more inspiring for being commonplace and unvarnished. Indeed, the honesty of the story allows the rousing songs uniting the women with their sisters protesting wrongs in Wapping and Belfast ("We Are Women, We Are Strong" and "Nice Girls") to do their inspirational work without a tinge of self-importance.

The story *about* the story, in fact, speaks to the women's courage in portraying themselves so self-deprecatingly and to the theater's courage in preserving their honesty. At the end the president of the mineworker's union, Arthur Scargill, asks the women to abandon the occupation. They had anticipated striding out in triumph but

BREN: Instead of saying

ALL (*sing*): We are women, we are strong—

BREN: We go

ALL: Yes Arthur (*all crying*)

GINA: It was terrible. After all the shouting and aggressibleness.

BRID: I want to re-write history. We're not 'avin that.

("Final Scenes," 12)

But, of course, neither Cheeseman nor the women do rewrite history, which reaches the New Vic stage shorn of the formal niceties that normally accompany "history" plays. Instead, Cheeseman marshals community resources to craft plays with the purpose of "giv[ing] utterance to the voice of the community itself" and of "reflect[ing] the life of the district in such a way that we, its voters in a democracy, really believe that we are important and that important things happen here."[14]

Nice Girls was performed within six months of its originating events, and *Fight for Shelton Bar* (1974), which opposed the shutdown of a local steel mill, was so current that the script was constantly altered in the course of its run to accommodate the most recent developments in the negotiations. But, as the originating events recede in time, it is not so much the memory of the "fight" that endures (at least for the observer from beyond the community)[15] but, rather, the memory of something broader and deeper. It would be accurate to say that, although the topics of Cheeseman's documentaries change, they share a single action: the making of the Midlands. Thus, while the railroad in *The Knotty* may indeed stand metaphorically for the road men travel, its uniqueness is a metonym for the making of Stoke. By the same token both the steel-making process and the negotiating process documented in *Fight for Shelton Bar,* like the play-"wrighting" process that documents them, are less illustrations than instances of the craft that gives the region its character. Collectively, the Stoke documentaries take on a sedimentary nature. They enact a living archaeology of the region, uncovering more and more of the past vertically (i.e., back in time) and horizontally (i.e., synchronically across the diverse human activities the land has sustained). And the spectacle of an audience of listeners, encircling the actors in the Victoria's theater-in-the-round, present at a poesis both collectively and anonymously created, itself recalls the ancient image of the rhapsode.

Play Making and Steel Making

When theatrical history tellings are collaboratively created and when the memories they are based on are generated by a circle of narrators and witnessed by a circle of listeners, their social function as co(m)memorations becomes more obvious. Historiographically sophisticated pieces, such as Cheeseman's, make no effort to suppress the playwright's role in shaping the material. Indeed, perhaps under the influence of postmodernism and contemporary historiography, playwrights have increasingly been drawn to staging openhandedly the encounter between history and memory as a way to revise majoritarian versions of the past, to put a human face on history, and to reconsider the capacity of the theater to make veridical truth claims.

While such lofty aims may have been faintly in the sights of the authors of *Steel/City,* we were in 1974 scrambling to climb on a bandwagon that was about to leave. Plans to celebrate the American Bicentennial were well advanced, and the University of Pittsburgh invited faculty members to suggest ways in which the academic community might contribute to a dialogue about local and national history. Elvgren, fresh from his research experience at the Victoria, proposed the writing and production of a Cheeseman-style documentary targeting some aspect of local history. The idea met with skeptical indifference from the faculty of the Theater Arts Division, except for its head, Favorini.

In retrospect the skepticism of the faculty may have been well founded. Neither of us was a Pittsburgh native, and neither had attempted anything but journeyman playwriting. Nonetheless, the idea appeared to serve departmental and institutional goals. The demise two years previously of the Pittsburgh Playhouse, then the only professional theater in the city, had left a void on the local scene that the University of Pittsburgh Theater had successfully begun to fill. A small but growing cadre of Ph.D. candidates in the department could be drawn on for research assistance. A pair of annual fellowships for graduate actors funded by the Charles E. Merrill Trust encouraged us to nurture dreams of more ambitious productions. And the chancellor of the university, Wesley Posvar, had proclaimed an urban mission for the institution.

Over the next year Elvgren (with Favorini assisting and attending) conducted a graduate seminar in documentary theater. The outcome of the seminar was to focus our attention on the steel industry as a topic for the projected documentary. (Among the many other topics considered, most promising was a dual history of the Pittsburgh Pirates and Homestead Grays baseball clubs.) Ambitious plans, requiring considerable financial support and involving the participation of significant segments of the university community, were conceived—and cut back. Some money was raised both from local steel companies (but not U.S. Steel) and the Steelworkers' Union—though both sides remained standoffish, as we could assure neither party of the play's sympathies.

That was because we didn't know ourselves what we would end up with. One of us was Republican, religious, and conservative, the other Democrat, agnostic, and liberal. One had been a union member, one not. Although we didn't realize it at the time, our differing orientations fostered the multivocality that lends the most successful documentaries historiographical credibility.

The latitude we allowed ourselves in developing the script taxed the generosity and patience of the production team. We had spent most of 1975 gathering primary source material (e.g., excerpts from George Washington's diary describing his discovery of the site of future Pittsburgh; the oath sworn by steelworkers initiated into the nineteenth-century forerunner of the

USWA), imagining potential scenes the material could support, and parceling those scenes out to one another for writing, critique, and rewriting. While we accepted Cheeseman's discipline of employing only primary source materials, we interpreted the condition more liberally than he would have at the time. For example, we created a scene using verbatim excerpts from the writings of Andrew Carnegie, Herbert Spencer, and the preacher Russell Conwell in which the three appeared to be talking with one another—although, so far as we knew, they were never actually in the same room together. Also during this time we secured a musical director/composer, Frank McCarty, from the Music Department and assembled hundreds of slides, for we knew that we wanted an efficient way of projecting the changing face of the city. Crucial to this process was our primary research assistant and dramaturg, graduate student Karen Byrne.

Going into auditions at the end of the year for a March 1976 opening, we had about two-thirds of the script written. The first act resembled a romantic epic, chronicling the settlement of Pittsburgh and the rise of the steel industry and its ambiguous genius, Andrew Carnegie. The second act felt like a tragedy, though with a strongly melodramatic cast. It staged the growing gap between rich and poor expressed in the burgeoning conflict between the industry and the people it consumed. That brought the story up to the failed Homestead Steel Strike and the founding of the United States Steel Corporation. As for the third act, Elvgren had a vague idea: to re-create the picnic, hosted by retired Jones and Laughlin steelworkers, that we had attended earlier in the year.

Byrne and Favorini were skeptical. The script we had developed thus far had a Brechtian, presentational feel, and we couldn't see how the picnic scene, which Elvgren wanted to carve out of oral history tapes (some recorded at the picnic and some transcribed from archives in Pittsburgh, at Penn State, and in Harrisburg) could jibe with the rest. Elvgren persisted and one day shortly before the start of rehearsals brought in a draft of the third act literally pasted up from bits of scores of transcripts. Favorini grudgingly admitted the material had dramatic potential. He revised the paste-ups to form a rough chronology of immigration, unionization, and domestic reminiscence from 1900 (where the second act ended) to the present and wrote three presentational flashback scenes to bridge the stylistic gap. We had a play.

But we didn't yet have a production. The initial indifference of the faculty was erased from memory by hundreds of hours of generous and heroic work. Partly because the script was so late in taking final shape and partly to serve the presentational idiom in which it was conceived, set designer

Henry Heymann devised a neutral playing area ringed with movable, double-tiered steel scaffolding, flanked, backed, and topped with projection screens. Costumer Heidi Pribram endured with aplomb the appearance and excision of characters during the rehearsal period. (Egregiously, we wrote in nonspeaking roles for our four young children, whom long hours away from home had made virtual strangers to us.) Our colleague, theater historian and mandolin picker David Rinear, was pressed into service as actor and member of the stage band. The cast, anchored by Emmy nominee and Merrill Fellowship holder William Wendt, and steelworker and part-time student Don Marshall, stuck by us through myriad script changes, large and small. They accompanied us to steel mills and talked with some of the people we had interviewed.

The outcome was more than gratifying; it remains perhaps the most moving and enriching production experience of our professional lives. Although reviews from the two major newspapers were mixed (one strongly favorable, the other not), word of mouth swiftly turned the event into the biggest hit the University Theater ever had. The *Pittsburgh Post-Gazette* on 19 March 1976 followed up its favorable review with an editorial. ("The Bicentennial here doubtless will have nothing with a truer Pittsburgh flavor than *Steel/City*. . . . Particularly effective is the third act, laid at a steelworker pensioners' picnic." "Ah, ha!" exulted Elvgren.) United Press International put a feature story on the worldwide wire, and the Smithsonian's field research coordinators, in their letter inviting us to the Festival of American Folklife, observed of *Steel/City:* "It asks its audiences to honestly confront their shared community experience, to see where they fit in a living continuum of history and tradition, and to understand the truth of what has been gained, what has been lost."[16]

For the revival during the summer we pared forty minutes off the script, dropping a framing device (an "alchemist" who had opened the play with a medieval formula for steel making), all the material prior to 1794, when Pittsburgh was incorporated as a borough, and a balladeer character. We had come to see more clearly that our subject was the alloy formed by the industry and the people, signified by the slash in the play's title. Funds raised from the Pennsylvania Humanities Council allowed us to augment the performances with panel discussions and town meetings conducted by a score of university faculty, union organizers, clerics, and community leaders on issues raised by the script: ethnic identity, local environmental regulations, labor history, and family storytelling. After each performance the audience was invited downstairs for coffee and cookies in the Social Room, where the cast chatted with audience members and encouraged them to tell their own family or workplace stories. Tape recorders on every table recorded the interviews for possible future use.

We enjoyed the positive response. But we were most thrilled with the reception accorded the play by its cocreators, the steelworkers and their families. We invited all of the pensioners from the picnic to attend the production on opening night in March. We hadn't seen them since the previous August.

It had been something to observe these men, mostly in their seventies, stripped to the waist, their aging frames still barrel-chested and bearing testimony to the strength it must have taken to survive ten and twelve hour days in the mills, six days a week. In this male-dominated milieu the women fixed salads and stuffed cabbage, while the men played roulette, threw horseshoes, and downed jiggers of slivovitz (plum brandy). After a while, the slivovitz began to do its work, washing away the unease occasioned by the tape recorders we had placed among the picnic tables. Stories were shared, their painful elements sometimes buried in bluster:

> RUDY: In them days throughout the mill you had mules.
> MIKE #2: In them days, if that mule broke his leg or something, you'd get fired. They could kill a man over there. That was nothin'. But it cost you a lot of money to buy a mule.
> STEVE: It ain't like in the movies where a man falls in a vat of steel, a ladle of steel, and they bury that.
> SAM: They don't bury that goddamn thing.
> FRANK: Where you gonna bury two hundred and fifty tons of steel . . . no way.
> ALL: Nah—no—I never heard of that. (*Laughter. But with an edge to it.*)
> STEVE (*bitter*): Sanitation gang. They called it the crippled gang. When a man got injured on the job, they'd put him on a lower job and also cut his pay. I wasn't bitter over the pay. I just couldn't go anywhere.
>
> (86)

We tried to leave intact ethnic or sexual tensions:

> FREEMAN PATTON (*angry*): How could my father be in sympathy with the strike? What did he know about the strike, what did he know about unionism? West Virginians, Polish, Hungarians, anything Caucasian got into the union, but no blacks. All my dad

knew was work. Anything that deprived you of your work he hated. Hunkies got in the unions but no blacks.

WALTER KLIS (*reacting to* PATTON *and advancing on him*): I was called a hunky a number of times. In those days I did resent it. I'd tell a guy off. I didn't care who he was.

ROBERT MILANOVICH (*stepping between* PATTON *and* KLIS; *changing the subject*): If you didn't know how to fight you didn't go out to play. (KLIS *and* PATTON *disengage.*)

JOHN MAGDIK: They should have sunk all the boats bringing Hungarians over here. (*To his wife.*) Then I wouldn't of had to put up with you. (*Laughter from the* MEN.)

MARY MAGDIK: The best thing you done in your life—you was nothing until you married a Hungarian! (*Loud laughter from the* WOMEN.)

(92–93)

Although we had explained at the picnic we were doing research for a play and urged all the pensioners to attend, we doubted they would come. We thought it would be just as difficult for them to imagine a play crafted from their words as it had been for some of us. The ephemeral art of the theater seemed a far cry from the fruits of *their* labor: the bridges they crossed every day, the rolled-steel automobiles they used to cross them. But evidently Sam Davich, who had for many years been the organizer of the picnic, took it upon himself to organize this outing, too. Sam was feeling a little deflated on opening night because, following his fourth heart attack, he was going to have to give up smoking. Eager to get his reactions, we tracked him down in the lobby after the first act and asked how he liked the show. His hands searched aimlessly for a cigarette that wasn't there. "It's okay." We think he was being polite. After the second act we checked in again with him. Warming to the union sympathies evident in act 2, he was more positive. But after the third act he was glowing. He couldn't stop shaking our hands. Well, we wondered, were we going to be invited back to the picnic next year. "No," he replied. "The old man who owns the farm, he's too sick to have the picnic, and his wife says it's too much work. There isn't going to be any more picnic. But that's alright," Sam smiled at us. "The picnic, it's there, on the stage, and it will be there forever."

We think it is true, as Mike Zahorsky told us, that even the principals involved didn't fully comprehend what all those years working and struggling in the mills were about until they saw it onstage. Mike had been president of the Steelworkers' local in Aliquippa, once a thriving steel town on the Ohio River, and his stories were among the most colorful we encountered. The same stories, his niece told us after a performance one night, had occasioned rolling of the eyes among the younger generation of the Zahorsky family. Not anymore. "I never understood my Uncle Mike until tonight."[17]

1992: A Postscript

In 1976 the public voice of the steel industry, both labor and capital, had been optimistic about its future in Pittsburgh. It would be twelve years before John P. Hoerr's *And the Wolf Finally Came* would chronicle the long history of shortsighted decisions that banished Big Steel from the banks of the three rivers. But, in the kitchens and parlors of the steelworkers' homes where we had set up our tape recorders, we often heard a different story. Sometimes old union organizers would ask us to turn off the recorders, as they deplored the deterioration of a work ethic, lamented the ignorance of the young about the fight for workers' rights, and spoke sadly of shrinking union membership rolls. But enough was spoken on the record so that the third act of *Steel/City* hit a prophetically elegiac note.

By 1992, the centennial year of the Homestead Steel Strike, a generation of Pittsburghers to whom its heavy industrial past was almost unknown, was coming of age. It seemed like a good time to revive *Steel/City*—particularly since the professional resources of the Three Rivers Shakespeare Festival could be marshaled to provide a more mature and skilled cast than the script had previously enjoyed. We decided to produce *Steel/City* without revision, partly because the play itself had by now become a document of the city's past.

The revival was not a satisfying experience. In a cruel irony a strike (or lockout, depending on one's point of view) shut down both major newspapers prior to the start of the festival's season, enveloping *Steel/City* and our other offerings that year in a cloud of silence. Although reviews in a faxed arts letter and in alternative newspapers were good, the revival failed to draw the crowds of its previous incarnation.

Furthermore, the play seemed oddly different in 1992 from what it had been in 1976. It had somehow become harder and colder. We could attribute only part of this feeling to changes in the staging (Elvgren again directing). For one thing the final scene of the second act depicting the formation of the United States Steel Corporation took on a darker tone with the introduction of a strong image (derived from the cartoonist Thomas

Nast) of J. P. Morgan as an octopus, literally hooking his tentacles onto his competitors. For another, while many of our student actors in 1976 had been sons and daughters of steelworkers and had either met some of the characters they portrayed in the third act or knew someone like them, the professional actors of 1992 had no such personal associations. We think that lent their portrayals a harsher, more Brechtian quality. But even more crucial, we subsequently concluded, were the changed social conditions.

In 1976 the elegiac note had been struck in the context of "Look! We've come through!" Dwindling membership rolls might be only temporary. Memories of the organizing struggle were *living* memories; many of the heroes still walked among us. But in 1992 the third act had begun to sound like a dirge rather than a paean, and the union leadership asked us to make cuts for the performance at the Steelworkers' Convention, to eliminate what they heard as "belly-achin'." We complied.

Our experience with two productions of *Steel/City* sixteen years apart made us sharply, and doubly, aware of the complexity of the "hermeneutic conversation"[18] joined by researchers, their subjects, and their audiences. Each production was imprinted with its distinct historicity, and so was each picnic. We even suspect that, if we could ask the same questions of the same pensioners today, their memories would offer different answers. So in what sense is the picnic, our template of Pittsburgh, "there" on the stage? The picnic became *our* picnic, an experience shared by our theater and its audience, instancing a kind of artistic citizenship worth repeating. In the original playbill we put it this way: "Despite its authenticity, *Steel/City* claims neither neutrality nor objectivity. Our point of departure was a determination to follow wherever the facts would lead us; our journey through the city's history left us keen to tell of what we have seen."

NOTES

Parts of this essay originally appeared, in different form, in the introductions to *Steel/City* and *Voicings* (ed. Favorini).

1. Gillette Elvgren and Attilio Favorini, *Steel/City* (Pittsburgh: University of Pittsburgh Press, 1992).

2. See the introduction to *Voicings: Ten Plays from the Documentary Theater*, ed. by Attilio Favorini (Hopewell, N.J.: Ecco Press, 1995).

3. "Though each region was encouraged to develop living newspapers on local problems, few were produced. The national office of the FTP wanted full documentation and proof they were factually accurate." See *Free, Adult, Uncensored: The Living History of the Federal Theater Project,* ed. John O'Connor and Lorraine Brown (Washington,

D.C.: New Republic Books, 1978), 14. Among produced Living Newspapers, only *Ethiopia* relied exclusively on primary source materials.

4. Ann Jellicoe, *Community Plays: How to Put Them On* (London: Methuen, 1987).

5. Cheeseman recently moved his company to the New Victoria Theater in New-castle-under-Lyme.

6. Peter Cheeseman, "Introduction" to *The Knotty*, "Created by the Victoria Theater Company working from historical research conducted by Peter Terson under the direction of Peter Cheeseman" (London: Methuen, 1970), xiv.

7. In an interview with Gillette Elvgren cited in the introduction to Elvgren and Favorini, *Steel/City*, xvii.

8. Ibid., 7.

9. Cheeseman, "Introduction," xiv.

10. *The Writing of History*, trans. Tom Conley (New York: Columbia University Press, 1980), 94.

11. Cheeseman, "Introduction," xii–xiii.

12. *Times* (London), 22 October 1993.

13. *Nice Girls* is unpublished. The typescript is page-numbered scene by scene, rather than consecutively.

14. From "The Role of the Vic Musical Documentary," MS, in the theater's *New Vic Documentary File*, 7.

15. Within the community it may well be different. Outcomes do matter: Shelton Bar was eventually shut down, but the Trentham Colliery is making a go of it in private hands. Irrespective of winning or losing, however, for the Cheeseman and the New Vic "to fight is to win," as the lyrics to "Nice Girls" proclaim.

16. Letter to the authors from Robert McCarl and Robert Porter, 1 April 1976.

17. *Steel/City* was followed in 1980 by *Hearts and Diamonds* (written by Favorini and directed by Elvgren), which applied the musical documentary mold to the intertwined stories of Lillian Russell and Willa Cather, both of whom spent crucial decades of their lives in Pittsburgh. But the most long-lived and extensive town-gown theater collaboration was the Three Rivers Shakespeare Festival, founded in 1980 and featuring for the next 15 years large numbers of Pittsburgh actors in its summer seasons. Touting its local origins from the outset, the festival's logo deliberately evoked the logo of *Steel/City*, substituting for an orange sun rising behind the cityscape the gleaming Shakespearean pate of the Droeshout engraving.

18. This coinage, based on Gadamer's notion of a hermeneutic circle, is from Eva McMahan, *Elite Oral History* (Tuscaloosa: University of Alabama Press, 1989), 5.

Harry Elam and Kim Fowler

Dreams of a City:
The East Palo Alto Project

East Palo Alto is an ethnically diverse, low-income community located one mile from Stanford University. During the first half of the twentieth century it was the hub of a thriving agricultural and floricultural industry. Since 1920 East Palo Alto has been a migration point for individuals and families seeking a less expensive alternative to the larger cities in the San Francisco Bay Area. The post–World War II growth of the surrounding cities and towns negatively impacted the then unincorporated area, which lost land and resources to its more powerful neighbors. The resulting economic decline led to the accompanying social problems of unemployment and crime. In 1992 articles in newspapers across the country as well as stories on national television news programs labeled East Palo Alto, California, the "Murder Capital of the Nation." Forty-two murders occurred that year in this small community of twenty-five thousand residents, the most per capita in the country. And so the media descended upon East Palo Alto to tell the story of another poor urban community in the United States ravaged by crime and violence. After sensationalizing the image of East Palo Alto, the television cameras and media outlets quickly departed. Consequently, they failed to report on how the community on its own initiative took corrective

Harry Elam is Christensen Professor for the Humanities, Director of the Introduction to the Humanities Program, Director of Graduate Studies in Drama, and Director of the Committee on Black Performing Arts at Stanford University. He is author of *Taking It to the Streets: The Social Protest Theater of Luis Valdez and Amiri Baraka* (1997) and coeditor of *Colored Contradictions: An Anthology of Contemporary African American Plays* (1996) and *A Critical Anthology: African American Performance and Theatre History* (2001).

Kim Fowler is the Program and Fundraising Associate for the Committee on Black Performing Arts. She has served as Assistant Director of Grants for the Arts and as Executive Director of Theater Artaud in San Francisco. She is a management consultant to arts organizations as well as a singer, writer, and performer who has authored solo and collaborative performance pieces for theater and dance.

action. Due in large part to neighborhood watch and citizens action programs, drug sales and the murder rate dropped precipitously. In 1995 only
one murder occurred in East Palo Alto, and yet this tale of recovery and survival, of self-determination in the face of great odds, has gone largely
untold. To many outside of East Palo Alto the stereotypical representation
of the city as a dangerous urban drug zone laden with crime, guns, and
urban gang violence persists.

The Stanford Committee on Black Performing Arts (CBPA) formulated the East Palo Alto Project (EPAP) as a way to combat these misper-
ceptions of East Palo Alto through theatrical performance. The CBPA envisioned EPAP as a collaborative "research-to-performance" project, joining
residents of East Palo Alto with staff, students, and faculty at neighboring
Stanford University and creating an alternative vision of the East Palo Alto
community. The project, which the CBPA eventually entitled "Dreams of
a City," sought to capture just that: the past and present dreams of the city's
residents for and of their community.

The CBPA based "Dreams" on the research-to-performance model
developed by the Rites and Reasons African-American theater project of
Brown University.[1] For more than twenty years Rites and Reasons has created theater projects through an interactive process: a research component
investigates particular issues, and then a commissioned playwright collabo-
rates with a director and a group of actors to dramatize the results of that
research. Adapting the Rites and Reasons formula, over a three-year period
Stanford students, staff, and faculty worked with East Palo Alto community
residents to research the history and evolution of East Palo Alto. Two
nationally renowned playwrights, Cherríe Moraga and Charles "OyamO"
Gordon, were commissioned to turn the research into two original one-act
plays. These plays, featuring casts of students and community residents, premiered in East Palo Alto on 10 November 1995. The following week they
played at Stanford University for six performances. The performances drew
sell-out crowds in both locations.

The achievement of this project, however, should not be measured as
theater projects in both the academic and commercial arenas are too often,
in terms of the final product, the critically reviewed performance. The
CBPA never expected the productions, cast with a mixture of students and
community people, experienced and inexperienced actors, to be viewed
through a professional lens. While the intent was to produce well-crafted
theater, the project has a broader social goal that parented its artistic elements. With this project the interactive learning process leading up to performance was truly as significant as the final sell-out performances. The pro-

duction process facilitated new understandings of East Palo Alto and forged new bonds of communication between the university and the community. The actual engagement of participants in the preparations for performance affected their perceptions of and relationship to East Palo Alto as well as to Stanford University. By examining the production process as an integral element in this "theater of community," our essay will explore how community theater can produce new configurations and definitions of community and can function as a critical element in achieving social change.

And yet, it would be naive to assume or even arrogant to pronounce that one performance project could alter ingrained perceptions of East Palo Alto. Consequently, our objective in this essay is to examine not only the achievements of "Dreams" but to discuss the deficiencies of the project as well. Moreover, we, the authors, recognize that we must investigate the politics of our own position. As cultural critics such as bell hooks note, a critic's own location and subjectivity, his or her position in relation to the subject of inquiry, are critical elements in his or her interpretation.[2] The notion of a disinterested, objective analysis is inherently flawed. Rather, we mediate past and present events through our own present circumstances. Where we position ourselves or are positioned informs how we read that text and in turn how we are read as critics.

Accordingly, our roles as operatives within the East Palo Alto Project must be acknowledged and interrogated, as it will figure into our analysis of "Dreams" (Harry Elam was and is the director of the CBPA and also directed the one-act play by OyamO; Kim Fowler, the Program and Fundraising associate for the CBPA, was the key fund-raiser for the project as well as a key contributor to and coordinator of EPAP). As representatives of Stanford and the CBPA, we were project insiders. We were also outsiders to the community of East Palo Alto. Neither of the authors has ever resided within the community. Our close involvement over three years with the project affected our own perceptions of and relationship to East Palo Alto, our concepts of community and community service projects, and our understanding of the collaborative process of performance as a catalyst for social change. Our shifting outsider/insider status not only influenced our participation in the project but will play a significant role in our examination of the process and the project. Through this critical analysis we hope to provide insight into the age-old and oft-debated questions of whether and how artistic performances can affect actual social conditions.

One of the tenets of current community service pedagogy affirms the idea that community service must address an actual need within the community. Too often community service volunteers have virtually viewed themselves as missionaries and naively imagined their projects as acts of ennobled altruism. Such an outlook, however, reflects the desires of the community service volunteer rather than those of the community residents and as a result does not foster an atmosphere of cooperation. The CBPA began EPAP wary of being perceived by the community as another unwanted research effort or service program that Stanford forced upon East Palo Alto. In the past Stanford students and faculty have used East Palo Alto as a laboratory to conduct social studies or as the basis for thesis projects and community outreach initiatives. Many times such usage has benefited the Stanford affiliates more than the East Palo Alto community. As a result, some East Palo Alto residents have acquired a certain reticence toward involvement with Stanford. Contrary to this history, the goal of EPAP was to create a truly collaborative process that reflected the community's own voice.

The process of achieving community involvement, however, was not always successful. At the project's inception the CBPA decided to set up a meeting in the community with residents to brainstorm about the project. The meeting was held at the East Palo Alto Senior Citizens Center, a centralized location, and was set for early evening, a time we hoped was convenient for people with families. The CBPA sent an invitation for this initial meeting to every household in East Palo Alto. Despite these "personal" invitations, only two East Palo Alto residents attended. Clearly, mass mailings from Stanford were not the way to generate community interest and involvement.

After this failed community meeting, the CBPA decided on a different strategy. We targeted certain community activists and organizers involved with the arts, culture, politics, and education in the city to be part of a task force. In organizing this task force, the CBPA purposefully sought representation from the various ethnic groups that reside in East Palo Alto. East Palo Alto is approximately 40 percent African American, 40 percent Latino, 9 percent Pacific Islander and Asian, and 1 percent white. The EPAP Task Force also included Stanford faculty, staff, and students and fluctuated between ten and thirty members through the duration of the project. It operated as the project's board of directors and advisors and became a vital component of and guiding force for the project.

From its initial January 1993 meeting to the production dates in November 1995, the task force met at least monthly. The frequency of meetings increased as necessitated by the demands of project programming. For the Stanford members of the task force as well as for the East Palo Alto residents, participation in the task force was a learning process. Task force gatherings facilitated new interactions between Stanford and East Palo Alto residents. Each group gained greater insight into each other and the workings of both Stanford and East Palo Alto. Involvement on the task force taught Stanford members that the goal of the project to serve the East Palo Alto community needed to supersede all else. Accordingly, when the CBPA director felt because of financial and technical reasons that it would be easier to premiere the shows at Stanford and not in East Palo Alto, the task force reacted decisively. Overwhelmingly, the members believed that a site within the city needed to be found for the premiere. They maintained that, if this project truly were to be a community project, then an East Palo Alto opening was critical. The task force compelled the director to understand the rationale for opening this project about the community in the community. As a result, the shows premiered in East Palo Alto.

New configurations of community and continuing negotiations of the divides between Stanford and East Palo Alto remained integral to the workings of the task force and the East Palo Alto Project as a whole. The key player on the task force and facilitator of this process of evolving community awareness and group consciousness was Elena Becks, the administrator for the CBPA. Becks, a lifelong resident of East Palo Alto and a community activist, functioned legitimately as an insider within both communities. She bridged differences and helped to mediate discontinuities.

With the assistance of Becks and funding from the deans of Humanities and Sciences, the CBPA in 1992 conducted a detailed search for a playwright. The objective of this hiring process was to find a playwright who could interface effectively with the East Palo Alto community, who had an established professional reputation, and who was comfortable working in the research-to-performance mode. The search committee, consisting of Becks, Elam, and Fowler, read published plays and scripts and conducted phone interviews with eleven published playwrights from around the country. Initially, the CBPA planned to hire only one playwright, specifically an African American. Since the principal agency involved with production was the Committee on Black Performing Arts, we originally felt that selecting an African-American playwright would be in keeping with the CBPA's programmatic philosophy. We also believed, however, that the playwright needed to be able to respond to the specific populations of East Palo Alto and the city's changing demographics. From the late 1980s into the early 1990s the population of the city of East Palo Alto dramatically shifted from being 90 percent African-American to being 40 percent African-American and 40 percent Latino. One critical goal of the project was to reach out to the growing Latino population of the city, and one way to do this was by locating a playwright who spoke to that constituency and who could address issues of bilinguality. As a consequence, two playwrights were chosen: Charles OyamO Gordon, an African American, and Cherríe Moraga, a Chicana. Each would create an original one-act play for the project, and the plays would be performed in tandem.

In their professional work and in their personal philosophies, Moraga and OyamO demonstrated a commitment to working with communities of color and with using theater as means to social awareness and change. Both OyamO and Moraga had strong professional resumes and experiences with the research-to-performance method. Prior to accepting the EPAP play-writing commission, OyamO had completed the critically acclaimed play *I Am a Man,* which examines the sanitary worker strike in Memphis, Tennessee, 1968, just before the assassination of Dr. Martin Luther King Jr. OyamO had studied historical records and interviewed former strikers as preparation for writing the play. In addition, he had previously worked with Rites and Reasons at Brown University on two separate research-to-performance projects. Bay Area playwright Moraga had based her award-winning play *Heroes and Saints* on historical research and personal interviews as well. This piece dramatizes the oppositional response of migrant workers to pesticide poisoning and systematic oppression in the community of McFarland, California. It sets the action in the fictional town of McGlaughlin, California.

In the fall of 1992, at the same time as the CBPA conducted the playwright search, it initiated the research phase of the project. The purpose of the research phase was to gather all the materials available on the history and development of East Palo Alto as a resource for the playwrights. Yet one of the difficulties for the CBPA in the research phase was finding social science faculty willing to supervise this process. Rites and Reasons research operated under the auspices of Professor Rhett Jones, a historian. The Stanford CBPA did not have the advantage of such a relationship with a faculty member experienced in historical research and as a consequence had to turn to a variety of alternatives, including the employment of a diligent core of student workers. Consequently, the research phase involved not only the collection of historical archives and recorded interviews but also a process of learning how best to assemble these materials.

In the summer of 1993 the CBPA hired students to audiotape oral histories of both long-term and newly arrived residents as background material for the plays. The CBPA purposefully employed Spanish-speaking students to interview Spanish-speaking residents. Questions for new residents, including immigrant families, generally focused on what brought them to the area, how their families existed economically, how they felt the town was changing, and their hopes and fears for the future. The students questioned longer-term residents about the general evolution of and their interaction with life and politics in East Palo Alto.

The CBPA also employed a student as an archivist. This student researched information available in surrounding libraries, from neighboring Menlo Park to San Francisco, thirty miles north. The archivist also went about the process of collecting all the Stanford materials on East Palo Alto. Over the years Stanford students had written dissertations, thesis projects, and term papers on aspects of East Palo Alto's social, political, and cultural developments. The CBPA's archival objective was to house these materials all in one central space and then to make them available to the playwrights as well as to future researchers from Stanford or the community.

As the research continued into the fall of 1994, we gained another student volunteer to EPAP, Lily Batchelder, a political science major, working on her senior honors thesis. She gathered information on the process on the long and involved struggle over incorporation, which East Palo Alto voters narrowly passed in 1987. Batchelder's research provided important background information for the playwrights. In addition, her thesis won the Firestone Award and the Golden Grant at graduation in 1994 for best senior honors thesis in political science.

Unlike the Stanford faculty, staff, and East Palo Alto residents involved in EPAP, the participation of students in the project was by necessity much more transient. Many, like Batchelder, graduated before the premiere of the plays in the fall of 1995. Accordingly, for them the process leading to production was clearly more significant than the final product itself. Most significantly for these students, the process brought interactions with community members not as research subjects but as collaborators on the project. As a consequence, this interaction compelled a reconsideration of the traditional roles of researcher and researched.

In addition to the employment of student researchers, the CBPA also initiated new academic courses that developed research materials. Anthropology professor Paulla Ebron taught a seminar, "From Research to Performance," in conjunction with the CBPA and the Urban Studies Program in the spring of 1994. This course taught students how to conduct oral interviews and other ethnographic research methodologies. It also examined how these oral interviews might serve as the basis for artistic collaboration. Ebron offered the course while playwright Charles OyamO Gordon was in residency. OyamO participated in the class and detailed for the students what he as playwright expected from gathered research materials. The audiotaped interviews from that class became a valuable resource for the project. During the fall of the next academic year, 1994–95, the other com-missioned playwright, Cherríe Moraga, taught a course entitled "El Sexto Sol," which sent students into the community to collect oral histories. Their oral interviews then became the basis for topical skits, or "actos," developed by the students and presented at an East Palo Alto community forum, "Comida y Conversacion," directed specifically at the Latino residents of East Palo Alto.

Perhaps the most significant research tool available to the playwrights was the collection of videotaped oral interviews gathered in conjunction with the production of a documentary video on East Palo Alto. This docu-mentary, the brainchild of Michael Levin, a video producer with Academic Software Development, a subsidiary program of the Stanford University Library, became a critical outgrowth and complimentary auxiliary of the theater project. In the fall of 1993 Levin approached the CBPA with the idea of developing a half-hour video documentary about the history of East Palo Alto as a component of EPAP. His original plan was to base the video documentary on oral histories of town residents, augmented by archival footage and documentation. The video, however, required much more than was first anticipated and eventually became the most time- and resource-consuming component of the EPAP project. The hour-long doc-umentary premiered in East Palo Alto in October 1996. To date the docu-mentary video *Dreams of a City: Creating East Palo Alto* has been shown on Public Broadcasting Service television in San Jose, California; at the Roxie Theater in San Francisco, California; at the national conference of the Council of Foundations in Washington, D.C.; as well as the Cinémathèque Festival in Los Angeles, California.

Despite the costs of the documentary video, its value to the creation and production of the plays cannot be overstated. While the plays presented views of the community and its history through the eyes of two playwrights and the representation of student and community actors, the documentary presented actual residents speaking in their own voices. Levin, with the assis-tance of community members and students, conducted over eighty hours of video interviews. He also gathered footage from local television archives and early videotapes and films of East Palo Alto's history. In addition, pho-tographs, flyers, and other archival materials were collected by town resi-dents. All of these materials proved vital to the playwrights in crafting their plays. The playwrights also used the videotaped oral interviews as the basis for characterizations as well as historical information. Throughout the pro-duction process Levin and the production crew held viewings of raw video footage. Eventually, the CBPA, in coordination with Levin, presented a rough cut of the video to the community. The documentary brought additional viewership, energy, and resources to the play productions.

As they began the writing phase of the project, the playwrights as well as the project organizers faced significant questions: How do you transform social and historical research into drama? How much should the plays created be a reflection of the playwrights' vision? Does the need to reflect the community's voice and to capture the history of the community constrain and even censor the playwrights? Moraga and OyamO confronted the problem of dramatizing the research materials quite differently. OyamO's play, *Dancing on the Brink,* was episodic in structure, while Moraga's approach in *Circle in the Dirt* was more linear. Moraga created a narrative based in the present realities of East Palo Alto that featured historical flashbacks. The citizens of the Cooley Apartment complex discuss the approaching demolition of the buildings and remember back to East Palo Alto's past. OyamO, on the other hand, set his play in the past, at an Muwekma Indian village. The Muwekma were the original residents of the area now known as East Palo Alto. When the Muwekma chief has a vision of the future, the play flashes forward and traces the evolutionary progress of East Palo Alto to the present day. Given a directive from the CBPA to focus more specifically on the Latino population of East Palo Alto, Moraga made *Circle* purposefully bilingual mixing in Spanish and touches of Chicano slang, *calo,* that were not present in *Brink.*

Despite these differences, there are also strong parallels in the two one-acts as well. Both playwrights concern themselves with the multicultural makeup of East Palo Alto, and the plays feature characters from a variety of ethnic groups. The central issue in *Brink* and *Circle* is land and the question of how land use, abuse, usurpation, and annexation have affected the lives of East Palo Alto residents past and present. Critical to both works, then, is a message of self-determination and self-definition. The playwrights reflected differing community responses to the problems East Palo Alto faced and urged its residents to search for common solutions. The plays encourage East Palo Alto citizens to take pride in their heritage and also to take the responsibility upon themselves to work for change and growth.

The decision to shape the plays as correctives rather than just celebrations of East Palo Alto reflected the social vision and theatrical philosophy of the playwrights within the scope of the project. Still, these authorial decisions were shaped by the process, negotiated at times through collective reworkings of the scripts. All along the way to production the plays were read and critiqued by the CBPA administrative staff as well as members of the task force. Both Moraga and OyamO took part in the "Community Forums" on the project and used them to mold their work. The three forums held became staged reading workshops for the playwrights' work that provided vehicles for interaction between the community and the playwrights.

The first forum was held in May 1994, during OyamO's residency at Stanford. He and Moraga created and presented preliminary sketches of their final work. At the second forum, held in December 1994, Moraga presented *actos* from students in her drama class as well as a revision of her initial EPAP play sketch. This forum was targeted to the Latino community and was facilitated by a Chicano member of the EPAP Task Force. The third forum was geared toward youth. Becks and Walter Matherly, the project's community liaison, contacted groups such as the Teen Home and enlisted the outreach capabilities of the Black Male Rebirth Project, a program of the local nonprofit Community Development Institute. Moraga presented a staged reading of the final draft of her play and again received feedback. The main concerns from the audience were the racial breakdown of the cast (the reading was done mostly with Latino actors playing across racial lines) and the omission of certain historical political movements. Moraga spoke of the challenge of creating a script from an overwhelming amount of material and the need to narrow the focus in order for the play to work dramatically.

The value of the community forum approach was evident with each succeeding forum and script revision. And yet, because of financial limitations, the forums primarily benefited Moraga. Funding prohibited flying OyamO in from Michigan for repeat visits. Immersing Moraga's play in the community in a variety of settings made it more representative of the community, without compromising its critical impact. The fact that Moraga lives in the San Francisco Bay Area and could easily commute to Stanford and East Palo Alto facilitated her ability to participate in all phases of EPAP. She was present during the research phase of the project as well as during the casting and rehearsal process. Moraga even added a character and adapted roles within her project play, *Circle in the Dirt,* after observing the talents of a Chicano father and his family who had come to the East Palo Alto community audition.

For OyamO, an associate professor at the University of Michigan, the involvement in the process was somewhat different. He did not have the luxury of proximity. OyamO was in residency at Stanford for four weeks in the spring of 1994, where he conducted interviews and analyzed research materials. During his residency at Stanford OyamO, like Moraga, became actively involved with the East Palo Alto community. In June 1994, however, he had to return to Ann Arbor, Michigan. He did not come back out to East Palo Alto until the fall of 1995 for the premiere. As a consequence, OyamO wrote his script from a critical distance, unlike Moraga, without the possibility of observing rehearsals and receiving immediate interactive feedback. OyamO stayed in phone communication with the director, Elam. He also received written critiques of his drafts from the CBPA and members of the task force. Interestingly, despite their disparate writing experiences, both playwrights remarked during the post-play discussion following the premiere performance about how much they felt a part of East Palo Alto and how they believed that they carried the community with them.

The actual process of rehearsal leading to the performance brought new problems as well as new configurations of community. Each play had a different director. Elam directed OyamO's *Dancing on the Brink,* and Roberto Gutierrez Varea directed *Circle in the Dirt* by Moraga. Each cast featured a combination of Stanford students and East Palo Alto community residents. Some cast members had never acted before. For some community residents this production marked their first experience at Stanford. For some Stanford students it represented their first foray into East Palo Alto. For other students participation in the production reaffirmed their commitment to community service within this ethnically diverse community. Because performers in each play held jobs and had families, issues of child care entered into the rehearsal plan. Unable to find or afford evening child care for the duration of the rehearsal schedule, parents brought their children to rehearsals. By default the stage managers became child care providers and the rehearsal space, playgrounds and child care centers. As a consequence, concentration during rehearsal was often problematic as the needs and volume of children could supersede those of the director and the rehearsal process. For those who had never previously been onstage the process of learning lines also presented new challenges. As a result, both of the playwrights had to change lines and cut speeches in order to accommodate the abilities of the performers.

Education and community building were critical to the rehearsal process. The actors learned acting techniques, but they also discovered more about East Palo Alto history and heritage. Early in the rehearsal schedule the cast for both plays viewed a first cut of the East Palo Alto documentary video. Later on, Ohlone Indian tribal leaders came to rehearsal to instruct the actors in authentic tribal movements and lore. The Ohlones are the descendants of the Muwekmas, the first residents of East Palo Alto. Members of the casts were also given research tasks to carry out on their own. All of these activities educated the cast about and affected their own perceptions of East Palo Alto.

Richard Schechner has theorized that "the essential ritual action of theater takes place during rehearsals."[3] Throughout the rehearsal process the directors actively engaged the Stanford student actors and East Palo Alto community actors in a dialogue about the issues expressed within the plays. Through these "rehearsal rituals" they all became increasingly aware and sensitive to the social agenda of EPAP. Whether or not this sensitivity and educational indoctrination made a difference in the final performances is debatable. What these activities do attest to is the significance placed on process.

The premiere in East Palo Alto occurred in the gymnasium of Cesar Chavez Middle School. The gym's daily usage by the school severely limited the time for load-in of the set and for technical rehearsals. The shortness of the technical rehearsal period combined with the actors' problems of memorization, concentration, and unevenness of stage experience made it difficult for the two directors to produce a coherent production and to follow through on their directorial concept. Compromises and adjustments had to be made. Directors and designers simplified and even eliminated lighting and sound cues as they all spent long evening hours in Cesar Chavez gymnasium.

Despite these disadvantages, the rehearsal and production processes did have special rewards. They instigated new interactions and interchanges in which students, Stanford Drama production staff, and community residents all participated. For all involved these processes were educational. They learned not simply about the making of theater but, even more important, about the politics of difference. In order for the production to work, differences needed to be respected and accepted. Community members and Stanford students came together in support of their united goal. At times the rehearsal process produced moments of what anthropologist Victor Turner terms *communitas,* "a spontaneous effervescence and feeling of wholeness."[4] At the technical rehearsal for *Circle,* as the hour drifted past one o'clock in the morning, well past the bedtime of the children and working parents involved, the cast did not despair, nor did they grow agitated; instead, they joined together in song and with a spirit of togetherness.

And yet, as Turner notes, the production of *communitas* is ephemeral. While those participating in the process may have felt a spirit of togetherness during the process of rehearsal, was this spirit sustained after the production ended? Did these Stanford affiliates and East Palo Alto residents continue to commune after the production? Were the perceptions each group had of the other changed forever? We have no qualitative data to provide concrete answers to these questions. Still, we would argue that the participation alone is critical indicator of and a key factor in assessing the efficacy of social change theater. Participatory involvement of the actors and production staff signified agreement with the overall strategy of the community theater performance.[5] This participation bolstered the performers' belief in the objectives of the project. And for some this produced a lasting value.

Concern with the lasting value of the project also produced other strategies in EPAP aimed at incorporating audience participation and involvement. The task force and CBPA did not want the performance to be viewed as an end in itself. They intended for the project to have a continuing postproduction impact. Vital to the EPAP plan for audience involvement and lasting significance were the incorporation of post-play discussions. Every performance of the plays in East Palo Alto and at Stanford was followed by post-play discussions. These discussions provided a vehicle for the audience to talk about the plays and the issues they raised and to address the representation of the East Palo Alto community in each piece. The CBPA and the task force selected different members of the community and members of the Stanford faculty active in East Palo Alto to lead these interactions with the audience. The reason for the facilitation was to ensure that the discussion focused on the issues presented rather than on critiquing the performers and the aesthetics of the performance. With these controls in place the post-play discussions allowed for a public dialogue on the concerns addressed in the plays and provided the opportunity for a broad cross-section of viewpoints to be expressed. A wide range of comments came forth, from critiques to reminiscences to appreciation for new insights. At one performance in East Palo Alto a middle-aged black man, a longtime resident of the community, noted that he had known little about the Latino community in East Palo Alto before seeing *Circle in the Dirt*. The spectators' involvement in the post-play discussion demonstrated their investment in the production and served to indicate the effectiveness of the community theater production and its messages. The post-show discussions, consequently, were as important as the plays themselves.

We must note that the responses to and participation in the post-play discussions at Stanford were markedly different from those in East Palo Alto. The differences in these interactions illustrate that the physical environment and cultural context for a performance can affect the production of community theater. In East Palo Alto, where the audience consisted largely of community members, post-play discussion participants spoke from experience and with vested interest in community. At one Sunday matinee in East

Palo Alto the majority of the audience stayed for the discussion, which lasted well over the allotted forty-five minutes. The conversation evolved from a critique of problems raised within the performance to an examination of community issues and a determination of action steps required by the community.

At Stanford the audiences consisted largely of people from outside the community. Some came to find out more about East Palo Alto; some came to be entertained. As a consequence, the questions during the post-play discussion tended to be more informational than probative. A sense of critical distance was more evident in the Stanford post-play discussions. Still, one of the most effective discussions at Stanford involved student volunteers from the Stanford Haas Community Service Center. Student service leaders facilitated the discussion, which focused on how best to implement service that truly served the community.

Perhaps one of the best indicators of the impact of the plays is their continued visibility in the community since the original production dates. Owing to the dedication of a group of East Palo Alto citizens, funds were raised to produce professional quality videotapes of both plays. These were then aired on Stanford's local television station, and over seventy-five copies have been distributed to individuals and organizations in the community. They also have become part of the resources available to teachers in concert with a curriculum guide that is being developed for the video documentary.

In her essay "Art on My Mind" bell hooks writes of the significance of defamiliarization in art "as a process [that] takes one away from the real only to bring us back to it in a new way."[6] The theater of the community process, of which EPAP is representative, is a concrete example of this process. The "real," in this case, a wealth of individual and communal historical data, provided the basis for a process through which participants, researchers, interviewees, and task force members interact, artists reflect and interpret, and audience members experience anew the "real."

In one instance artistic process not only reflected but anticipated reality. Early in 1995 a vibrant member of the task force, East Palo Alto resident and activist "Brother Anthony" Morris, died of AIDS. His death had a significant and indelible impact on the processes leading to production. The memorial services for Brother Anthony brought together his family and friends as well as other East Palo Alto residents and task force members, including Stanford staff. Participation in this event made all gathered feel a part of a community united in the loss and the tragedy of AIDS. The task force determined that the premiere of "Dreams" would be dedicated to Brother Anthony. In creating *Circle in the Dirt,* playwright Cherríe Moraga

Circle in the Dirt by Cherríe Moraga. East Palo Alto Project, co-produced by the Committee on Black Performing Arts and the Drama Department, Stanford University, California, November 1995. Photograph courtesy of Alex Stewart.

modeled a character on a videotaped interview of Brother Anthony. Moraga's character in the play, Reginald, eventually dies of AIDS. Unbeknownst to Moraga, who did not serve on the task force and never interacted with Brother Anthony, this theatrical creation reflected his real life.

No one involved with any part of this process of developing theater from the community came away without having some perception of what was "real" about East Palo Alto altered; no one came away untouched by an insight, incident, or individual relevant to the town. If theater as a change agent is a goal, this process provides a rewarding and productive means of achieving it.

NOTES

1. For more information on Rites and Reasons, see Rhett Jones, "Politics and the Afro-American Performing Arts in Environmental Perspective," *Callaloo* 5, no. 12 (May 1982): 175–94; and "Finding the People's Ideology: Black Theatre at Brown University," *Black Scholar* 10, no. 10 (1979): 17–20.

2. See bell hooks, "Is Paris Burning?" *Black Looks* (Boston: South End Press, 1992), 145–56; See Stuart Hall, "New Ethnicities," *Black Film / British Cinema* (London: ICA Documents 7, 1988), 27–31.

3. Richard Schechner, *Performance Theory* (New York: Routledge, 1988), 104.

4. Victor Turner, *The Anthropology of Performance* (New York: PAJ Productions, 1986), 133.

5. For further discussion of audience participation and efficacy, see Harry J. Elam Jr., *Taking It to the Streets: The Social Protest Theater of Luis Valdez and Amiri Baraka* (Ann Arbor: University of Michigan Press, 1997).

6. See bell hooks, "Art on My Mind," *Art on My Mind: Visual Politics* (New York: New Press, 1995), 4.

Jan Cohen-Cruz

Speaking across Communities: The Liz Lerman Dance Exchange

The Liz Lerman Dance Exchange production of *Shehechiaunu* exemplifies the growing movement among professional companies not only to make work with nonprofessional collaborators but to do so beyond the boundaries of any one particular identity group: to speak across communities, as it were. Choreographer Lerman, artistic director of the company, grounds the piece in her favorite Jewish prayer, Shehechiaunu, or Sustenance, usually translated as: "Blessed art thou, Lord our God, Ruler of the Universe, for keeping us alive, sustaining us, and permitting us to behold this day." She thus honors a collective source of her own Jewish identity. But she ties that history to those of other people, first by retranslating the prayer, "Isn't it amazing that, given all our different histories, we've gathered together at this moment?" She further extends her circle by creating about as multicultural a company as exists in the dance world. Finally, she seeks out audiences that are just as diverse and involves them in the production from early exploratory workshops right through to finished performances. Integrating dance, storytelling, characterization, and music to explore a century of interactions, overlaps, and frictions among various ethnic, racial, religious, and sexual legacies in the United States, *Shehechiaunu* pries community-based performance beyond the identity politics with which it has been so fiercely connected for a good twenty years.

In her 1993 keynote address to the Association for Theatre in Higher Education, Anna Deavere Smith acknowledges the importance of professional artists of the 1970s and 1980s who "tried to start theatres of their own

Jan Cohen-Cruz is an Associate Professor of Drama at New York University, where she directs the theater component of a project placing young artists in community-based internships. She is on the faculty advisory committee of the new Tisch School of the Arts Center for Art and Public Policy. Her writing on related subjects includes *Playing Boal: Theatre, Therapy, Activism,* coedited with Mady Schutzman; and *Radical Street Performance: An International Anthology.*

that were about *them*. . . . Asian American . . . Black . . . Gay . . . Latino
. . . Women."[1] But she attests that the time has come to educate artists who
can speak for all of us or at least for more than themselves, challenging professional artists to move out of their own cultural "fortresses" and find the
"specialness" in the world around them. Lerman has facilitated scores of
community-based workshops for nearly thirty years, in addition to her professional projects. She has more recently been puzzling over how to present
community revelations to audiences beyond the makers' own realm,
including professional contexts. Both Lerman's and Smith's projects are
variations on what I am calling cross-community professional art.

Even without the crossover element, balancing professional and community-based commitments is both compelling and problematic. Close
contact with communities offers artists the opportunity to expand and grow
humanly, keeping the horizons of their world broader than their former circle of acquaintances. For professional performers, facilitating workshops
breaks the passivity that sometimes comes from not being the director of a
company. Community connections provide outlets for artists' political and
social visions, too, such as the sense of injustice that not everyone has equal
access to art making. Communities, artists, and audiences alike have much
to gain from material developed cross-culturally. But how do artists balance
this dual agenda in terms of fund raising, time, and energy? Having introduced art to a community, what happens when the artist leaves? How do
artists balance facilitating the artistic expression of others with their own
personal creative desires? How do artists negotiate professional standards
with the radically democratic spirit of community art? And what about the
artist's public identity, given the tendency for community work to be seen
as amateurish? I turn to *Shehechianu* to consider such questions.

Lerman started the project off, as is her way, with a series of questions,
explored through movement and storytelling in three contexts: within her
company, in short workshops (a half-day to two weeks) with interested
people around the country, and at an extended residency in Portsmouth,
New Hampshire. The questions included: What is the meaning of the
prayer in relationship to your own cultural history? What has sustained you
in the face of the wounds you have suffered? Are you to remember and be
burdened by those memories or forget and move on? Do you see other
choices? After developing the theme in these three formats, the piece was
shaped by Lerman's highly trained dancers under her direction. So *Shehechianu* is "community-based" in several senses—as an expression of the company, of specific geographic communities (particularly Portsmouth), and of
the United States itself, even with its history of conflicting subcultures.

Unlike the performers in some models of community art—such as the ubiquitous "of the people, by the people, and for the people"[2]—the dancers in Lerman's company are professionals. They join through auditions, not by simple membership in a given population. Lerman is clearly looking, however, for movers who can do more than her technique. The company members who helped create *Shehechianu* range in age from their twenties through their sixties and are Puerto Rican, Filipino, African-American, Jewish, Catholic, gay, and straight. The diversity of the company mirrors the diversity of the audiences that Lerman is committed to reaching. Indeed, the *San Francisco Chronicle* described the Dance Exchange as "an opportunity to see America dancing." In contrast to orthodox community arts' emphasis on participatory democracy, here we have an instance of representative democracy; that is, the company members serving as representatives of a range of ethnicities, races, religions, and sexual preferences.

Lerman needs this broad cross-section of dancers for the themes she is drawn to artistically. In *Shehechianu* the process of creation featured an exploration of multiple American legacies, relying on the full participation of company members. Their research included not only archival work at libraries and museums but also extensive family interviews. Rome Quezada, for example, investigated the impact on his Filipino family of the display of Filipinos at the 1904 St. Louis World's Fair soon after the United States had won the island as war booty.[3] The prayer weaves through the piece, reflecting the dancers' personal histories. At one point, for example, it is intoned by African-American Gisel Mason. "Given our different histories," she laughs bitterly, as she bends and picks . . .

While Lerman is not bound to the "of the people, by the people, and for the people" model of community art, elements of direct democracy are nonetheless present. One level takes place within the company. Lerman describes her choreographic role as "creating an environment in which people can do their best work,"[4] in contrast to her "own rotten experiences in other people's dance"—being told exactly what to do. As a choreographer, she observed that the creation improved when the dancers participated in the process of making it. Indeed, a keystone of community-based art is that the people performing it have a unique and illuminating relationship to the material created.

Another level of direct democracy takes place with nonprofessional artists. For *Shehechianu* Lerman instituted the Sustenance Project to provide a way for people all across the country to examine what sustains them, via workshops, conferences, courses, and residencies. She did so because, in her experience, sometimes people who have not been asked to think about things, particularly via movement, do so in fresh and interesting ways. Her job as the professional artist in those settings is to see and hear the bits of fresh insight when they arise. Thus, community expression constantly enriches the Dance Exchange as a professional company.

In Portsmouth, New Hampshire, where the most extensive community work was done, a range of workshops was set up, including one for officers' wives, middle school students, Ballet New England, Isle of Shoals Board Company personnel, a local color guard, and an "All Come Artists" group open to any interested residents. Lerman believes in the power of art to help people work through the issues her questions raise, not just reflect on them. She refers to the work the company did in Portsmouth as a literacy project "because it's letting a community know something about its history . . . [and] how it is to use art in their life, or why certain artistic principles might be useful to somebody in their life." For example, the workshops manifested the loss of tradition in Portsmouth. With the decline of the shipping industry there was also a decline of accompanying ceremonies featuring marching bands and parades that had brought the community together in expressive and meaningful ways. The Dance Exchange thus revived an experience of group expressivity; time will tell if it continues. The residency also led area residents to examine repressed controversies about the yard's role in the environment, the economy, and military-civilian relations. On a personal and political level the differing views—of a contingent opposed to the shipyard (which is a nuclear plant) on environmental grounds and a group in favor of it as the number one employer in the region—were articulated and heard. And, besides its experiential value for the participants, some of the texts and movements developed there were integrated into *Shehechianu,* as I will describe.

The Dance Exchange started work on *Shehechianu* with the prayer itself, both the shape of its Hebrew letters and their meaning. They talked with Hebrew scholars about the root meanings of the words. Different translations offered different movement ideas; for example, one word of the prayer, *vihichianu,* can be understood as "caused us to reach" or "caused us to endure." Company member Rome Quezada explored its meaning: "My first impression of [these] Hebrew letters was that of uncontrollable energy that seemed to bounce right off the page."[5] This he translated into swirling and pulsating movements emerging from that moment of his own life, itself characterized by both reaching and having to endure. Another company member, Jeffrey Gunshol, explained: "I was drawn to the letter that represents Adonai, which means 'Lord' . . . [and] has two hooks near the top. So I am jumping into the air while hooking my fingers and knees."[6]

Signaling a relationship between cross-community professional art and postidentity politics, Jewish symbols are not assumed to speak only to Jewish audiences nor expected to be performed only by Jewish performers. Rather, forms and stories from one cultural experience are made available to a diversity of people to explore. This is a familiar goal in community art, in which affirmation of each group's cultural identity is often the basis for exchange. But, as the old saying goes, "the lyfe so shorte, the crafte so long to learn." Often the community art of one group, which works internally because of the participants' familiarity with it and one another, is not potent to "outsiders"; they just don't speak the language. Perhaps everyone *could* be an artist, but reaching a larger audience entails some mastery of craft. Extending such work beyond the community of origin may depend on a role for professional artists.

Dancer Celeste Miller[7] makes a distinction between community-informed and community-based art. She acknowledges the value of input from "social workers, teachers, nurses, health care workers, administrators, electricians, mothers and others who work with me on projects. But there is a difference. I eat, breathe, sleep, die over this art stuff." Miller speaks of community art as "a consciousness on the part of the artist that the artistic work has the potential to meaningfully impact the human condition . . . challeng[ing] the artist to envision a wide range of potential for these activities."[8] Lerman agrees with Miller's sentiment but says she would not make the distinction in the same way, seeing her role as "remaining open to see the beauty of what people without art training do and make it work." Indeed, Lerman distinguishes between "creative process" and "art making." The former is the free exploration of themes at which time the artist tries to make people feel relaxed, comfortable, and confident and simply encourage the flow of material. The second phase is the editing and shaping of the material into something that can be articulated to an audience that was not part of the creative process. Some community projects stay in the first phase.

Lerman is currently focusing on how to bring community groups into the second phase. She sees a fallacy in the idea that only in community art do artists worry about hurting participants' feelings in the editing process. Rather, she finds it to be a touchy area in professional companies with collective processes as well. In both cases the director/choreographer contends with conflicting loyalties—to the work of art, to the participants, to the audience. Lerman believes that artists need to get tough without being mean, to use their editing skills without being unduly authoritarian.

In *Shehechianu* Lerman's company used its command of craft to shape the responses garnered in the three contexts. Like a coat, the prayer took the shape of its wearers, referencing both the multicultural and multigenerational company as a site "where many different histories come together" and the United States itself. The piece evolved into a triptych zooming in first on the 1904 St. Louis World's Fair, then on critical midcentury moments in two U.S. cities, and, finally, on *this* moment, at the edge of the millennium.

Part 1, "Faith and Science on the Midway," opens with an evocative sense of beginnings. The characters appear all in white. It is the beginning of the piece, the beginning of the century. As "Faith and Science" unfolds, the company represents the fair's attractions, within which are embedded stereotypes of cultural "others" displayed for their entertainment value that continue to (mis)shape perceptions of different groups to this day. These images also bespeak the personal histories of the dancers. Rome Quezada does the dance of a Filipino on the midway, naked except for a white cloth covering his genitals. Judith Jourdin, as an exoticized Palestinian Jewess with a large fake nose, tells the audience about the letters in *Shehechianu* as her two assistants dance a hoochie-coochie. Peter Dimuro plays a congenial white anthropologist, measuring the head of the pygmy Otabenga, a particularly painful display. Andy Torres, a dark-skinned Latino, plays a carnival barker selling cure-all potions but moving in the physical "Stepin Fetchit" language of nineteenth-century minstrelsy, which has plagued the representation of African Americans since before the Civil War.

Juxtaposed against these large racial and cultural representations are small, detailed movements—"The essence of life is in smallness." We are thus brought into the uniqueness of the individual dancers, beyond their cultural markers. Is this also a clue to the bizarre mosquito character, bearer of malaria, the first in a series of plagues including cancer and AIDS that scourged the century? Why is this bearer of bad news so cute, too cute, so round and lyrical? The piece contains a certain amount of mystery. The company thus resists the equation that accessibility to broad audiences means aesthetic simplification. But Lerman does include a guide for looking at art in the program when the company performs for audiences new to dance.

Part 2, "Bench Marks," starts in the ship building town of Portsmouth, N.H., after World War II and later shifts to Washington, D.C.—not insignificantly, the Dance Exchange's hometown and most frequent performance venue—also in the 1950s. We witness moments in which core elements of human sustenance, namely love and work, are in social crisis. The Portsmouth section focuses on the latter, by way of the collective history of workers and their families. Indeed, fourteen minutes of *Shehechianu* are accompanied by an audiotape culled from Portsmouth stories. Images, too, are drawn from former shipyard workers. In one segment the dancers are lying on the floor doing work gestures they learned from ship builders as, on tape, a Portsmouthian recounts a story about twelve generations of her family who worked there. Peter DiMuro confirms: "Portsmouth feeds our art. We are pushed to explore new metaphors. You don't put it together in the same way because you have different ingredients."[9]

The D.C. section was a breakthrough for the company, which for years had been trying to connect with the local Washington, D.C., gay community. Here, depicting a time when gays and lesbians in the U.S. government were hunted out and ejected from their jobs, the piece suggests complications between work and love. One section danced to the tune of "Young at Heart" is unabashedly romantic, with pleasurable couplings of various sex, race, and age combinations. There's also a woman in love with babies and another in love with her vacuum cleaner. Gay love is complicated with spies lurking in bushes, shifting the mood from nostalgic romance and satire to ruinous memories of exceptional intolerance. The Washington, D.C., gay press, which hitherto had not reviewed the Dance Exchange because it is not a strictly homosexual company and Lerman is not gay, covered this piece and has continued their alliance with the company ever since. One gay journalist did comment to a gay member of Lerman's staff, however, that the piece was not "gay enough" for him.

This anecdote raises interesting questions about identity politics and art. People from groups that have been under- or misrepresented understandably want to see their lives mirrored on the stage. A piece like *Shehechianu,* which speaks to common struggles among various cultural groups, is asking spectators to identify with more than one primary group, with all due respect for differences. As Lerman states: "Are you less gay if you get immersed in a piece that is not just about gayness? How can you be your hyphenated self? Hadn't we all better learn? And isn't sitting in a theatre for two hours a good place to practice?"

Part 3, "The Skin Soliloquies," evidences how our different histories affect the way we relate to one another in the present. Characters from earlier in the piece arrive at the edge of the millennium and consider holding onto their historical scars or forgetting their pasts. One carries a box, one a sphere, one the branch of a tree. Quezada's character speaks an evocative text about the geography of the body: "My spine is a mountain range of the future. I can't see it. My toes are the archipelagos. If something happens, maybe it'll sustain me."

The dancers, friends, fellow travelers, comfort one another. A hand reaches down, lifts someone up, and their heads rest on one another's shoulders. One kisses another's cheek. Others take hands, balance, twirl, leap around, and give more kisses. Pass the sphere, one to another. Sometimes they appear to be carrying the weight of the world on their shoulders; other times the sphere is a playful, oversized beach ball. And another kiss. Andy sings: "Don't know why, there's no sun up in the sky, stormy weather," evoking the emotional geography of the loss of the sustenance of love. The space is empty but for an enormous panorama with tree, sky, and Hebrew letters floating on a scrim. *Baruch, atah, adonai. . . .*

Gisel Mason ponders: "Wouldn't it be amazing to be seen without my scars? Scars on my knees from bending, picking. On my chest from Otabenga's chest. Can't forget, your water fountain is over there. I'm trapped by my own skin." Picking up Andy's minstrel waiter shuffle from part 1, she mutters, "I'm going as fast as I can." Mason then asks for us all: "Is my worth always to be measured by the weight of my burden? Do I diminish my ancestors if I move forward? Do I diminish myself if I look back?"

In part 3 we have arrived at the edge of the century as in a vast wilderness. Is this where Moses saw the burning bush? Both are evoked by *shin,* the first letter of *Shehechianu*—looking like three flames reaching upward or Moses with his two arms stretched high. Indeed, throughout the piece the dancers raise their arms up to the sky or, more often, out to one another. Or is this that famous landscape, barren except for a single tree, from *Waiting for Godot?* For these characters are also trying to figure out how to go on.

One of the biggest problems in negotiating the worlds of professional art and community may be mainstream critics. Robert Brustein, for example, a veritable dean of American drama for over thirty years, contrasts art that is "useful . . . [such as] outreach programs, children's projects, access for the handicapped and artists in schools" with art that is validated through its "creative contribution."[10] Lerman faults such a bifurcated perspective on the prevailing notion of professionalism:

> You are a dancer if you take two technique classes a day, wait tables, behave and dress a certain way, perform once a year. . . . You are not a dancer if you teach dance in a senior center. You are a social worker. You are not a dancer if once a month you work with the rabbi at the synagogue. You are a liturgical something. In other words the narrow definition of dance as art led to a narrow practice.

Lerman is suggesting that the problem lies with an idea of professionalism that devalues community, indeed devalues any performance with a larger frame than a proscenium stage.

Other impediments arise from the community end of the spectrum. Some people feel that community art may only be done by nonprofessionals, about their own issues, and for audiences of their peers. Professional artists who orchestrate large community groups in their own professional pieces are sometimes accused of co-opting or using the participants.[11] While this is surely something to guard against, professionals who choreograph community groups with their permission need not be categorically condemned.

Clearly, this is a moment when art with a community component is groping for more diverse ways of defining itself. (It is, in fact, reminiscent of the shift in the early 1970s from feminism to feminisms.) Some of the most respected practitioners in the field do not, or no longer, subscribe to the term *community art* at all. Dudley Cocke, director of the Appalachian-based Roadside Theater, decries the term's lack of specificity: "all theatre comes out of and expresses concerns of a community, though for much of the theatre activity in this country that is a community of wealth and privilege."[12] They have renamed their practice grassroots theater, whose defining characteristic is "to preserve and express the values of those without privilege" even while "given its voice by the community from which it arises."[13] Whit MacLaughlin, until recently of Bloomsburg Theatre Ensemble, emphasizes an ethical dimension of "community-concerned" art, which serves as a sort of forum for its audience:

> The play, the mode of its creation, the economics of the piece, the spatial context of the production, the situation wherein the piece has been assembled somehow "harmonize" in a way where all of the above resonate within a viewing community. . . . And it doesn't necessarily mean that folks have to produce a play about "golf" for a "golfing" community, if you know what I mean.[14]

John Malpede, performance artist and founder of Los Angeles Poverty Department (LAPD), a company largely composed of homeless people, prefers the term *art,* finding *community* to be a code word for social work or therapy. These two extremes—a theater defined by giving voice to disenfranchised people and a theater that wants no distinction made based on its constituents—mark the breadth and diversity of this moment in what used to be called community art.

The process by which Lerman came to ground professional dance in community contexts suggests that "community-based professional" work may simply express a conception of art per se. In the early 1970s Lerman studied the Graham technique in Washington and did guerilla theater in Boston. In 1974 she spent a requisite season living in New York City, struggling to make it as a "pro," earning her living as a go-go dancer. Finally fed up, she returned to Washington, D.C., to pursue the integration of her various passions: "I had the idea that dance could belong in a community and that there would be a mutual change in both the dancer and the community if it were there." She applied political organizing principles to dance— "meet people on their own turf, affirm what they already know, bring them together"—as a way to build community. She had experimented with some of this approach in a production of *Alice in Wonderland,* in which she cast a mother and daughter as the big Alice and little Alice, and everybody knew it was a mom and daughter. For Lerman that did not take away from the product but enriched it. She rejected the modernist notion of art as a self-contained system in favor of a model of art planted in people's lives. One of her inspirations was "the passion play at Oberammergau, where who gets to play Jesus is an issue in that community and the person who is chosen brings himself to that. And the knowledge you have about him filters into what you see."

Exchange with a range of communities has in fact elucidated her sense of art's extraordinary scope. She describes, for example, a residency with particularly troubled kids:

> And the woman who was liaison could not believe the changes in those kids. And I said, "Yes, it's too bad we're going." And she said, "No, it's a great thing you're leaving." And I said, "What?" Because one of my issues has been who's going to sustain it? And she says, "Look, these kids have never completed anything in their whole lives. They never complete a year of school, their families are coming and going, they never live more than a few months with anybody. You are giving them their first experience with a beginning, middle, and end, the first time they can appraise and own accomplishments, the first time they are learning how to say good bye." This is fantastic. In that moment I'm completely elevated, transformed in my understanding of yet another function of art that I never knew.

Lerman's deep connection to art that flows out of everyone's life exists comfortably along side that which takes place in professional performance spaces. She revels in the intensity of long technical rehearsals, insisting: "I think I'm the better for having both. I don't see why we can't practice the art of dance and have those things and many more. That seems much more what the role of an artist should be."

The broadening of the basis for including artists in a dance company has been one of Lerman's major contributions to the professional art world. She first did so in the 1970s, drawn to working with older people by her own mother's death. She soon became smitten with the older dancers' "impact on an audience, their incredible openness to learning, the beauty of their movements, and what they had to teach me about dancing." Incorporating older people into her work, in which the thrill, as she puts it, cannot possibly be seeing how high someone's leg is going to go, has had the salutary effect of weaning audiences from the habit of overvaluing technique. So the inclusion of older people has also illuminated the richness of community art. Contrary to the stereotypic conception of community-based art as an oxymoron, this reflects one of Lerman's basic criteria for artistic merit—how committed and connected a person is to the movement: "And if I don't see THAT on stage I'm bereft." Thus, a deepening of the artistic experience—the emphasis on an aesthetic of commitment as well as technical prowess—takes place concomitantly with a focus on communal representation.

Community workshops have, in fact, helped Lerman define a whole set of criteria for art that she has observed in people without training as well as those with it. She uses the example of seeing a woman in a nursing home make a marvelous little movement with her forearm. She observed the woman exhibiting four characteristics: 100 percent commitment to the movement, an understanding of why she was doing it, revelation of something about herself and her world, and overcoming some kind of hurdle in the process. For Lerman this adds up to art. But the challenge, states Lerman, is how to retain all that in front of an audience. Without training, experience, and technique to fall back on, there's a good chance that the woman will lose confidence in front of strangers, certainly if she's asked to perform repeatedly. On the other hand, professionals sometime mask revelation in technique. So Lerman continues to find sustenance in projects that combine community and professional elements.

Soon after her mother died, Lerman created a piece called "A Woman of Clear Vision." This rubric also applies to her and is at the heart of why I marvel so at her work. The clarity of Lerman's vision prompted her to include older people in her company when technique was still the dominant artistic measurement. She recognized the power of community-based workshops both as a rich art activity in itself and as source material for professional work before such a practice was accepted. The subject matter she takes on, as in *Shehechianu,* extends art well beyond formal considerations. Her concept of community applies to her company as well, translating into dancers who also speak, cocreate, and co-teach, even though such thorough collaboration may be considered passé, a thing of the 1960s. Lerman has, in effect, found a way to pursue proficiency in dance without privileging form over content. She's found a way to work with communities that is not parochial. At each juncture she has assessed what would move her further along a meaningful road, not getting caught up in either/or thinking— either community or professional venues, teacher or artist, body or mind. Having decided to make art the "organizing principle" of her life, she "stretched and pushed and pulled at that boundary in order to make room for *the other things* that feel so essential to me as a person and to art—and ultimately to the life that art is supposed to serve." To my mind the result is art with a sense of group significance and the kind of heart more often found in community settings but with the degree of proficiency and complexity more expected in the professional world. And, finally, she is bringing revelations discovered and expressed among distinct groups into cross-community contexts. While *Shehechianu*'s point of departure is distinctly Jewish, the expression spun out from it and the intended audiences are broadly multicultural. Intertwining community and professional art, as with *Shehechianu,* stretches both fields and perhaps eradicates the difference between them entirely.

NOTES

1. Anna Deavere Smith, "Not So Special Vehicles," *Modern Drama: Plays, Criticism, Theory,* ed. W. B. Worthen (Fort Worth, Texas: Harcourt Brace Publishers, 1995), 1080–81.

2. See especially Richard Geer's essay by that name in *High Performance* 16, no. 4 (#64, Winter 1993). In fact, see this whole special issue, subtitled "Local Life Aware of Itself: Alternate ROOTS and the Partnering of Artists and Communities."

3. Rome Quezada to the author in a telephone interview, 19 September 1997.

4. Unless otherwise indicated, all comments by Lerman in this essay come from interviews I did with her in New York City, 21 January 1995; and over the telephone, 28 June 1997 and 22 January 1999.

5. Rome Quezada, quoted in "From Meaning to Movement," *Exchange: A Publication of Liz Lerman Dance Exchange* (Spring 1997): 2.

6. Jeffrey Gunshol, quoted in ibid., 2.

7. In September 1999, Miller joined the Liz Lerman Dance Exchange as an artist-in-residence.

8. Celeste Miller, from e-mail message musing on community arts, 8 January 1999.

9. Quoted in D. Quincey Whitney, "Week of Dance Fetes Portsmouth's Past," *Boston Globe,* 15 September 1996, NH 20.

10. Robert Brustein, "Culture by Coercion," Op-ed page, *New York Times,* 29 November 1994, A25:3.

11. For the harshest condemnation of such work as "victim art," see Arlene Croce, "Discussing the Undisscussable," *New Yorker* (26 December 1994–2 January 1995): 54–60.

12. Dudley Cocke, Harry Newman, and Janet Salmon-Rue, *From the Ground Up: Grassroots Theater in Historical and Contemporary Perspective* (Ithaca, N.Y.: Community Based Arts Project, Cornell University, 1993), 13.

13. Cocke, 13, 81.

14. Whit MacLaughlin, in an e-mail exchange, 8 January 1999.

PART 3

Empowering the Audience

Community-based performance seeks to improve a community's condition and its ability to satisfy its needs in political and social arenas. Of course, projects can vary greatly in the way that democracy is conceived, what constitutes such improvement, and the process adopted to achieve it. Securing a better position within current institutional arrangements, confronting those arrangements, enabling individuals to recover their sense of their own value, creating public recognition of a marginalized community's cultural tradition—these are only some of the approaches through which a community might be empowered. This diversity among performance projects sometimes indicates real differences in goals and attitudes, but, more often, the work is seen as simply one effort out of many participating in a larger, highly complex, always fallible, and constantly renewed struggle for cultural democracy and social change.

The essays in part 3 illustrate the wide range of approaches through which community-based performances strive to empower a community and the differing ways in which the functions of community-based performance take concrete form. Anne Basting's essay on a voting rights project offers a good example how community-based theater can be used to encourage marginalized communities to exercise the powers that the existing social system offers them. In the process, however, this project fostered understanding and coalitions across generational lines, countering the enormous pressure exerted by politicians and advertisers to divide the young and old. In effect, the project worked to give both generations greater power in two ways: by turning them into stronger voting blocs and by subtly realigning the groups so that they saw themselves as potential allies rather than inevitable competitors.

The use of theater for specific political goals also appears in Susan Suntree's essay. Over seventy organizations formed a coalition to call attention to a local environmental issue. Mainstream institutional channels were unresponsive or unavailable, so an alternative avenue was taken instead. A theater troupe created for the campaign produced a commedia dell'arte satire in order to attract publicity. But it faced serious obstacles, including lack of public space, clashes with the police, and blacklisting of actors. Suntree analyzes the effect of these obstacles on the work and its reception.

Both Basting's and Suntree's essays concern projects ultimately aspiring to address a large audience. The former sought to empower certain substantial communities; the latter might be construed as a "special interests" campaign, but clearly it would benefit the general public. The next two essays concern projects that instead aim primarily to assist and empower a specific group of people, as individuals. The Puppets in Prison project described in Marcia Blumberg's essay conducts workshops with the involuntary and unstable community of prison inmates, producing puppet plays that explore issues of violent crime and especially the rapidly worsening AIDS pandemic. Not only do inmates and prison officials obtain vital information, inmates participating in the workshops become peer educators who, often for the first time, are able to express their fears and improve their sense of confidence and self-worth, all of which has a liberating effect upon them.

As Susan Haedicke explains, a similar approach is also the basis of Robert Alexander's Living Stage work, which uses performance workshops to increase participants' artistic abilities and self-esteem and thereby their practical effectiveness. The teenaged African-American mothers participating in the workshops not only develop a sense of community but also establish ties with a larger community of artists and social activists. An unusual facet of this program is that the focus is on creating art: therapeutic benefits are seen as an added boon that arise when art becomes a way of life.

The subsequent essays return to projects that strive for community empowerment but by using the community's cultural heritage either to preserve a community against a precarious future or to enact direct political interventions. Tori Haring-Smith reports on how colonizing forces have endangered the continuity of Egypt's oral culture. Theater is helping to maintain a major portion of that heritage, yet it must alter this legacy in order to save it. Implicitly, this work is an act of resistance against a danger coming to the community from outside.

Not far from Egypt there is, instead, a community that has come from outside whose culture is now endangered by its new homeland. Rob Baum tells how the Falasha (Ethiopian Jewish immigrants to Israel) face poverty, indignities, and the loss of their cultural identity, but a dance troupe has sought to sustain at least one aspect of that culture and, in doing so, has won recognition for the community and generated both community and national pride. Even though the troupe itself is apolitical, it has reshaped both the national and the ethnic political landscapes of Israel.

The appropriation of cultural tradition is a key aspect of the Korean performance genre *madang kut,* but in this case it is used as a way to address national political issues directly. Dong-il Lee describes how *madang kut* combines an ancient shamanic ritual performance with political content, providing the democracy movement with a new type of protest theater that has succeeded in politicizing and mobilizing large numbers of people. Most crucially, it replaces slogans with narratives of oppression placed within sacred occasions that are communal, participatory, and transformative.

Like Lee, Diana Taylor discusses performances that invoke what one might call a "double memory"—of indigenous cultural traditions and of more recent political atrocities—as a mode of intervention. When the Peruvian company Yuyuchkani sustains these memories, it sustains the social life and sense of identity that keep an embattled community from joining the ranks of the disappeared, and it reminds urban audiences in particular that what they cease to remember will leave them dismembered. Resuming the themes of the first section, memory is part of what defines community itself. The connection between performance and memory, Taylor argues, not only has political implications for a community's existence; it also bears ramifications for our understanding of performance itself.

In the final essay local culture serves as a means for both collective political intervention and individual empowerment. Mary Ann Hunter analyzes the *Skate Girl Space* project, formed in inner-city Brisbane, Australia, in response to young women's desire to develop skateboarding skills and challenge male skateboarders' domination of a "public" space. Here the cultural activity in question is not part of a long-standing tradition but, rather, a form of contemporary youth culture. The ramifications of this point are extensive. Rather than preserving community by rescuing a tradition from oblivion (a strategy that in some cases provides a community with a needed sense of identity and self-worth but in others amounts to nostalgia), *Skate Girl Space* joins forces with a living cultural practice characterizing a relatively new type of community. Moreover, Hunter argues that the celebratory epics that community-based theaters so often produce have wound up playing safe; their effectiveness and relevance must be sharply questioned; in contrast, she says, projects like *Skate Girl Space* suggest new directions that community-based performance should pursue if it is to sustain its vitality. Thus, part 3, and the book, closes by interrogating the strategies that community-based work has adopted; whether they are in fact still alive; and how they must change for community-based performance to go forward.

Anne Davis Basting, with Peggy Pettitt

Generations as Communities: Elders Share the Arts and *Bushwick, Why Vote?*

Surveys suggest that Americans don't tend to think of a "generation" as a community. For various reasons, from ageism to an antimarketing backlash against the promotion of products geared toward Generation X, only one-third of Americans openly identify themselves as being part of a particular generation.[1] But one's location in history and one's role within one's extended family are certainly responsible for shaping who and how one comes to know oneself. While my mother remembers where she was when Kennedy and Kennedy and King were shot, the memory that fuses time and place for me is the vivid image of the *Challenger* bursting into flame and smoke against a clear blue sky. Not only do historical conditions and events unique to one's lifetime shape people, but throughout the twentieth century American culture has also increasingly sought to divide and isolate people according to their ages. If we are to seek an end to ageism or, at very least, an understanding across ages, we must acknowledge and work through generational differences.

Anne Davis Basting is a playwright, scholar of performance studies at the University of Wisconsin–Oshkosh, and author of *The Stages of Age: Performing Age in Contemporary American Culture* (1998). Under a National Brookdale Fellowship she is running creative storytelling workshops with young adults and people with Alzheimer's disease in Milwaukee and New York, a project that shares participants' stories with their communities through a website and a professionally produced play in both cities.

New York–based actress and playwright Peggy Pettitt has created award-winning one-woman shows and facilitated community-based theater since 1975. From 1984 through 1996 she worked with Elders Share the Arts, where she developed many plays and formed the Pearls of Wisdom, a team of older women storytellers from across the five boroughs. She continues to work closely with the Bushwick community.

New York City–based Elders Share the Arts (ESTA) is one of a handful of community-based arts programs that identify generations as communities and seek to bridge the widening fissures between them.[2] For more than fifteen years ESTA has been working in impoverished neighborhoods in the New York area, acting as a conduit for older men and women to shape and share their memories and opinions with their communities at large through the visual arts and storytelling. In the 1990s ESTA expanded its focus to include intergenerational projects between school-age children (from grade school to high school) and older adults within the same neighborhoods.

Building coalition and understanding between generations is a vital part of community-based work. I share ESTA's history and practices here as both a positive model and one that points to potential trouble spots in inter-generational arts programming. My focus here is on generational relationships in ESTA's 1996 production of *Bushwick, Why Vote?*

Shaping Generations: Trust No One Over . . . ?

Relationships between people of different generations (roughly twenty years each) shape and are shaped by their historical contexts. Over the last decade scholars have created several models of generational boundaries. While these generational divides differ in title and are often off by one or two years, they share a common recognition of the effects of key political and social events in each generation. The 1960s youth movement, for example, can be associated in part with the inevitable collision between what Neil Howe and William Strauss describe as the members of the ideal-istic Baby Boom generation (born between 1943 and 1960) and the more civic-minded GI generation (born between 1901 and 1924).[3] Suspicious of their elders' strict social mores and their trust in the greater good of govern-ment interests, the youth movement of the 1960s warned against trusting anyone over thirty.[4]

Relationships between Boomers, the Silent generation (those born between 1925 and 1942), and their own children are radically different. Coming into adulthood during the 1960s meant that Boomer and Silent parents turned the focus from their children to themselves and were less likely to repeat the strict gender and social roles of their parents without questioning them. Boomer and Silent generations were much more prone to treat their children as peers, creating a phenomenon variously called "the hurried child" or "the disappearance of childhood."[5]

The generation born roughly between 1961 and 1981 is known by a variety of names, letters, and numbers, the most common being Generation

X. According to Bureau of Education statistics, more than 40 percent of "Xers" are children of divorce. The emotional strain of divorce aside, the real tragedy of the rise in divorce is that the concept of child support was a massive, systematic failure. Some states have begun to enact stricter laws in the last several years, threatening, for example, the loss of one's driver's license unless payments are made. But of the nine million women raising children alone in 1981 only 59 percent were awarded child support. Only 23 percent received any payment at all. The breakdown of child support, along with cuts in governmental services to children, contributed to their becoming the most impoverished age group in 1974. By 1984 the number of children in poverty had increased by two-thirds.[6] Today one in five children lives in poverty.

In spite of these figures, Xers and their followers, the Millennial generation (born after 1981, according to Howe and Strauss) report friendly relationships with their parents. So what is the source of the much reported fear of rising intergenerational tensions? Demographics. Anticipated increases in life expectancy and the impending retirement of the Baby Boom generation will create an unprecedented imbalance in the ratio of workers to elders in the U.S. economy. In 1900 there were roughly seven elderly to every one hundred people of working age. By 2030 this figure is expected to rise to thirty-eight to one hundred.[7] This demographic challenge is compounded by several factors. First, those over eighty-five, the fastest-growing age group in the United States, also require the most health care services. Second, those past retirement are predicted to continue working later into life. And, third, younger workers are finding it harder to get and keep jobs that pay a living wage. Debates over Social Security reform, over exactly how to and who will pay for the aging Baby Boomers, are predicted to ignite lasting tensions between the young and old.[8]

Reciting ratios of workers to dependents and sketching broad generational boundaries paint intergenerational relationships with enormous brush strokes that inevitably miss location-specific details. ESTA's work with the Round Table Senior Center (RT) in Bushwick, a neighborhood in Brooklyn, New York, reveals a unique tale of fractures between generations and the first steps toward healing those fractures through a performance that encourages political self-empowerment.

A Neighborhood in Brooklyn

Bushwick is now largely a poor African-American community in the northern end of Brooklyn. When Christine Cutchin first became politically involved as a State Committeewoman in the Bushwick community in 1968, it was predominantly peopled with Italian and German immigrants. By 1973, however, the area had shifted to include African- and Caribbean-Americans as well as a rich variety of Latinos. As is common with poor, immigrant neighborhoods, waves of migration often leave older residents isolated when younger family members move on in search of better jobs. Crime and fear were crippling Bushwick's multiethnic senior community.

In 1973 Cutchin helped found the Round Table Senior Center in the hopes of providing a place where the area's seniors might safely come together without carrying with them the neighborhood's racial and ethnic hierarchies. Cutchin chose the name because, she said: "At a round table, no one is at the foot of the table. There are no hierarchies." Today, the Round Table reflects its namesake, drawing its current 2,630 members from the surrounding communities of Bushwick, Bedford Stuyvesant, Ridgewood, Williamsburg, and East New York, and including Chinese, Italian, Latinos from Puerto Rico, Costa Rica, and Spain, Virgin Islanders, African Americans, and Eastern European Jews. The vast majority of Round Table seniors live alone and in poverty.

Elders Share the Arts and Round Table first began collaborating in 1989, when Cutchin and her program director, Verneal Kizer, cautiously measured ESTA's motives. "We had had people come out [to the center] to pick the senior's brains for stories, and not give them any recognition when it was over. They came and they went. So at first we weren't sure if ESTA would just do more of the same," said Kizer. But RT's partnership with ESTA proved to foster deep bonds among participants and challenge the seniors toward surprising growth. "Since my seniors joined ESTA," said Cutchin at ESTA's 1996 Living History Festival at St. Ann's Church in Brooklyn, "I don't recognize them. Once upon a time they were afraid to speak. Now you can't shut them up."[9]

Since its beginning in 1979, ESTA has sought to empower seniors in what founder Susan Perlstein calls "underserved" neighborhoods by encouraging them to become storytellers. ESTA facilitators lead a series of thirty weekly workshops that culminate in a Living History Festival each spring in which each of the twenty-five neighborhood programs share their stories with one another and the public at large. ESTA expanded its programming in the mid-1990s to include collaborations between seniors and children within the same neighborhood, with the aim of dissolving fears and biases in both directions. In 1995 Perlstein received a grant to support *Why Vote?*, an intergenerational program that would bring young and old together to share stories about the importance of voting. Tapping into the momentum of the successful workshop group Pettitt had been leading at Round Table, ESTA began the *Why Vote?* program in Bushwick with a collaboration between a dozen RT seniors, two students from East Brooklyn Congregational High School (EBC), a student at Long Island University (LIU), and a student at New York University.

ESTA facilitator and then performance director, Peggy Pettitt, led the workshops and production of the flagship *Why Vote?* in 1995. Over the next two years *Why Vote?* expanded to other communities served by ESTA and, at this writing, is poised to develop its own intergenerationally constructed website. The model of the original *Why Vote?* project is helpful in establishing the importance of intergenerational work. Students and seniors eloquently voice the project's positive impact on their lives. *Bushwick, Why Vote?* (*BWV*) also points to some potential difficulties other groups might face in working to bridge generations as well: being sure to acknowledge cultural changes that face young adults and being sure to assess the soundness of a "family" model as a basis for intergenerational alliances for individual troupe members. I will elaborate on both the value and potential traps of intergenerational work as I describe the shaping and production of *BWV*.

Confronting Fears of Youth and Age

The students involved in *BWV* were mainly united by their ages and an interest in theater. Thelma Lenton and Sue Frias were both enrolled at EBC High School, but Gabrielle Bayme (NYU) and Vladimir Auguste (LIU) were outsiders of the Bushwick community. None of the students knew one another before the program began.

On the other hand, the dozen black, older adults who had been meeting at Round Table for several years were a much tighter group. They shared common experiences of aging, Christianity, and neighborhood. Some had migrated to New York from the South, while others had been born in the New York area. All shared a general history of oppression.

As is traditional in ESTA's intergenerational programming, Peggy Pettitt worked with the seniors and young people separately at first, allowing those in each group to voice their worries and/or preconceptions about the other. She also used these early sessions to describe the task at hand to each group and sense their reactions to it. According to Pettitt, the students had heard of the famous figures from the civil rights movement but really had no idea that they were surrounded by people who had firsthand knowledge of the atrocities of Jim Crow. The older adults, on the other hand, doubted that the young people would have any interest in hearing their stories.

Stereotypes were rampant and predictable. The seniors for the most part imagined "bad" kids, the kind you "hear of on the news." Sue Frias, from EBC, who worked as a dispatcher at a volunteer ambulance corps, said she never really considered that older people in her neighborhood could be active citizens. To Frias they were simply people who were sick. LIU student Vladimir Auguste explained his friends' resistance to the elderly: "I think most young people don't think they have anything to gain by talking to old people. I think they are afraid to age themselves. They don't want to think about it."

Pettitt is a skilled storyteller as well as a tremendously dedicated and inspirational facilitator who connects deeply to the communities with whom she works. In her late forties during the formation of *BWV*, Pettitt forged connections with and between both age groups by finding common interests and sharing in their everyday lives. She visited participants when they were sick and attended family funerals; she came to them when crises blocked participants from being with the group. To mark the rehearsal as a sacred space, she created a participatory ritual for each rehearsal/gathering. Tapping into Round Table's emphasis on spirituality as well as the interest in music shared by the younger and older participants, Pettitt framed rehearsals with song, discussion, and prayer. She also extended the standards of respect and sense of family that Christine Cutchin had built over the twenty-five years of Round Table's existence—standards that require, for example, that every member of Round Table be referred to by his or her title and last name (Mr. Cherry, Miss Hall, etc.) and a sense that everyone who enters Round Table's doors is welcomed into an extended family.

This strong sense of family permeated the rehearsals and helped to dissolve the initial hesitancy between the young and old participants by providing them with an established role to play in one another's lives. Frias, who had imagined the seniors to be sickly and distant, was surprised that on the first day "everybody said hello to me as though they knew me. Everybody saw me as their granddaughter or their little niece and I felt really at home. On that first day I felt at home." Pettitt's approach of shaping the group into an extended family during rehearsals was effective in alleviating the fears each group carried to that first day of intergenerational rehearsals.

In intergenerational work in general it is important to recognize that there is a difference between idealized family relationships and everyday families. While the family model, long established at the Round Table, worked well for *BWV*, practitioners should feel out the appropriateness of this model

in their own groups. Using the family as a model for intergenerational relationships can also backfire if younger or older members of the group have
particularly bad experiences with families in their own lives. Vladimir
Auguste hinted at this problem when he blamed his friends' negative attitudes toward the elderly on the tensions within their own, multigenerational
families: "I don't know, I look at some of my friends who have grandparents
living in the house and I see the generation gap right there within their families." While family models offer immediately recognizable roles for old and
young alike, they can also inadvertently replicate some of the troubles haunting generational relationships within families across the United States today.
Friendship in which there is mutual respect, support, and playfulness can
serve as an alternative model for intergenerational relationships. Again,
Auguste pointed to this possibility himself when, after a moment of
reflection on the stress in his friends' families, he continued, "But for me, it's
like we [he and the older performers] are friends, you know?"

A benefit the family model offers is a chance for group participants to
fill the gaps within their own families. If there are no grandparents or there
are other troubles, the group offers support for those whose families have
been fractured. Pettitt said that for the several older members of the group
whose children and grandchildren had problems with drugs or had little
hope for the future, working with the young people gave them a chance to
channel their own hopes and guidance. The older people gave the kids a
chance to make up for grandparents some had never known.

One danger of the family model is that the surrogate grandchild/parent
role might not necessarily expand the roles of older adults or children within
their communities. If the value and treatment of the generations are to
change in any significant way, young and old also need to see one another
as citizens and artists as well as family members—something *BWV* clearly
accomplished through its call for civic activism. The fears and apprehensions
that each group carried to the first joint rehearsal shifted and dissolved as the
rehearsals grew into full production. In addition to the emphasis on the family model, older and younger members of *BWV* were in fact drawn together
by common goals for artistic success and for convincing audience members
that voting is crucial to creating social change.

The Medium and Message of *Bushwick, Why Vote?*

Over the months of once-a-week rehearsals Pettitt encouraged students and
seniors to share their stories about voting. Why was it important? What

were their memories of it? If they didn't vote, why not? The students told of their disbelief in the system, of a paralyzing apathy and cynicism that had rotted any sense of citizenship among their friends. Older adults, on the contrary, shared tales of the fight for the right to vote and of covert and sometimes gruesomely overt violence meant to keep them from exercising that right.

Any sharing of stories across generations will help develop a greater sense of understanding between them. But encouraging both young and old to vote is of particular importance in the contemporary political scene. According to Susan MacManus's study of the voting patterns of young and old in Florida, young adults will lose the battle for generational equity if they do not mobilize as a voting bloc. If Baby Boomers continue to out-number and outpower (in voting and donating to campaigns) Xers and Mil-lennial generations, it will be Boomers who guide the actions of politicians. This is only a bad thing if each generation fights solely for its own interests. Encouraging today's older voters, who have the best voting record of any age group, to understand the needs of children can in turn encourage politi-cians to recognize the same needs. A joint vision reflecting the needs of all generations is crucial as Americans renegotiate a contract between genera-tions regarding financial support and responsibilities.

In early spring of 1996 (rehearsals began the previous fall), Pettitt began to shape the shared stories of voting into script form. Keeping the form true to her emphasis in rehearsal, Pettitt created a piece based on a three-gener-ational family. The seven short, realistic, and comic scenes were divided by songs that invoked the spirits of ancestors, RT's Christian/spiritual base, as well as memories of the civil rights movement—a crucial part of which was the fight for voting rights. "This Little Light of Mine," for example, book-ended the first two scenes—monologues exploring the importance of vot-ing from two different generational positions. In the story that followed, two high school–aged sisters (Lisa and L.C.) and their mother learn the value of voting from their Grandma and Aunt Jerry. The process of creating and performing *BWV* was clearly effective in solidifying bonds between the two generations of actors, in fueling confidence among individual actors, and in beginning the long process of increasing political involvement in an impoverished community.

BWV begins by drawing fairly stereotypical, generational depictions of its characters. Grandma tells the same horrid story over and over again. Mom loses her job and becomes addicted to soap operas. L.C. is a selfish teenager who monopolizes the phone. Aunt Jerry is the play's sage, and, after an initial bout of cynicism, Lisa echoes Jerry's wise advice. These

broadly drawn characters enable the ensemble to move the play quickly and
clearly toward its lesson: the urgency of voting. Grandma's graphic stories of
lynchings end up convincing L.C. of the need to be politically involved:

> Back then we didn't have choices. We were told what to do. So we
> voted for the right to choose. Listen to me. Don't be too sure it can
> never happen again: lynching, tar and feathering, burning homes. . . .
> Read your history. . . . Read one of them books. (*She pats L.C.'s back-
> pack.*) There's nothing in there! You're just wearing that because it
> matches your clothes. When I was your age we children didn't have
> books and pencils and if we wore bags on our backs it was for carrying
> wood or coal. We worked hard. We didn't have the privileges you
> have today.[10]

Worn down by Grandma's exaggerations, repetitions, and chiding,
L.C. finally offers to accompany her to the polls. Aunt Jerry's persistent dia-
tribe about voting eventually moves Lisa to register and Mom to admit that
she doesn't know how to vote or even who is running for office. "Isn't it
strange," says Mom, "I know who's doing what to who on those soap
operas but I don't know who's doing what to who in politics."[11] While the
play begins in generational stereotype, it moves toward more nuanced
intergenerational relationships. Both Lisa and L.C. listen to and side with
their elders, and L.C. is stunned by her selfishness (she wants to go on a ski
trip) in the face of her mother's job loss. The danger of using stereotypes to
move the plot, however, is always that the play might simply reinforce
images of being repetitious and obsessed with the past. The troupe's
tongue-in-cheek performance style let the audience know that the stereotypes were just that—and the actors, as both young and old revealed in pre-
and post-show discussions, were clearly much more complicated than those
two-dimensional caricatures could contain.

BWV emphasizes the activism of the 1960s in order to compel action
among today's youth. The introductory remarks by the students, for example, show a direct link to the 1960s. Both Bayme and Auguste wrote introductions, and, depending on availability, for each performance one would
speak as a voice of youth. Both of their monologues hark back to the
activism of the 1960s as a model for contemporary student political involvement. Auguste's speech addressed the change in student activism: "Today,
lack of understanding the voting process and general apathy keeps us slaves
to the idea that our vote does not count. But several generations ago students took it upon themselves to teach others how to participate in the

democratic process of voting."[12] Bayme fingers her generation's apathy even more directly. She recalls the frustration that grew from a class in which students complained of social ills but did nothing to solve them:

> So we all just sat there debating and complaining about things that should change. Our teacher commented that "yeah, if this was the sixties or seventies we'd be out there picketing or sitting on their doorstep!" We all laughed, then one of us pointed out that maybe this is why the media has labeled us "Generation X" and portrays us as apathetic whiners.[13]

Borrowing examples from the past helps put today's situations in perspective, letting young adults see that drastic changes have occurred in the past and that culture can change again. *BWV*'s call for change and its success at getting audience members to register to vote after performances speak to the power of this approach. Caution should be taken as well to acknowledge the unique cultural landscape in which young adults live today. Student audience members can easily interpret a regaling of the past to be "out of date" or not applicable to their lives. A careful assessment of how the times have changed and, along with them, how activism, politics, and the condition of youth have changed in kind would make it clear to students that recreating 1960s activism is not the goal. Audience feedback underscored this point. While *BWV* did successfully register audience members to vote after nearly every performance, Auguste told of one performance at LIU after which a young man stood up and objected to the play's message. Said Auguste: "This guy stood up and he was like 'I know you guys, you know I respect you, you've done all this for us, but it doesn't really relate to us now.' And I remember I pointed out that what he's saying is pretty true, because I see this in other students." Pettitt explained that on the whole this kind of response was rare for *BWV*, but I include it here to suggest that other groups working intergenerationally should be aware of how easily models from the past can be misinterpreted or, worse, simply excused.

Difference Doesn't Mean Division

Round Table member Carrie Raeford's memories of the silent humiliation she suffered riding on the back of the bus as a child are certainly different than Sue Frias's memories of a post–civil rights movement childhood in one of New York's poorer neighborhoods. Both Raeford and Frias shape and are shaped by the historical events and social conditions in which they have lived. And both Raeford and Frias condition and are conditioned by culturally pervasive biases against what are today too often depicted as violent, apathetic youth and feeble, helpless age.

Working together toward a common goal of encouraging young adults to vote, younger and older members of *BWV* both recognized and accepted differences between their generations. Whereas the seniors began with nightmarish visions of the "bad" kids on the evening news, their views changed over the course of the project. Randall Cherry, the only man among the RT seniors, put it this way: "A funny thing, people do not talk about the good kids today. And you got plenty of good kids." Margaree Hall, who designed the backdrop for *BWV,* explained it succinctly, "I enjoy working with the young people. I learn from them and they learn from me."

The lessons Vladimir Auguste learned from working with the older performers included how to plan for his own retirement: "I think I should save money, invest in the stock market for my retirement fund." Auguste said he also learned how not to waste time in life worrying about "being so cool" and how to anticipate change. Frias's expectations of what the seniors would be like were radically different than the reality. Said Frias, "They weren't what I thought they would be, like, you know, in wheelchairs and all lame and everything. They are very vibrant, full of life people."

For complex financial and personal reasons Pettitt left ESTA after *BWV*'s first year. After a challenging transition from Pettitt's facilitation, Perlstein and ESTA hope that the 1998 program can reach a wider audience by designing a website to post information about the political process and debates about generational alliances. In a time when political analysts are sounding alarms about the coming of intergenerational warfare, the rare foresight of ESTA and groups such as Oakland, California–based StAGE Bridge and Pittsburgh's Generations Together are taking steps to join generational forces in a common fight against passivity, poverty, and ageism by first recognizing generations as communities and then working to find common ground between them.[14]

NOTES

1. See Cheryl Russel and Susan Mitchell, "Talking about Whose Generation?" *American Demographics* (April 1995): 32–33.

2. Other groups of this type include StAGE Bridge, an intergenerational storytelling and performance group based in Oakland, California; Roots & Branches Theater based in New York City; and Generations Together based in Pittsburgh.

3. William Strauss and Neil Howe, *Generations: The History of America's Future, 1584–2069* (New York: Morrow, 1991).

4. I use Strauss and Howe's titles for the Baby Boom, Silent, and GI generations here because I find they resonate with popularly used terms. Strauss and Howe are problematic, however, for their close ties to the Concord Coalition and their clear political aims to incite a sense of generational inequity in the hopes of prompting major reform in entitlements. For other divisions of generations, see Susan MacManus, *Young v. Old: Generational Conflict in the 21st Century* (Boulder, Colo.: Westview, 1996); and Fernando Torres-Gil, *The New Aging: Politics and Change in America* (New York: Auburn House, 1992).

5. See David Elkind, *The Hurried Child: Growing Up Too Fast Too Soon* (Reading, Mass.: Addison-Wesley, 1988); and Neil Postman, *The Disappearance of Childhood* (New York: Vintage, 1994).

6. See Geoffrey Holtz, *Welcome to the Jungle: The Why behind Generation X* (New York: St. Martin's Press, 1995), 45–50.

7. MacManus, *Young v. Old*, 11.

8. See ibid.; and Peter G. Peterson, "Social Insecurity: Will America Grow Up before It Grows Old?" *Atlantic Monthly* 227, no. 5 (1996): 55–74.

9. I interviewed Cutchin and Kizer in June 1997. I interviewed Auguste and Frias in November 1996. The senior members of Round Table's Intergenerational Ensemble were interviewed several times, during my visits to Pettitt's workshops in the fall of 1995 and at the May 1996 Living History Festival.

10. Peggy Pettitt, in collaboration with the Round Table Intergenerational Ensemble, *Bushwick, Why Vote?* MS, courtesy of Elders Share the Arts, 1996, 13–14.

11. Ibid., 16.

12. Ibid., 4.

13. Ibid.

14. Thanks are due to Peggy Pettitt, whose passion and vision for community-based theater in particular and people in general are an inspiration to all those who contemplate doing this work. Our long and heated conversations are like stuffing yourself in a raucous, delicious restaurant, one at which I hope to have the pleasure of dining for years to come. I would also like to thank the administrators and members of the Round Table Intergenerational Ensemble for sharing their project and their stories with me.

Susan Suntree

FrogWorks in Los Angeles

At dawn on 2 July 1996 three activists, their wrists handcuffed inside steel pipes, locked on to bulldozers at the Ballona Wetlands. Ballona is the final vestige of a wetland that once covered twenty-one hundred acres in Los Angeles. Today barely a thousand acres remain of this magnificent ecosystem. Not only is it the last coastal wetland and large open space left in Los Angeles, where 97 percent of all wetlands have been destroyed; it is an important stopover on the severely threatened Pacific Flyway for migratory birds and the location of significant Native American sites. This is where Wall Street bankers Morgan Stanley, Dean Witter, and Goldman Sachs, partnered with DreamWorks SKG (the movie studio created by Steven Spielberg, David Geffen, and Jeffrey Katzenberg), plan to build a gigantic city, called Playa Vista.[1] Corporate welfare, totaling almost a half-billion dollars in city and state taxes and bonds, has shored up the project. Playa Vista would be the largest development in the history of Los Angeles and would leave barely two hundred acres of a so-called Wetland Restoration on a section where building is impossible anyway because of the high water table. The intimate relationship between environmental and social justice issues manifests clearly in the community struggle to save the Ballona Wetlands.

At the demonstration supporting the handcuffed activists, I picked up a bullhorn and explained for two hours to an audience of rush-hour trapped motorists why helicopters, police cars, fire trucks, and people carrying banners had converged at Jefferson and Lincoln Boulevards near Los Angeles International Airport. In the aftermath the coalition Citizens United to Save ALL of Ballona grew to include over eighty political, church, and environ-

FrogWorks continues Susan Suntree's investigation, as a poet and playwright, of the interactions between theater and nature, activism, and community. The several years she spent as a resident artist and consultant in theater and mask making for disabled adults and her ongoing examination of theater's range of concerns and modes of participation inspire her work. Suntree thanks the FrogWorkers, audience members, and community supporters whose thoughts have contributed to this essay.

mental groups, which work to save the Ballona Wetlands according to their particular resources. My offering, because of my background in environmental and outdoor performance, was to gather a troupe of players and take the issue directly to the community through street theater.

I first discussed this idea with Andrea Hodos, a dancer interested in social justice issues, and Allaire Paterson-Koslo, an actress active in environmental work. We named our troupe FrogWorks, a reframing of Dream-Works, and found a nonprofit sponsor in the Wetlands Action Network to coproduce with my company, Theatre Flux. Our director, Zoey Zimmerman (MFA, Yale School of Drama), brought to our work her extensive experience in both community-based and professional theater. Based on transcripts of speeches by the politicians and developers promoting Playa Vista and on inspiration from the San Francisco Mime Troupe and the Chicago-based Ladies against Women, I wrote a commedia dell'arte–style script that evolves along with the Playa Vista controversy. We decided our troupe would be a mix of activists and theater artists to introduce performance skills to activists and activism to actors through the practice of street theater while also promoting art as environmental action.

Pulling together our FrogWorks community, however, was more difficult than we expected. Rehearsals for the twenty-five-minute piece took almost three months and included over a dozen cast changes. Allaire (who plays the Frog), Zoey, and I struggled to find people who would do this type of theater. Our current troupe, who are Jewish/Anglo/American mix and live in various areas of the city, has worked together for a year and a half. During this time we've seen our Frog actress become pregnant and give birth, our stage manager/costumer/musician, who is a visual artist, take on a speaking role, and our activist-turned-actor leave his job as an aerospace engineer to become a videographer. And all of us have grown enormously in our understanding of and respect for the immediacy and effectiveness of the marvelous art of street theater.[2] Additionally, our troupe includes at least one or two supporters who hand out our flyers during performances.

Our play, "THE AMAZING Unveiling and Startling Origins of WETLANDS Land," follows the tragic last day of a homeless mother frog as she confronts a chorus of three Suits: Rob McLiar (Rob McGuire), representing the developers; Spielkatzengef (Spielberg, Katzenberg, and Geffen), the movie guy turned real estate tycoon; Ruth Gallivanter (Ruth Galanter), the threatened area's city councilwoman; plus Mayor Dick (Riordan) and (now former) Governor Peter (Wilson) and recently Governor Gray (Davis) represented by puppets who pop out of the developer's pockets. As the struggle to save Ballona evolves, so does the cast of characters. In addition to the new governor puppet, Rob McLiar now transforms into a Wall Street banker.

The Suits repeat the actual words and deeds of the developers and politicians they represent, so these facts can be critiqued by the audience. When the play begins, the Frog appears to be just another street crazy, while the Suits are responsible leaders acting in the best interest of the people. By the play's end these positions are reversed. The Frog is clearly the one telling the plain truth.

Our script is divided into three acts: a mini full-length tragicomedy complete with numerous references to Spielberg films, American patriotic iconography, *Angels in America,* and Shakespeare (*Hamlet* and *Macbeth*). We intend our performance to have two surfaces. When we perform outdoors, our colorful costumes and vigorous acting style appeal to children and adults distracted by shopping. When we perform indoors, nuances emerge: word-play, allusions, and visual puns. We use puppets and masks to enhance the symbolic function of our visual presentation, including a frog mask inspired by E.T. (who was modeled after a frog) and sunglasses worn by the Suits in act 1. They remove their shades as they expose their true natures. The stage manager, who introduces the show and distributes props, punctuates the action with musical accompaniment played on instruments that hang from her costume.

In each act we repeat our primary concerns so people walking by don't have to stay for the whole show to get the point. To make sure we communicate our views clearly, the performance is structured so that key information is repeated in three formats; we want the audience to see it, hear it, and read it. The action of the play itself is a flow of visual and aural images allegorically representing the problem. When the Frog is gagged at the beginning of act 1, she continues to fight back by holding up large signs so the audience can read facts that counter what the Suits are saying. During the performance the audience receives a flyer that reiterates our key concerns and lists actions they can take to save the Ballona Wetlands.

Throughout the play we encourage our audiences to question their thinking about crucial assumptions raised by the Ballona controversy. When, in the second act, the Frog asks audience members to join her in building her Frog Home, which the Suits immediately destroy, we invite people to identify with the Frog's plight and see its connection to human homelessness. A subsequent scene includes "Spielberg's List"—an operatic roll call of Ballona's endangered species, which are then swiftly executed along with the Frog. In this case our intention is to provoke questions about personal and cultural attitudes toward nature while referencing Spielberg's popular film *Schindler's List*. We create an image of the common bias in which nature, like certain ethnic groups in recent history, has limited legal standing and is viewed either as raw material to be exploited or as a hindrance to be destroyed.

The ritualized garroting of the Frog by Rob McLiar and Ruth Gallivanter, which Spielkatzengef directs and films, is the emotional center of our play. It takes place after the Suits march onto her last hideaway, playing "The Marine's Hymn" on their kazoos and waving an American flag labeled with a large green dollar sign. They plant the flag in her shopping cart, replicating for a moment the famous statue of the planting of the flag at Iwo Jima, a gesture, like the use of the American flag, meant to provoke questions about patriotism and citizenship. After her martyrdom the Frog is resurrected as a winged and haloed angel, equipped with the magical power to stop the action and sing the truth.

Getting FrogWorks to the community is not easy. Looking back at the period of our play's inception—August to October 1996—I see the serious, unanticipated obstacles that we faced casting it and finding space to perform it. Los Angeles is a car-cultured, ethnically segregated megacity, having very little history of street theater. It is infatuated with its Hollywood moguls. Paradoxically, it is a city that loves to play outdoors and lately has become a center of environmental and social activism.

Since the whole city needs to know what is at stake if Playa Vista is built, our challenge is how to identify and approach communities in such a huge and rambling metropolis. The proposed development's central location, gigantic size, and citywide impact mean that everyone will be affected if it is built. For example, the predicted ten tons of new air pollution generated every day will billow across all of L.A.'s already brown skies, but it will especially pollute South Central and East Los Angeles, where onshore breezes carry the smog. Los Angeles's Mediterranean climate suggests a city that assembles outdoors, yet it has extraordinarily little public or open space (the nation's lowest percentage). People do tend to congregate by ethnicity and class and to form communities based on their work or personal interests through mediums of communication and travel. Since there is little public transportation, many people expect to commute by car not only to work but also to associate with friends and family and to join in activities that interest them. But freeways don't provide points of congregation as do mass transit stations. We faced the dilemma of creating street theater for a city where there aren't very many people on the streets.

In all of Los Angeles there is perhaps only one truly public space, the

After invading her wetlands home and killing everything that lives
there, Ruth Gallivanter (*left*) and Rob McLiar (*right*) execute the
Frog. Venice Boardwalk, Venice, California. Photograph courtesy of
Greg Sotir.

Venice Boardwalk, where performers can still arrive and present their acts
with minor restrictions and where, amid the hawkers and chainsaw jugglers,
people of various ethnicities, economic classes, and personal interests con-
verge. The only other public area where performers are regularly allowed to
mingle with shoppers is Santa Monica's Promenade, but the city requires an
entertainment license. The license application's requirements characterize
L.A.'s limited access to public space: over a hundred dollars in fees; answers
to such questions as each performer's height, weight, eye and hair color; and
driver's license and social security numbers, followed by a police check.[3]
The first time we performed on the Promenade, our presence provoked an
argument between policemen, who disagreed about whether or not we had
a free speech right to perform without the license.

Subsequently, we discovered that, indeed, we do have this right, and
we often perform on the Promenade so we can engage people attending the
many movie theaters located there, especially when DreamWorks films are
playing. We also perform for schools, colleges, and universities and at club
meetings, conferences, rallies, and churches throughout the city. Usually

we're invited, but occasionally we just show up. Our theater catches people's attention and makes them laugh as it presents them with Playa Vista's potential impact on their lives. We find that each performance creates a small community of concern—sometimes fragile and temporary and sometimes lasting—within the larger round of neighborhood and metropolis.

Lack of public space in Los Angeles not only makes finding places to perform perplexing; it also leaves the city with almost no tradition of street theater. Consequently, most people, including actors and activists, don't have an aesthetic, personal, or political frame for this kind of experience, which made casting for FrogWorks quite difficult. Most nonactor activists are unprepared for the time and energy commitment theater requires, while professional actors want to perform where agents and casting directors can see them and where they will be seen and reviewed as performing in a "legitimate" arena. We found ourselves faced with the weakened, but still kicking, modernist attitude that sets art against activism. Meanwhile, neither activists nor actors were prepared for the demands of street theater.

Performing on the street is like volunteering to be a rock in a river: our form is reinvented by the flowing course of the audience—where they decide to stand, if and when they decide to leave, whether or not one or more of them is drunk and wants to join us or heckle us. Wherever we perform, including DreamWorks movie premieres or opening nights on Hollywood Boulevard, we might be heckled, enthusiastically applauded, or ignored. Our reviews are instant. When we first started performing, a man who identified himself as an accountant for a major studio put fifty dollars in our collection hat saying he agrees with us that the wetlands should be saved. Fairly often, adults as well as children cry and call out "No!" when the Frog is murdered. Others, of course, shout, "Spielberg would never do that!" Audience response is as varied as the weather, though about a year ago we and our flyer distributors noticed a distinct shift. When we first started performing, most people seemed perplexed or left quickly when we offered a postperformance discussion. The unabated grassroots fight to save the wetlands, however, has finally begun to permeate public awareness. Now when we go out, people often request a flyer and comment that they know about the issue and support our position. Although some still advise us that "you can't fight city hall," as Allaire says, "At least we are acting."

As we confront the perils of performing street theater in L.A. and the obdurate issue of artistic legitimacy, we FrogWorkers find ourselves in a wonderfully paradoxical position. Our transgressions make us dangerous, and our vulnerability gives us power and attention—people are afraid of us and for us. Audiences know we are taking on the titans not only of Los

Angeles but of the state and even the world, since some of the investors are among the richest people on the planet. That we would do something as quixotic and risky as political street theater, performing without the protection of even a stage, speaking up unequivocally to people and institutions that make most people feel afraid and impotent, shines on us a klieg light of legitimacy. We up the ante of what people might expect of their public spaces, of art, and of themselves as citizen. The troupe members' struggle, however, to make time for FrogWorks and its unique requirements while attempting to make a living takes a toll. And some of us hope that in the process we won't be professionally maimed by the entertainment industry.

A serious issue that especially concerns every professional member of our troupe is the fear of being blacklisted by Spielberg, Katzenberg, and Geffen. This is not a petty anxiety given the extraordinary power of these three men and the corporations they represent individually and together as DreamWorks. Actors well-known in Hollywood for their social justice and environmental activism have remained conspicuously silent about the Ballona Wetlands controversy.[4] When asked about this in an interview, Andy Goodman, president of the Environmental Media Awards, put it succinctly: "This is a company town. It doesn't pay to go against the company."[5] As corporations grow and the public sphere shrinks, the power of the very wealthy to influence artistic as well as social and political decisions becomes more invasive. Producing FrogWorks exposed to us the local sway of these powerful forces.

The threat and promise of Hollywood bounty cast an onerous shadow. Steven Spielberg, known as a major Democratic Party financial mainstay, gave fifty thousand dollars to Republican Pete Wilson's presidential campaign in 1996. A promise from Wilson of forty million dollars in state subsidies for Playa Vista soon followed. Shortly before the board of a prominent local arts organization, 18th Street Arts Complex, was to discuss a resolution to join the coalition, it received a phone call from one of its funding sources, the Geffen Foundation (a major Los Angeles art funder), questioning its stance on the issue. This kind of inquiry is most unusual and was interpreted by the center's codirector as an attempt to quash coalition support. In 1997 DreamWorks invited the executive directors of Greenpeace, the Sierra Club, and the Surfrider Foundation, all coalition members, for individual private meetings with the apparent intent to dissuade them from supporting the coalition. Hollywood megamoney, a critical source of funding for political, environmental, and arts organizations, exerts a dismaying new kind of censorship.

FrogWorks faced this very problem in April 1997, when we performed for two assemblies at Manual Arts High School, located in South Central Los Angeles. We were invited by the history department, where we were warmly received by the faculty and students. We brought with us a speaker, maps, charts, flyers, and information from the Sierra Club and, as usual, listed phone numbers of the developers, moviemakers, and politicians involved. A week later we learned that several students actually followed through and made the calls we suggested. I was told by a faculty member that the students readily understood the politics of rich and poor exemplified by the corporate welfare being dished out to DreamWorks. Some of the students also showed up at a rally held at the wetlands a few weeks later. Others, however, felt disillusioned and despairing because, yet again, adults they might admire turned out to be untrustworthy. Shortly after the students phoned, DreamWorks retaliated with an angry phone call to the administration about our presence on campus. In Los Angeles, as in the rest of the state, public agencies like schools must often augment their budgets by petitioning private foundations and donors. FrogWorks was abruptly uninvited from participating in a Manual Arts High School educational fair, where at first we had been asked to perform.

Our troupe was central to the planning for Earth Water Air Los Angeles (EWALA), a four-day ecopolitical performance and trek that I conceived and which Jan Williamson art-directed. Like a medieval mystery play that entertains as it models community values, we urged people to see Los Angeles as a vital landscape having intrinsic worth but with precious little open space left to save. In the fall of 1996 one of EWALA's organizers sent letters to local and state politicians asking for their endorsement as part of our fund-raising campaign. Suddenly, in March our unknown trek was on the front page of the local papers as, one by one, the endorsing politicians held press conferences announcing that they had been deceived because they didn't know we were protesting Playa Vista and DreamWorks when we said we were walking to save the Ballona Wetlands. One senator's letter to us was openly copied to DreamWorks's public relations director.[6]

None of this last-minute chaos stopped us. In April 1997, and again in 1998, we commenced our forty-two-mile walk from the Ahmanson Ranch, in the oak woodlands bordering the San Fernando Valley, where another immense development is planned, along the course of the threatened Los Angeles River, to the Ballona Wetlands.[7] We carried thirteen-foot-tall puppets representing the elements, huge banners announcing our purpose, ribboned dream-catchers, and, in 1998, we wore headdresses of local animals created by art students at Roosevelt High School. Over fifty students from Roosevelt, located on the eastside in Boyle Heights, joined us for a half-day of trekking. Banging up against the limits of public space, playing our kazoos and drums, and explaining through bullhorns, we spilled over the narrow sidewalks into the traffic. We draped our banners over the railings of freeway bridges and struggled through the wind tunnels created by the tall buildings on Wilshire Boulevard. All along the way people came out of their homes and businesses or stopped their cars to ask what we were doing. At parks, schools, universities, and street corners FrogWorks performed, demonstrations and teach-ins were held, and over five thousand informational flyers were distributed by the approximately one hundred young, old, abled, disabled, and racially diverse people who participated each year.

Each time FrogWorks performed, we adapted our work to our audiences, which included Latino children at Balboa Park, students at UCLA, and bar patrons on Santa Monica Pier. The trekkers saw our play several times, memorizing the lines and joining in, á la *The Rocky Horror Picture Show*. One of the children who trekked even created a role for himself and joined the cast. The Ballona activist community's generous appreciation revealed to us how much our play, with its satiric humor and review of the facts, helps to rally the troops and cheer them on.

Like proverbial weeds poking through cement, FrogWorks implicates its audiences in the fate of the Ballona Wetlands. When we try to hand out our flyer before we start performing, we are usually rebuffed or ignored as though we were homeless beggars. But once the play starts, like an invisible curtain, resistance tends to dissipate. Our play is a keen tool for the imagination and emotions, revealing the essence of the problem through its allegory, hyperreality, and humor. If audience members have never heard of the Ballona issue, then seeing FrogWorks even for ten minutes alerts them to the controversy. Artistically, we feel our work responds to the challenges posed by the art educator, Kees Vuijk, when he was questioned about Dutch public policy and the arts: "Is this art sufficiently itself? Does it make use of the freedom available? Is it filling the space open to art in our culture?"[8]

FrogWorks began performing in October 1996, and since then we have had a wonderful, weird, challenging run in which we've performed for thousands of people.[9] We know we are upholding the venerable lineage of street performance as we confront a local manifestation of megacorporate will contesting the well-being of the local environment, a confrontation seen more and more frequently in the streets. We have seen how street theater climbs over the barriers of media neglect and even hostility, allowing us to engage people directly within the context of their daily lives. Our intention is to present an entertaining, informative, emotionally affecting play that alarms people and persuades them to take our flyer, read it, and take action. We want our audiences to form a community of concern, to help us spread the word about how some of the richest men in the city have been offered millions of tax dollars to destroy the last wetland in Los Angeles. FrogWorks is part of a citywide effort by people who envision not more cement and pollution but a green, nourishing wetland that serves the whole community of life in Los Angeles.

NOTES

1. On 2 July 1999 DreamWorks announced that it was permanently withdrawing from the Playa Vista development. Currently, Wall Street bankers Morgan Stanley Dean Witter, and Goldman Sachs and investor groups Pacific Capital and Oak Tree Capital form the consortium known as Playa Capital.

2. The original stable cast (1996 to early 1997) included Allaire Paterson-Koslo, Jonathan Hayles, Erika Ackerman, and Susan Suntree. The current cast includes Allaire Paterson-Koslo, David Koff, Rob Kinslow, Dennis Olivieri, Susan Suntree, and Jan Williamson, who also took over costume and prop design from Oksana Korsun. Zoey Zimmerman continues as our director. Our website is www.thelyp.com/ewala.

3. In October 1997 the Santa Monica City Council lowered the entertainment license fee but added more restrictions. Since then license requirements have been debated and changed several times partly in response to a street performer's lawsuit.

4. In 1997 actors Ed Asner, Esai Morales, and Martin Sheen spoke out against the destruction of the Ballona Wetlands in the documentary film *The Last Stand,* directed by Sheila Laffey and Todd Brunelle.

5. "DreamWeavers," *George* (March 1997): 92.

6. Barbara Boxer, letter to Mary Altman, 7 March 1997.

7. The 1999 trek was a two-day event (17 and 18 April) that attracted over 500 participants from all parts of the city, several prominent local politicians, and environmental leaders. In 2000 EWALA participated in Earth Day LA with environmental groups from across the country, students and teachers from Roosevelt High School, indigenous Native Americans, FrogWorks, and other local artists.

8. Kees Vuijk quoted in Ritsaert Ten Cate, *Man Looking for Words* (Netherlands: Theater Institute, 1996), 117.

9. DreamWorks's withdrawal from the Playa Vista development prompted us to create a new play, "Saving Private Pickle Plant," which we scripted collectively and debuted in December 1999. Since then, FrogWorks has performed in front of three Morgan Stanley Dean Witter offices and, in January 2000, spent five days performing in New York on the steps of Wall Street in front of the corporate offices of Morgan Stanley, Dean Witter and at the Esperanza Garden, which was bulldozed a few days later. In August 2000, FrogWorks performed during various events protesting outside the Democratic National Convention in Los Angeles to call attention to how a giant global bank makes environmentally ruinous local investments.

The work to save the Ballona Wetlands continues with growing public support. Meanwhile, the Los Angeles City Council recently voted to give Playa Capital a $468 million package of both interest-free and Mello-Roos Bonds. The Mello-Roos bonds would be repaid by business owners and residents of Playa Vista and would finance the developer's version of wetlands restoration even as Playa Capitol continues to assert in its publicity statements that it is paying for the restoration. There are now four lawsuits pending against various aspects of the development and over ninety members of the coalition Citizens United to Save ALL of Ballona.

Marcia Blumberg

Puppets Doing Time in the Age of AIDS

Over the centuries puppetry has developed into a multifaceted art form that includes ritual, folk art, plays, and a popular entertainment especially geared for children in the interrelated genres of theater, the movies, and television. In pre- and postelection South Africa puppets have played an important role in breaking new ground.[1] Peter Larlham's 1991 essay about theater in transition documents various events, including Gary Friedman's Puppets against AIDS, and lists some defining features of South African theater:

> a theatre that addresses issues of immediate relevance to South African society with a de-emphasis on producing Western works; play making rather than working from preexistent scripts—the actor is regarded as a role-maker rather than an interpreter of roles; a theatre that assists in re-education after the long period of enforced censorship and disinformation.[2]

In an unusual mode puppetry is fulfilling these criteria and making a radical contribution toward theater as a transformative force in South Africa at a significant time when, in the opinion of a local AIDS expert, Dr. Clive Evian, "the South African epidemic is one of the most explosive in the world . . . and will have devastating consequences for the country."[3] As the brainchild of puppeteer Gary Friedman, a pilot project developed out of ten years of work with puppets to promote HIV/AIDS awareness. Puppets in Prison utilizes the stark locale of a prison environment to intervene through

Marcia Blumberg is a Research Fellow at the Open University, England. Her involvement with the Puppets in Prison project stems from her conviction of the relevance of theater to productive societal change. Puppets in Prison forms part of a cross-cultural study, "Staging AIDS: Theatre as/and Activism," now in progress. She coedited *South African Theatre as/and Intervention* with Dennis Walder and is completing *Engendering Intervention in Contemporary South African Theatre*.

the medium of puppetry in the harsh reality of oppressive structures, brutal practices, and the ever-growing AIDS pandemic.

My essay situates this puppet project in its specific national and sociopolitical coordinates at the nexus of theater as an interventionary force in the prison milieu and the AIDS pandemic. In historicizing the context for these complex issues, it is valuable to analyze the role of one South African prison in the history of the nation. Although the criminal and the political grounds for incarceration were often deliberately blurred and regarded by some as equivalent in the apartheid discourse, Robben Island, a political prison from 1667, has since 1961 assumed a unique position as the bastion of the liberation struggle, signifying courage, survival, and the dream of free-dom. Leaders of then-banned political organizations kept faith with their ideals despite the harsh conditions and physical demands. Nelson Mandela articulated the dilemma: "The great challenge is how to resist, how not to adjust, to keep intact the knowledge of society outside and to live by its rules."[4] Strategies to enact this challenge involved the often surreptitious circulation of reading materials, a determined effort among prisoners to share their knowledge, whether teaching rudimentary reading and writing, upgrading skills, or keeping one another apprised of the latest political developments, and participation in weekly performances of poetry, story-telling, and dramatic material.

Robben Island also provides a context for theater in prison as a vehicle of intervention. *The Island,* devised in 1973 by Athol Fugard, John Kani, and Winston Nshona, gives spectators a window on a world that, John Kani reminds us, "we never talk about, no one can write about, the press cannot talk about, not even white South Africans, free as they are can talk about."[5] Yet this collaborative work evokes salient aspects: the opening scene, which includes a sequence of "back-breaking and grotesquely futile labour"[6] (which can take an interminable stage time of ten minutes or longer); the complex bonding communicated by the two actors and prison inmates, John and Winston; the power of theater to voice protest, here in the form of the play-within-the-play, *The Trial of Antigone,* derived from Sophocles's tragedy. Since the playlet is performed at the prison concert, *The Island's* spectators watching the action on the bare stage are cast in the added role of prison audience; unlike the prison inmates, they are free to leave the theater and necessarily occupy spectatorial positions synonymous with the prison warders (guards). In the moments of enforced complicity spectators hear Winston's Antigone refuse to remain silent in the face of injustice and voice his resistance to Creon and other authority figures. Theater within this prison setting focuses upon rights and rituals of ancient Greece and at the same time speaks to the oppressive structures that expose problems of race, class, and gender roles as well as restricted liberty for the vast majority of South Africans until 1994.

Robben Island in the mid-nineteenth century also served as a hospital for the mentally ill and from the last decade of that century until 1930 functioned as a leper colony. A book on Robben Island addressed to high school teachers and students sets tasks in each section; one proposed debate, titled "Are AIDS Victims the 'Lepers' of the 1990s?"[7] refers to a reprinted 1994 local newspaper report suggesting that children in Swaziland infected with HIV/AIDS should be barred from school, since they have no future and are damned by divine punishment. Notwithstanding the highly contested word *victim* so reviled by people living with HIV/AIDS, many of whom courageously face daily hurdles and prize their empowerment, however much illness may create challenges, the analogy between AIDS and leprosy raises Paula Treichler's concern that "AIDS is simultaneously an epidemic of a transmissible lethal disease and an epidemic of meanings or signification."[8] While ignorance, bigotry, and discrimination spawn fear and stigmatization of people infected with HIV/AIDS, the distrust of official policy bred during the apartheid years exacerbates the complexity of the issues.

The AIDS pandemic in South Africa constitutes different demographics from that of North America or Britain in that those infected with HIV or living with AIDS are mainly black men and women; statistics also show that approximately one in four black babies is born seropositive.[9] In fact, the term *child-headed household* is now used when both parents have died from AIDS-related causes. Mary Crewe explains how apartheid structures have affected the AIDS crisis:

> There is little doubt that AIDS has generated a good deal of angst in South Africa. Although it is a new disease, it is laying bare and exacerbating the social prejudices, the economic inequalities, discriminatory practices and political injustices that have been the cornerstones of apartheid.[10]

Here Crewe insists on an awareness of differentials of marginalization and their effect on the situations of people living with HIV/AIDS. In her 1992 report on an "AIDS and Lifestyle Education Project Undertaken in Rural Zululand," Lynn Dalrymple provides extensive analyses of the methodology and rationale for drama education rather than conventional teaching around the issues of HIV/AIDS. Among many aspects she highlights the work of Paulo Freire, whose *Pedagogy of the Oppressed* challenges what he calls "the banking concept of education," which supposedly deposits information into putatively empty vessels and calls instead for "learning through doing"[11] and an understanding of how society functions. This DramAidE project provides for participants' active involvement and has made such an impact that related programs have started in Grahamstown and Johannesburg.[12]

Gary Friedman has also made a marked contribution to this field of AIDS awareness; his work particularly epitomizes the transformative potential of puppet theater. Returning to his homeland in 1987 after training in Paris with the Muppet master, Jim Henson, Friedman founded the African Research and Educational Puppetry Programme (AREPP), which is a community-based educational trust. The group's first project, "Puppets Against AIDS," is periodically updated and takes life-size puppets onto the streets to perform for adults outside health clinics, at the mines, taxi ranks, and other street venues; transportable theatrical projects such as the group's consciousness-raising version of Punch and Judy also visit factories and offices. Different shows geared for audiences at primary, junior high, and secondary schools approach HIV/AIDS issues from various perspectives and employ a range of puppets and media to entertain and involve spectators and concomitantly engage pressing issues.

In 1994 Friedman left AREPP[13] to tackle new challenges, including a pilot project, "Puppets in Prison." This peer group educational theater program developed for prisoners directly confronts the nexus of apparently unrelated but vital issues in a postelection South Africa: violent crime on an unparalleled scale and the rapidly increasing AIDS pandemic. Gary Friedman acted upon his belief that "without the element of risk—in life, in theatre—things are not worth doing."[14] For this innovative project, undertaken in 1996, twelve[15] long-term prisoners were selected to participate in an eight-week workshop from a section of Diepkloof Prison, Johannesburg, that houses inmates from the ages of eighteen to twenty-four years and offers no recreational facilities. His modest proposal should be compared with another approach to theater as a supposedly interventionary vehicle: Mbongeni Ngema's lavish 1995 musical, Sarafina 2, purported to be an entertaining as well as educational production about AIDS and issues of safe sex. Scandalous budgetary demands (over 14 million Rand, approximately 3.5 million dollars) funneled into salaries and promotional excesses resulted in the discrediting of officials, including the Minister of Health and the return of funds to the European Union; the closure of the production within a few months hinged on these factors as well as inflated ticket prices and the musical's poor critical reception. Most significantly, the lack of advice from activists, health professionals, and people from the communities who are most affected not only demonstrated arrogance but resulted in poor and irresponsible communication about salient issues within the framework of the production. Adele Baleta discloses that "Dr. Evian, a public health physician, saw *Sarafina 2* and described it as a 'slap in the face to AIDS health care workers struggling with meagre resources.'"[16] The gross wastage is easily assessed when calculations demonstrate that the *Sarafina 2* budget would have funded over 150 Puppets in Prison workshop series (at a cost of approximately ninety thousand Rand each).

Unlike the *Sarafina 2* situation, health professionals initiated the prison project with sessions on AIDS awareness and its impact on the prison community, in particular. Friedman and Nyanga Tshabalala provided training in puppet making, acting, and rudimentary set design. Most important, they created a safe space and engendered a collaborative process based on a growing trust in which prisoners/puppeteers utilized the opportunity to share personal experiences and fears about HIV infection, AIDS, rape, prostitution, gangsterism, and other related scenarios that eventually constituted the narratives of the puppet playlets. Friedman emphasizes that "puppets can do and say things that real live actors wouldn't dare do."[17] Ventriloquizing their stories through the mouths of the puppet characters has a liberating effect, since the actors can communicate their concerns in a narrative that engages sensitive and even dangerous issues, yet there is no direct line of retaliation, since it is the puppet character and not the actor performing his own story. These "created performers,"[18] a term coined by Eileen Blumenthal, although manipulated and spoken by the actors, mediate between the embarrassment or shame of personal revelation and the necessity to impart educational material in dramatizations that entertain the audience and empower the actors who know that their performances are relevant to the prisoners' lives. Adele Baleta explains the process: "The workshop is presented to up to 50 inmates a day and is constantly revised and reworked."[19] These sessions culminated in performances for high-profile officials from the Department of Correctional Services (DCS), other prisoners, and warders; the latter frequently occupy contradictory positions as agents for forced prostitution and other coercive situations and are totally ineffectual in imparting information on AIDS awareness to inmates, who regard them with distrust.

A detailed evaluation of the process and the final performance product of Puppets in Prison by Renee Bub and Dr. Clive Evian demonstrates an overwhelmingly positive reception by the various audiences. The few negative comments from prisoner/spectators were content related and spoke particularly about absences—issues they regarded as especially pertinent but which the narratives had failed to include. Bub and Evian cite the opinions of some inmates: "There was no depiction of warders. If you did it would make it more real to our day-to-day lives and problems"; and "Yes it is realistic to prison life, some of the time. But the warders selling juvenile prisoners to older prisoners was not revealed."[20] Hazel Friedman assesses the warders' absence from a different perspective: "Their exclusion is perhaps one of the loudest statements prisoners can make about temporarily reclaiming power through theatre in a place where they have been stripped of it completely."[21] Despite her view of their envisaged empowerment to enact the scenario within the inmate hierarchy, the prisoners' comments insist on greater complexity within the narratives and representations that conform more closely to the reality of their prison world.

For the project the group chose to work with two kinds of puppets. Glove or hand puppets in the format of a Punch and Judy show were situated in a puppet booth fashioned from a tent. In addition, large rod (body) puppets were played in front of the booth in full view of the audience. Puppeteers used their arms as the puppet's arm and showed the manipulation of the rod puppet. Small microphones worn by the actors/manipulators amplified their voices during the performance. The twelve prisoners each created a character, developed a narrative, and made an appropriate puppet in one of three playlets. These constitute rudimentary scripts that fall within the general rubric so apt for prison life: "love has no bars." In analyzing these scenarios, all of which revolve around networks of power and sexual relationships, the performed narratives are examined in conjunction with a video of workshop sessions and remarks by the puppeteers, newspaper reviews, and a thirty-eight-page evaluative report of the project to assess it as a vehicle of transformation and rehabilitation, albeit on a small scale.

The first scenario centers on a male prostitute dubbed Sharon Stone whose relationships with two inmate "bosses" demonstrate a sexual and material economy that also involves the transmission of HIV. Cas St. Leger identifies the complex relationship between actor/creator and character:

Sharon Stone would never have recognized herself. . . . Anonymous in drab prison garb and hidden behind the puppet stand, which is light years away from seaside Punch and Judy shows, 20-year old Johannes Mmusi from Alexandra [township] was at Sharon Stone's controls. . . . The dread locked Sharon Stone represents a gay prisoner in drag. The words "she" speaks in a hodge-podge of South Africa's official languages are the proud creation of Mmusi.[22]

These observations also expose displacements of race, gender, and sexual orientation in the embodiment of the particular construction, which takes into the heart of a restrictive locale identity issues only recently addressed in South Africa by antidiscrimination laws. Since eleven of the twelve prisoners in the group were black, these shifts constituted a sense of realism for the creators and prison audience alike, all of whom seemed to value that aspect of the scenarios as a basic necessity for peer identification and awareness raising.

The playlet's plot line is simple and direct. When the rich boss, Tshepo, falls ill, the doctor's diagnosis of AIDS takes them all by surprise. This reaction is quite understandable on an individual level but also represents a different form of denial: an initial widespread disbelief in the existence of AIDS that stems from the apartheid years, when distrust and misinformation were engendered and manipulated by the dominant power structures. Tshepo's death, while accelerated and far-fetched in terms of a lived reality, nevertheless foregrounds the effects of risky sexual practices and negligence about health care and testing. This condensed time sequence equates AIDS with death and provides a simplistic and terrible certainty that elides the possibility of years of living with HIV, especially at a time when antiviral cocktails have shown promising results. Yet perhaps this situation more accurately exposes the reality of the AIDS pandemic in South Africa and other parts of the continent, where exorbitantly priced medication is just not a viable option, since poverty and deplorable conditions often prevail. Since Tshepo and the poor boss, Spiwe, have had sex with Sharon Stone, they are both fearful and engage in mutual blame. Sharon's cough necessitates a doctor's visit, which includes an HIV test; the importance of retaining "her" role as prostitute in the prison hierarchy prompts a decision to remain silent about the test results: "'I am only responsible for me and nobody else,' growled Ms. Stone, 'girlfriend' of prison 'bosses' Spiwe and Tshepo." St. Leger further clarifies the situation: "Johannes and his fellow prisoner-puppeteers . . . believe they have a responsibility to each other."[23] This exposure of Stone's bravado, or perhaps what she considers a necessary lack of knowledge in order to survive the prison locale, emphasizes the antithesis. The actors, whose serostatus was unknown to Friedman, displayed concern about HIV; from the beginning of the workshops they developed a sense of motivation particularly within their roles as peer educators, who in the final analysis could feel responsible for saving lives.

The second playlet focuses upon rape, a practice prevalent in prison but here performed as a sexual initiation rite into the dynamics of gangsterism. When Bra Biza, the knife-wielding boss of a prison gang, who is also HIV-positive, hears about a new inmate, he sends his "guard" Roger to procure

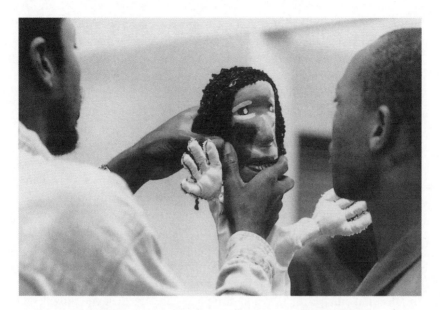

Puppeteer Nyanga Tshabalala (*left*) and inmate Johannes Mmusi (*right*)
engage with Mmusi's creation, Sharon Stone, a puppet representing a
gay prisoner in drag, in the Puppets in Prison workshop held at
Diepkloof Prison, Johannesburg, 1996. Photograph courtesy of
Gisele Wulfson.

the young prisoner for himself and promises the newcomer material com-
forts: "clean bedding, soap, cigarettes." Biza's act of rape accompanied by
the youngster's screams for mercy loses none of the horrific violence when
enacted by puppets. The lack of physical and emotional inhibitions of puppets adds to the potential for increasing the severity of the violence, yet the
human involvement is never forgotten, as the actors manipulating the puppets are fully visible; this linkage emphasizes egregious modes of behavior in
and out of prison. When Roger take his turn to repeat the violent act, the
intervention of the former guerilla fighter, Sporo, who has lost a friend to
AIDS, provokes a fight in which Bra Biza stabs Sporo and Roger and tri-
umphantly declares to the audience, "I am boss." Daryl Accone reports
Gary Friedman's assessment of this moment: "To watch the delicacy of a
huge guy manipulating a glove puppet, a character that has been stabbed to
death with a pair of scissors, is amazing."[24] The exchange of commodities
and sexual favors in an oppressive hierarchy of machismo and territorial
claims raises questions of danger within prison culture that places the transmission of AIDS in juxtaposition with other, more familiar concerns. The

message is always one of fear and spells out the equation, AIDS = death. This scenario uses the viral threat as subtext while showing a trajectory of violence that begins with the circulation of power within a gang and enacts rape as an extreme form of sexual violence that can result in death.

The third scenario dramatizes what the first playlet debates. Boss "owns" the cell and protects his "girlfriend," Maria Podesta, in exchange for loyalty and sexual availability. Sexual relationships are demonstrated in an unusually graphic way by the construction of a "Mdiya-diya." This tentlike structure of sheets around a bed offers privacy of a sort so that other inmates know and hear what takes place without seeing it. What may seem a creative solution to an expected event is in the context of this prison performance a daring act, since the authorities deny that sexual relationships occur in prison and therefore forbid the distribution of condoms. Other characters bring AIDS awareness to the fore: the puppet, Special, knows about AIDS from life on the outside, and the doctor discusses sexually transmitted diseases and advises Maria, who is wracked by pain, to abstain from sex. While this decision enrages the boss and disrupts his life, the dialogue provides an opportunity for discussion and information on many issues, including the benefits of monogamous relationships and the necessity for condom use. Rafiq Rohan reports Gary Friedman's dilemma: "We may teach the prisoners about HIV and AIDS and the use of condoms but we cannot distribute condoms. This dichotomy . . . creates difficulty and is cause for great frustration."[25] Describing the situation as a "health time bomb," an editorial in the same newspaper argues:

> It appears that everyone except the Minister [of Correctional Services] is aware of the looming threat. . . . It would be highly irresponsible for the department to take the position that because it is not permitted, sex among prisoners is not happening. Equally dangerous is the rather puritanical view that to provide prisoners with condoms, as they should be, would encourage sexual relations behind bars.[26]

This scenario also proves reductive of the many complex nuances of the issues it raises, but, unlike the two preceding playlets, it moves from violence and harshness to an insistence on the necessity of dialogue and understanding other perspectives.

Baleta suggests the anticipated trajectory of Puppets in Prison: "Friedman had submitted a one-year budget of less than one million Rand. . . . The plan was to train eleven groups of prisoners, who through the medium of puppetry, would educate their peers in jails in all provinces."[27] The significant projected continuance of puppeteers to train other prisoners and impart skills and vital aspects of AIDS awareness was aborted due to lack of funds despite high praise from the DCS, an African National Congress (ANC) cabinet minister's statement on video that this program should be implemented in every prison in South Africa, and the known statistics that approximately 20 percent of the Diepkloof prisoners were diagnosed with HIV/AIDS. Internal government political feuding has proved an immense obstacle to the project. Gaye Davis argues that the "chief casualties of the conflict between the correctional services minister [Dr. Sipo Mzimela], and then ANC Member of Parliament, Carl Niehaus [now an ambassador in Europe], are the prisoners, prison staff and prison reform."[28] Mzimela has been criticized for hasty decisions, lack of consultation with parliamentary committees, and morale problems at a time when violent crime continues to escalate. Moreover, dire overcrowding in prisons has led the authorities to consider and reject the proposed conversion of disused mine shafts into prison cells in favor of prison ships anchored in naval dockyards. While these suggestions elicited outrage in certain quarters, a report from the *Herald Sun* reminds us that "South Africa has one of the world's highest crime rates, and has already granted amnesty to some prisoners to relieve a growing burden on the prison system."[29] In an address on penal reform Jody Kollapen notes the untenable conditions, which he attributes to gross overcrowding, militarism within the correctional system, and the lack of effective educational and vocational opportunities:

> Within the prison system hundreds of thousands of abuses of human rights took place [under apartheid] and still continue. . . . [W]e need to transform our system not because others expect us to do it but rather because we as South Africans believe that the system is wrong, that it negates the very ideals we fought for and that it negates the important features of a democratic society.[30]

Although conditions at many of the correctional facilities are deficient and even dangerous, recidivism is high. Nyanaga Shabalala explains that for many young black South Africans the lack of education, skills, jobs, and opportunities combined with the high cost of basic necessities for living often translates into a desire to be caught and sent back, since life may be easier to handle in the structured environment of the prison.[31]

The Diepkloof project was not reinstated, and each time I hear the participants' views on the video or read the evaluation report I feel a combination of anger, a sense of their betrayal and wasted opportunities, and a fear for their futures. John Sloop considers rehabilitation of prisoners an out-moded process yet at the same time offers Edgardo Rotman's deeply felt argument for "rehabilitation not as something granted to the criminal but as a human right. . . . [I]t is the task of society to provide all outlets for the cul-tivation of human independence and self-determination."[32] The rehabilita-tive function of Puppets in Prison is clearly articulated by the puppeteers involved. They reiterated how the program served as a turning point in their lives when, for the first time, they formed long-term goals and future visions. Most notable was their increased confidence and sense of self-worth; their newly learned skills and significant roles as peer educators trans-lated for them into the potential for a viable future, especially when AIDS education addresses life and death issues and the other interconnected prob-lems of violence that form a cycle that impacts on life both in and outside prison.

During the workshop the puppeteers also developed a commitment to the project and to its participants, learned a self-activated discipline, and practiced physical training and meditation; the creative and performance aspects offered them a special opportunity in an otherwise harsh prison rou-tine that allowed no recreational outlet. Their understanding of stigmatiza-tion came through clearly in the workshop and discussion process but is less prominent in the scenarios than the ramifications of the existence of the virus and the prevention of its transmission. Nevertheless, the process as a whole is markedly different from the situation outlined by Philippa Garson in a 1994 report:

> One of the HIV-positive inmates in a Johannesburg Prison describes the level of stigmatization: he no longer has a name, no longer has rights. "My name is HIV or AIDS kaffir." Most of them receive no counseling and the news of their status is often given in public as they wait in line with other prisoners. Even their food is labelled HIV.[33]

These intolerable acts of discrimination and harshness are even more oppressive by virtue of their containment within a prison environment and exacerbate the stress and vulnerability of people already coping with the virus.

The demise of the Diepkloof project occurred despite many initiatives on the part of Gary Friedman and others as well as critical appraisals such as the one from Daryl Accone: that this project "may well provide the blue-print for HIV and AIDS education in our jails."[34] The comprehensive eval-uation report, which analyzes many aspects, concludes with overall praise for the project as "an excellent AIDS initiative that gave audiences important information about AIDS and also served to stimulate further interest in and discussion about the disease." Yet it was also threatening on other counts: "Certain of the prison staff felt that 'Puppets in Prison' was giving a negative message to the outside world. Furthermore they were shocked by some of the feedback they received pertaining to the programme. As a result they were not comfortable with the programme."[35] Nevertheless, a second workshop was held in January 1997 at the Ekuseni Youth Development Centre in Natal involving a new group of prisoners and scenarios. An invitation for another workshop in 1998 and the reported benefits of the first, like that of the Diepkloof project, mark this puppet theater as a transformative vehicle but remind us that these initiatives are tenuous unless funding is available for support. Reporting on a South African theater festival at Lincoln Center, New York, during August 1997, Donald G. McNeil Jr. warns that

> South African theater is in some danger of dying, not for lack of topics to write about, but because crime is choking off audiences. Theatregoers are nervous about driving downtown at night to venues like the world-famous Market Theater. Theater in black townships is "literally dead" because of crime, [Duma] Ndlovu said.[36]

How fitting that this vital theater project within prison should have gained support and gathered momentum, yet its limited deployment relates directly to paucity of funds and governmental inaction. Puppets in Prison fulfilled an opportunity to confront violence on all levels and procure greater well-being in this time of AIDS.[37] Now more than ever, its demise should be countered by renewed efforts and an urgent realization: in the postelection transition period doing time can be synonymous with a productive use of time.[38]

NOTES

I acknowledge sincere appreciation to Gary Friedman and Nyanga Tshabalala, who inspired me with their commitment and who generously provided me with interviews, e-mail correspondence, video, scripts, and evaluation reports that brought to life a process that I couldn't witness. A warm debt of gratitude also to Stephen Barber for his inspiration and ongoing engagement with my work. Special thanks to the Social Sciences and Humanities Council of Canada for a postdoctoral fellowship supporting my work.

1. Highly innovative puppeteers are Handspring Puppet Company's Basil Jones and Adrian Kohler, who have collaborated with artist and filmmaker William Kentridge on three internationally acclaimed productions: *Woyzeck on the Highveld* (1993), *Faustus in Africa* (1995), and *Ubu and the Truth Commission* (1997). Their multimedia cross-cultural revisionings of canonical texts transform conventional readings and dazzle spectators with brilliant theatrical values that utilize the collaborative efforts of actors, puppeteers, animated drawings, magnificently carved puppets, and haunting music. The latest production is the most pared down but superbly explores the complex nexus of representations of the controversial Truth and Reconciliation Commission, historical process and artistic licence, the impossible dilemma of amnesty and the bartering of justice for truth and reconciliation, and various Ubu figures in revisioned forms that satirize national and cultural stereotypes. Notwithstanding tremendous critical success in Europe and mostly favorable reviews in South Africa the response of local spectators is revealing: some gave a standing ovation, others sat stony faced without applauding, while a few walked out to refuse engagement with the disturbing scenarios.

2. Peter Larlham, "Theatre in Transition: The Cultural Struggle in South Africa," *Drama Review* 35, no. 1 (Spring 1991): 211.

3. Clive Evian, "Latest AIDS Epidemic Update," *AIDS Management and Support* (May 1997).

4. Penny Nyren, ed., *Dreaming of Freedom: The Story of Robben Island* (Johannesburg: Sached Books, 1994), 60.

5. W. B. Worthen, "Convicted Reading: *The Island,* Hybridity, Performance," *Crucibles of Crisis: Performing Social Change* (Ann Arbor: University of Michigan Press, 1996), 174.

6. Athol Fugard, John Kani, and Winston Nshona, *The Island, Statements* (Oxford: Oxford University Press, 1974), 47.

7. Nyren, *Dreaming of Freedom,* 37.

8. Paula A. Treichler, "AIDS, Homophobia and Biomedical Discourse: An Epidemic of Signification," in *AIDS: Cultural Analysis/Cultural Activism,* ed. Douglas Crimp (Cambridge, Mass.: MIT Press, 1988), 32.

9. In a report by R. W. Johnson in the *Times of London* that appeared in Johannesburg on 26 April 1997, South Africa's health minister, Dr. Nkosana Zuma, unveiled new figures showing that the number of people infected by HIV rose in a year by 33 percent. In 1996 about 2.4 million people, or 6 percent of the population, were HIV-positive, a rise of one-third over 1995. These statistics should be read with the knowledge that there is underreporting in the wake of social stigma and medical confusion about the syndrome in a country where tuberculosis is rife and other diseases also take a huge toll. Inexplicitness about sexual practices and modes of transmission of the virus, to avoid offending conservative African social mores, exacerbates the problem when misinformation results from understatement and veiled allusions. While the average time for conversion from an HIV-positive status to full-blown AIDS seems to be twice the length (about ten years) of that occurring in the rest of Africa, probably in light of relatively better health care and food, it also means that more people are able to transmit the virus for a longer period, especially in a situation where initiatives in AIDS awareness are inadequate.

10. Mary Crewe, *AIDS in South Africa: The Myth and the Reality* (London: Penguin, 1992), 54.

11. Paulo Freire, *Pedagogy of the Oppressed,* trans. Charles A. and Maria-Odilia Leal McBride (New York: Continuum, 1989), 58, 59.

12. Michael Carklin's detailed description and analysis of methodology used in the Grahamstown DramAidE project form part of his article "Rainbows and Spider-webs: New Challenges for Theatre in a Transformed System of Education in South Africa," in *South African Theatre as/and Intervention,* ed. Marcia Blumberg and Dennis Walder (Amsterdam: Rodopi, 1999).

13. Gordon Billbrough is now at the helm of AREPP; it has continued to develop the initial programs and is also offering new material.

14. Daryl Accone, "Master Puppeteer Gary Friedman Pulls Strings, Not Punches, as He Unmasks Us," *Sunday Independent,* 21 April 1996, 4.

15. In a discussion on 7 July 1997 in Grahamstown Gary Friedman explained that there were initially fifteen members in the group. One dropped out of the project; two others tried to escape by jumping off the roof. One broke his neck and died; the other was caught and put into chains.

16. Adele Baleta, "AIDS 'Made Real' for Inmates," *Weekend Argus,* 21–22 June 1996, n.p.

17. Fiona Chisholm, "It's Soweto II—The Puppet Show," *Cape Times,* 22 March 1996, 13.

18. Eileen Blumenthal, "Life and Death of Puppets," *American Theatre* (January 1997): 17.

19. Baleta, "AIDS 'Made Real' for Inmates," n.p.

20. Renee Bub and Clive Evian, "A Qualitative Evaluation of the "Puppets in Prison" Programme Conducted in Johannesburg Prison," June 1996, 17.

21. Hazel Friedman, "Puppets Get behind Bars," *Weekly Mail and Guardian* 12, no. 15 (12–18 April 1996): 25.

22. Cas St. Leger, "No Stone Unturned," *Sunday Times,* 7 April 1996, 3.

23. Ibid., 3.

24. Accone, "Master Puppeteer," 4.

25. Rafiq Rohan, "MPs Hear about Sex in Prison," *Sowetan,* 20 March 1996.

26. "Sowetan Comment," *Sowetan,* 20 March 1996.

27. Baleta, "AIDS 'Made Real,'" n.p.

28. Gaye Davis, "Mandela Steps in to Cure Bad Blood in Prisons," *Weekly Mail and Guardian* 12, no. 12 (22–28 March 1996): 13.

29. "Outrage over Mine Jail Plan," *Herald Sun,* 6 March 1997, 26.

30. Jody Kollapen, "Transformation and the Challenges Facing Corrections in South Africa," address delivered at a Penal Reform International Seminar, London, 19 May 1995, *Penal Lexicon,* 3 November 1997, 1–5.

31. At a meeting in London on 14 September 1997 with Gary Friedman and Nyanga Tshabalala, Tshabalala explained why Ekuseni offered a more promising environment for the project. At Diepkloof, where prisoners were often moved around, gangsterism was rife and participants left their separate enclaves to work together for four hours each weekday and virtually occupy another world from their usual prison routine. On their return to the cell the boss and gang members often berated and effectively punished them for their participation in a project that gave these individuals "unearned" prominence. In contrast, Ekuseni is a rehabilitation center for youth with ongoing educational and vocational programs to equip inmates for reintegration

into society. The Ekuseni Workshop, held 7–23 December 1998, marks the final stage of "Puppets in Prison."

32. John M. Sloop, *The Cultural Prison: Discourse, Prisons and Punishment* (Tuscaloosa: University of Alabama Press, 1996), 199.

33. Philippa Garson, "The 'AIDS Kaffirs' of Johannesburg Prison," *Weekly Mail and Guardian* 10, no. 30, 29 July–4 August 1994, 4. *Kaffir* is an offensive, abusive term for a black person in South Africa.

34. Accone, "Master Puppeteer," 4.

35. Bub and Evian, "Qualitative Evaluation," 36.

36. Donald G. McNeil Jr., "A New Stage for South Africa," *New York Times*, 6 July 1997, 2:5.

37. In "The Deadly Gender Gap," an article in the *Village Voice*, 30 December 1998–5 January 1999, Mark Schoofs reports: "Just last week a South African activist, Gugu Dlamini, was stoned and beaten to death by her neighbours, furious that she had spoken out about her life with HIV." When stigmatization combines with violence to enact such brutality in the world outside prison, how much more complex is the experience of HIV/AIDS within the prison community. This incident occurred at the same time that the final Puppets in Prison workshop was completed at Ekuseni.

38. I would like to honor the memory of the South African activist Simon Nkoli, who died of AIDS-related causes on 30 November 1998. His warmth, vitality, gentleness, and resolute commitment touched me, as did his life and legacy of activism, which will continue to make a difference in international venues and throughout South Africa, particularly in Johannesburg and Soweto, where he founded GLOW (Gay and Lesbian Organization of the Witwatersrand), TAP (Township AIDS Project), and PAMP (Positive African Men Project).

Susan C. Haedicke

Theater for the Next Generation: The Living Stage Theatre Company's Program for Teen Mothers

On 12 May 1993 Lachan Richardson, a young woman from Anacostia, in Washington, D.C., testified before a House of Representatives Subcommittee on Appropriations for the National Endowment for the Arts:

> Maybe when you think about funding the arts, you think about entertainment. That's not what it is all about. I would like you to think instead about young people. Young people, like me, not just watching the arts, but actually using the arts every day of our lives. For me and my friends, art is a life-line. The arts have changed my life. . . . I am seventeen years old and I attend Ballou High School in D.C. I also have an eight-month old baby girl. I am a participant in the Living Stage Theatre Company's Teen Mothers of Today Project. . . . By coming to Living Stage and doing theater I have a whole new outlook on life.[1]

Teen pregnancy prevention has become a high priority for lawmakers, but few programs exist to help young women who already have children. Living Stage Theatre Company, an outreach venture of Arena Stage in Washington, D.C., created just such a program. This community-based theater, located in a renovated jazz club on Fourteenth Street, was founded in 1966 by Robert A. Alexander who served as its director until 1995. The company rarely gives public performances, and instead the four to six professional actors create theater with underserved populations: those Alexander calls the "forgotten people"—emotionally or physically disabled children, teens at risk, the elderly, the poor, and inmates of D.C. prisons. At Living Stage, the audience-participants attend performance-based workshops usually on a weekly basis over a year or more. With the actors they create characters and improvise scenes exploring a wide range of issues that are of particular importance to the participating group. These scenes are never rehearsed and developed into a public performance for an outside audience, but instead are used to understand, analyze, and explore solutions to a specific problem that the members of the group face in their daily lives. Thus the emphasis is on the process rather than the product.

The theater space plays a significant role in making the spectator feel comfortable as a collaborator in the making of the "performance": the large room looks more like a child's playroom than a theater. A coat tree covered with hats and pieces of brightly colored cloth, a ladder, a seven-foot-high arch like those found in playgrounds, and several large red, blue, and yellow cubes are scattered around the room. The participants are encouraged to use the tambourines and other simple musical instruments or the art supplies during the workshop. Through these participatory performances Living Stage strives to awaken the imagination and the consciousness of the spectator/actors so that they become more aware of the social situation that circumscribes their lives and more critical and creative in their approach to what needs to be done to improve their condition.

The primary goal of the teen mother program, like all Living Stage programs with other disadvantaged populations, is to empower the participants to speak up for themselves and to determine their own futures "through creativity [which] will not only affect the lives of individual mothers, but also will radically impact the ways in which the mothers interact with their children: social change through art one child at a time."[2] My use of the term "empowerment" here is based on the concept of *conscientization* introduced by Paulo Freire, who developed a literacy program that not only taught reading and writing but also critical thinking about one's world. Freire claims that the hallmark of oppression is a passivity and an unthinking acceptance of one's reality and that to be fully human, one must be active and reflective. In *Pedagogy of the Oppressed* he examines how the process of conscientization occurs through dialogue as people begin to understand institutional injustices and contradictions and learn how to utilize their power, however limited, to challenge the powerful and change their reality. Through "problem-posing education" in which students "produce" and "act upon" their own ideas rather than "consume" the ideas of others, in which they participate in knowledge construction, they "emerge from their *submersion* and acquire the ability to *intervene* in reality as it is unveiled."[3] For Freire, empowerment is the process by which people assume control over their lives by wresting their destinies from those who make their decisions for them and by passing their new-found knowledge on to others.

Participatory research,[4] the grassroots action that grows out of Freire's ideas, offers specific groups with little power and few resources a strategy by which they can work together toward social justice: to understand what they need to better their lives, to decide how to attain it, and to take effective action toward improving their conditions, achieving "material well-being and sociopolitical entitlement."[5] With the help of an outside researcher or leader, the people come together to analyze their situation and to determine collective action. John Gaventa, director of the Highlander Research and Education Center in Tennessee, explains: "Participatory research attempts to break down the distinction between the researchers and the researched, the subjects and objects of knowledge production by the participation of the people-for-themselves in the process of gaining and creating knowledge. In the process, research is seen not only as a process of creating knowledge, but simultaneously, as education and development of consciousness, and of mobilization for action."[6] Participatory research is primarily about the right to speak. "True speaking," warns bell hooks, "is not solely an expression of creative power; it is an act of resistance, a political gesture that challenges politics of domination that would render us nameless and voiceless. As such, it is a courageous act—as such, it represents a threat."[7] Thus participatory research is about intervention for the purpose of social transformation.

The teen mother program at Living Stage and, in fact, all of the theater's work with various disadvantaged groups use the principles of participatory research in the performance workshops to empower their audiences. Many practitioners and theoreticians working with the Freirean model of development have found that participatory research releases people's creativity.[8] Instead of relying on participatory research to release creativity however, Living Stage begins with the creative process, using it to lead to social action. The primary popular mobilization strategy used by the theater company shifts the participants into the "subject" position as it transforms passive spectators into active artists which, in turn, strengthens their self-reliance, willingness to express their thoughts and feelings, cooperation with others, and confidence to test new solutions on real-life problems. For Alexander, artists are people who respect themselves and expect to be taken seriously; artists communicate their thoughts and feelings to others without fear of what they might think.[9]

The goal, however, is not "to make professional theater workers of these young women, but to have an impact on their perception of themselves in relation to the rest of society."[10] Transforming spectators into artists, insists Alexander, does "more than validate their creativity: it empowers them to change things for the better"[11] because "in re-experiencing their artistry, they will be able to articulate their needs, articulate their hopes, and feel that they do make a difference."[12] Jennifer Nelson, a former actress and associate director with the company, insists that "because the work reaches so deep, [the spectator/actors] can take creative chances and do things that they might never try in any other environment." That experience of living out of the imaginative part of themselves, she continues, enables them to "become rooted in healthy behavior, even when they are not in the workshop setting."[13] In his work with various populations Alexander has found that, "Audience members become creators when they talk about the experiences of the characters. If you can make choices in the imagination, you can make choices in life."[14] Augusto Boal agrees when he writes, "The liberated spectator, as a whole person, launches into action. No matter that the action is fictional; what matters is that it is action!"[15]

Like participatory research this work "restructures [the] relationship between knowing and doing, and puts the people in charge of both the production and the utilization of knowledge."[16] Paulo Freire admits that "Participatory research is no enchanted magic wand that can be waved over the culture of silence, suddenly restoring the desperately needed voice that has been forbidden to rise and be heard. . . . the silence is not a genetically or ontologically determined condition of these women and men but the expression of perverted social, economic, and political structures, which can be transformed." But it is through participatory research that they learn to be "the masters of inquiry into the underlying causes of the events in their world"[17] and that knowledge is inextricably linked to social action.

The teen mothers project creates a community of artists/social activists through which the young women *remake* society for themselves and their children, first in their imaginations and later in their actual lives. It is community which empowers the young women by providing them with a support network that contributes to increased self-esteem and improved life skills and thus advances their chances for an independent and productive adult life. It is a community which affects social change on two levels: in the individual lives of the teens as they learn to speak for themselves, to work cooperatively, and to expect respect not only from family and friends but also from institutional representatives—teachers, social workers, police, employers—and in the next generation as the young mothers transfer these newly learned skills to their children. The micro-level claim of individual empowerment is, of course, circumscribed by the lack of clear or measurable examples of macro-level social transformation, yet individual success stories abound as Lachan Richardson testified to Congress. In one case, a teen was able to stand up to the doctor called in by the day care center who prescribed ritalin to control her active two-year old. The young mother insisted on further tests that showed that her son was not clinically hyperactive but was responding to his environment. As his mother developed self-confidence and creativity in her parenting skills, the child calmed down without drugs.[18]

Participatory Research and the Program for Teen Mothers

In 1991 Living Stage inaugurated the first three-year long program for D.C. teen mothers, aged thirteen to seventeen, and in 1994 began its second. All the teenagers decided to keep their babies, and most remained in school, in grades 8 through 10 when their babies were born. Some had more than one child. All were African-American. Some lived with their own families, others with friends or in shelters. At the beginning of each program the young mothers had limited verbal skills and low self-esteem; some even reverted to childlike behavior such as hiding behind others and thumb sucking. Their attention spans were short, their hopes for the future stopped at high school graduation, and they were fatalistic about their lives, their communities, and the world. Yet, in spite of their poverty, their weakened emotional conditions, and frequent condemnations of their choices from family, teachers, social workers, and peers, the young women were survivors and their love for and pride in their children were strong.[19] Living Stage works with these positive characteristics and does not moralize or show the teens what they did wrong. Instead the actors explore with the young women what they can change and encourage them to see their lives as works of art and, therefore, within their power to design.

Each program is structured to be a cumulative process of empowerment. The first year establishes the foundation by increasing the teens' capacity to work together, by creating a safe environment in which they can experiment with new ideas and behavior, and by allowing them to play as children. This play not only enables them to finish their own childhoods interrupted by the adult responsibility of motherhood, but it also encourages them to experience the joy of children's games so they can become better companions for their own children and to enhance their imaginative abilities, an important tool in problem-solving. In *Playing and Reality,* child psychologist D. W. Winnicott claims that play helps children organize their experiences and establish a dialogue between their inner worlds and external reality. The second year builds on this foundation of stronger imaginations as it increases the teens' independence by helping them master skills like problem-solving and conflict resolution through the use of improvisation where they experiment with approaches and solutions to problems they may face in the actual world. Alexander claims that "inherent in any work of art are problems to be solved and the process of wrestling with those problems expands children's growth effectively and cognitively."[20] They also learn to read aloud, write and tell stories, create costumes, and paint—activities important for creative parenting. The second year also focuses on parenting skills by exploring the developmental stages of a child's behavior. The third year emphasizes conflict resolution. At the end of each year, outside evaluators measured substantial improvements in the self-confidence of each of the young women and in their resilience, creative problem-solving, social and parenting skills, and the ability to play.[21]

According to Park and others, every participatory research project begins by identifying and defining a problem that affects the group and by establishing its scope and impact. The same is true in the teen mothers program where the central problem to be analyzed and tackled is overcoming the internal and external obstacles to good parenting that the young women face. Contributing to this problem are issues of lack of self-esteem, violence in personal relationships, and institutional hurdles in the form of social workers, teachers, family members, doctors, or day care providers. Each of the workshops targets a specific aspect of the central problem and its related issues.

In an early workshop with the first group of teen mothers, the actors created a scene in which a white store owner accuses an African-American teen of shoplifting and demands to search her. She responds by cursing him. An African-American policeman arrives and yells at her for making a bad name for black people, an action that hurts and confuses her. Several other incidents occur that humiliate her and highlight her apparent powerlessness until she finally runs into her friend who hands her a gun so she can rob and perhaps even kill the store owner. At this moment the scene was frozen. The teens offered endings from killing the store owner to not taking the gun but never entering the store again to saving the store owner from a white woman who was robbing the store and then demanding an apology. They adopted roles in the scene, performed the endings, and experienced the consequences of their choices. After the improvised performance they decided on titles ("Happy," "The Young Black Hero," "Black and White People Fighting Together") and discussed real-life incidents of such accusations, what they did, and whether they would do something different now.[22]

During the third year with the first group, the Living Stage actors began a play at the lunch table as they and the teens were finishing the meal. It dramatized an argument between a teenaged boy and his girlfriend who had a baby. The fight exploded into the hall and down the stairs into the theater with the teen mothers running to keep up. The girl accused the boy of flirting with other girls, and she was desperate with jealousy (a situation easily recognizable for the teen mothers). At the moment of crisis when the scene could easily turn violent, it was frozen and discussed. The young women then divided into three groups to create different endings, all which explored resolutions without violence or abandonment of mother or child. These endings were gradually developed into a list of "commandments" for respect in a relationship that they decided to live by.[23]

Clearly, the Living Stage actors, like the outside researchers in participatory research projects, play a significant role in focusing the problem and guiding the process of discovery and analysis. Intervention in some form is a requisite to participatory research because while the problem is experienced on a daily basis, it may not be clearly articulated. In addition, the very powerlessness of the group or the lack of a clear community, often evident with urban groups in developed countries, prevents them from formulating a plan of action. The actors at Living Stage function as intervening "participatory research researchers" in a number of ways. In determining the scenes for which the teens create an ending, the actors can focus attention on significant issues in their lives—being a small child, date rape, family conflicts—or on historical and cultural information that helps them understand their roots and the sociohistorical forces that contribute to the societal injustices they experience—a racial incident from America's past, an African village at various times in its history, Kwanzaa celebrations.

As the teens become comfortable developing endings, they are introduced to "environments," and thus the actors, like researchers in participatory research projects, further the process that Freire insists is essential to *conscientization*—creating new leaders. With the young women the Living Stage actors establish a place (an African village four hundred years ago or today, a zoo, a hospital, a fairground, a courtroom, a fashion show) in which the action will occur, and the actors and participants alike create characters who would be found there. According to Oran Sandel, current director of Living Stage, the character choices of the Living Stage actors are based on the character choices of the participants so that the actors "wedge themselves firmly into the fabric of the situation" where they can heighten the environment and push the participants beyond stereotypes and the known.[24] Sometimes the beginnings of a scenario are offered; sometimes just the situation. The action develops according to the participants' needs, and often multiple "scenes" occur simultaneously, and time, place, identities, and relationships are fluid. Audience members are encouraged to "try on" roles on the other side of the power dynamic and create an authority figure who responds to their needs. Although the actors help guide and deepen the experience through the interactions of their characters with those of the participants or through "side-coaching" (asking questions about the inner life or past experiences of the participant's character), the action is determined by the audience/actors. They can experiment with actions and get immediate feedback on their choices from the reactions of others as they work through issues similar to what they face in real life. Again like outside researchers the Living Stage actors must trust the audience/actors and give them the space to experiment and explore. As Freire warns, "a real humanist [researcher] can be identified more by his trust in the people, which engages him in their struggle, than by a thousand actions in their favor without that trust."[25]

While the scene within the environment may parallel situations from their actual lives, it never represents an enactment of their own story. This strategy frees the spectator/actors from aspects of the actual event that blocked creative solutions the first time; it opens doors to new possibilities. "When you create a character," explains Alexander, "the character can do anything because it is not you. When you create a character, the imagination sets you free from your worldly body, your specific situation, your life. The creation of stories allows you to tap into areas that have remained hidden because you're afraid or ignorant. When you live as an artist, you become healthy and compassionate."[26] D.W. Winnicott's formulation of the development of the child "from *me* to *not-me* to *not-not-me*" in *Playing and Reality,* as adapted by Richard Schechner to the rehearsal process in *Ritual, Play, and Performance,* provides insight into the significance of the distance between the individual (me) and the character role (not-me) and the new person (not-not-me) at the end who has learned from the experience.

One environment set up a scene in which family members from the country and the city met for the first time in many years to attend the funeral of a fifteen-year-old boy who died in a drug-related incident. Each teen created a character for the improvisation: the dead boy's mother, father, sister, great-grandmother, the preacher, and others. Each character had a fully developed life: for example, the sixteen-year old sister of the dead boy was a struggling photographer on welfare with a two-year-old daughter. She chose her career when her brother gave her a camera. The environment exposed family dynamics, disputes, and jealousies and in one memorable scene, worked through intense grief. As the family was standing around the casket the sister, enacted by one of the teens, began to sob uncontrollably. No one was able to comfort her, not the preacher, her parents, her daughter: no one could stop her wailing or could convince her to carry on. Finally, one of the actors adopted the role of her dead brother whose spirit returned to earth. He spoke to her imploring her to be calm and to stay strong for the children. This entire scene was improvised by the workshop participants who worked through loss and grief in the roles of their characters. The Living Stage actors followed their lead.[27]

In another environment the teens split into small groups, each of which "created" a country. They determined the physical attributes of the landscape and the people, the climate, and the history, and they explored how these aspects formed the basis of their culture. They also established the governmental structure, the economic system, and the social policies. Once the national identities of each country were established, the groups met to discuss issues of mutual concern. Treaties, alliances, and animosities developed among the various groups over the issues. Jennifer Nelson observes, "The questions and comments were insightful, and showed that they had no problems making sophisticated connections between contemporary political and social realities."[28] In the tradition of participatory research the participants began to move into the role of the new leaders, even though at this point it was still what Boal calls "fictional action."

Another environment met some of the real-life needs of the teens in addition to providing them with a place to practice new behavior. The Living Stage company realized that the young women lacked basic products for child-rearing. Alexander went to the Board to ask for donations, and at the next workshop, the mothers entered a "bazaar" full of cribs, strollers, diapers, toys, and clothing. Each participant received a bag of beans and haggled with the actors, now merchants, for the purchase of their items. When they ran out of beans, they reassessed their purchases and "sold" some to buy others. At the end of the workshop, they went home with their purchases.

One other major project was the making of a video entitled "That's My Mommy!" The teens wrote the script from improvised scenes which dealt with childhood fears and dreams. They performed the play and filmed it. Once the video was completed, each received a copy to show their children. Teachers at the schools attended by the teens remarked on the significant improvement in the girls' attentions spans, organizational skills, and creative problem-solving in the classroom after this project.

The Wishes Mural. Each teen traced her silhouette and inscribed her
goals for her future on the front and the aspects she wanted to leave
behind on the back. Teen Mothers of Today Project, Living Stage
Theatre Company, 1991–94. Photograph courtesy of Living Stage
Theatre Company.

What enables the young women in the teen mothers program to take
risks, both artistic and personal, is the safe environment created by the company for the participants: a tangible example of the psychological process
"holding." This loving, safe, and supportive context allows the teens to grow
and increase self-confidence and self-worth which, in turn, improves their
chances for accomplishing what they want. Dr. Margaret Beyer, an outside
psychologist evaluating the program, found that Living Stage "designed
holding into all aspects of the teen mother program," especially through the
creation of a loving family which offered trust, warmth, touching, and a
sense of belonging and through opportunities to experience success.[29] Thus
Living Stage begins to establish community bonds among the teens. Nelson
insists that "When the person feels cared for, she can freely ingest new information or even process previously held information in new ways. This gen-
tle yet aggressive approach is crucial when dealing with young people whose
earliest memories are of being under attack; seeing parents and friends abused
and killed, seeing every dream ridiculed or destroyed."[30] In his welcoming
remarks to the first group of teen mothers Alexander introduced this concept
of "holding" in words the teens could understand: "We will all be working

and living part of our lives together over the next three years, so we're entering into a friendship and a relationship that will last forever. . . . This is a safe
place, so take chances, really fly. In here, you can be who you want to be in
the deepest part of your soul, and no one will laugh or disrespect you."[31]
These words receive reinforcement every minute in the performances where
each participant's artistic choices are validated. "The creative process,"
explains Nelson, "is in no way limited or diminished by one's economic,
educational, or social status and so it ipso facto carries no possibility of failure, which is the motivating factor for opting out of the mainstream. Living
Stage creates an atmosphere in which everyone participating is successful; in
which each person can be recognized for the gifts that she/he has; and in
which whatever opinion one has about the world can be expressed freely. . . .
One of the advantages that Living Stage has when dealing with our specific
clients is that we accept them as they are and look for ways to help them recognize possibilities within their own context."[32]

Such programs as the one for teen mothers at the Living Stage not only
affect the workshop participants, but the next generation as well: the young
mothers begin to interact in more positive ways with their children as they
read aloud, create stories, and take excursions to museums, zoos, and festivals. In addition, they begin to model alternative behavior like rejecting
shabby treatment by boyfriends or standing up for what they believe in.
Although almost impossible to measure, it is here that the participatory
research techniques used by Living Stage may achieve social transformation
by breaking the cycles of pessimism and violence. Creativity, says Alexander, teaches individuals "to daydream, to imagine possibilities, and to stick
up for themselves and their hopes. Creativity enables them to communicate."[33] As Lachan said to Congress, "When you think about funding the
arts, remember me and my baby and all the other people like me who have
come to understand more about ourselves and our world through the arts.
For us, the arts are an encouragement to go on with our lives."

NOTES

1. 1993 Folder of Documents, Living Stage Archives, Washington, D.C.

2. Robert A. Alexander, personal interview, 13 October 1995.

3. Paulo Freire, *Pedagogy of the Oppressed,* trans. Myra Bergman Ramos (New York:
Continuum, 1989) 100–101.

4. There is a wealth of material available on participatory research (also called participatory development or participatory action research). Two journals with several articles focusing on this development strategy are *Convergence* and *Community Development
Journal.* Authors that I have found most helpful are Bonnie J. Cain, Orlando Fals Borda,

Budd L. Hall, Yusuf Kassam and Kemal Mustapha, Patricia Maguire, Mohammad Anisur Rahman, and Rajesh Tandon.

5. Peter Park, "What is Participatory Research? A Theoretical and Methodological Perspective," *Voices of Change: Participatory Research in the United States and Canada,* ed. Peter Park, Mary Brydon-Miller, Budd Hall, and Ted Jackson (Westport, CT: Bergin & Garvey, 1993), 2.

6. John Gaventa, "Participatory Research in North America," *Convergence* 24.2–3 (1988): 19.

7. bell hooks, *Talking Back: Thinking Feminist, Thinking Black* (Boston: South End Press, 1989), 8.

8. Muhammad Anisur Rahman, "People's Self-Development," *Community Development Journal* 24.4 (October 1990): 307–14.

9. Robert A. Alexander, personal interview, 18 February 1996.

10. Jennifer Nelson, "Evaluations of the Teen Mothers of Today, 1991–2," Living Stage Archives.

11. Nathan Paige, "The Living Stage Theatre Company," *The Cleveland Call and Post,* May 1989.

12. Robert A. Alexander, transcribed interview, 1982, Living Stage Archives.

13. Jennifer Nelson, "Living Stage: The Improvisational Process and the Myth of the Black Underclass," Living Stage Archives (August 1988): 17.

14. Ann Greer, "Imagine It First: Robert Alexander's Living Stage Targets Tough Issues for Youth," *American Theatre* (July/August 1988): 27.

15. Augusto Boal, *Theatre of the Oppressed* (New York: Theatre Communications Group, 1985), 122.

16. Park, 4.

17. Paulo Freire, "Foreword," *Voices of Change,* ix–x.

18. Robert A. Alexander, personal interview, 9 October 1995.

19. Robert A. Alexander, personal interview, 8 October 1995.

20. Robert A. Alexander, "What Are Children Doing When They Create?" *Language Arts* 61.5 (September 1984): 479.

21. Margaret Beyer, "Evaluations of Teen Mothers of Today, 1991–94," Living Stage Archives.

22. Living Stage Production Reports, December 23, 1991, Living Stage Archives.

23. Production Reports, Spring 1994.

24. Oran Sandel, personal interview, 28 June 1996.

25. Freire, *Pedagogy,* 47.

26. Robert A. Alexander, personal interview, 18 February 1996.

27. Production Reports, December 30, 1991. (A video of this improvisation is available in the Living Stage Archives.)

28. Nelson, "Myth," 12.

29. Beyer, "Evaluations."

30. Nelson, "Evaluations."

31. Production Reports, December 23, 1991.

32. Nelson, "Myth," 3.

33. Robert A. Alexander, personal interview, 18 February 1996.

Tori Haring-Smith

Preserving a Culture through Community-Based Performances in Cairo

Before I came to Egypt I associated this country with icons of preservation: the pyramids, the Sphinx, the Rosetta Stone. Having lived here since 1996, I now have a very different sense of Egypt's relationship to its past. Simply put, Egypt's culture is in danger of disappearing, thickly covered over as it is by layer upon layer of colonizing influences. The physical monuments remain (some of them), but the culture is disappearing. The Bedouins are being settled, the Nile bridged and dammed, and ancient songs and stories are being forgotten. McDonalds, Kentucky Fried Chicken, Xerox, Panasonic, Kodak, Demi Moore—these are quickly becoming the culture of contemporary Cairo. Along with this cultural loss has come a loss of identity, a disintegrating sense of self.

Nowhere is this more apparent than in the Egyptian theater. The first recorded performance of a European play took place here 150 years ago, and since then the theater has developed as an essentially Western form. The commercial theaters are dominated by domestic farces, while the impoverished private companies superficially ape European experimentalism, both scrupulously censored for any shred of explicit sexuality or political critique. Only in the last few years has there been any evident interest in building a theater rooted in Egypt's indigenous arts.

The man who has spearheaded this movement and remains its most

Tori Haring-Smith was the Chair of Performing and Visual Arts at the American University in Cairo and the Artistic Director of the Wallace Theatre in Cairo from 1996 to 1999. Before that, she was a professor in the Theatre and English Departments of Brown University from 1980 to 1996 and dramaturg for the Trinity Repertory Company from 1990 to 1996. She is now Executive Director of the Thomas J. Watson Foundation. Her current research focuses on new and experimental voices in Egyptian theater, with special attention to women's work.

prominent and successful leader is Hassan El Geretly. El Geretly's theater company, El Warsha (The Workshop), was founded in 1987. Since then, the membership of the group has changed, of course. People have come and gone, but consistently some members have been amateurs (previously bakers, secretaries, students) and others theater professionals. Because El Geretly often holds open rehearsals, there is certainly the sense that the boundaries of the group are permeable. El Geretly, however, does not accept casual comers. He likes to build long-term relationships based on a mutual understanding of mission. His is not a weekender's theater, but it does draw from all segments of society. Currently, for example, several members of his troupe have come from a choir school for Muslim and Christian children that he has supported in rural Minya.

El Warsha's first projects were to translate, adapt, and perform contemporary European works (Pinter's *The Lover* and *The Dumb Waiter,* Kafka's *The Penal Colony,* Handke's *The Ward Wishes to Become a Guardian,* and Fo's *Waking Up*) on the Egyptian stage. Hassan El Geretly has been characterized in this period as "casting around for a compass to help him find his own cultural bearings after his long expatriate years."[1] By 1989, when El Warsha "Egyptianized" Jarry's *Ubu* plays, creating a close connection with the audience by adding material from popular culture, the members felt like "people building their own temple in other's holy land,"[2] a phrase that captures both the desire for dialogue and the discomfort with it that characterized these early years. Their adaptation of the *Ubu* canon (called *Dayeren Dayer*) was set in Mamluk Egypt, a time of continuous, horrific bloodshed as one sultan after another fought his way to power. The narrator of the piece, Ibrahim, was a traditional shadow puppeteer, who recounted the stories of violence as a contrast to his own faithful pursuit of the arts. This was the first time that El Warsha used traditional shadow play. Performed in the courtyard of a sixteenth-century house, the story literally pulled its audience back in time. They sat, like the spice merchants that used to frequent the house, and listened to a tale both lyrical and political. El Geretly's early attempts to create typical middle-class pseudo-European theater had been unsatisfactory, but with *Dayeren Dayer* he found his voice. He told Laura Farabough: "I recognized in this very old art form . . . a liveliness, and humor, and spirit that is deeply Egyptian. It's not so much that I wanted to make a shadow play, as that I wanted to capture this imagination and put it into the theatre."[3]

The *Ubu* project marked the beginning of El Warsha's long and fruitful research in Egyptian folk art. As part of their adaptation of *Ubu,* the group became associated with the few surviving masters of the traditional shadow puppet play. Before they joined El Warsha, one of these three artists was still working occasionally at *moulids* (saint's birthday feasts), another performed for handouts on the street, and the third was making money as a plumber. The craft was clearly dying until El Warsha found a way to integrate it into its contemporary performances. Now the troupe not only incorporates shadow plays into cabaret evenings like *Layaly El Warsha* (Nights of El Warsha), but it also uses the nonlinear structure and the rhythms of the shadow plays to shape their own work.

This is the most important feature of El Warsha's developing theatrical form. They do not perform the traditional street arts as ossified museum entertainments for tourists. As El Geretly puts it, "It is not enough that this [Egyptian] culture provide the subjects of the stories; it has to become the object of our work. This turns out to be almost impossible to achieve if we are using European techniques which have been developed for centuries to express an outlook so different from our own."[4] Although some critics of this early work faulted El Warsha for stealing business from the shrinking market in folk art, the shadow puppet master Hassan el Farran wrote: "I must admit, working with El Warsha has developed our work: shadow-play has come back, and I find the means to innovate. Without them, I think we would have given up this line of work."[5] The combination of folk art and contemporary theater in El Warsha is simultaneously preserving the traditional arts and enlivening the contemporary theater.

In 1993 El Warsha produced its first fully Egyptian play: *Ghasir el-Leil* (Tides of Night). For this piece the troupe began with the traditional story/ballad (*mawwal*) of Hassan and Naima, a real-life Egyptian Romeo and Juliet from the early twentieth century. The members interviewed people who had known the couple and produced a show told from many perspectives and through different forms of art, including shadow puppetry and dervish dances. The result was "truly Egyptian in spirit but in no way 'touristy.'"[6]

El Warsha's successful association with the shadow puppet masters led them to seek out masters of other dying folk arts like public storytelling and stick dancing (a civilized form of dueling in which men carry a stick in one hand, usually balanced vertically, and then swing it at their opponent/partner in fierce, sweeping arcs). El Geretly brought masters of these and other arts to Cairo to rehearse with the troupe, and soon they were training young actors in their craft. The troupe quickly embraced folk art as a powerful means of defining a culture, as a repository for human feeling and experience, from which to draw strength in unsettled times, and build upon when the instability is over. Folk art is the coin whereby collective emotions are exchanged: all types of folk art have a common root in people's experience. The energy in folk art is massive: it is akin to the lava within a slumbering volcano, which erupts periodically to reshape the world.[7]

One of the folk art masters who came to work with El Warsha was Sayed El Daoui, an epic singer and probably the only man alive who knows the entire *Al-Sira al-Hilalayya*, a million-line epic, once the core of oral culture here. A newspaper reporter profiling El Daoui described him:

> Sayed El-Daoui has probably told more stories than any other man on the planet. The verses in his head outnumber all those written by Walt Whitman, Ahmed Shawqi and a dozen other poets from a dozen other nations combined. If Sayed El-Daoui were to tell every story he knows, one after the other, without stopping, it might take six months or more.[8]

Al-Sira al-Hilalayya is Egypt's *Iliad,* and Sayed El Daoui is like one of Homer's relatives who has memorized the entire work. Yet, when he was first asked to perform with *El Warsha*, El Daoui had not sung large sections of the epic (like "The Book of the Orphans") for twenty-five years. Since 1993 El Warsha has been intensively experimenting to find a theatrical form that will allow the troupe to perform this epic in a way that is true to the rhythms and structures of Egypt's traditional street arts and that will connect contemporary audiences to the epic, not distance them from it.

Like *The Iliad* and *The Odyssey, Al-Sira al-Hilalayya* is the foundation book of a people; quoting Bridget Connelly's book *Arab Folk Epic and Identity,* El Geretly calls it "the autobiography of the Egyptian South."[9] The story, a complex hero's quest tale, recounts the history of the Egyptian people's migration from Arabia to Egypt and their battle at Tunis. At the center of the story are the escapades of Abu Zeid El Hilali, a warrior who is "a model of manliness and dignity and a Don Juan to boot."[10] The events are not entirely historical but, like Homer's tale, weave together history with ethics and mythology into a complex fabric of romantic passion, spectacular battles, tribal politics, loyalty, revenge, and reconciliation. The story comes from the eleventh century, but the epic itself dates from the fourteenth century. It consists of four major books, each of which in turn consists of many subbooks and, within them, substories. The recording of Sayed El Daoui telling "The Orphan's Tale" (Book iv) has already consumed thirty-five tapes, and it is still far from over. El Warsha has been working on one sub-substory, "The Sons of Rageh," which recounts how two young boys defied the formidable general of Tunis during the besieging of that city. This story alone took five cassettes to record.

El Warsha is, of course, interested in preserving this epic poem, but even more important for them is to reanimate Egyptian culture and theater. The troupe knows that merely recording the epic could freeze this dynamic art—killing it in the act of preserving it. For this reason the way that the members work on the enactment of the story receives as much or more of their attention as the story itself. Their goal is not to be archivists but, rather, to redefine theater by producing theatrical pieces based on the epic. To accomplish this, however, has required the development of a new kind of theatrical performance. El Geretly explains: "We would like to talk *with* rather than *at* the audience, in a dialogue based on emotions, where all parties have a common background to fall back on. If folk art and theater do not interact through living artistic experience, both run the risk of degenerating into empty rituals presided over by high priests who profit by them, while concealing their demise from the public at large."[11] What they have discovered is that revitalizing the *enactment* of the folk art—specifically the way it relates to the audience—is more fundamental to sustaining a culture than merely preserving the precise *content* of its cultural artifacts.

From the beginning the group rejected the performance practices of contemporary Egyptian theater, seeing it as distanced from real life on the streets. El Geretly echoes writers like Joseph Chaikin and Peter Brook when he describes contemporary performance as "self-generating."[12] Too often, he says, commercial actors pattern their performances not on real life but on the performances of other actors. In his opinion these actors have lost contact with reality, and so their art has lost contact with real people. Instead, El Warsha began to study performance through storytelling. But soon it also rejected conventional storytelling as too often directed *at* the audience rather than *to* them. The actors observed storytellers whose eyes never made contact with those of the audience, who literally and figuratively never made contact with those they were addressing. Another storyteller was visibly upset when some latecomers entered her performance space. She could not adapt to her hearers. El Warsha knew that the stories it was working on were "suffused with the spirit of the people and imbued with the souls of the great story tellers of the past," yet the members were muffled when they were cut off from dialogue with the audience.[13]

At present the group is mixing elements of storytelling and dramatic performance to form a new kind of enactment, most closely resembling story theater. El Warsha's performances typically take place in tents and the courtyards of 400-year-old homes, not in formal theater buildings. The audience sits on two sides, facing each other, the performers moving between them. Since thrust and arena staging are hardly known in Egypt, the experience of seeing performers against the backdrop of other audience members is shocking. The state-run "experimental" theater building in Cairo also has railroad-style seating, but the stage is so wide that neither side of the audience can see the other. The El Warsha arrangement actually recalls the seating for Egyptian funerals (also held in tents on street corners) in which rows of men sit facing one another. Those watching the play come from all segments of Cairo society: theater aficionados, diplomats, business-men and women, artists, taxi drivers, fruit sellers, police officers.

The master storyteller still presides over the action, but others in the group take on characters, echo ideas chorally, and support the words with action. The master storyteller, musicians, and other singer/narrators who enact the story sit in two lines in front of each side of the audience, almost blending into them. The master storyteller is simply in the middle of one of these two lines, sitting next to the *rababa* player, who accompanies him. When the performers are seated, they are spectators and musicians. When an actor/singer "enters," he or she simply stands and draws attention before moving to the center of the acting area. Sometimes actors sing solos as their entrance pieces, beginning in the position of a musician and only gradually separating themselves from the crowd to become a featured player—at least for a while. When an actor's segment of the story is completed, he or she returns to the group of musicians. If the piece is performed in a courtyard, the architecture of the building is often woven into it so that characters can establish a doorway as a house entrance, for example. Even upper stories overlooking the courtyard are used for chases and distant scenes. In these cases actors may enter without going directly from the seated company to the acting area, but one still feels that, if the spirit moved a member of the audience, he or she might just stand up and join the fun. Indeed, the audi-ence often does join in the singing of popular songs and the repeated choric sections that punctuate the piece. The players and the audience are inte-grated into the same space. And there are none of the ubiquitous gray wooden blocks that Egyptian theater designers love to use on their stages. If El Warsha needs a chair, its designers find something on the streets (crates, carpets, saddles, discarded chairs held together by bits of string) and bring it into the space. El Warsha's set designer, Tarek Abou El Fotouh, explains, "Ordinary chairs have within them a sort of history, a link with the people and the place, and as such are far richer than the poor, stunted fossilized cliches trapped within theatrical walls."[14]

Like the epic stories they perform, this theater seems to come quite literally from the people. The boundary between the players and spectators is blurred and permeable. The performance exists within the community as well as before its eyes. This impression is always heightened by the visible presence at the side of the acting area of Hassan El Geretly, standing proudly, watching his actors, and clapping along to the music. He is clearly neither performer nor spectator but both simultaneously. Not only the physical boundaries of the performance but also its temporal margins—the beginning and end—defy the usual theatrical conventions that separate the tale from the audience. After the crowd has gathered, El Geretly walks to the side of the playing area and casually welcomes the audience in English and Arabic, explaining the story in English for those who do not know Arabic. Even as the play proceeds, spectators wander in from the street, crowding at the entrance to see what is happening. At the end the performers take a bow, but then the musicians often stand around casually and play familiar pieces to amuse the audience; some people remain and sing, while others may leave the space. Like a wedding or a funeral, performance bleeds into real life. The communal aspects of El Geretly's theater are essential to his project. Whereas traditional tourist performances of indigenous arts typically "other" the performers, exoticizing them and separating them from the spectators, El Warsha players seem indistinguishable from the crowd of onlookers except for their temporary roles as performers. It is clear that the audience recognizes what they are seeing as their own art, the art of the feasts and street fairs.

This commitment to communal enactment has radically altered the relationship of the players to one another and to the epic. Traditionally, the epic was always told by a solo, male voice—the voice of authority. Now all company members, male and female, are learning the piece. The story moves from person to person within the troupe, each adding his or her energy to it. And so its meaning once again circulates among all those involved; the story is alive and dynamic, not static. In a recent performance of *The Sons of Rageh,* for example, two sixteen-year-old boys from the children's choir in Minya enacted the roles of the defiant soldiers who insult the venerable general of Tunis, played by the master storyteller. The old man reacted almost viscerally to their challenge. The moment shimmered; it was impossible to separate the master storyteller challenged by his pupils from the aged general insulted by his underlings. The story came to life, born again in the midst of the audience. The ancient words became a contemporary scene through the process of enactment—a perfect example of Richard Schechner's maxim: "Theater and ordinary life are a mobius strip, each turning into the other."[15]

Although this kind of performance is new in Egyptian theater, its combination of storytelling and enacted improvisation in fact reflects the essence of the Egyptian epic. The richness of the poem relies upon improvisation. *Al-Sira al-Hilalayya* exists not only as lines to be memorized but also as a basic storyline along with thousands of different narrative formulas that can be used to generate the narrative itself. These formulas encode the ethics and the philosophy of the piece. They can, therefore, change in context—depending on where they are used in the story or who the audience is. Each time the master tells the story, it may be slightly different, influenced by his mood and his audience. Each segment of the epic, then, has infinite possibilities in the telling. Like life, it is not fixed. El Geretly explains that the story contains "everything possible," not just "only what we know already."[16] When the El Warsha actors first encountered this kind of performance, they found it very difficult; they were accustomed to a more controlled theater, with, for example, exact cues for their entrances and exits. The master, however, always told the story a little differently anyway. Gradually, the El Warsha actors have learned to work in this improvisatory mode, and now they say they can sense "when the idea is completed" and so know when to speak. They don't need exact cues anymore. Now the group's practice is to work through individual stories, bringing characters to life through improvisation, adding characters occasionally, and developing the music of the piece. In this way the lively spirit of the epic is being preserved as well as its narrative content. And audiences have come to expect this kind of variation. They will come to several nights of "the same" El Warsha production, wondering what play the actors will construct that particular night.

Because this process involves using the ancient narrative as a basis for telling contemporary stories—stories of the actor him- or herself—it involves new training for the actors. And the presence of the actor within the story—his or her active participation in its development—allows energy to pass directly between the actors and the audience. The story becomes a means of communicating with the spectator. Eye contact become "I-contact." The actors strive to appear "naked" before the audience, not hiding behind characters and plot but interacting directly with the audience, using the tools of storytelling and theater to speak directly to them. Khaled Goweily, a writer for the troupe, explains:

El Warsha performs *Spinning Lives* at the British Council in Cairo, Egypt. As usual, musicians sit immediately in front of the audience, which flanks the performance space. Photograph courtesy of Khaled Goweily.

Our relationship with storytelling, for example, reflects the love of intimate interaction between story teller and audience, between enchanter and enchanted. The audience, enchanted with their own imaginations, become children once again, full of wonder as the words reach them, clothed in images, sounds, colors and feelings flowing through them with astonishing fluidity, taking them faraway and returning them but not unchanged: they return filled with wisdom, rich in imagination and images, and yet more importantly, haunted by a mysterious yearning that will be a part of them forever.[17]

This work recalls the way in which groups like the Open Theatre and the Living Theatre strove for direct contact with the audience.

This process of improvisation within a formulaic structure may in fact be the only way of preserving the epic that is the story of the Egyptian people. Although El Daoui remembers the overall story and has mastered its structuring devices, he has to improvise in order to fill in the lacunae. He cannot teach all of what he remembers to his new apprentices. In the words of El Geretly, the story is "unraveling." Yet "there is enough pattern still visible that you can guess about what's not there."[18] This is what El Warsha has observed with the art of stick dancing as well. As the new practitioners of this art practice what they know of it, "the bits that have vanished re-emerge."[19] Recreating the piece by coming to understand its essence, its basic structure, and the means by which it is self-generating will allow the epic to become once again a living part of the culture. El Geretly defines their intentions, saying, "We are citizens and want culture to develop. The intervention, the making, the oeuvre, is to do with theater. It is a joy to have the epic preserved, but it is not our function. It is a by-product of what we do."[20] In other words, this theatrical group is preserving an epic that encodes history and morals not as data but as living art. In so doing, they are not removing a text from the community that created it, but they are teaching the community how to keep the text alive, evolving, and growing.

There have, of course, been problems with this approach, and not everyone agrees with it. Some critics believe that, in altering the performance of the epic, El Warsha has violated it. The group has been repeatedly criticized by some quarters for playing around with this kind of traditional material. Some of the original group members also left when the group moved from conventional theater work to this new performance style—they said it wasn't "theater." Others criticize the group's reliance on foreign funding sources and their active participation in international festivals.

Yet such criticism is diminishing as the group's work spreads and brings more attention to Egyptian culture. El Geretly is interested in disseminating his work through founding a school for actor training. And El Warsha has begun to collaborate with several groups within Egypt and internationally in order to find ways of preserving traditional arts through revitalizing contemporary performance. In Upper Egypt it has collaborated with two projects: a theater for children and a choir school where Christian and Islamic children work together. It also supports a group of musicians in Port Said who are reconstructing the culture of that city, which was severely fragmented during the 1967 and 1973 wars. Through an Arab theater festival the group has collaborated with a Jordanian company, Al Fawanees (The Lanterns), which is also exploring modes of performance. El Warsha wants to encourage such groups to remain autonomous—to remain free.

Most community-based theater addresses issues of immediate social or political concern (rights of the poor, abortion, the environment). El Warsha's act of cultural preservation may seem much more remote from the immediate needs of the community. But, in fact, it addresses one of the most important problems facing the country—loss of self. It is not surprising that one of the formative narratives in this culture is *A Thousand and One Arabian Nights*. Just as Sheherazade told tales to survive, so this culture must learn to create and recreate itself through its own foundational stories. The work of El Warsha has helped save the epic from extinction, but it has done so much more. The old masters are once again passing on their arts and so have become ten times more alive. The company has found a way to bring the ancient stories into the present—to hand them over to the audience, where they can live and become part of the community again. And the very notion of theater has been redefined in a way that makes it central to cultural preservation, not ancillary to it. This is a country where surviving is an art, and, as El Warsha has demonstrated, art is part of that survival.

NOTES

1. Nehad Selaiha, "Taken at the Flood," *Al Ahram Weekly,* 14–20 October 1993, 10.

2. "El Warsha's Progress, 1987–1997." Private publication of El Warsha.

3. Quoted in Laura Farabough, "Al Warsha in Cairo," *Theatre Forum* (Spring 1992): 6.

4. Ibid., 11.

5. El Warsha, "Papers of El Warsha," 28. Private publication of El Warsha. For a discussion of criticism of El Warsha, see Alan Wright, "Reviving the Spirit, Resisting Decay," *Al Ahram Weekly,* 21–27 October, 1993, 10.

6. Sarah Enany, "Waves of Passion," *Cairo Today* (October 1993): 47.

7. El Warsha, "Papers," 9–10.

8. Tarek Atla, "Healing for Hearts," *Al Ahram Weekly,* 15–21 February 1996, 9.

9. Interview with Hassan El Geretly, 6 July 1997, citing Bridget Connelly, *Arab Folk Epic and Identity* (Berkeley: University of California Press, 1986).

10. Atla, "Healing."

11. El Warsha, "Papers," 10.

12. Interview with Hassan El Geretly; Joseph Chaikin, *The Presence of the Actor* (New York: Atheneum, 1972), 6–8; Peter Brook, *The Empty Space* (New York: Atheneum, 1980), chap. 1.

13. El Warsha, "Papers," 6.

14. Ibid., 15.

15. Richard Schechner, *Between Theater and Anthropology* (Philadelphia: University of Pennsylvania Press, 1985), 14.

16. Interview with Hassan El Geretly

17. El Warsha, "Papers," 13.

18. Interview with Hassan El Geretly

19. Ibid.

20. Ibid.

Rob Baum

Eskesta in Israel

In only two years a group of Ethiopian-Israeli students without conventional performance training, professional aspirations, or financial connections became the nationally celebrated Eskesta Dance Theatre, attracting financial backing and an international performance schedule. In order to appreciate Eskesta's significance and swift acclaim, one must appreciate this Ethiopian community's history before and after its prophetic "return" to Israel.

An Unwanted People

Ethiopian King Ishaq declared in 1415: "He who is baptized in the Christian faith may inherit the land of his fathers; otherwise, let him be a *Falassi*." Thus, condemned *Falasha*, "peasants without land," Jewish Ethiopians were now legally "outsiders" and "strangers," "foreigners" to Ethiopia. Through a series of bloody wars, exclusive laws, and humiliating customs, *Falasha* were denied public normalcy: prohibited from status positions, land ownership, weapon usage, open worship, community benefits. Living in the social margin, indigenous Africans without a home, this persecuted people called itself Beta Israel, "House of Israel," identifying its citizenship with its originary land. For Beta Israel believed themselves the descendants of King Solomon and beautiful Ethiopian Queen Sheba, tracing their bloodlines to the twelve tribes of Israel. In Ethiopia Jews took up whatever work was permitted—occupations ill paid and feared by Christians and Muslims alike—typically, clay pottery, weaving, and ironwork. People capable of these

---

Because of her background in African dance, art, and culture, and in dance generally, Rob Baum was an outside advisor to the original team that determined support for Eskesta. Since that time she has followed the progress of the members, many of whom became her students at the University of Haifa. She now teaches performance theory, movement, and feminist theater at a New Zealand university.

crafts were said to cast the "evil eye," *buda* (witches) who fly through the air.

Due to the length of historical separation, it was difficult for world Jewry to accept this mysterious African people as Jews. Unlike Diasporic Jews, Beta Israel were estranged from Hebraic writings, cut off from centuries of Jewish thought and practice, and astonished to learn that Jews existed elsewhere. In 1973 Israel's chief rabbis acknowledged Beta Israel as descendants of the Tribe of Dan believed to have been lost in the Exodus three thousand years ago: it was thought that only two tribes had survived this holocaust. When Ethiopia refused emigration, Israel's remarkable Mossad (Intelligence) infiltrated Ethiopia and the Sudan, preparing "Operation Moses" (1984–85) and "Operation Solomon" (1991). Clandestine immigration began through pipelines in Sudanese refugee camps. Accustomed to institutionalized anti-Semitism, Beta Israel endured harsh treks, bandit attacks, and the squalor, torture, and death of Sudanese way-stations to reach the modern marvel of Israeli rescue. These shared experiences foster a community history in Israel.

While seeking to efface cultural differences, Ethiopians endured new ordeals in Israel involving settlement and legal status. To ensure *Halakhic* (legal Judaic) conformity, Israel's Chief Rabbinate (the government's religious arm) required mass "conversions" of *olim hadashim* (new immigrants)—redundant and humiliating for Ethiopians who had been circumcised at eight days old and ritually immersed at onset of menses, marriage, and childbirth. The passive Beta Israel began to develop a political character: organizing moratoria; demonstrating before the Knesset (House of Parliament); threatening to return to Ethiopia via Egypt—a dramatic invocation of a *common* Jewish history.[1] Through these protests the community won limited concessions and religious autonomy. Years of bad blood climaxed in 1996 with the "accidental" release of a news story revealing that blood drawn from Ethiopian *olim* is routinely discarded for fear of HIV. The event let loose waves of outrage at the implication of African *primitiviut* (backwardness, ignorance), an inferior otherness whose blood is worthless. As demonstrations, moratoria, and violent outbreaks made daily headlines, Ethiopian representatives materialized, establishing a new Israeli voice. In this tumult Eskesta Dance Theatre emerged.

The People's Voice

Asked about the company's rapid success, Eskesta's founder and artistic director admits surprised delight.[2] Ruth Eshel had experienced Beta Israel culture at weddings and bar mitzvahs; teaching choreography at University of Haifa, she watched Ethiopians "moving differently" than other students.[3] "Struck by their creativity, their natural abilities," Eshel encouraged self-expression outside of class, offering rehearsal space and personal time.[4] Enthusiastic word-of-mouth brought the first eleven members informally together. Within a year they had coalesced into Eskesta Dance Theatre, named for shoulder movements unique to Ethiopian dance.

In rehearsal students flourished; in performance energy evaporated. Early presentations were predictably mixed, featuring compelling, spectacular movement, poignantly restrained gestures, and embarrassed faces, particularly among the women. Ethiopian cultural disapproval for public display caused movement potential to diminish under scrutiny: Ethiopians eschew "stardom" as counter to communal ethics. Disregard for even the "Oriental" (Middle Eastern) sense of "time" made rehearsal schedules into wishful notions as members were absent or late or vanished mid-session. Throughout Israeli society cultural differences generate severe problems. *Mizrachi* (eastern Jewish) concepts of time and responsibilities to employers and colleagues versus loyalty to family and friends, significance of meetings and contractual agreements, school and work obligations, and ramifications of premarital and nonmonogamous sexual activity are inconsistent with those accepted in Israel.[5]

Although dancing with Eskesta early on guaranteed a small stipend, travel, stage experience, and prestige in the Ethiopian, student, and general theater communities, none of the group's original members remain. One reason is that students—Eskesta's population—are often a family's chief financial support. Another is the continual demand for what Westerners view as "rehearsal." As this community theater bases its productions in primarily "inherited" or transmitted movements known to and publicly enacted by native Ethiopians, the need for daily or even weekly rehearsal seems unreasonable. Even the improvisatory dance Eshel prizes and encourages in rehearsal is perceived as a natural element of African dance, paradoxically expected in the rigorous reenactment of masked and unmasked dancing. *Improvisation* is thus interpreted literally as ideas conjured on the spot and on the stage, as happens in jazz music. But, while Western jazz riffs occur between prescribed or prescribable intervals, African dance theater starts when ready and ends when done. Western time eludes Eskesta.

Despite this ongoing concern, Eshel's vision and audiences' interest helped overcome cultural prohibitions, and members saw material advantages in being cultural messengers. In adopting Western production aesthetics, Eskesta increases performance value, but members, community, audiences, and Beta Israel's own future will determine whether Eskesta's development corrupts cultural values or accommodates global pressures. Israel's war-rocked society grants surpassing significance to military achievement and respect: Ethiopians are considered exemplary as soldiers and fighters— well disciplined, extraordinarily strong, and having much stamina. Yet traditional Beta Israel family structure is gone, succumbed to horrific death rates during immigration, modern Israeli demands (e.g., compulsory military service), high unemployment, and difficulties in adult Hebrew language acquisition. Changes in standards of living from the *Aliyah* (immigration to Israel), with its gifts of housing, clothing, food, *ulpan* (intensive language immersion program), and medical benefits, to citizenship, with its temporal and financial demands, contributed to ghettoization of Beta Israel in the Holy Land. Once-dominant fathers must rely upon their children to translate vital documents, impart news, negotiate family needs, fight wars, and support households. As an urban social event, Eskesta stages the inescapably darker Jewish body, providing a socially acceptable platform for Amharic (Ethiopia's native tongue) and other defining Beta Israel affects. As a cultural theater project, Eskesta promises Beta Israel elders acknowledgment in Israeli macro-culture, while its youthful composition symbolizes the Ethiopian community's growing source of power and self-determination.

Community Theater in Israel

Despite the number of cultures in Israel there is not a profusion of regional dramatic offerings or community theater companies, due in part to Zionism's contemporary mandate to produce melting pot "Israelis" as an act of national survival. After Habimah (Russia's Art Theater) Inbal was the first community theater success. Built upon *Temani* (Yemenite) folktales, authentic colorful costumes, and *Mizrachi* movement styles, choreographer Sarah Levi-Tennai's original choreography redefined the Zionist ethic while giving Yemenite immigrants special recognition. Israel proudly claimed Inbal as an indigenous company. Inbal's directive to reproduce Yemenite folk history and culture using biblical/folk-based narratives pushed productions toward dance theater.[6] Neatly occupying the place vacated by Inbal in its highly politicized demise (1996), Eskesta followed this model in performing community culture.[7] Many of Israel's cultural communities yearn for such a legacy in the fragmentation and ghettoization of modern Israeli city life but lack the strength, leadership, and single-minded passion to create it. Ruth Eshel's drive and commitment (coupled with then-company principal Zena Arkhadi's) are reminiscent of the shared genius of Levi-Tennai and her lead dancer, Marguerite Oved. Israel's military existence strains artistic groups, whose young members are subject to draft and front-line battle and whose older members face near-eternities of *miluim* (active reserves). Immigrants' superpatriotism sometimes proves a negative, as when an Eskesta member was imprisoned because pride constrained him from admitting to being a student and thus temporarily exempt from army duty.

The fledgling company has been warmly welcomed by Israeli institutions. In its first full year Eskesta played Israeli cultural and school venues and invitational events in Paris and New York. Now officially under the aegis of University of Haifa's Department of Theatre, funded by Israel's Joint Distribution Committee, Eskesta combines folk, artistic, and pedestrian movement; training in traditional *Falasha* vocalizations by an Ethiopian *kess* (diasporic rabbi); ancient Ge'ez songs from Ethiopia's Jewish populations (Gondar, Minjar, and Gojjam regions; Semien mountains); spoken Amharic; accompaniment on native drums, stringed and wind instruments; and Eshel's guided improvisations. Early productions sported white gauzy one-pieces and bright red, yellow, or green T-shirts over white cotton trousers; recent performances incorporate several dress changes, including genuine Ethiopian festive kaftans—heavy garments of thick white cotton embroidered with red and yellow designs, belted by long, colorful strips of woven cloth. Eskesta's most recent performances boasted four male/female "pairs" and three male dancer/musicians, although women also play some percussion instruments.

Eskesta does not see itself as political—a relative term in Israel, where Hizbollah terrorists periodically explode bus stations and downtown cafés, the Holy City of Jerusalem is a capitol divided between warring factions, and ultrareligious Jews violently protest the existence of a Jewish state. Eskesta nonetheless offers to exorcize community ghosts while celebrating historically repressed Jewish traditions, and in Eskesta's maturity it should move beyond representation to presentation and begin explicitly to educate Israeli audiences familiar with Ethiopian aesthetics to Beta Israel conditions, values, and concerns. Eskesta does not thematically specify, and may not consciously register, its intentions, yet one can discern performative subtexts and tones of a modern narrative voice. Several of Eskesta's original pieces ambiguously portray social issues—primarily aspects of disease, communal care, and mundane dangers. In one segment healthy men in the central circle (symbolizing a village square) become afflicted with fits of shaking—limping on unstable legs, falling to the ground, and clinging childlike to

Eskesta Dance Theatre. Photograph courtesy of Biton, University of
Haifa, Israel.

other men as they are lifted and half-dragged/half-carried to the outskirts of
the "village," where the palsy as suddenly ceases. One reasonable interpretation would ascribe this illness to the indigenous Ethiopians' trauma, suggesting an infirmity issuing from geography itself, which fails to harm inhabitants once they leave. This is consistent with the experience of Beta Israel,
whose physical health in Ethiopia was endangered by peculiar, untreatable
diseases and whose spiritual health languished under the onus of anti-Semitism. To the starved and dying refugees in the Sudan, Israeli Mossad agents
must have seemed miraculously healthy, able literally to lift and carry Beta
Israel from certain death to wellness and well-being in Israel. The piece also
points out the necessity of depending upon and trusting in others, taking
care of one's own and "sharing the burden." In this way Israel's socialized
health care programs and new immigrant facilities replicate the Beta Israel
community structure in Ethiopia as communal caregiver.

Other pieces treat elements of contest and conquest, with men and
women pairing off (the choreography is emphatically heterosexual) to enact
courtship rituals through corporeal isolations, one couple displaying neck
movements, another concentrating upon the chest, another using hip isolations, and the last group the shoulders, including the famous *eskesta*. This seg-

ment flows into another in which men leave their "conversations" and try to dominate one another, while women "talk" alone or in the company of several men. The women's attempts at flirtation invariably fail, as the men focus upon other men with only proprietary interest in women; the homosocial subtext is invigoratingly candid. At last the men good-humoredly "fight" through *eskesta's* mediation until the most flexible dancer has won out—to group approval. This piece is tremendously popular with modern Israeli audiences, who enjoy "tribal" Africana without extrapolating Israeli rituals of courtship and aggrandizement. One of the most virtuosic pieces employs the high jumping movements associated with Zulu and Massai peoples. The men stomp in an inward-facing circle, rhythmically pounding the ground with tall wooden staffs, then begin to jump and outjump each other vertically while brandishing their staffs and striking the ground. With the air of a pregame "pep talk," this battle vignette always seems far too short (easy to say from a seat in the house) and vaguely hypnotic.

An important aspect of Eskesta is its emphasis, through symbolic movement, upon the prayer and religious devotion vital to continuance of Beta Israel in the *Galut* (Diaspora). The gesture (hands placed together, fingers pointing upward, head bowed) is inauthentic to Beta Israel[8] but communicates to audiences familiar with Christian ritual behavior from cable television and foreign movies. More successful integrated actions are attitudes of prayerfulness, as when Eskesta members gaze upward and, arms upraised, tap rain or dewfall to their faces or stand in a circle harmoniously chanting in call-and-response or a capella. Women's winnowing actions with hand-woven native baskets, an agricultural motif, also creates the impression of prayerfulness through repetitive circulation and soft susurration as they throw out handfuls of grain.

Eskesta's frequent carries always involve men body-lifting men, likely a trace of Orthodox Jewish codes of religious separation. Because Ethiopian aesthetic values are not seated in Westerners' dangerous concepts of beauty, abstract work leans heavily upon mimesis, mixing pedestrian with ritualistic movement. The body lifts are awkward but fresh, more practical than "aesthetic." From a Western perspective Eskesta members have scant "formal" dance training, but African cultures (generally speaking) exhibit an *informal* degree of dance training without parallel in Western cultures: the complex rhythms and motions of *eskesta* shoulder dance, pervasive in community life, are not "taught" but learned, inculcated through observation and imitation at an age when Western babies are clinging to trouser legs. The ability to portray sophisticated tempos and subjects of a lost village life, set against the excitement of *eskesta,* is refreshing in Israel's urban environment. On the local scene companies resemble German or North American modern dance or (at their best) Pina Bausch's performance politics. Previous experiments in founding Ethiopian dance troupes in Afula, Nazareth, and Petach Tikva did not succeed; as Eshel writes, "much of the authenticity and beauty of the dances is lost as they try to adapt the dances for the stage, replacing the original forms and rearranging them with banal choreographic patterns copied from commercial video cassettes of Ethiopian folk dances."[9]

Ironically, as artistic director, Eshel risks following the path she denounces. The company's somatic concentration has already shifted from Ethiopian folk and mimetic improvisation to aesthetic dance choreography, as Eshel deliberately emphasizes the nonmimetic, abstracted impulses of the members. Although its latest nonindigenous work retains much of the folk-based novelty, it begins to spotlight technical deficiencies: Eskesta cannot compete with the modern dance training of Israel's Batsheva ensemble or Kibbutz Dance Company. Eskesta's artistic success and funding depend upon its reception as a community production representing one of Israel's respected minority populations. The restricted integration of Western aesthetics may not harm Eskesta in Israel, but international comparison with Alvin Ailey (rather than, e.g., Dance Theatre of Senegal) would be unfavorable.

Summary

Beta Israel negotiates a duality of diasporic traditions, whether as Jews in the Galut or as Africans in Israel. Its members continue to experience the duality known to Jews everywhere of being at once inside and outside culture, expressing (or by law concealing) nationalism and religious/cultural fidelity. Through melding of "wax and gold," to paraphrase an Ethiopian maxim, Beta Israel is surviving instant modernity by assuming a collective community stance. Simultaneously, Eskesta blends ethnicity and artistry, virtuosity and naïveté; captivates audiences; and inspires a national, "homegrown" awareness of Israel's ethnic diversity and latent community power. Though not overtly political, Eskesta cannot fail to influence public opinion about African Jewry while seducing the cynical, secular Israeli population into familiarity with—and admiration for—rich Ethiopian traditions. Coming home through Eskesta Dance Theatre, Beta Israel brings fresh blood to Israel's cultural scene and, with its international promise, another means of bridging distances between Israel and the "outside" world.

NOTES

1. Associated Press (Jerusalem), "Police Fire on Protesting Ethiopian Jews," *San Diego Union-Tribune*, 29 January, 1996, A:6.

2. Ruth Eshel had a distinguished career in Israel as a solo dancer before beginning her academic career. Eskesta marks Eshel's artistic comeback: she accompanies the troupe, announces performances, and demonstrates gestures from the coming dances.

3. Eshel, private conversation, late 1996.

4. University of Haifa, "Ethiopian Student Dance Troupe Headed for Paris . . . and Beyond" (press release), Focus 12.1 (Spring 1996): 1. See also (author unknown) "An Ethiopian Surprise," *Israel Dance Quarterly* (October 1996): 26–27.

5. Modern Israel's *Sephardic* (Spanish and North African Jews) majority is governed by an Ashkenazi minority. Thus, the standards that Israelis apply themselves conflict with much of the modern world.

6. Very briefly (and without qualitative judgment), "pure dance" companies eschew clear narrativity, preferring "dance for dance's sake": Merce Cunningham is pure dance; Martha Graham is "dance theater." Pure dance companies uphold different aesthetic mandates than companies seeing themselves as theater: community theaters commit to portraying political issues, often at regional/local levels, whether or not they pose solutions to problems.

7. Although a second Inbal flew from its ashes, it lacks Levi-Tannai's vision and fire and tends to remount old works.

8. Former members have complained to me about incorporation of "inauthentic" gestures (especially this one), arguing that they have no place in Beta Israel life, are strictly Eshel's conceptions, and led to their abandoning the company. Audiences do not notice or accept the gestures as stylistic. Obviously, the *Ashkenazi* and professionally dance-trained Eshel's own abstract tastes have an enormous effect upon the Ethiopian performances. But without such a driving force Eskesta has no chance of survival in this society.

9. Ruth Eshel, "Shoulder Dance, Dance Traditions of the Ethiopian Jews," *Israel Dance* (1993): 68.

SUGGESTED READING

Bulcha, Mekuria. *Flight and Integration: Causes of Mass Exodus from Ethiopia and Problems of Integration in the Sudan.* Uppsala: Scandinavian Institute of African Studies, 1988.

Erlikh, Hagai. *Ethiopia and the Middle East.* Boulder, Colo.: L. Rienner Publishers, 1994.

Levine, Donald Nathan. *Wax and Gold: Tradition and Innovation in Ethiopian Culture.* Chicago: University of Chicago Press, 1965.

Rapoport, Louis. *The Lost Jews: Last of the Ethiopian Falashas.* New York: Stein and Day, 1980.

Safran, Claire. *Secret Exodus.* 1st ed. New York: Prentice Hall, 1987.

Turner, Victor. *The Anthropology of Performance.* New York: Performing Arts Journal, 1988.

Wagaw, Teshome G. *For Our Soul: Ethiopian Jews in Israel.* Detroit: Wayne State University Press, 1993.

Wubneh, Mulatu. *Ethiopia: Transition and Development in the Horn of Africa.* Boulder, Colo.: Westview Press, 1988.

Dong-il Lee

Contemporary *Madang Kut* of South Korea

On 9 April 1994, at West Gate Independence Park in Seoul, Korea, the Committee on Democratic Student Coalition Movement produced *Memorial Kut for the Victims of the Democratic Youth and Student Coalition Incident*. This contemporary *madang kut* (yard play) was performed by the People's Kut Performance Troupe "MamPan" and Shaman Dongho Choi to appease and cleanse the oppressed spirits of the victims of the Second People's Revolution Party Incident, otherwise known as the Democratic Youth and Student Coalition Incident, which had occurred twenty years earlier.

Sources and Character of *Madang Kut*

The new theater genre called *madang kut* arose in the 1970s, along with several other forms of contemporary progressive theater, which have proven to be a powerful artistic instrument for politicizing and mobilizing a large number of people in South Korea. *Madang kut* usually refers to outdoor ritual drama dealing with social issues. It delivers the democratic movement's propaganda messages but not by way of raw slogans. Rather, it narrates the oppressed situations and hard realities of marginalized people within the framework of folk traditions of masked dance drama and shamanistic ritual. Both of these theatrical forms have a long history in Korean performance.

Dong-il Lee is Assistant Professor of Theater and Film and Executive Director of the Twenty-first Century Research Institute of Arts Management at Dankook University in Seoul, Korea. He was founder and artistic director of Theatre MU and guest director at Heart of the Beast Mask and Puppet Theatre and at Mixed Blood Theatre Company in Minneapolis, Minnesota. In 1999, he was artistic director and executive producer of "DMZ 2000," a millennium project in the demilitarized zone near the border of North and South Korea and the largest performance project in Korean history.

Elements of masked dance drama originated early in Korean theatrical history, but the form really developed both in rural or village festivals and at court during the fourteenth century. These masked performances focused on dance, song, music, and masks, but pantomime and witty exchanges were important elements. They were held outdoors, so settings were minimal, and instead the emphasis was on the costumes, masks, and movement, which was stylized and often quite complicated. It is only in recent years that texts have been written down and published; before that, the episodic dramas were created collaboratively by village actors who improvised the plot line, and they were transmitted orally. Characters who appeared in one scene might never reappear later, and much of the dialogue consisted of improvised banter mocking excessive behavior or poking fun at local social issues. While the particulars vary, the common element running through all masked dance drama and influencing *madang kut* is the satiric representation of male authority figures: the corrupt local official, the lascivious Buddhist monk, the power-hungry aristocrat, the abusive husband—individuals who "should" command respect. Taking the people's perspective, these plays ridicule the indiscretions and crimes of the leaders and thus subvert the established social system through performance.

Performances of *kut* lead the participants to discover the contradictions, structural conflict, and spiritual contamination that need to be exorcized from the community. The performances dramatize the basic assumptions and values in the culture and either reconfirm them without changes or reconstruct them during the *kut* performances by acts of transformation from *han* (deep sorrow, suppressed emotion, restless remorse) to *shinmyong* (ecstatic joy, entrance of the spirit into the body, divine order). A shaman/actor leads the ritual—which consists of dance, song, music, chant, oracle, storytelling, mime, costumes, and symbolic props—to invite the spirits to participate and to create a state of balance. These techniques transform the awareness of time, space, and characters not only in the performers but also in the spectators, who both watch and participate in the performance. When the spirit enters into the participant's body and mind during the *kut* performances, it purges all the contaminated forces of conflicts and produces a spiritual experience of transformation.

The *kut* performance has an open plot that can accommodate unexpected moments as it is created somewhat improvisationally by putting episodic events together. It transforms ordinary time and space to a sacred time and space, and it transforms a shaman/actor into an eternal medium providing efficacy and entertainment to the spectator. Each scene depends on aural and visual metaphors expressed through song, dance, and mime, rather than plot, and the shaman/actor's ability to perform between present and heightened reality while manipulating degrees of intensity determines the success of the performance. But the help of the participants (performers, musicians, and spectators) cannot be underestimated. *Kut* demands more of an audience than "willing suspension of disbelief" as promoted in Western culture; rather, it requires the "spect-actor" (to use Boal's term) to be a participant. The performance is a mutual transformation that cannot exist without the collective effort of the participants.

Madang kut draws on these traditions of masked dance drama and *kut* to create a new form of theatrical presentation. The performances attract popular audiences with plays portraying contemporary sociopolitical events satirically and in so doing revive the folk tradition of social satire in masked dance drama. But, in addition, this public open space or gathering site where communal events happen also has a religious connotation of a sacred place where the village ritual *kut* can be performed. Thus, *madang kut* exists on the threshold of the secular and the sacred as a place of transformation where both worldly and religious matters can be performed without restrictions on participation.

The braiding of masked dance drama and shamanistic ritual occurs in the structure of the performance as well, since the open episodic form of masked dance drama easily incorporates diverse shamanistic rituals to allow the theater to function as an open forum anticipating spectators' participation and communication. But, most of all, the enthusiastic energy of transformation created during the performance enables the spectators to become the protagonists in their own play and to resolve the conflicts of the community as they shift from being passive spectators into slogan-chanting demonstrators. Many mass demonstrations are initiated or animated by the *madang* performances that follow the cycle of clash, deconstruction, and reconstruction through transformation from *han* to *shinmyong*. As a result, *madang kut* has become a profound instrument for democratic reform.

The Performance: A Description

Memorial Kut for the Victims of the Democratic Youth and Student Coalition Incident commemorates events of May 1974. These events occurred after a series of decrees by President Park JeongHee attempted to crush any signs of radical or even democratic resistance. Each decree provoked large demonstrations against Park's dictatorship, and a new organization emerged: the Democratic Youth and Student Coalition. Feeling that his rule was being challenged, Park used this new organization as a political scapegoat and deliberately plotted an "incident" as a pretext for repressing the resistance movement. In May 1974 the Korean Central Intelligence Agency announced that it had uncovered a violent coup plot against Park's regime and arrested 1,024 people; 180 of them were eventually prosecuted. Twenty were sentenced to twelve to twenty years in prison, 21 were given life imprisonment, and 8 received the death sentence. Even though six months usually elapsed between sentencing and execution, the 8 sentenced prisoners were executed just nineteen hours after the final appeal was turned down. The bodies of these victims were cremated by the police against the wishes of the families.

The *Memorial Kut* has three major sections, each of which has several parts braiding together shamanistic rituals of *kut,* the political events of 1974, and memorial tributes. The first section consists of the shamanistic ritual of opening. In front of Independence Gate the People's Kut Performance Troupe "Mampan" starts to play traditional music using various gongs and drums. Dressed in black and holding pictures of their loved ones, the families of the victims, those executed in the aftermath of the fabricated conspiracy, follow a tall flag and march in one line toward the performance area, located in front of the symbolic death chamber house. After playing music and dancing around the house, the performers move into the death chamber and lay two long pieces of cotton cloth, one black and one white, on the floor. These cloths symbolize the long suppressed feelings of restless resentment (*han*). The performers tie one end of the cloths around a rail in front of the death chamber and bring the other end out into the performance area in a ritualistic manner, accompanied by music and dance. The shaman then brings a small table set with knives, a rice bowl, a bowl of rice wine, fruit, and dried fish—an offering to the victims—to the performance area. He then picks up the bowl of rice wine and spills it on the ground, after which he bows to the spirits in the four directions. These movements represent a shamanistic ritual inviting the spirits of the victims and invoking their participation in the ritual of cleansing. This initial transformation creates a sacred, infinite time and space and expresses the desire and the possibility to return to the free and eternal chaos in which the participants, including both the spirits of the victims and their family members, can be reunited.

This second section follows the arrangement of a conventional contemporary commemoration ceremony and starts with a one-minute silent tribute to the victims. This is followed by a series of activities to set the context and remind the participants of the events and their significance, thus placing the political events within the ritual context. After opening remarks by the chairman of the Committee on the Democratic Student Coalition Movement, each of the incident victims is introduced. Memorial addresses by other progressive leaders follow to activate the audience. Then ByongRan Moon reads a memorial poem, and the Seoul Workers' Choir sings memorial songs. A resolution is announced, and the victims' families are introduced. The scene concludes with a ceremony of incense burning and wreath laying.

The final section of the *madang kut* consists of three scenes. The first is a shamanistic ritual of cleansing. Three female performers dressed in white traditional mourning clothes enter the stage. Each dances around the stage as if she were transformed into the character of the victim. Dramatic movement sequences using traditional and contemporary dance techniques portray the victims' long-suppressed agony in symbolic forms. From this dance of agony (*han*) the dancers move to the dance of joy (*shinmyong*), in which they use more dynamic movement sequences in collective forms. Each dancer then grabs a long knotted white cloth, which symbolizes the *han* of the victim. The performers dance with it in circular movement patterns to untie the knots, symbolizing the release of the spirits from long-suppressed resentment. After completing this dance of ritual transformation, they exit to the opposite side from the death chamber in a single line, connected by the cloth held above their shoulders.

This liberation dance shifts from a slow style of individual movements to a fast style of collective movements and integrates contemporary dance sequences in between. The dance signifies the transformation of the spirits' emotional states; it is not only an expression of the profound will of the victims to be liberated from the cruel chain of oppression but also a firm statement of resistance against the oppressors. The scene gives the victims' family members a great sense of relief as they find themselves liberated from the oppression of forced silence, since, under the military dictatorship, they were falsely accused of being communists or communist sympathizers. Their human rights were violated, and even their daily activities as ordinary citizens were greatly restricted.

The second scene is a shamanistic ritual of releasing *han*. Shaman Dongho Choi enters the stage, wearing a long blue waistcoat with a colorful belt over traditional clothes and holding a shaman's bell in his right hand and a white cloth in his left. Two musicians (a woman playing an hourglass-shaped drum and a man playing a large gong) sit on a straw mat in front of him. He begins a shaman song of greeting for the spirits, and, as he starts to dance, holding several pairs of *sangboks* (white cloths of the deceased), he moves to the upper-left-hand corner of the performance area and grabs the end of the long white fabric tied to the death chamber rail. By this ritual act of connecting a long piece of white fabric to the *sangbok,* the spirits of the victims are given symbolic form, and Shaman Choi becomes the victims' medium. Choi brings the *sangbok* to the families of the victims and speaks the victims' last words that they wished to deliver to their families before they were executed. Many family members and spectators cannot hold back their tears during this scene, and some of the family members stand, embrace the *sangbok,* and talk to the spirits of the victims amid their tears. Like the first scene, in this ritual Shaman Choi tries to appease the victims' spirits by reuniting them with their beloved families using his body as an medium. This act of ritual transformation purges all the contaminated forces of oppression and produces a spiritual experience of transformation.

The final scene, the Resurrection Dance of Flags, has two parts. In the first, Shaman Choi reenters the performance area, arrayed in a traditional general's costume and hat. He holds a knife in each hand. He starts to dance with the knives, leaping and spinning around in a fast tempo while pointing the knives to his neck from time to time. He then grabs a *chakdu*—two sharp blades wrapped by white fabric—and gently cuts several parts of his body, first his arms, then his legs, face, and mouth; but, miraculously, the blades do not actually cut him. Suddenly, he runs and with leaping movements climbs up onto the platform located between two bamboo poles covered with colorful flags and balances himself barefoot on the sharp blades. Shaman Choi's transformed energy reaches its peak when he is able to dance barefoot on the two sharp blades in a state of trance. Shaman Choi describes this movement: "It was possible only because of the help of the invited spirits and participants. They were intense—their long-suppressed feelings of resentment were so strong. They were not ordinary wandering spirits, but those of great patriots. When I received their powerful spirits, it was relatively easy for me to dance on the blade with confidence and dignity. Also I felt very strong energy from the spectators, especially the family members of the victims. It was heartbreaking for me to be a victim because I could feel the severe pains, but at the same time, I would like to give courage for the future generation of activists by dancing on the *chakdu*." During this dance the family members and spectators are stunned and remain intensely focused. Choi proclaims *gongsu* (divine oracle) to the spectators, who believe it to be the words of the spirits. After giving the oracles, he comes down from the platform holding the *chakdu* on his shoulder and dances with the spirits to send them back.

This scene is regarded as one of the highlights of the whole *kut.* Its success requires intense concentration of energy from all the participants and spectators to achieve a collective transformation. The scene allows the participants to confront a direct and immediate manifestation of the invited spirits of the victims in the form of *gongsu* through the communal sharing of *shinmyong* (joy), but for Shaman Choi it is a direct confrontation with his fear of death. By transforming those fears with the help of spirits and spectators, he is able to perform this dangerous act of symbolic death and resurrection.

In the final segment Shaman Choi replaces his traditional general's costume with one with long white sleeves and begins to dance in preparation for the departing ritual for the invited spirits. Family members and musicians hold each end of a long white fabric, symbolizing the road to the other world, which is stretched tightly across the performance area from upstage to downstage. Shaman Choi dances with the white *sangbok,* jacket, and trousers that are the embodiment of the spirits and places them on the long white fabric road. He sings the shaman song of departure while playing the *bara*. Then he places himself at one end of this symbolic road and pushes his body through the middle of the fabric, splitting it in half. This ritual act represents the paving of the road. Then, standing in the middle of these strips of fabric, he lifts a strip on one side of his body and places it on the opposite shoulder. He alternates this motion in a fast dance until he ties himself up. Caught between these strips of fabric, he faces a group of family members sitting on one side of the performance area and spreads his arms wide, recalling the image of the victims who died on the gallows. He is transformed into a victim and narrates a long-suppressed feeling of resentment. After calming his emotion, Shaman Choi begins to untie the fabric quickly. He approaches the family members of the victims and invites two of them to help him move forward to cut the chain of oppression, symbolized by the twisted rope of white fabric, which is blocking the road to the other world. He places the white mourning clothes on a straw mat and asks the spirits to begin their journey to the other world, leaving all sorrows behind. In this final scene of sending-off and reintegration, all the invited spirits are sent away to the place where they belong. The *kut* ends with the sharing of food and drink with participants and uninvited wandering spirits.

Conclusion

Madang kut uses ritual enactment to reconstruct a collective life of harmony based on the spirits of playfulness and inclusiveness. By transforming socially oriented theater into a shamanistic ritual act, the performers and spectators can create collective ecstatic moments, a truthful portrayal of reality, a practical method of social change, and a healthy image of the people—the four essential elements of *madang kut*. This transition from theater to ritual allows a constant invocation of social memories and realities that, in turn, transforms silenced histories of *han* into healthy histories of *shinmyong* and also offers possibilities for constructing an alternative history.

KOREAN REFERENCES

Cho, Dong-il. *HanGuk GaMyonGeuk ui MiHak* (The Aesthetics of Korean Masked Dance Drama). Seoul: Han Guk Il Bo Sa, 1975.

Choe, Hiwan, and Im, Jintaek. *HanGuk ui MinJoong Geuk* (People's Theater of Korea). Seoul: Chang Bi Sa, 1985.

Chung, Jichang. *Seo Sa Geuk, Madang Geuk, Minjok Geuk* (Epic Theater, Madang Theater, and People's Theater). Seoul: Chang Bi Sa, 1989.

Im, Jintaek. *MinJoong YeonHee ui ChangJo* (A Creation of the People's Play). Seoul: Jip Mun Dang, 1981.

Kim, Taegon. *Hanguk Musok Yongu* (A Study of Korean Shamanism). Seoul: Jip Mun Dang, 1983.

———. *Hanguk Mingan Sunang Yongu* (A Study of Folk Religion in Korea). Seoul: Jip Mung Dang, 1983.

Lee, YoungMee. *Minjok Yesul Undong ui Yoksa wa Eeron* (The History and Theory of the People's Cultural Movement in Korea). Seoul: Han Kil Sa, 1991.

Minjok Kut Hoe (People's Council on Kut). *Minjok kwa Kut* (People and Kut). Seoul: Hak Min Sa, 1978.

Park, Inbae. "Norae Pan Kut Chang Jak Bang Bop kwa Yoenchul Ron" (The Method of Creation and Direction for *Norae Pan Kut*), *Journal of the People's Theatre and Arts Movement* 3 (Fall 1992).

Diana Taylor

Yuyachkani:
Remembering Community

"In Quechua, the expressions 'I am thinking,' 'I am remembering,' 'I am your thought' are translated by just one word: Yuyachkani," the noted Peruvian commentator Hugo Salazar del Alcazar wrote in one of his many pieces on the Yuyachkani theater group.[1] The term *Yuyachkani* signals embodied memory and blurs the line between thinking subjects and the subjects of thought. "I" and "you" are a product of each other's experiences and memories, of historical trauma, of enacted space, of sociopolitical crisis. But how is "embodied" memory different from "archival" memory, usually thought of as a "permanent" and tangible resource of materials available over time for revision and reinterpretation? Embodied memory, transmitted through performances stored in what I call a "repertoire" of gestural and oral traditions, usually gets thought of as ephemeral, nonreproducible knowledge. There is a long tradition, which in the Americas dates back to the Conquest, of thinking of performance as that which disappears without a trace, as that which cannot be contained or recuperated through the archive. Part of the colonizing project consisted in discrediting autochthonous ways of preserving and communicating historical understanding. As a result, the very existence/presence of these populations came under question. The Huarochirí Manuscript, written in Quechua at the end of the sixteenth century by Friar Francisco de Avila, sets the tone: "If the ancestors of the people called Indians had known writing in early times, then the lives they lived would not have faded from view until now" (41). The very "lives they lived" fade into "absence" when writing alone functions as archival evidence, as proof of presence.

Diana Taylor is Professor and Chair of Performance Studies at New York University. She is the author of *Theatre of Crisis: Drama and Politics in Latin America* (1991); and *Disappearing Acts: Spectacles of Gender and Nationalism in Argentina's "Dirty War"* (1997). She has coedited six books on Latin/o American theater and performance. She has worked closely with the Grupo Cultural Yuyachkani in Peru since the mid-1990s.

310

Yuyachkani, Peru's foremost collective theater group, sees itself implicated—both as product and as producer—in various modes of cultural transmission in an ethnically mixed and complex country. For the past twenty-eight years the group has participated in at least three interconnected survival struggles—that of Peru, plagued by centuries of civil conflict; that of the diverse performance practices that have been obscured (and at times "disappeared") in a racially divided, though multiethnic Peruvian culture; and that of Yuyachkani itself, made up of nine artists who for decades have worked together in the face of political, personal, and economic crisis. In adopting the Quechua name, the predominantly "white," Spanish-speaking group signals its cultural engagement with indigenous and mestizo populations and with complex, transcultured (Andean-Spanish) ways of knowing, thinking, remembering. Yuyachkani attempts to make visible a multilingual, multiethnic praxis and epistemology in a country that pits nationality against ethnicity, literacy against orality, the archive against the repertoire of embodied knowledge. In Peru the urban turns its back on the rural, and languages (Spanish, Quechua, and Ayamara) serve more to differentiate between groups and silence voices than to enable communication. Yuyachkani, by its very name, introduces itself as a product of a history of ethnic coexistence. Its self-naming is a performative declarative announcing its belief that social memory links us, implicates us, in the transitive mode of subject formation.

Yuyachkani's work has drawn on Peru's archive and repertoire not only to address the country's many populations but also to elucidate the multiply constituted history. Some dance, sing, speak, or otherwise perform historical memory, while others access histories through literary and historical texts, maps, records, statistics, and other kinds of archival documents. Their practice of drawing from all the various sources urges us to ask the following questions: What is at risk politically for marginal populations in thinking about performance as that which disappears? Because the live exceeds the archive, just as in other ways the archive exceeds the live, does that mean that performance leaves no trace? Whose memories "disappear" if only archival knowledge is valorized and granted permanence?

While Yuyachkani incorporates indigenous and mestizo sources and ways of remembering in their work, contradictions abound. How can a group, made up predominantly (but certainly not exclusively) of urban, white/mestizo, middle-class, Spanish-speaking professional theater people think/dance/remember the racial, ethnic, and cultural complexities and divides of the country without glossing over, minimizing, or misrepresenting the schisms? Who exactly is thinking whose thought? Thought and remembrance, as the name *Yuyachkani* makes clear, are inseparable from the "I" and "you" who think them. As a group made up mainly of Limeños (from Lima), does Yuyachkani have access to the memories of the Andean communities? How to avoid charges of cultural impersonation and "appropriation"?

One obvious response to this danger of cultural trespassing that threatens practitioners lies in simply turning one's back on the rural indigenous and mestizo populations and tacitly accepting that "performance" in the Americas is a European practice carried out by and for white urban audiences. The indigenous and mestizo practices, one can argue, belong to a self-contained, parallel circuit of cultural (and economic) transmission—oral, mythic, calendar-based fiestas, rituals, and festivities. "Theater" practitioners, then, might decide to stick to European repertoires and archives. If, conversely, one acknowledges that indigenous and rural mestizo populations also have deeply rooted performance traditions that make up part of the rich repertoires of the Latin American countries, then how do artists from all ethnic backgrounds approach their multiethnic, transculturated traditions—one that is a product of cultural multiplicity?

Thinking about how performance participates in and across these networks of social memory allows us to consider cultural participation more broadly. Social memory assumes that "Peruvians," for example, are a product of, and participants in, mutually constituting historical and cultural processes. But social memory is, of course, constituted not only by what communities remember but also by what they choose to forget. "Perú es un país desmemorizado" (Peru is a *de*-memorized country), Teresa Ralli, an actor of Yuyachkani told me, and the *de* captures the violent refusal at the heart of a country that does not recognize or understand the realities of its many parts.[2] Peruvians participate by forgetting, not just by remembering. Therefore, it's not a question of *if* but, rather, *how* they participate.

Yuyachkani, one of Latin America's most important collective theater groups, actively stages Peru's social memory. Actors Teresa Ralli, Rebeca Ralli, Ana Correa, Débora Correa, Augusto Casafranca, Julian Vargas, Amiel Cayo, the director Miguel Rubio, and the technical director Fidel Melquiades (most of whom have been in the group since it started in 1971) have worked together close to thirty years, a momentous achievement, given the severe economic and political hardships they have faced. Only a couple of other Latin American collectives—La Candelaria and Teatro Experimental de Cali (TEC), both from Colombia—boast similar accomplishments.

This group of nine has made visible a series of survival struggles culminating in the recent atrocities associated with *Sendero luminoso* (Shining Path), which left some thirty thousand people dead and eighty thousand homeless. Perhaps as daring, however, Yuyachkani has insistently re-membered Peru as one complex, racially, ethnically, and culturally diverse country. The white, Westernized Lima, built with its back to the Andean highlands, affords Yuyachkani one of the spaces to stage this remembering for urban audiences. They perform throughout the city, staging "public acts" on streets, in schools, on the steps of the national cathedral, and in orphanages, cemeteries, jails, and government buildings. This citywide staging follows the tradition practiced in indigenous and mestizo festivals and fiestas: everyone participates in the procession and festivities by following the actors from place to place, by talking, discussing, celebrating, and being part of the all-inclusive event. Everyone—even the social outcasts and the dead—are invited to join in the celebration. The physical movement of the procession itself encourages urban Limeños to follow the lead of their rural *compatriotas* (compatriots). These embodied enactments help urban audiences recognize that they have forgotten a great deal and need to remember their role in the national community.

Yuyachkani also stages street performances in nontheatrical spaces throughout the country. Their *pasacalles* (literally, "through the streets") follow in the indigenous and mestizo custom of theatrical street processions. Recognizable characters from traditional and popular culture—musicians, masked figures on stilts, characters from *comparsas* ("houses" of festival bands and dancers)—parade through the streets inviting spectators to join in. These parades, as Ana Correa describes them, end in a fiesta in which participants talk and get to know one another. The *pasacalles* simultaneously affirm the validity and dynamism of these performance practices and open the arena for intercultural conversation. Drawing from Western models such as Brecht's political theater and Boal's "theater of the oppressed" as well as Quechan and Aymaran legends, music, songs, dances, and popular fiestas, Yuyachkani asks spectators to take seriously the coexistence of these diverse ethnic, linguistic, and cultural groups. These performances, then, broaden the experience of those who agree to follow these actors physically through all the different spaces. These routes become the new "memory paths"[3] that allow participants to recognize and bear witness to Peru's history of extermination and resistance, alienation and tenacity, betrayal and remembrance.

When Yuyachkani began working in the early 1970s, the members of the group saw themselves as politically "committed" popular theater practitioners. Popular theater of the late 1960s and early 1970s, with its *by* the people *for* the people ethos, challenged the systems that placed *Theater* with a capital *T* and *Culture* with a capital *C* in lofty, aesthetic realms, beyond the reach of working-class people and racially marginalized communities. Popular theater groups in Latin America and the United States (Bread and Puppet, San Francisco Mime, El Teatro Campesino, to name just a few) tended to work as "collectives." The members of Yuyachkani, for example, meet every morning at their "Casa Yuyachkani" and work on developing new material and ideas. They have lunch together in their communal kitchen and meet again in the afternoon to rehearse or warm up for an evening performance. Like all collective theater, they rejected the playwright- and "star"-driven theatrical models that dominated highbrow and commercial theater.[4] They took the theater out of elite spaces, staging free performances that had to do with the real-life economic and political conditions of working people. Political and economic issues took precedence over aesthetic concerns. They toured their shows to rural communities that never really had access to theater and involved spectators in many aspects of the productions. Working under the Brechtian influence, popular theater in Latin America was closely linked to strikes and other class/labor struggles.

As I have argued elsewhere, there are some fundamental limitations and built-in contradictions to "popular theater," no matter how important and laudable the projects have been in general.[5] Popular theater at times presented an oversimplified and programmatic view of conflict and resolution. In Latin America and elsewhere popular theater was often animated by Marxist theories. Progressive, at times militant, university students and intellectuals instructed the disenfranchised about how to improve their economic lot or lead a more productive life. Because Marxism privileged class, anticapitalist, and anti-imperialist struggles at the expense of racial, ethnic, and gender conflict, its implementation in popular theater groups in Latin America ran the risk of reducing deep-seeded cultural differences to class difference. In Peru, and other countries with large indigenous and mestizo communities, the "proletariat" in fact consisted of indigenous and mestizo groups who lived on the margins of a capitalist society for various reasons—including linguistic, epistemic, and religious differences not reducible (though bound into) economic disenfranchisement. A call for solidarity organized around anticapitalism allowed for rampant, unthinking trespassing on cultural, ethnic, and linguistic domains. Furthermore, the "popular," as understood by some of its activists, became entangled with fantasies of a simple, pure world existing somewhere beyond the grips of capitalism and imperialism. The less the practitioners truly knew the communities they were engaging, the more the discrepancies in power and the lack of reciprocity threatened to place them in positions of moral superiority reminiscent of religious proselytizers.

These problems plagued the initial endeavors of Yuyachkani. The marginalized groups they were addressing in their own country had their own languages, expressive culture, and performance codes that the group knew nothing about. Miguel Rubio recalls how during that first play, *Puño de Cobre* (1971), in which they performed for miners during a particularly brutal strike, the actors (dressed in jeans and T-shirts) played a variety of roles and characters. After the performance one miner commented: "Compañeros, that's a nice play. Too bad you forgot your costumes."[6] Unlike some of the other popular theater groups of the period (both in Latin America and the United States), who set about to enlighten an exploited population, Yuyachkani realized that they needed enlightening: "Much later," Rubio continues,

> we understood why the miners thought what they did. We had forgotten something much more important than costumes. What they wanted to tell us was that we were forgetting the audience that we were addressing. We were not taking their artistic traditions into consideration. Not only that, we didn't know them! The miners came from rural areas rich in cultural traditions. They were right. How could they imagine a play about them that did not include their songs, or the clothing of the women who so proudly conserve their traditional dress, or the figures who tell stories as they dance?

This became the beginning of the ongoing education of Yuyachkani. The group's theater no longer became "about them" but was about a more complex reflection on Peru's ethnic and cultural heterogeneity. They added members from these rural communities to their group; the actors learned Quechua; they trained in indigenous and mestizo performance practices that included singing, playing instruments, dancing, movement, and many other forms of popular expression. They expanded the notion of theater to include the popular fiesta, which emphasized participation, thus blurring the distinction between actor and spectator. Performance, for Yuyachkani as for other popular theater groups, provided an arena for learning—but here it was Yuyachkani learning "our first huaylars, pasacalle, and huayno dance steps[;] between beers and warm food, we started to feel and maybe to understand the complexity of the Andean spirit."[7] Performance did indeed offer enlightenment and intergroup understanding—but Yuyachkani admits to having taken the first steps in learning about rural populations by participating in their cultural practices. According to Hugo Salazar del Alcazar, this was the first phase of Yuyachkani's development, which focused primarily on political issues.[8]

Since those beginnings Yuyachkani has continued to train in various linguistic and performance traditions to offer a deeper vision of what it means to "be" Peruvian, one that reflects the cultural, temporal, geographical, historical, and ethnic complexity of that articulation. This includes the layering and juxtaposition of the diverse traditions, images, languages, and histories found in the country. Poised between a violent past that is never over and a future that seems hopelessly prescripted, their performances represent images and scenarios that live and circulate in a variety of systems and forms—from the media, the children's stories, martial arts, silent movies, to indigenous myths.

This second phase of Yuyachkani's development, according to Salazar, focuses more on the cultural debates around "lo nacional." The group studied José María Arguedas's work on Andean myths and performances to understand the ancient traditions that persisted in contemporary cultural practices. A play such as *Los músicos ambulantes* (*The Travelling Musicians* [1983]) draws from the famous folktale "The Musicians of Bremen" and Arguedas's *Todas las sangres* to tell a humorous and beautiful story of homelessness, social injustice, and the importance of working together. In an aesthetically rich performance full of masked figures, music, dance, and comic routines, the little red hen, the mangy dog, the wily cat, and the limp donkey realize that, for all their differences and incompatibilities, they're better off together than apart. The play works on different levels for different audiences. In one sense the play is an important reflection on Peru's racial makeup. The dog represents the Creole Limeño, from the *barrios altos,* or poor sectors of the city. The hen stands for the Afro-Peruvian populations. The cat comes from the *selva,* or the Peruvian Amazon valley, while the donkey represents the *cholo serrano,* the mestizo from the Andes. These figures, all of whom have been persecuted, beaten, and exploited, come together to rebel exuberantly against the *patrón* (boss). The negotiation among them requires that they get to know one another—to recognize one another's strengthens and what each contributes to the group. But it also requires that the group respect each member's individuality.

On this, more personal, level the play summed up Yuyachkani's predicament at the time. How, as Miguel Rubio asks, does the group allow each member to flourish individually without threatening the existence of the whole? Yet, even for those who do not get the racial or personal subtext of the performance, the play is enormously appealing—sparkling with humor, energy, music, and intelligence. This play rejoices in the fact of transculturation, for the only music these characters can create requires a bringing together of the various distinct elements and traditions. The music from the jungle harmonizes with that from the Andes, the coastal plains, and the Afro-Peruvian communities. The play ends as a fiesta, with actors and audience dancing and singing together. The play's national and international popularity has enabled Yuyachkani to buy its cultural center, Casa Yuyachkani. Because this play is so well-known, moreover, these characters can intervene in the national drama. When the economic situation in Peru gets particularly critical, for example, the little red hen of the production (Ana Correa) performs an *acto público* by joining the line of retired people waiting for social security monies to complain about being penniless. "Cómo como?" (How am I to eat?), she demands impatiently, as she clucks and struts about.

Yuyachkani has developed more troubled plays to think through the civil violence and the apparent impossibility of respectful coexistence in a country torn apart by injustice and rage. *Encuentro de zorros* (1985) draws from ancient myths of "el zorro de arriba" and "el zorro de abajo," preserved both in Peru's repertoire and archive.[9] The legend of the two foxes was already considered ancient when it was first written in the sixteenth-century Huarochirí Manuscript, and it was reworked in Arguedas's famous "El zorro de arriba y el zorro de abajo" (1968). The foxes, symbols of change, appear in moments of extreme social crisis. In their first apparition, some twenty-five hundred years ago, they met to decry injustice. Their role, as they describe it, is to devour the world and create a new one. Yuyachkani uses the myth to again think through Peru's geographic, ethnic, and linguistic schisms—the *zorro de arriba* represents the populations from the Andean highlands, while the *zorro de abajo* typifies those from Lima's coastal region who meet once again in the violent throes of mass migration due to Peru's civil war of the 1980s and 1990s. Beggars, thieves, and drunken clairvoyants push a Mother Courage–type cart and offer a grim perspective on Peru's urban landscape.

Rather than a respectful coexistence, these characters show a world devastated by criminal violence, displacement, and unemployment. The world is turned upside down, "parents against children, children against parents, the living against the dead and the dead against the living." *Retorno* (1996) shows the aftermath of Peru's "dirty war." As a reenvisioning of Beckett's *Waiting for Godot, Retorno* stages the despair and isolation of those who have nowhere to go. Two men stand at a crossroads. They, like many of their *compatriotas,* have been left stranded and disoriented. Their villages have been destroyed, their harvest lands burned. They wait. Will someone come by and lead them somewhere, anywhere? They pass the time by engaging in a mestizo ritual of lighting a cross. Small candles illuminate the stage and surround a large Christian cross. But the ritual has no meaning any longer; their acts don't resonate; their voices have no echo. They feel as desperate when they complete the ritual as they did when they stated it. There is no going forward, no going back, no home to return to.

Two of Yuyachkani's best-known pieces are also from this period— *Contraelviento* (1989) and *Adios Ayacucho* (1990)—again focusing on the conflict between the military and *Sendero luminoso* that annihilated indigenous and rural mestizo communities. *Contraelviento,* one of Yuyachkani's largest and most spectacular pieces, restages the testimony of an *indígena* survivor of the 1986 "massacre of Soccos" in Ayacucho. "Disappearance" and mass murder, as in other Latin American countries in the 1970s and 1980s, had become common political practice. What happens when, as Adorno asks, genocide is part of our cultural heritage?[10] Even if we respond to Adorno's often-cited concerns about the ethical implications of representing violence, especially the offering up of the victim's pain for the viewer's pleasure, other questions remain. How can theater compete with the theatricality of political violence? Miguel Rubio sums up the challenge: "Nothing that you create on stage can be compared with what is happening in this country."[11] Furthermore, the heightened spectacularity of political terrorism, as I argue elsewhere, forces potential witnesses to look away.[12] It blinds the very spectators that theater calls on "to see."

In the most lyrical of forms *Contraelviento* succeeds in posing the most urgent questions. How do populations remember and deal with trauma? How can indigenous and mestizo communities address genocidal policies and practices that are often not acknowledged by the national or international community? How can atrocity be "remembered" and "thought" when there are no witnesses or no recourse to the archive? Whose memories disappear when scholars and activists fail to recognize the traces left by embodied knowledge?

Adios Ayacucho takes the question of witnessing further—the dismembered victim of torture and disappearance is forced to act as sole witness to his own victimization. In this crime without a witness no one but he himself can demand that justice be served. No documents, photos, or gravestones attest to his annihilation. Only his bones, shoved in a plastic garbage bag, serve as evidence of an event that left no other material evidence.

Yet, while no external witnesses exist, *Adios Ayacucho* affirms the vital role of what Dori Laub calls the "the witness from inside" or "the witness

Adios Ayacucho by Grupo Cultura Yuyachkani. Photograph
courtesy of Herman Schwartz.

to oneself." This witness from inside, though impossible, according to Laub,
in the context of the Holocaust that "made unthinkable the very notion that
a witness could exist," because it allowed for no "outside," no "other," is
nonetheless posited as the only hope for justice in the Andean context.[13]
The victim reconstitutes himself by finding his scattered body parts. Little
by little, he reclaims his human form. Finally, he finds his face; finally, he
finds his voice, which will proclaim the violence done to him and his community. He not only voices his denunciation, over and over again, but he

determines to take a letter to the president of the republic, outlining the violence he has suffered. This letter, finally, will make it into the archive, a testimony of the erasure of mestizo and indigenous populations. This haunting image from *Adios Ayacucho* suggests the way in which Yuyachkani layers its approach to representing violence. The clothes laid out in memory of the dead re-presents the missing body of the victim of disappearance, even as it echoes an ancient burial practice. These practices are alive; other bodies will perform them just as the man fits himself back into the waiting clothes. Andean performance practices, this shows, are not dead things, fading from view. Nor do they function in a parallel universe. These traditions continue to allow for immediate responses to current political problems. Every response to political violence carries with it a history of responses, conjured up from a vast range of embodied and archival memories.

The third stage in Yuyachkani's development illustrates how each of the members has developed individually and independently even as they maintain their strong working and individual ties to the group. Teresa Ralli created the closest thing Yuyachkani had done in terms of solo performance, *Baladas del Bien-Estar,* in which she sings and acts Brechtian songs and poems accompanied by a pianist. Rebeca Ralli and Julian Vargas developed two pieces for two characters, *No me toquen ese vals* (1990) and *Serenata* (1995). The female members of Yuyachkani wrote, directed, and acted in a *La Primera Cena* (The First Supper), a play that brings three childhood friends together to reflect on their lives as women in Peru. Sometimes the entire company works on a production, such as *Hasta cuando corazón* (1994), which captures the loneliness of poor city dwellers, crammed into tenements, waiting for something: a lost love to reappear, a better job, a new life. Sometimes just one or two of the actors create and act in a production, while others are running workshops, directing, or somehow developing their special interests.

Through each of these periods, however, Yuyachkani has worked to reveal the "past" in the present. They function as witnesses to the premodern living conditions of some Peruvians in the country today and the postmodern loneliness and alienation of others. For them performance is not about going back but about keeping alive. Its mode of transmission is the repeat, the reiteration, the "yet again" of the twice-behaved behavior that Richard Schechner defines as "performance."[14] The violence of the past has not "disappeared." It has reappeared in the violent response against the miners's strike (1971), in the massacre of Soccos (1986), in the displacement of local populations caught between *Sendero* and government forces, on the empty streets of Lima in the 1980s and early 1990s, torn and made strange by the violence. Their work of those years recounts the ideological ruptures and personal losses caused by the terror tactics and forced migrations of the period. And all the while the group was undergoing its own crisis. As its stance remained nonviolent throughout this period of civil upheaval, its members received threats from both *Sendero* and military sympathizers. It even lost two of its own members, who disagreed with its nonviolence position.[15] The remembering was always past, present, and seemingly future. As Rebeca Ralli puts it, the group's work represents the struggle for survival of the Peruvian people even as it represents Yuyachkani's own struggle to survive both as individuals and as a group. "We put up with so much just to be able to live, just to be able to create."[16]

Yuyachkani's performances make visible a history of cumulative trauma, an unmarked and unacknowledged history of violent conflict. As in *Adios Ayacucho,* the attempts at communicating an event that no one cares to acknowledge need to be repeated again and again. Part of the reiteration stems from the traumatic nature of the injury. Cathy Caruth argues that the obsessive repeats occur because "the event is not assimilated or experienced fully at the time, but only belatedly, in its repeated *possession* of the one who experiences it. To be traumatized is precisely to be possessed by an image or event."[17] The same, Caruth's proposes, occurs with historical understanding: "For history to be a history of trauma means that it is referential precisely to the extent that it is not fully perceived as it occurs" (8). Trauma produces dislocation, a rupture between the experience and the possibility of understanding it. But trauma, as Caruth's notes, "opens up and challenges us to a new kind of listening, the witnessing, precisely, of *impossibility*" (10). For members of traumatized communities, such as the Andean ones Yuyachkani engages with, past violence blends into the current crisis. The trauma of the persecuted and deracinated indigenous and mestizo populations is a "symptom of history," as Caruth puts it: "The traumatized, we might say, carry an impossible history within them, or they become themselves the symptom of a history that they cannot entirely possess" (5).

The retelling and reenactment, however, pose problems of legitimacy. While the performances capture the ongoing nature of the violence against indigenous peoples, it complicates a historical accounting. What is time without progression? What is space without demarcation? What happens to a people's concept of history when markers are few or known only through a performative repeat?

Most writing on atrocity insists on fixing the time and place of the traumatic wounding. Situating the event in a temporal and spatial frame establishes that vital "outside" that Laub refers to—the space in which witnessing can take place. The telling of atrocity tends to unfold as narrative, setting the stage to enable the act of bearing witness, however retroactively, even to events that had no witnesses.[18] The traumatic *recall* is performative—that is, a *living through*, "repossessing one's life story through giving testimony [which] is itself a form of action, of change, which one has to actually pass through."[19] Each attempt at communication is also a repeat, as the person who survived the trauma tries to transmit it to another person outside the experience—the one who bears witness and accepts the burden of performative contagion. Like performance, the recounting involves bracketing, framing, setting up the scene. "Listen to this," says the victim, the narrator, the testimonial writer. "Look at this," say the survivors who return to the place, the *lieux de mémoire*,[20] or the photographers, playwrights, and filmmakers who need us to recognize something with our mind's eye, if not firsthand with the eye itself. In trauma the past is replayed in the present—both as a symptom of distress (as in flashbacks) and as part of the healing process (reclaiming the experience).

The undifferentiated, reiterative nature of Peru's traumatic history folds seamlessly with the Andean paradigm of memory (summed up in the Inkarrí cycle), which defies the fixity of a before and after. "Inkarrí's dismembered body (whose severed head has been taken, variously, to Cusco, Lima or Spain) is coming together again, underground. . . . The lower world, region of chaos and fertility, becomes the source of the future, an extension of the belief that the dead return to present time and space during the growth season."[21] Faced with the consciously deployed strategy of colonial dismemberment, the myths offer the promise of re-membering. "Perú es un país desmemorizado," as Teresa Ralli put it. Who can say, after five hundred years of ongoing conquest and colonization, where the memory of trauma is situated, whether it is individually or collectively experienced, if it is experienced belatedly or continually embodied, and how it passes from generation to generation? We only know from myths and stories that Peru's indigenous populations see themselves as the product of conquest and violence. Violence is not an event but a worldview and way of life.

Yuyachkani, it seems to me, intervenes in this problematic in two fundamental ways—one having to do with the transmission, the other with the role and function of witnessing. In regard to the first: Yuyachkani understands the importance of performance as a means of re-membering and transmitting social memory. Its use of ethnically diverse performance traditions is neither decorative nor citational—that is, Yuyachkani does not incorporate them as add-ons to complement or "authenticate" its own project. The group's commitment to enter into conversation with rural populations has led its members to learn the languages, the music, and the performance modes of these communities. Rather than attempt to restore specific behaviors, that is, re-creating museum pieces that somehow replicate an "original," they follow the traditional usage of reactivating ancient practices to address current problems or challenges. Moreover, Yuyachkani does not participate in the reproduction and commodification of "popular" culture. The group's texts do not circulate. Other actors or companies do not perform its plays. The only way one can access its work is by participating in it—on the streets as bystander caught up in the action, in Casa Yuyachkani as spectator and discussant, or in the many workshops open to students from around the world. New, younger members are joining the group, and they, too, are Yuyachkani. They will not act "like" Yuyachkani but "be" Yuyachkani, adopting and adapting the character of the group itself. Their performances, just like the performances they draw from, are inseparable from them as people. The "I" who thinks and remembers is the product of these collective pre- and postcolonial performances.

Furthermore, unlike groups that appropriate the performance practices of others, Yuyachkani's work does not separate the performances from their original audiences but, rather, tries to expand the audiences. The productions are not about "them"—the indigenous and mestizo others—but about all the different communities that share a territorial space defined by pre-conquest groups, colonialism, and nationalism. Yuyachkani attempts to make its urban audiences culturally competent to recognize the multiple ways of being Peruvian. In addressing Lima audiences, however, Yuyachkani feels it has to start "from zero."[22] The country's theatrical memory, much like its historical, cultural, and political memory, has been deracinated. These performances remind urban audiences of the populations they have forgotten. Storing and transmitting these traditions proves essential, because, when they disappear, certain kinds of knowledge, issues, and populations disappear with them. These traditions—the street procession, fiestas, songs, masked characters—bring together Creole, mestizo, Afro-Peruvian, and indigenous expressive elements, each vital to the deeply complicated historical, ethnic, and racial configuration of the actual political situation. Performance provides the "memory path," the space of reiteration that allows people to replay the ancient struggles for recognition and power that continue to make themselves felt in contemporary Peru.

This brings us to the second point: looking at performance as a retainer of social memory engages history without necessarily being a "symptom of history"—that is, the performances enter into dialogue with a history of trauma without themselves being traumatic. These are carefully crafted works that create a critical distance for "claiming" experience and enabling, as opposed to "collapsing," witnessing.[23] This performance event has an "outside," which is what, according to Laub, allows for witnessing. Yuyachkani, as its name indicates, hinges on the notion of interconnectedness—the "I" who thinks/remembers is inextricable from the "you" whose thought I am. The I/you of Yuyachkani promises to be a witness, a guarantor, of the link between the "I" and the "you," the "inside" and the "outside." Yuyachkani becomes the belated witnesses to the ongoing, unacknowledged drama of atrocity and asks its audience to do the same. Here its practice points to a radically different conclusion than the one Adorno arrived at in "On Commitment." Representation, for Yuyachkani, does not further contribute to the desecration of the victims, turning their pain into our viewing pleasure.[24] Rather, without representation viewers would not recognize their role in the ongoing history of oppression, which, directly or indirectly, implicates them. Who, *Adios Ayacucho* asks, will take on the responsibility of witnessing? The witness, like Boal's "spect-actor," accepts the dangers and responsibilities of seeing and of acting on what one has seen. And witnessing is transferable: the theater, like the testimony, like the photograph, film, or report, can make witnesses of others. The witness sustains both the archive and the repertoire. So, rather than think of performance primarily as the ephemeral, as that which disappears, Yuyachkani insists on creating a community of witnesses by and through performance.

These understandings of the political and historical importance of performance counter the performance as pathology model that assumes in theory, at least, that the need for repetition disappears when the wounding is healed. Treatments for post–traumatic stress disorder try to minimize the anxiety and depression that are triggered by the flashbacks. A successful outcome, in the best of all possible worlds, would mean the end of the performative repeat. At the same time, Yuyachkani counters the performance-as-disappearance of colonialism, which pushed autochthonous practices into the oblivion of the ephemeral, the unscripted, the uncontrollable. For many of these communities, on the contrary, when performance ends, so does the shared understanding of social life and collective memory. Performances such as these fiestas, parades, and theatrical productions warn us not to dismiss the I who remembers, who thinks, who is a product of collective thought. They teach communities not to look away. As the name *Yuyachkani* suggests, attention to the interconnectedness between thinking subjects and subjects of thought would allow for a broader understanding of historical trauma, communal memory, and collective subjectivity.

NOTES

1. Hugo Salazar del Alcazar, "Los musicos ambulantes," *La escena latinoamericana,* no. 2 (August 1989): 23.

2. Personal interview, Paucartambo, Peru, July 1999.

3. Thomas A. Abercrombie, *Pathways of Memory and Power: Ethnography and History among an Andean People* (Madison: University of Wisconsin Press, 1998), 6.

4. The anti-star sentiment was of course often contradicted in the group's makeup with the director functioning as leader and even guru. See Yolanda Gonzalez-Broyles's study on the Teatro Campesino as an example.

5. Diana Taylor, *Theatre of Crisis: Drama and Politics in Latin America* (Lexington: University of Kentucky Press, 1990), chap. 1.

6. Miguel Rubio, "Encuentro con el Hombre Andino," *Grupo Cultural Yuyachkani, Allpa Rayku: Una experencia de teatro popular,"* 2d ed. (Lima: Edición del 'Grupo Cultural Yuyachkani' y Escuelas Campesinas de la CCP, 1985), 9.

7. Brenda Luz Cotto-Escalera, "Grupo Cultural Yuyachkani: Group Work and Collective Creation in Contemporary Latin American Theatre" (Ph.D. diss., University of Texas, Austin, 1995), 116.

8. Hugo Salazar del Alcazar, interview in "Persistencia de la Memoria," documentary video on Yuyachkani.

9. "Encuentro de zorros" was based on a text by José María Arguedas entitled "El zorro de arriba y el zorro de abajo" and was cowritten by the group and Peter Elmore. "Adios Ayacucho" was based on a text by the same name by Julio Ortega.

10. Theodor Adorno, "On Commitment," *Aesthetics and Politics,* ed. Ernst Bloch et al. (London: Verso, 1977), 189.

11. Cotto-Escalera, "Grupo Cultural Yuyachkani," 156.

12. Diana Taylor, *Disappearing Acts: Spectacles of Gender and Nationalism in Argentina's "Dirty War"* (Durham, N.C.: Duke University Press, 1997).

13. Dori Laub, "Truth and Testimony: The Process and the Struggle," in *Trauma: Explorations in Memory,* ed. Cathy Caruth (Baltimore, Md.: Johns Hopkins University Press, 1995), 66.

14. Richard Schechner, *Between Theater and Anthropology* (Philadelphia: University of Pennsylvania Press, 1985).

15. Qtd. in Cotto-Escalera, "Grupo Cultural Yuyachkani," 98.

16. Interview, Rebeca Ralli, Casa Yuyachkani, June 1996.

17. Caruth, *Trauma,* 4–5; hereafter cited in the text.

18. Laub, "Truth and Testimony," 70.

19. Shosana Felman and Dori Laub, *Testimony: Crisis of Witnessing in Literature, Psychoanalysis, and History* (New York: Routledge, 1992), 85.

20. Pierre Nora, *Les lieux de mémoire* (Paris: Gallimard, 1984), qtd. in Dominick LaCapra, *History and Memory after Auschwitz* (Ithaca, N.Y.: Cornell University Press, 1998), 10.

21. William Rowe and Vivian Schelling, *Memory and Modernity: Popular Culture in Latin America* (London: Verso, 1991), 55.

22. Rubio, *Allpa Ravku,* qtd. in Cotto, *Trauma,* 115.

23. See Cathy Caruth, *Unclaimed Experience* (Baltimore: Johns Hopkins University Press, 1997); and Dori Laub's notion of the "collapse of witnessing" in "Truth and Testimony," 65.

24. Adorno, "On Commitment."

Mary Ann Hunter

No Safety Gear:
Skate Girl Space and the
Regeneration of Australian
Community-Based Performance

In one of the rare comic skits presented on the otherwise uninspiring Australian television parody "Fast Forward," a young man stands in court awaiting his sentence for a criminal offence. It is likely that the man will be handed a community service order or a jail term. After stern deliberation the judge sentences the offender to "200 hours of community theater." This play on the common parlance *200 hours of community service* is accompanied by great gales of recorded studio laughter and, one may presume, similarly audible sighs of resignation from former community theater practitioners across the country. . . . What has become the current public perception of community theater in Australia? Does it have relevance or a future when tired models of practice become the object of derision and a test of endurance for audiences?

The death-knell for a certain emblematic style of community theater has been sounding in Australia for quite some time. In a 1993 essay provocatively titled "Wanted (Presumed Dead): Community Theatre in Victoria," Geoffrey Milne lamented the disappearance of professional theater for, by, and about communities in the Australian state of Victoria, which at that time was being socially and culturally ravaged by its government's overtly economic-rationalist priorities.[1] Likewise throughout Australia, community theater's demise has been framed by funding agency agendas, and it has been well documented how government prerogatives have determined both the

Mary Ann Hunter is a Lecturer in Drama and Performance at the University of Queensland, Brisbane. She completed her PhD in 1999 and was recently a Teaching Fellow at Nanyang Technological University, Singapore. In 1997, she was awarded the Philip Parsons Prize for Performance as Research (Australasian Drama Studies Association) and continues to be actively involved in community-based research and performance.

mortality rate of community-based companies and the life expectancy of new approaches.[2]

Practitioners of the 1980s boom of community theater have become particularly disillusioned with notions of voice, identity, and representation in community-based performance as the foundations of "community" have become increasingly unstable in Australia's linguistically and culturally diverse society. And, as David Watt's description of the "celebratory epic" suggests, when these shifting boundaries of (and allegiances to) community become too time- and money-consuming to negotiate, a glossy street parade-style of community theater is the preferred option for arts practitioners and funding agencies.[3] As a result, in the 1990s the very definition of *community theater* finds itself at the mercy of an obsessively cautious, and in many cases banal, model of practice. As for any critique of an aesthetics of community-based performance, postmodern suspicions of a perceived reliance on authentic voices and boundaried communities have discouraged the kind of vigorous attention and debate that this field—which was formerly so important a mode of social criticism and political action—should deserve.

In his study of British community-based performance, *Theatre and Everyday Life,* Alan Read declares that community arts and political theater are outmoded forms of reference that "limit thought to partitioned realms which have very little to do with the complexity of real contexts."[4] While I agree with Read in his implication that all theater is political, difficulties arise in trying to avoid these terms of reference when dealing with practices that are community based. Particularly given the current connotations of the term *community theater* in Australia, this raises the question of how to reframe an investigation of a type of participatory, nonrepertory, nonamateur but not always fully professional performance practice that aims to have some political and community efficacy. Where do I begin when the goalposts are continually shifting?

These are just some of the dilemmas involved in tackling the "art form formerly known as" community theater in Australia. The attempt to negotiate a site for performance that is moving beyond a once gloried past is fraught with melancholic self-examination, reevaluation, and recategorization: is the "art form formerly known as" community theater still valid in the 1990s? Is it even worth posing the question?

My answer is a resounding, but carefully qualified, yes on both counts. To evoke the postmodern once again, if community really is a nonstatic, continually evolving process of relations (as those few who are working innovatively in the field believe), surely self-questioning, reevaluation, and general gloom mongering are the essential stepping stones for negotiating a site for performance that defies static categorization.

My aim in this essay is to highlight regenerative approaches to community theater that are emerging from this process of questioning and reevaluation. But there are two catches. One, the practice is not termed *community theater* anymore. And, two, despite its tenuous position as "community cultural development" in government cultural policy, this body of work is no longer afraid to be overtly critical of, nor criticized by, its participating community. The Backbone Youth Arts's *Skate Girl Space* project is an example of this "art form formerly known as" community theater, evoking the political function of earlier community-based performance in Australia rather than the term's celebratory connotations. This 1996 youth arts project was a gesture of radical social action reminiscent of the political performance that defined the term *community theater* twenty years ago, regenerated with a contemporary feminist attitude that demanded community-based solidarity and action while disrupting, on a number of levels, the very notion of community itself. While acknowledging major tensions and further political repercussions (manifest in the violent reaction of some spectators to the performance), I suggest that the project is an example of an important regeneration of community-based performance that refuses a routine sense of celebration and thus functions without the safety gear of conventional community arts practice.

By describing the project as "youth arts," I am cautious. Like the terms *community arts* and *community cultural development,* it is slippery terminology. The category youth has been variously described as rebellious, antiauthoritarian, deeply conservative, at the forefront of social change; under twenty-five, under thirty-five, "the young at heart." Across the category there are also distinctions of gender, race, sexuality, class, ability, education, and locality. So, when coupled with the equally diverse and pliable concepts of arts and culture, the result is a heady mix of confusing and stereotypical images of "youth cultures": raves, skateboards, religious rallies, cyber-realities, crime, drugs, fashion, girl guides, and sole parenthood, to name a few. Add to this the retro-perspective of adults surveying the under twenty-fives, and these images are sometimes further framed by nostalgia or fear.

Vered Amit-Talai refers to a particular anthropological problem arising out of "the tendency to identify cultures with community."[5] She observes that "within such a perspective, the very concept of youth culture becomes for all intents and purposes untenable unless we can assert that youths form their own separate societies."[6] To address this, Amit-Talai proposes an activity-oriented view of culture that presumes that "youthful cultural strategies [diverse as they are] will emerge from and be addressed to the exigencies of the situations in which they are implicated and the constraints which age restrictions impose on the range and nature of that involvement."[7] This allows the view that "youth is peculiar in status, expectations and involvement,"[8] without assuming any ageist, limiting, or essentializing notion of a youth culture or of youth. So, too, Johanna Wyn and Rob White describe youth cultural activity as a constant dynamic process, "not only in the sense of different and rapidly changing influences in one's cultural universe, but as well, with respect to the levels of participation by young people in actively constructing their cultural life."[9] It is on the basis of these activity-centered understandings that I use the terms *youth arts* and *youth cultures* in the following discussion.

In the early 1990s Brisbane-based La Boite Youth Theatre evolved into Backbone Youth Arts due to a recognition that theater, in the narrowly defined traditional sense of the word, was not a significantly meaningful "youthful cultural strategy" for most young people. Informed by Paul Willis's concept of a "grounded aesthetics,"[10] Backbone Youth Arts and a number of other former youth theaters around the country have expanded their work beyond conventional theater skills workshops to promote and encourage young people's own preferences in cultural activity and performance. For Backbone Youth Arts this transition has thematically focused on young people's experience as critical consumers in their everyday life; whereby a critical examination of the media and advertising industry's processes of production (particularly their representations of age, gender, and cultural difference) has informed the young participants' devising of contemporary performance. In all Backbone projects young people are positioned as the primary creators and artists, often working in conjunction with established arts workers.

A participant-managed performance group of young women has developed as part of Backbone Youth Arts' program. This group, called the Hereford Sisters, began in 1993 with the aim of encouraging young women's diversity, creativity, and cultures through physical performance and movement. Managed by a fluid membership of young women and facilitated by Backbone Youth Arts' artistic director, Louise Hollingworth, the Hereford Sisters process provides "a means for young women to occupy . . . decision-making positions of management and control"[11] in the arts industry. Following a number of performance projects exploring topics such

as eating behaviors, romance, and safety, the members of the Hereford Sisters consciously shifted their issue-based focus beyond the conceptual space
of the private to the public with the 1996 *Skate Girl Space* project.

Skate Girl Space centered on young women's relationship to public
space, particularly in inner-city Brisbane. Funded by the local Brisbane City
Council and sponsored by various skateboard companies, *Skate Girl Space*
initially emerged from young women's requests to develop skateboarding
skills in an arts framework. From there it evolved as an opportunity to
express their concern about access to the heavily male-dominated territory
of public outdoor parks. The project then became a major component of
the expansive Girls in Space arts and cultural action research program,
which later involved Backbone and four other organizations in identifying
and promoting young women's public space needs in Brisbane.

The *Skate Girl Space* project both utilized and challenged contemporary
youth cultures such as skateboarding in a six-month workshop and devising
process. The members of the Hereford Sisters researched and comanaged
the process, with Louise Hollingworth and dramaturg, Louise Gough, and
participated in skateboarding and physical theater workshops to hone their
skills in performance.

A narrative that parodied the vernacular of commercial skateboarding
culture and the genre of the American western resulted. Titled an action
plan, the script for the project's culminating performance event was structured more like a film treatment than any theater script: each scene
identified in relation to a specific context, task, and tension.

> *SCENE 1*
> CONTEXT: Heroes (the performers) have been told this was a free
>   tradin' town. They arrive to find it is inhabited and constructed.
>   They explore this weird place cautiously.
> TASK: Establish relationship between heroes/villain/society.
> TENSION: From the heroes perspective the relationships are not as
>   they expected.[12]

Focused on themes of territory and belonging in both form and content, the performance incorporated video images that critiqued prevalent
commercial skate culture attitudes toward women, people with low levels
of skateboarding skill, sacrosanct "peak traffic times," and skate fashion.
These images, in conjunction with the performance narrative, sought to
respond to skate culture as a mode of cultural consumption and social
identification through comic exaggeration and extension. The performance

employed the tropes of the American TV western to make ironic the idea of spatial frontiers and territorial conquests in the skate space. The performers decided to foreground their physical presence in the site-specific setting by utilizing a "parodic self-consciousness"[13] in costuming: fusing dance party and glam fashion with American western boots and fringes and, in so doing, overcoding a girlish stereotype. In this way their highly visual presence in the space commented on the prescriptive behavior of those who dominated the space. The issues and the gender formerly invisible in this space thus became extraordinarily visible and political.

Leading up to the performance event at the Paddington Skate Park, the thirteen-member Hereford Sisters team developed their basic skateboarding skills at night because, as unskilled riders, they were unable to access this public space during daylight hours due to the "heavy traffic" of skateboarding regulars. Throughout the process Louise Hollingworth consulted with the Paddington Skate Park Committee, a group of young men who voluntarily maintained this popular skateboarding site in Brisbane's inner city, and made special arrangements to gain access to the site on the day of the *Skate Girl Space* event for a technical run.[14] Despite this consultation, the performers experienced sexual harassment and physical and verbal abuse from a number of regular park users, to an extent that necessitated a police presence during the final rehearsal. As a precursor to what was to be a very tense event, the Hereford Sisters became acutely aware that this public space was exclusively male expert skaters' territory.

The early evening event featured large-screen video projection and a live "all-girl cow-poke" band set among Paddington Skate Park's skate ramps and bowls, the unique features of the park making an innovative performative landscape for the young Hereford artists and their audience. Dressed in their colorful mismatched gear, complete with the odd ten-gallon hat, the performance opened with the Hereford Sisters entering the park space as a skateboard-toting posse ready to explore and pioneer new territory. Placed firmly in the physical theater realm, the performers engaged in a feminist "doing" of performance, merging skateboarding and physical and comic skills in sequences, such as a "tick-tack skateboard tap," to confront the physical space and the dominant "law/lore" as expressed by the electronic image of authority, Sheriff Stiffy.

The audience was supposed to move around the space simultaneously with the performers as they explored the park, assessing the situation and constructing strategies for defiant occupation. But the day's earlier disruptions undermined the event's production values and impacted the performers' attitude to their spectators. The inability to stage an adequate technical run prior to the performance contributed to the failure of the outdoor sound system, so that the bewildered audience of five hundred had only the performers' visual coding and the singularly clear voice (ironically, that of the male Sheriff Stiffy) to make meaning of the haphazard goings-on. To make matters worse, a core of intoxicated male skaters and female companions also heckled the performers, at one point interrupting the production altogether by throwing a glass beer bottle onto the stage area.[15] Consequently, the narrative's clever "ramp thwackin', whip crackin', side splittin'"[16] conceptual and language play was largely lost on an audience whose members were left to assume mistakenly that this performance was essentially about girls-as-goodies versus boys-as-baddies. Although the piece was attempting to articulate the diversity of community and expose the power structures operating within the construction of regional and age-specific ideas of community, these aspects of the event contributed to a far more antagonistic treatment of the issues at hand. As the *Skate Girl Space* program prophetically stated,

Anticipating free tradin' space they discover all is not as it appears. . . . [T]his town is inhabited and has its ways. The unwritten lore is articulated when they meet face to face with Sheriff Stiffy. Stiffy acts as the mouth piece for BIG BAD BEEF's code of operation [BIG BAD BEEF being the space personified]. The scent of a SHOWDOWN wafts in the breeze.[17]

The performance narrative was intentionally left open-ended with a playful finale featuring live-to-screen video footage of the hero-performers "riding off into the sunset" (to cross at traffic lights on the street adjacent to the skate park). As young women denied equitable access to the realm of public space, these final images may have represented a return to the private gendered space of home and bedroom; that is, if it weren't for the deliberately defiant "in your face" attitude expressed directly, by each departing performer into the face of the live-to-screen camera. In this quick, aggressive succession of close-up facials, these young women were declaring that they would be back and would not be ignored. After the finale most of the crowd lingered in the space bemused. The hecklers—themselves resistant to this "performance of resistance"—continued to disrupt proceedings by physically scuffling with the remaining Hereford Sisters, again necessitating an intervention by police.

A far cry from celebratory community theater, the performance had

Publicity photo for *Skate Girl Space* by Hereford Sisters. Hereford Sisters, *from left to right:* Jacki McKean, Kellie McBride, Melissa Fox, Leanne Sales (*at far back*), Marion Woodhead, Zoe Green (*scooter*), Freya Dwyer. Photograph courtesy of Rebecca Harbison. (Backbone Youth Arts Inc.)

many detractors. What right did these women have to waltz (at times literally) in a culturally specific space, to declare a showdown with the young men who regularly used it? Haven't young men themselves been marginalized in their access to appropriate public space facilities? How were other skateboarders expected to react to the perceived generalizations made about male skateboarders? If the project aimed to get girls skating in Paddington, why didn't they practice elsewhere to hone their skills, just like everyone else?

These are valid questions that, to effect long-term community development, were later addressed by young women and men together in Paddington. To avoid the violence, critics of the process suggested that the entire project should have been more of a collaboration than a liaison with the young male skaters who used the space. Yet this leads to questions about the very purpose of community-based performance. Whose community are we talking about? Whose voice and representation are we talking about? Who is the public of *public space?* And what does this say about the concept of community?

The *Skate Girl Space* project was regenerative as community-based performance for its bold enactment and interrogation of community on a number of levels. While "celebratory epic" models of community theater attempt to achieve community cohesion—sometimes by celebrating diversity, sometimes by responding as community to adversity—*Skate Girl Space* provoked, agitated, and disrupted community to enable community action.

First, on a philosophical level this government-supported project enacted and interrogated the principles of community cultural development, cited by Fiona Winning as "Diversity, Access and Participation."[18] *Skate Girl Space* aimed to empower young women to access and self-manage processes of cultural production. This was facilitated by the experienced Backbone Youth Arts director and further guided by the narrative- and performance-shaping skills of the dramaturg, Louise Gough. The skate expert, video artist, musicians, and physical theater workers who facilitated the process also supported the young participants' skills development, enabling a process of community expression through performance to occur. On this level the project demanded local government attention to the fact that young women were invisible in the current discourse and provision of public space. In the tradition of earlier political Australian community theater, the project was an opportunity for a previously disempowered and marginalized group of people to enact community to effect social change. By physically occupying the Paddington Skate Park, which few women had traversed, and by satirizing the idea of territory, frontiers, and unwritten lore, the young women of *Skate Girl Space* resisted and challenged the assumptions about public space as community space. They delivered a clear message about the inequity of public space use and provision and the reliance on essentialized notions of "the public." Their performance also demonstrated that the idealized notion of "free access" operates as much in the cultural and social realms as in the purely economic, an aspect overlooked in the use and provision of "free" public space.

Second, the project both regenerated and challenged perceptions of age-specific community. This age-defined community context was reflected in the fact that Backbone Youth Arts, as host organization, was a youth-specific company and worked with other youth-focused organizations to support young people's own "youthful cultural strategies." Yet, on this level, *Skate Girl Space* also challenged the assumption that youth constitute a community of common interest, particularly as consumers of commercial culture. For example, as part of the performance-devising process, the participants of *Skate Girl Space* examined the commercial culture of skateboarding and its sexist representations of women as passive fashion objects. During their research the Hereford Sisters found it almost impossible to locate images of women actively skating in any of the current issues of the major skateboarding magazines.[19] This effectively debunked the idea that there exists a community of youth, young consumers, or even young skateboarders, resisting and disrupting the idea of an age-defined community with gender-specific perspectives. The performance of *Skate Girl Space* foregrounded this by depicting, on the wide screen, only one male character: a disembodied, electronically mediated, all-seeing, all-authoritarian talking head, Sheriff Stiffy, who laid down the law/lore on what to wear and what not to do as a (presumably male) skateboarder. The use of this omnipresent character also satirized, on a wider scale, the hegemonic systems of power and authority that operate in the media construction of youth in consumerist late-capitalist societies.

Third, the project was site specific and both engaged and provoked a regionally based community. At the time of the project the resources of Backbone Youth Arts were centered in inner-city Paddington, and Louise Hollingworth initiated ongoing consultation and coordination with community groups in the same region. At the same time, as a site-specific project in public space, *Skate Girl Space* resisted the ideals of regional community cohesiveness and shared living space and questioned the concept of value-free recreation. Inequities of public space provision were exposed in the process, revealing an erroneous assumption on the part of local government authorities that community is a regionally specific given with common recreational and cultural needs that can be universally met by conventional public facilities.

There is no doubt the *Skate Girl Space* performance event was disturbing. The disruptions that occurred were a very public manifestation of overlapping tensions among the gendered, age-specific, and regional communities involved. In the short term the event may have further limited young women's access to the Paddington Skate Park—the public space of their regional community. But, far more important, *Skate Girl Space* was a politically radical gesture from a group of young women critical of a sexist commercial culture that colonizes so-called public space with unwritten lore, critical of the invisibility of young women within debates about public space, and critical of unnecessary resort to violence.

While this performative action could be interpreted as political in itself, the reactions of the spectators to the event also made it politically perilous. Carlson states that "the central concern of resistant performance arises from the dangerous game it plays as a double agent, recognizing that in the postmodern world complicity and subversion are inextricably intertwined."[20] Carlson suggests that this "double operation"[21] may sometimes merely reinforce stereotypes, risking an essentialized us/them approach to domination and subversion. The Hereford Sisters' flouting of skate lore and their lack of high-level skateboarding skill, for which the inner-city skate park is renowned, punted on this hazardous game: the resultant dynamic among performers, spectators, and police almost countersubverting the project. While this danger was well acknowledged by the event's coordinators who, with the Hereford Sisters, had planned specific strategies to deal with the potentially violent situation,[22] their aim was to create a new space not only for "girl" skaters but for others denied access in the public and community realm.

A highly potent aspect of the Hereford Sisters' work was their commitment to the subversive and parodic self-consciousness of their political "double-coding." This "doing" functioned neither as a whole community celebration nor solely as a resistance against hegemonic forces. The performers were not resisting the act of skateboarding itself, for they themselves were doing it. They were not resisting or denying the right to develop and perform high-level skill, for they themselves were parodying their own lack of skill and were seeking out the unspoken rules pertaining to the display of such skill. Rather, their performance aimed to expose disempowering representational processes and the lack of access and opportunity that occurs when community and community space are dominated by particular interest groups that codify the space with highly discriminatory and exclusionary politics. The tensions that did arise indicated that *Skate Girl Space* was indeed a timely and relevant call for recognition and action.

Thus, *Skate Girl Space* was both a process of participatory community-based cultural production and a feminist commentary on dominant modes of cultural production and consumption in public space. It functioned as a politically charged message about the inequitable opportunities for young women to claim and share cultural space. Significantly, these strategies have a history that highlights the symbiotic relationship between feminist and community-based approaches to political performance practice in Australia.[23]

Currently, arts funding bodies and those responsible for the management of public outdoor spaces are besotted with the equation: *community-based arts activity plus young people (in public space) equals good community crime prevention.* But issues of public space and youth arts are more complex than that. By problematizing these recreation issues with questions of "whose space?" and "who is the public anyway?," *Skate Girl Space* facilitated young people's expression on a wider range of interrelated cultural issues, such as marginalization, identity, gender, access, and diversity. This was evident not only in the performance narrative but also in the spectators' responses (violent and otherwise) and in the community and media debate that followed the event, thus regenerating the principles of effective community theater for social change. If *Skate Girl Space* was a dissatisfying performance, this was because it became recontextualized by the very issues it set out to address and not because it wasn't celebratory or professional or didn't meet the mythical criteria for "excellent" cultural product at the behest of funding bodies. The Hereford Sisters and Backbone Youth Arts showed that, while the term *community* arguably becomes less useful in increasingly diverse and electronically mediated societies, the function of community-based performance does not. People coming together for an amount of time to participate in the expression of their common experience or concerns and to interrogate further the assumptions placed on regional, age-based, gender-specific, and commercially defined communities is an important political exercise.

In 1997 the Hereford Sisters embarked on a follow-up project, Risk8 Theatre, using the idea of positive negotiation of risk as a focus for their work. In particular, the troupe aimed to "negotiate daredevil tricks with a board in space + physical theatre" to create a "new performance language."[24] This approach is indicative of a wider shift in the uses of space, body, and language in youth-specific performance in Australia, perhaps also generating a revamped aesthetics of community-based performance. For the Hereford Sisters a continuing parallel investigation of consumer cultures, particularly the power relationships that operate within them, is leading to innovative intersections of form and content, an emerging signature feature of their work being the fusion of video art with physical theater in live performance.

Gay Hawkins has described how community arts in Australia negotiated a place in cultural policy by defining itself as oppositional to perceived elite culture, on the one hand, and mass-mediated culture, on the other—the result being an overvalorization of context over content.[25] Yet, by developing out of young people's diverse interests, needs, and preferred cultural processes, organizations like Backbone Youth Arts *question* context *through* content and generate new processes (and content) in doing so. In this type of community-based performance, context and content inform, challenge, and create each other in much the same way as a contemporary "genre of feminist theater" conflates form and content for political effect.[26] This provides the framework for serious, engaging, and sometimes dangerous arts practices to occur, one in which political efficacy and cultural value are inextricably linked.

In *Cultural Studies and Cultural Value* John Frow examines the dilemmas associated with making value judgments within and between what he terms "regimes of cultural value."[27] What is unique and important about the participatory community-based performance of Backbone Youth Arts and other politically effective youth arts and community cultural organizations is their recognition that many regimes of value operate integratively across the field. They refuse to be constrained by a singular regime of value or models of practice predetermined by government funding agencies' agendas for community cultural development. To ask honestly of community-based performance, "the ethical and political questions—who speaks? Who speaks for whom? Whose voice is listened to, whose voice is spoken over, who has no voice?"[28] is to risk creating more division than celebration—particularly when diversity within so-called community is at issue. It is only by acknowledging the nature of community cultural development work—its processual approach and its span across cultural and social regimes of value—that this division can lead to positive social action. This poses a direct challenge to policy makers and to the arts industry primarily concerned with categorization of arts industry sectors.

Perhaps it has been the case that, in fighting for a place in cultural policy and the cultural industry, community theater in Australia has tried valiantly to create a singularly appropriate regime of cultural value, one that offers criteria for evaluation and benchmarks for development. Yet I believe that the strength of community-based performance lies in the way it intersects with a range of regimes of value and thereby defies categorization. *Skate Girl Space* illustrates how this intersection can sometimes result in collision and confrontation and yet make for effective community cultural development. Far from being dead, the "art form formerly known as" community theater continues, transformed in different sites and contexts to effect social change.

NOTES

1. Geoffrey Milne, "Wanted (Presumed Dead): Community Theatre in Victoria," *Australasian Drama Studies* 23 (1993): 147–60.

2. For general discussions about community theater in Australia, particularly its links with government policy, see ibid.; and Richard Fotheringham, ed., *Community Theatre in Australia,* rev. ed. (Sydney: Currency, 1992); Gay Hawkins, *From Nimbin to Mardi Gras: Constructing Community Arts* (St. Leonards: Allen and Unwin, 1993); David Watt,

"Community Theatre: A Progress Report," *Australasian Drama Studies* 20 (1992): 3–15; David Watt, "'Excellence/Access' and 'Nation/Community,'" *Canadian Theatre Review* 74 (1993): 7–11; Fiona Winning, "Cultural Policy and Community Theatre," *Australasian Drama Studies* 22 (1993): 73–78.

3. Watt, "'Excellence/Access,'" 9.

4. Alan Read, *Theatre and Everyday Life: An Ethics of Performance* (London: Routledge, 1993), 1.

5. Vered Amit-Talai, "The 'Multi' Cultural of Youth," in *Youth Cultures: A Cross Cultural Perspective,* ed. Vered Amit-Talai and Helena Wulff (London: Routledge, 1995), 224.

6. Ibid., 224.

7. Ibid., 231.

8. Ibid.

9. Johanna Wyn and Rob White, *Rethinking Youth* (St. Leonards: Allen and Unwin, 1997), 85.

10. Paul Willis, *Moving Culture: An Enquiry into the Cultural Activities of Young People* (London: Calouste Gulbenkian Foundation, 1990), 14.

11. Julia Postle, "Accessing the Performing Body," *Real Time* 12 (1996): 33.

12. Backbone Youth Arts and Louise Gough, "Skate Girl Space Action Plan," MS. First performed as *Skate Girl Space* at Paddington Skate Park, Brisbane, 13 October 1996. Dramaturg: Louise Gough; director: Louise Hollingworth; associate director: Gillian Gardiner; video artist: Rebecca Harbison; associate video artist: Ayesha Muthalib; promotions: Eimear Quinn; "Sk8" facilitator: Hap Hathaway; physical theater facilitator: Sara Ritchie; costume construction: Karen Blinco; production manager: Denbi Newton; Hereford Sisters performers: Carolanne Sampson-Beechley, Zoe Robinson, Claire Mannion, Leah-Jett Pellinkhof, Tamara Miller, Marion Woodhead, Leanne Sales, Kellie McBride, Freya Dwyer, Zoe Greenhalgh, Roxanne, Jacki McKean, and Melissa Fox; Sheriff Stiffy: Jean-Marc Russ.

13. Marvin Carlson, *Performance: A Critical Introduction* (London: Routledge, 1996), 175.

14. Louise Hollingworth, personal interview, 18 October 1996.

15. The event was publicized as a drug-free and alcohol-free event, and there were no refreshments on sale.

16. Hereford Sisters, *Skate Girl Space Program* (Brisbane: Backbone Youth Arts, 1996), n.p.

17. Ibid., n.p.

18. Winning, "Cultural Policy," 74.

19. Louise Hollingworth, "Skate Girl Space," workshop, Youth Arts Queensland Artex Conference, Brisbane, 19 July 1996.

20. Carlson, *Performance,* 173.

21. Ibid., 173.

22. Hollingworth interview.

23. Feminists' leading roles in the development of community-based performance are evident in the influential work of women's theater groups such as Vital Statistix and Home Cooking Company, particularly during the 1980s, and the ongoing work of directors such as Fiona Winning, formerly of Death Defying Theatre, and Theresa Crea, of Doppio Teatro. While references to community-based performance are common in

studies of feminist theater practice (in particular the work of Peta Tait), reciprocal acknowledgment of feminists' contribution to the development of community-based approaches is yet cursory. Perhaps this is due to the fear of limiting the perception of "the art form formerly known as" as a prescriptively gendered practice?

24. Freya Dwyer, "1997 Boundary Busting Initiative," *A Moo Zine* (December 1996): 17.

25. Hawkins, *From Nimbin to Mardi Gras,* 163.

26. Peta Tait, *Converging Realities: Feminism in Australian Theatre* (Sydney: Currency; Melbourne: Artmoves, 1994), 2.

27. John Frow, *Cultural Studies and Cultural Value* (Oxford: Oxford University Press, 1995), 151.

28. Ibid., 161.

Index

Cover photos are from the following productions (clockwise, from top left):

Memorial Kut for the Victims of the Democratic Youth and Student Coalition Incident (1994), Korea. Photo: Dong-il Lee

Podrum (1996) by Scot McElvany and Mladi Most, Bosnia. Photo: Uli Loskat

Contraelviento (1989) by Grupo Cultural Yuyachkani, Peru.
Photo: Miguel Villafane

Walk Together Children (1996), College of William and Mary. Photo courtesy the Department of Theatre and Speech at the College of William and Mary.